I0715363

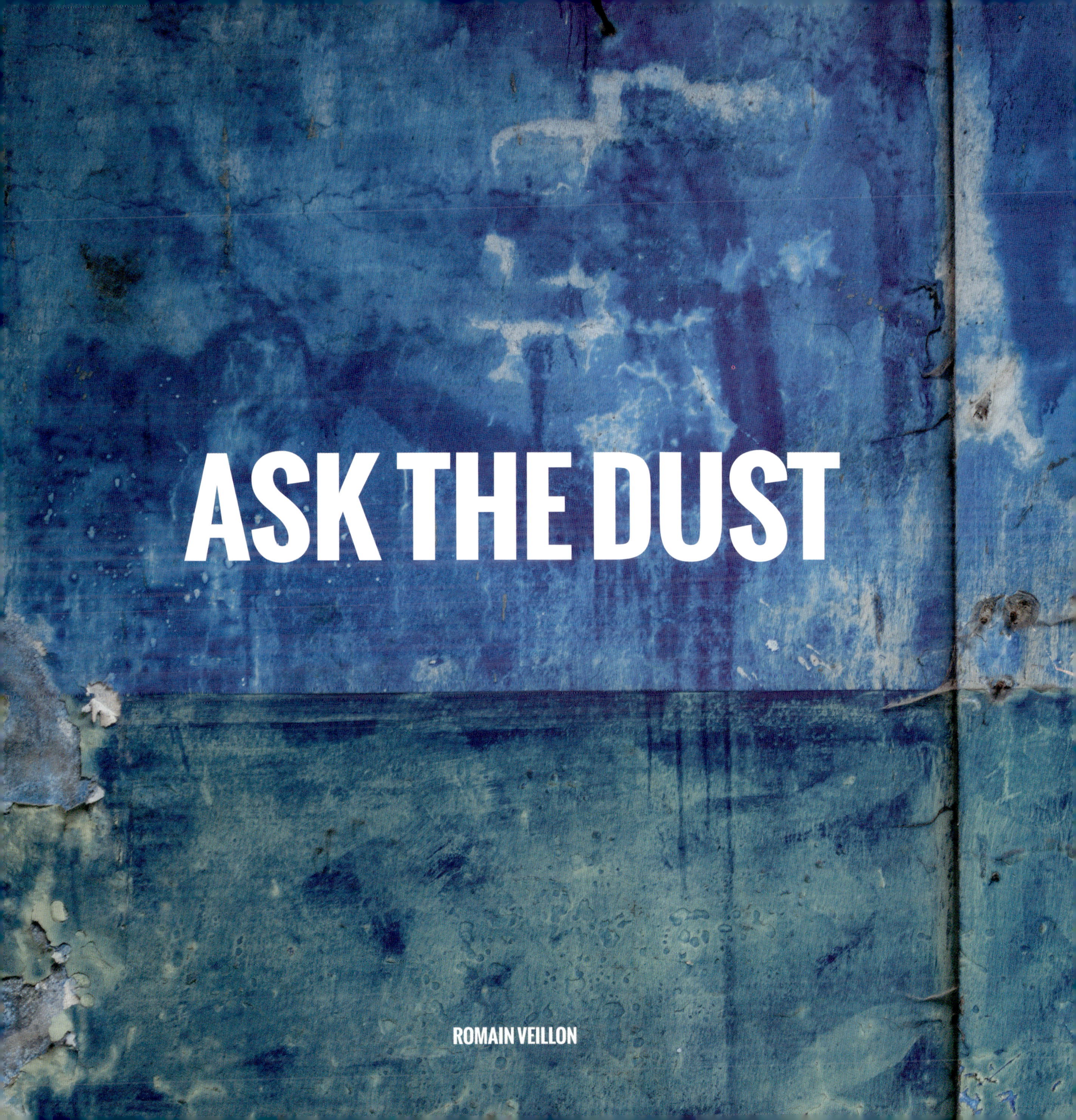
ASK THE DUST
ROMAIN VEILLON

ASK THE DUST

No part of this publication may be reproduced or transmitted in any form or by any means without the prior permission of the publisher. Any copy of this book issued by the publisher as a paperback or hardback is sold subject to the condition that it shall not by way of trade or otherwise be lent, resold, hired out or otherwise circulated without the publishers' prior consent in any form of binding or cover other than which it is published and without a similar condition including these words being imposed on a subsequent purchaser.

The information and images in this book are based on materials supplied to the publisher by the contributors. While every effort has been made to ensure its accuracy, Pro-actif Communications does not under any circumstances accept responsibility for any errors or omissions. The copyright with regards to all contributions remains with the originator.

This is a book about Urban Exploration. As publishers we're obliged to say it's not meant to encourage trespass where it is illegal. So we are.

A catalogue record for this book is available from the British Library.

First Edition 2016
First published in Great Britain in 2016 by Carpet Bombing Culture.
An imprint of Pro-actif Communications
www.carpetbombingculture.co.uk
email: books@carpetbombingculture.co.uk

©Carpet Bombing Culture. Pro-actif Communications

Photography and text by: Romain Veillon

ISBN: 978-1908211361

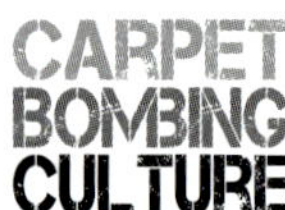

www.carpetbombingculture.co.uk

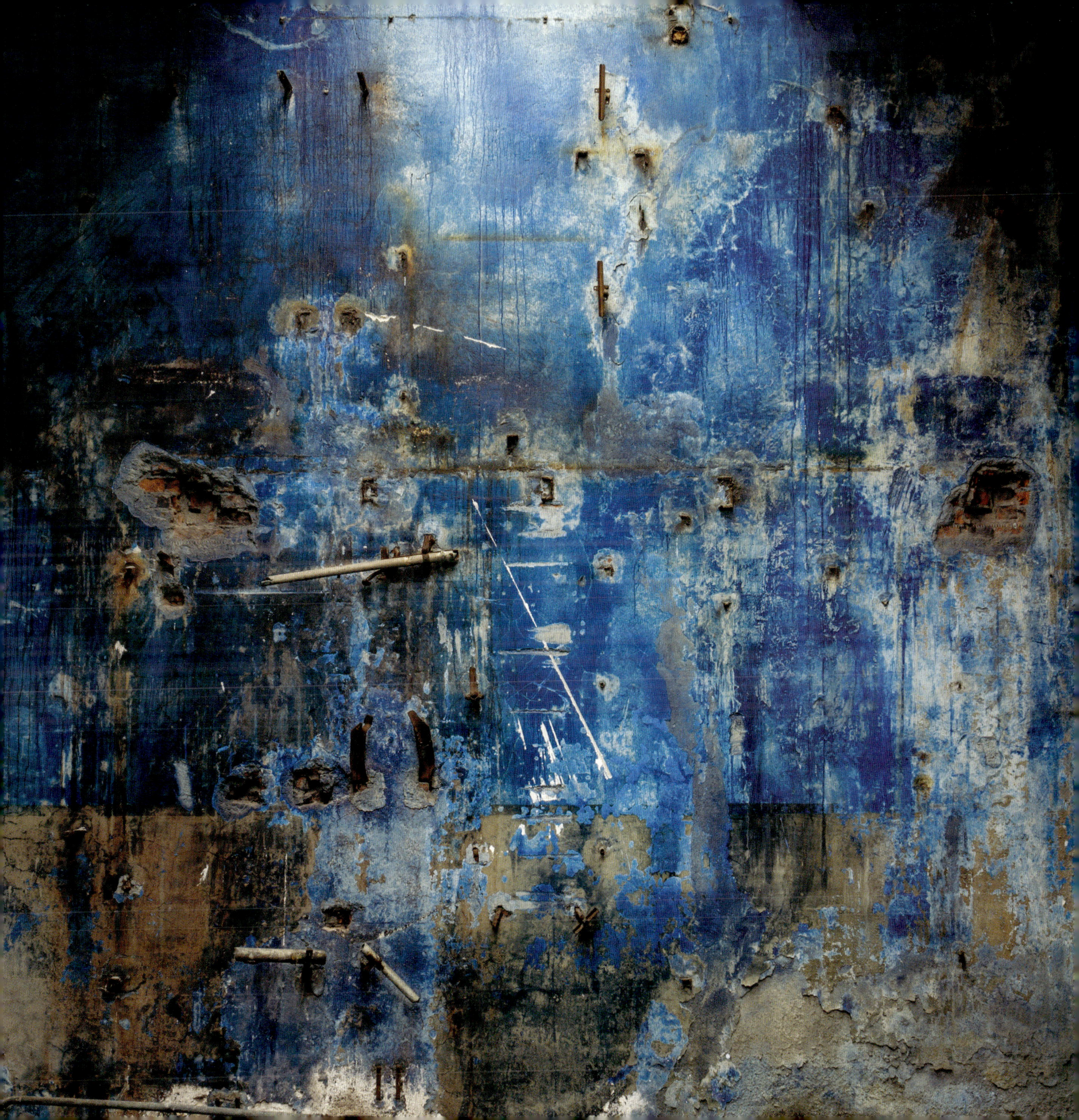

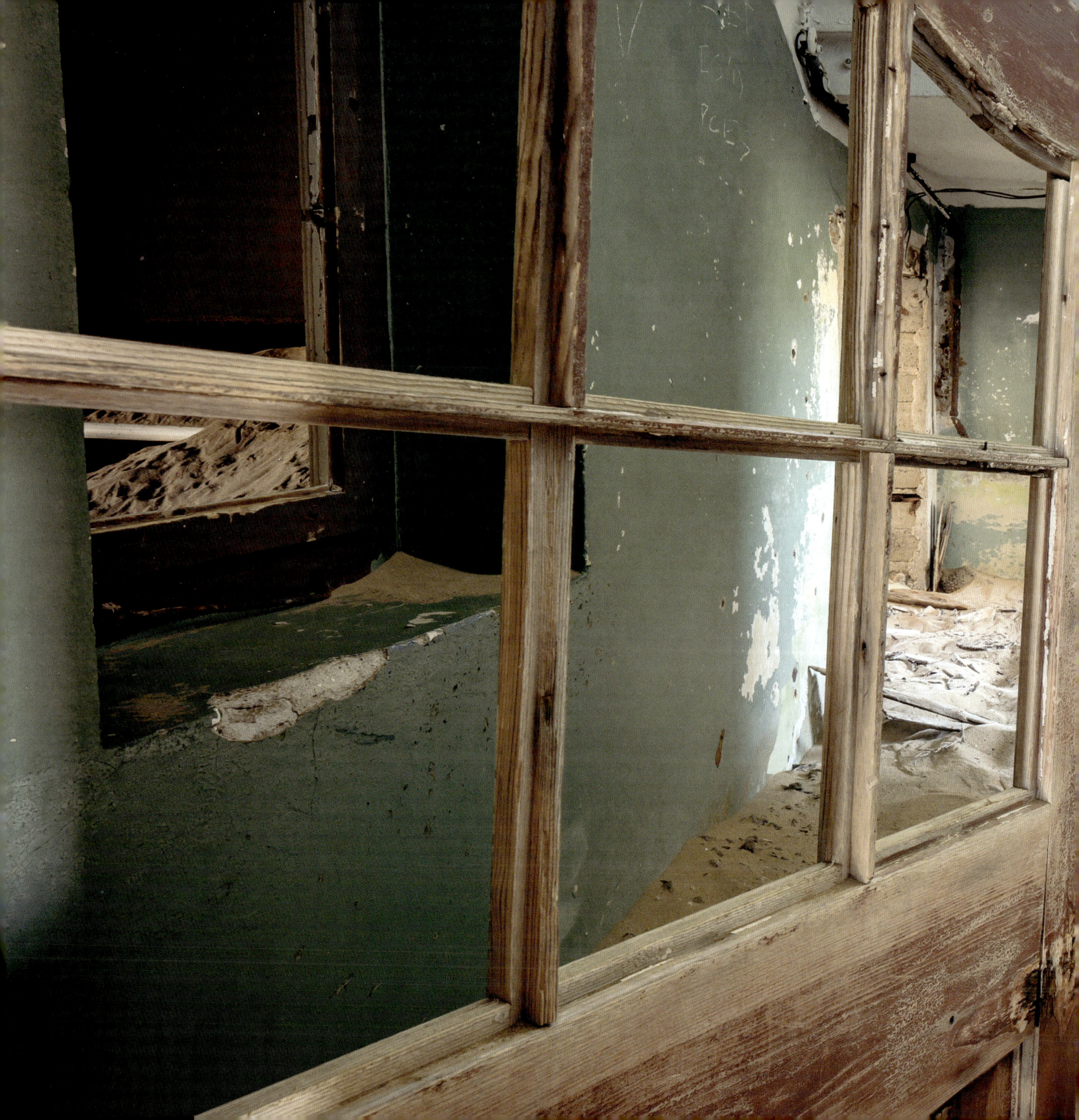

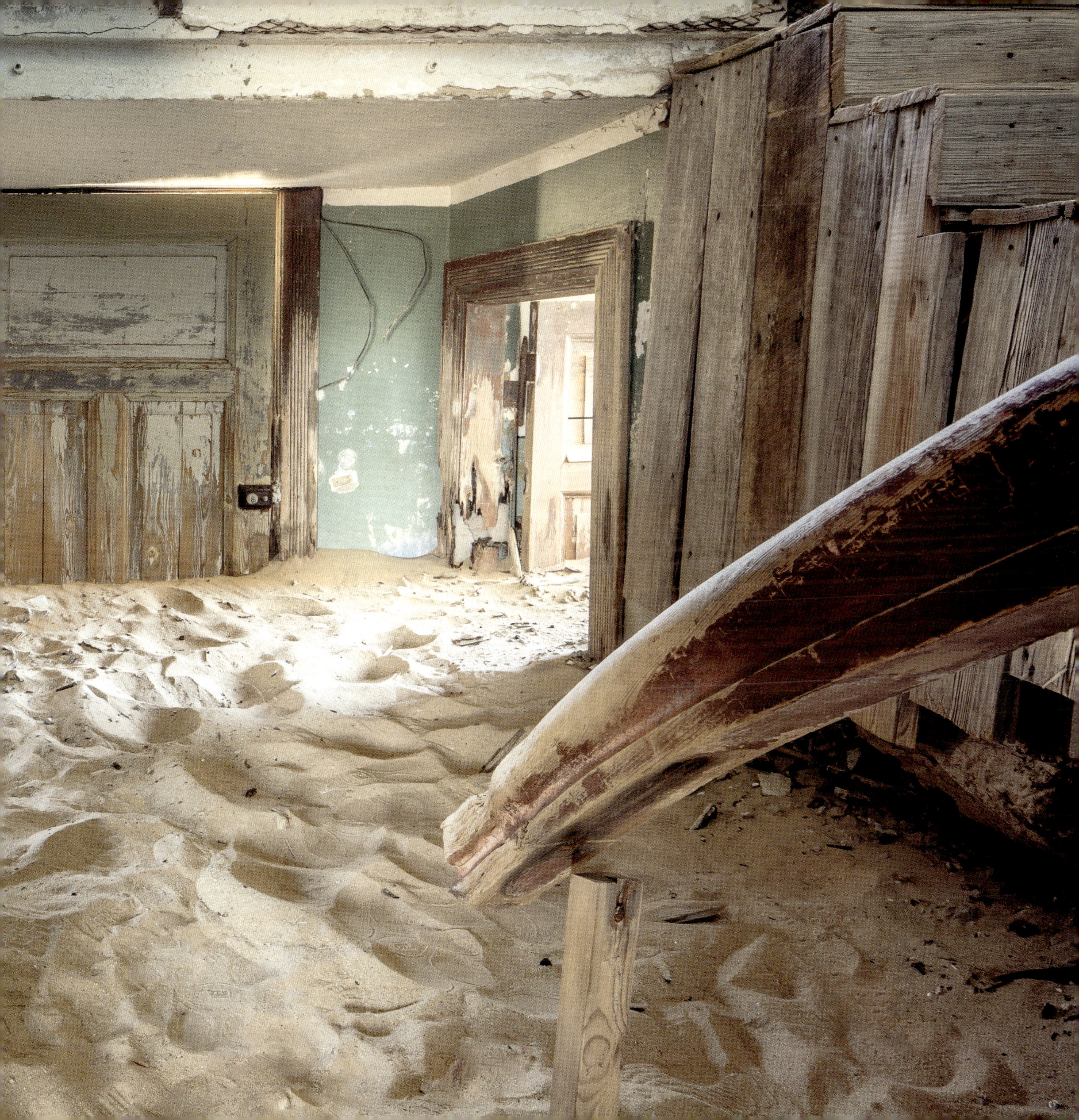

INTRODUCTION

"Ah, Los Angeles! Dust and fog of your lonely streets, I am no longer lonely. Just you wait, all of you ghosts of this room, just you wait, because it will happen, as sure as there's a God in heaven."

John Fante, Ask the Dust

Abandoned buildings are in mourning. They grieve for the lives that their residents have left behind. Rotten teddy bears, old wedding photographs or decomposing hats are the only remains that we can touch. In their halcyon days, these buildings were the foundation upon which men and women built their lives; where they worked, played, slept, prayed or were healed. Now they are shut away, scattered across the world, buried under the dust and crying in silence like the ghosts of history.

From the middle ages to modern times, through the Renaissance and the Century of light, humankind has always been fascinated by ruins. We are drawn to that special atmosphere captured in the ruins of our past. But why? Why are we captivated by these images? What do we see in these images that draws us so deeply into our own imagination and memory?

The TATE Britain Exhibition "RUIN LUST" (March-May 2014) revisited this enthusiasm, tracing a heritage back to 19th Century painters like Turner and Peter Van Lerberghe. The success of this exhibition proves that this is not something new or a passing fascination. Thus, examples of this love of derelict places are everywhere.

What defines the ruin? Is it the aspect of destruction? The invasion of vegetation? The absence of human life? I believe that there is no wrong answer here. They are all part of the equation. What the ruin is to you will depend on the moment you choose to look at it.

For a long time in Western Europe, the meaning of ruin was the chaos that emerged from aerial bombing attacks and the remains of the bombed cities after the great wars. Artistic creation, however, can use the ruins as a point of origin for imagining the legacy of our kind and to bring a creative force out of the chaos. Photographing these locations as art is to lay down a challenge to time itself, shouting "we are here and always will be!"

If the ruins speak to everybody, and they do, there must be a reason. Through modern movies, books, architecture, video games, even fashion designers, inspiration has been taken from abandoned buildings and integrated into their own art. We have even coined the phrase "Ruin Porn" to suggest that we watch the ruins as we watch pornography, for immediate pleasures.

When we speak about abandoned buildings the first word that comes to my mind is childhood. It is no coincidence. Everyone has a recollection of the old warehouse down the street or the collapsing little cottage in the wood where they first dared each other to explore, enjoying the first shivers of real fear.

Just ask people around you and you will collect dozens of unique stories. Everyone will be glad to tell a part of their life that was hidden for a long time in the back of their mind. Maybe we need to question our past to have a better understanding of our place on earth. Or sometimes it's just nice to recall lost emotions.

We are now facing a period of uncertainty to a degree that humankind has almost never before encountered. There are multiple causes, and we all have a personal perception on them. There have never been so many conflicts in the world. Terrorist attacks multiply, the environment is slowly but surely being destroyed by humanity…

Looking to the future is not a joyful thing to do right now. All civilization will come to an end. This memento mori reminds also us that each of us will eventually fall. Seeing what our house or office could look like in a few decades can be seen as an exaltation of our fears.

Perhaps we are missing the most obvious reason for our fascination with ruins, the simplest motivation of all. We are mesmerised by the past of other people's lives. Humans are completely absent from these places, yet their presence is everywhere. Any object or piece of furniture is a clue of what used to be their everyday life and routine. Thanks to a simple image, we can imagine the stories that hide behind them.

Who used to live in this house? Why did this factory close? What was this patient's disease? Did these two lovers stay together until the end? What kind of people frequented this dance hall? How many love stories began in this theater?

We can come up with hundreds of tales for every location we step into. We give a background and an aesthetic to the decline of a place. And it's true that it's an incredible feeling to recreate a life from clues and to make of it our own unique story. You are creating your own imaginary novel where you decide the fate and the destiny of the characters.

We all have our personal reasons, but I believe I share the same fascination as everybody else when I wander into these buildings. For me, I think it comes from my childhood and the hours I spent exploring the old warehouses of the transport factory my grandmother owned. Or all the hours I spent with my friends playing and talking in an old castle near my school where we used to meet after class. With time,

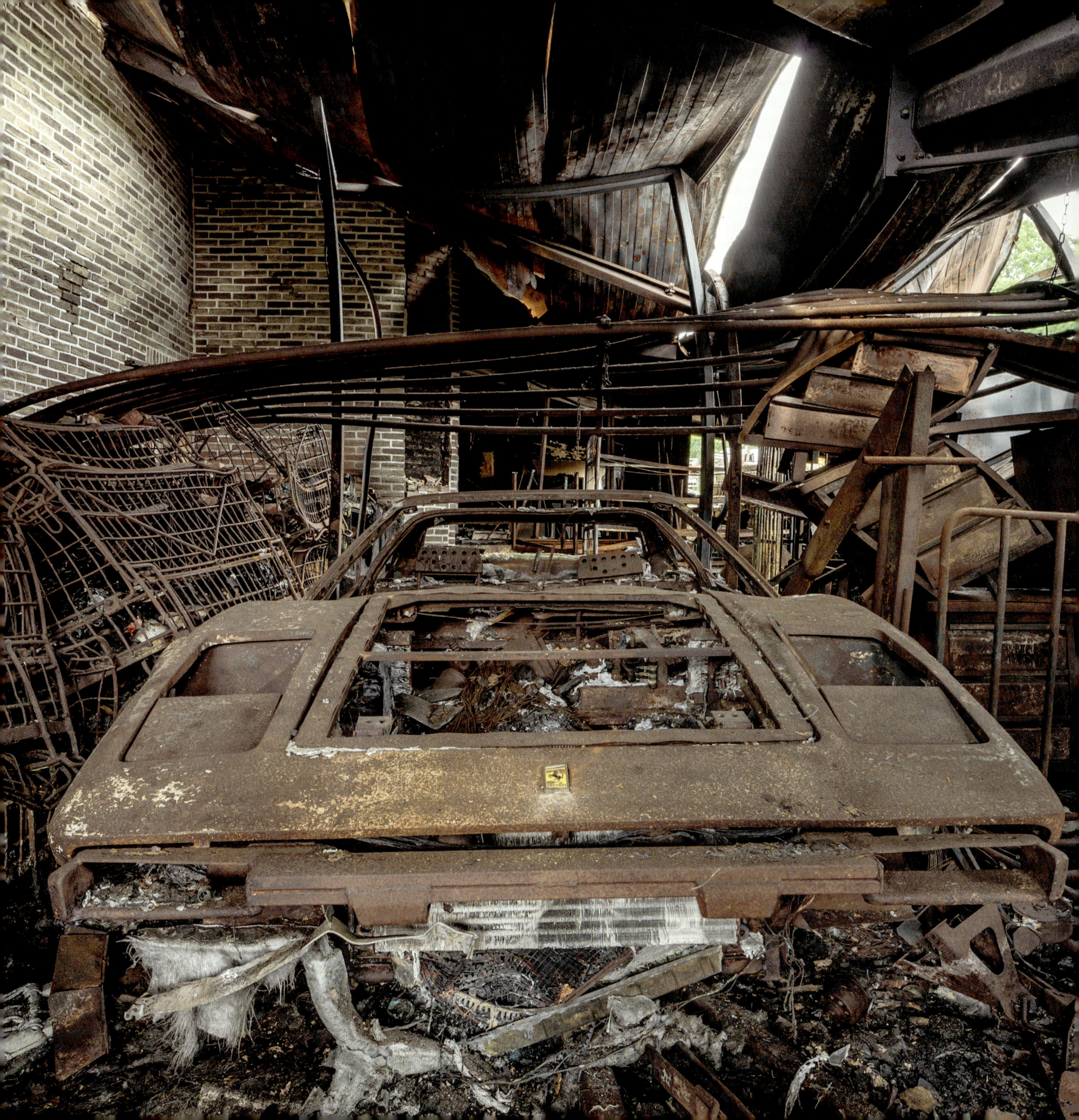

these memories were transformed into something special. I see myself as an adventurer trying to find the entrance of a locked castle, avoiding traps and discovering a secret ancient relic.

Furthermore, it takes me back to that seminal period of my youth. I remember in particular a teacher who was an inspiration to me at that time and how he used to teach his class in a very interactive way, based on exchange and self-learning. I loved the way he encouraged us to learn in our own way. And I think the fascination I have for places left by man comes from that, the fact that it is permanently tied up with my personal history.

The use of lighting in my photographs is also essential to me. Thanks to a very powerful light that I strengthen to a high level, I bring back some life to these deserted places. The light is a way of putting a presence there if only just for an instant, illuminating ghosts of the past, so that we can try to imagine the revival of the place for a few moments. In the end, we can leave sadness and nostalgia behind us and return with a smile on our face.

Wind in the curtains. Shadows on a wall. A ray of sun in a doorway. These things remind us that time can be uncertain. Like an hourglass, light tells us time has stopped there but will start again one day. Until then, let's appreciate this little piece of past we can admire one last time before it fades away.

As one of my favourite quotation states: "It's not the destination, it's the journey", which sums up exactly the way I work and my approach to capturing the spirit of these places around the world. Because, alongside these pictures, I think it is important not to forget all that's come along with these travels. And especially, the incredible opportunity to meet and discover people and cultures everywhere. For me, it is as equally important.

The idea we have discussed here of the uncertainty of the future, I think should push us to be closer to each other. And I hope that every time I visit a new region, there will be a chance to make new friends, to learn about new customs, to take time to think about what really matters, not only for myself but also for the man next to me.

I will never forget the man who comes back every day to Epecuén to remember how it was before the flooding; the woman telling the sad story of her family in front of their former house or the old timer who tried to fix the church he used to pray in when he was a child. These are the stories I want to tell.

During the last few years, I have tried to capture the essence of this feeling around the world. In this book, I will introduce you to the incredible destiny of the ghost town of Kolmanskop in the Namibian desert. Built from scratch after a diamond rush, Kolmanskop prospered during forty years but was abandoned as quickly as it was built after the diamonds ran out. Now only the last traces of civilization remain in the desert where the sand slowly reclaims its history.

I will focus on the flooded city of Epecuén in Argentina to show how man was obliged to flee after the catastrophic flooding of the town. Thirty years on, the water is receding and we can rediscover what relics stand in this city petrified by salt as if we were rediscovering the lost city of Atlantis.

I will also take you wandering with me to several strange and incredible abandoned places across Europe (France, Belgium, Luxembourg, Germany, Italy, Hungary, Poland, Bulgaria, Ireland, Portugal) to give you a taste of what marvels man left behind. Castles, houses, factories, hospitals, churches, all these locations have something in common.

Even if they are very different in their nature, it's a perfect summary of what our civilization would have looked like today if man had disappeared from this earth.

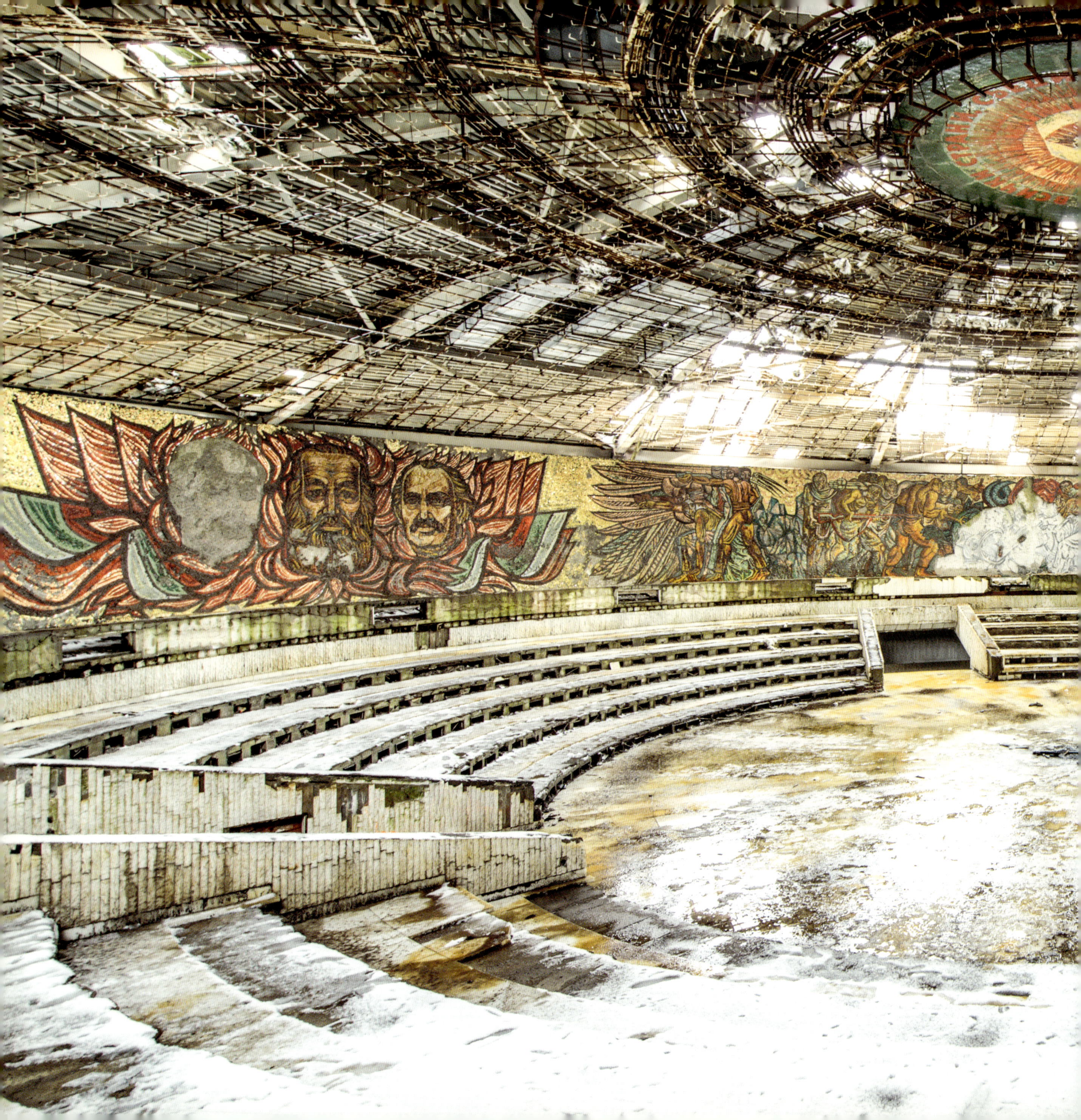

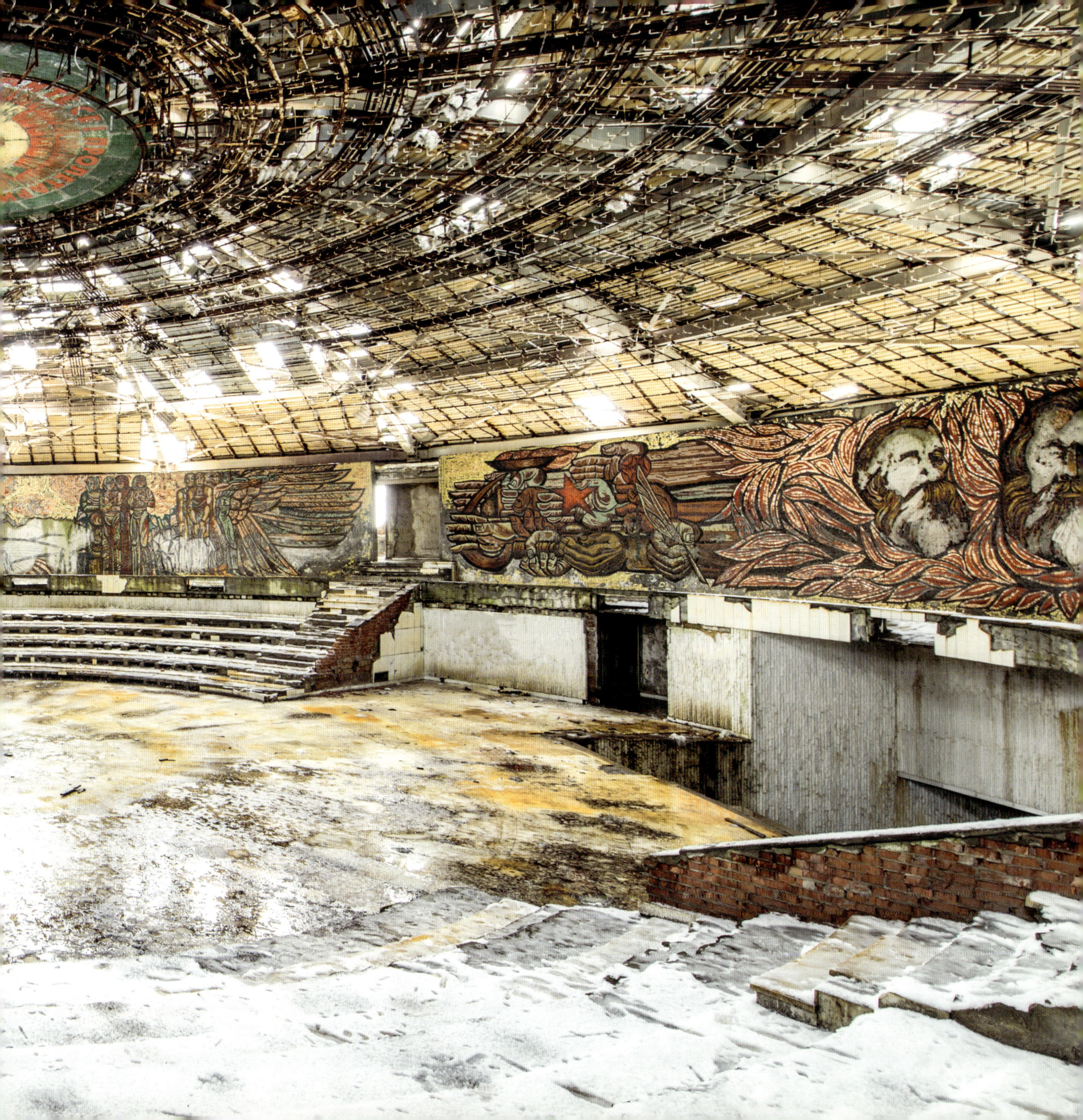

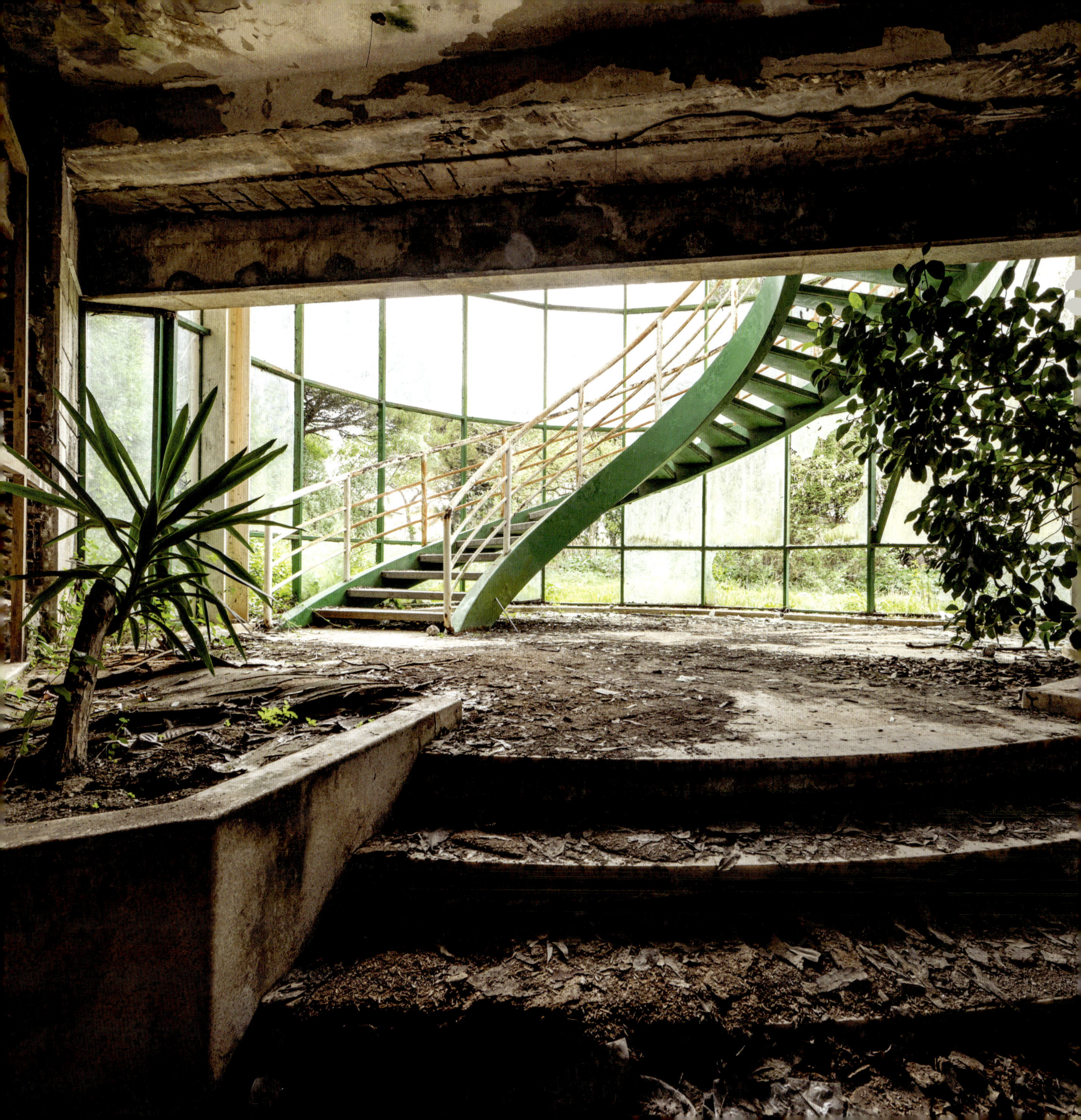

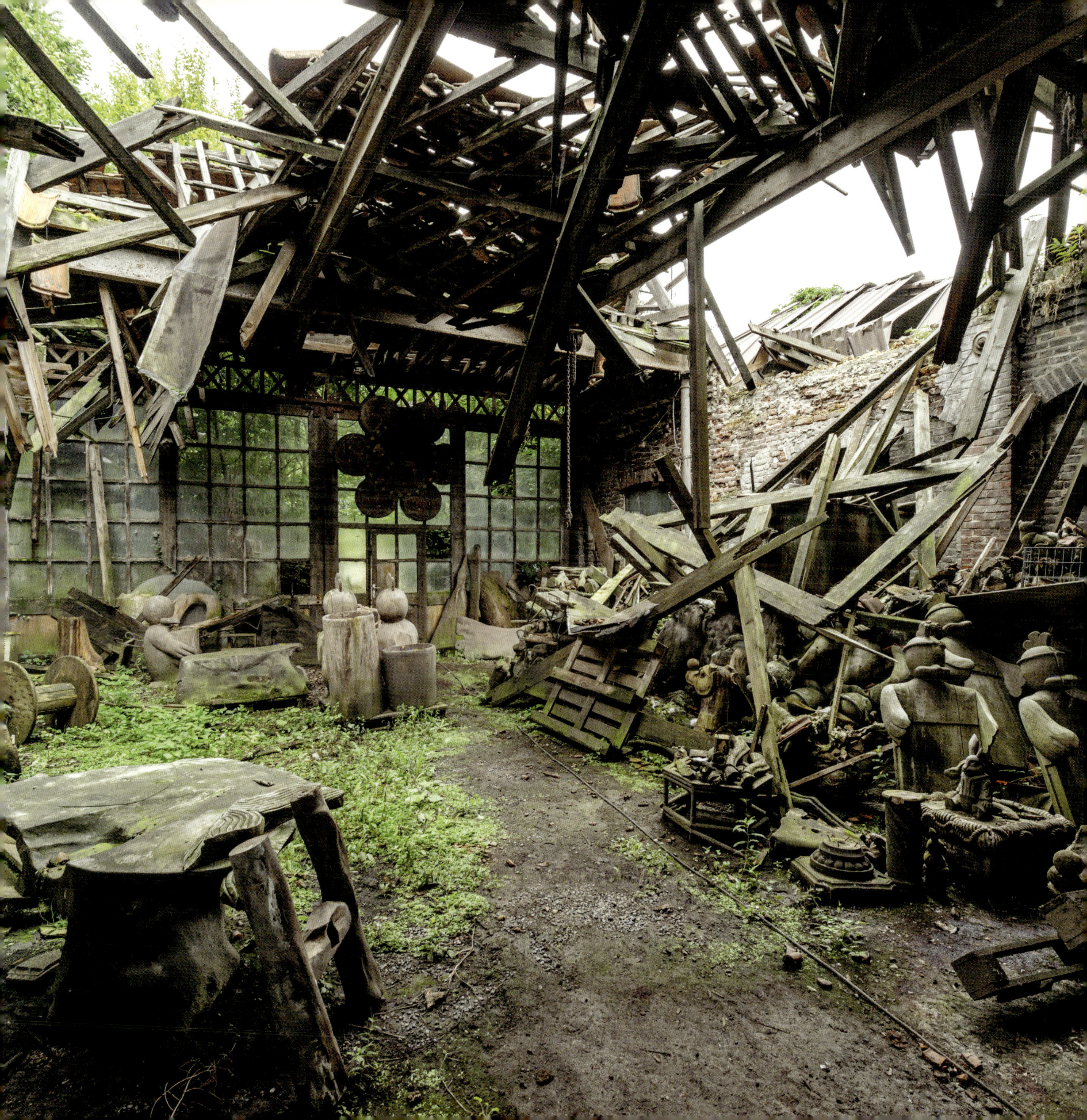

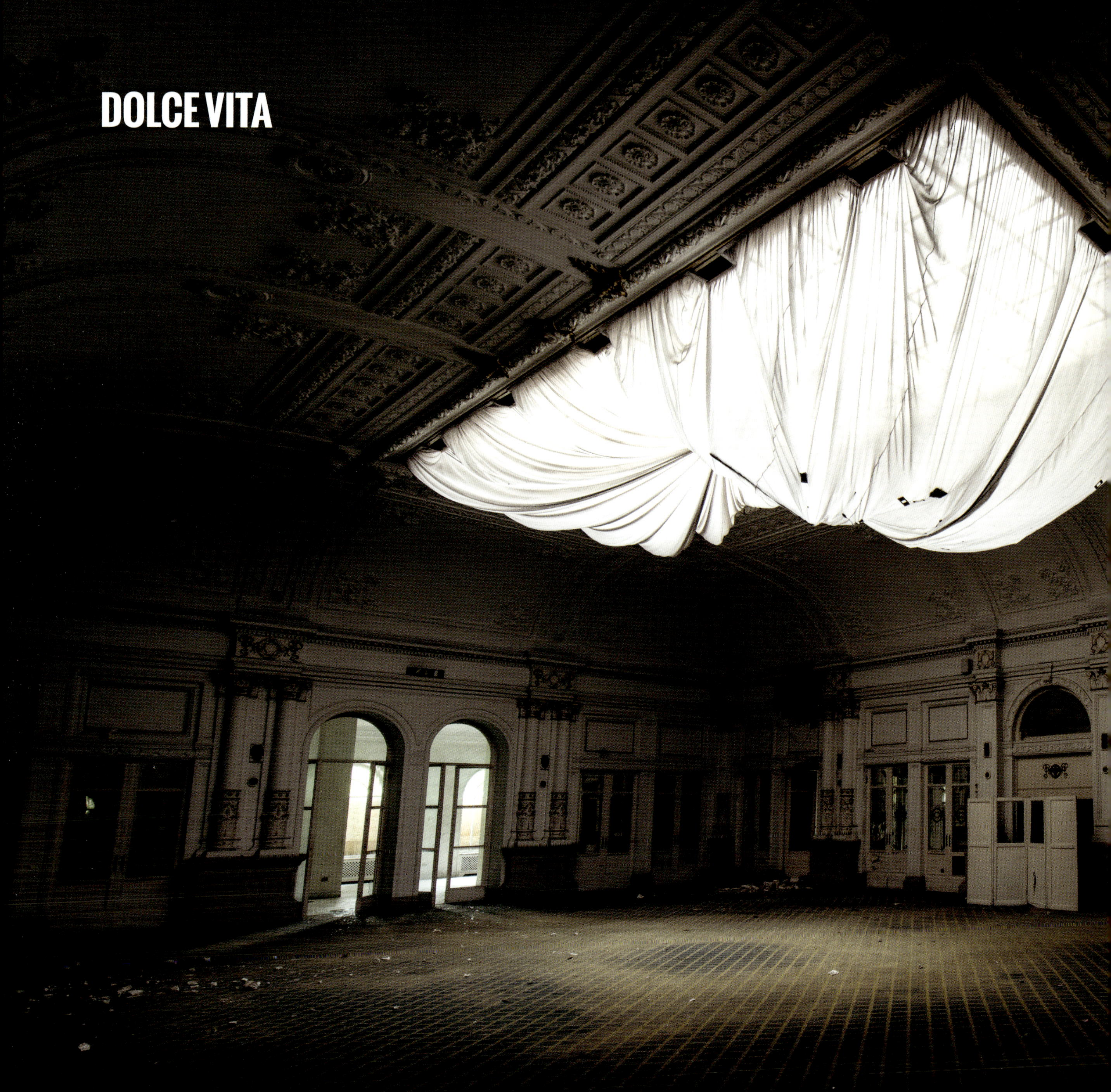
DOLCE VITA

If there was an iconic place where imagination could really fly and create the most amazing stories, it would be in the places where we used to enjoy ourselves after work or on vacation and where we tried to escape our lives for a moment. It can be a trip to the cinema to see a movie or a play at the theatre; for some others, an afternoon swimming and tanning by the pool. It was playing piano for hours to relax or going to the gym with friends and the chance to unwind while others will prefer to go to a bar, a ballroom, a casino or a nightclub to dance, play and have some drinks.

As a result of the industrialization of the western world and the appearance of leisure time for the masses, a new era developed where people began to discover a wide range of activities to fill their newfound spare time.

These activities were created so people could fill their time with a completely new form of entertainment. Thanks to the evolution of modern culture, this revolution was expressed in the construction of buildings centred on pleasure for the working class. Each of them was an illustration of a particular time in a specific place, which tells us a lot about the leisure habits of the region's population.

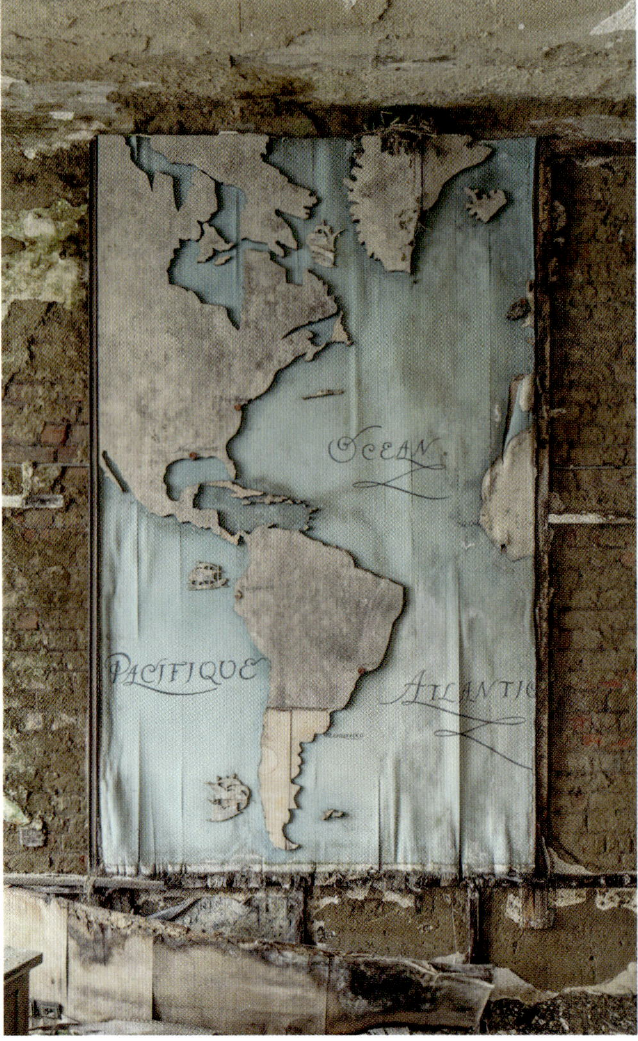

When open, life was everywhere, but now we can really feel the loneliness of these places. We often say abandoned buildings are where time has stopped, this is just the natural effect of abandonment. Here, we were having fun and wanted to extend this moment as much as possible. But finally, now they are forgotten, full of memories that will last forever.

We can say that these places were what our dreams were made of and the reason why we loved being there. We imagined going out with the girl of our dreams in a nightclub, of becoming a great basketball player, of swimming in the blue sea of the Caribbean, of getting drunk with new friends in a bar, of embodying the hero of the movie, of getting rich at the casino or being a famous musician. It was the way to escape for an hour or two and imagine what life could be if things were different. And when the curtains closed, these fantasies disappeared forever. They were usually the part of our childhood that we left behind, but we're always happy to stumble upon it again.

These places were, most of the time, where large numbers of people gathered together. They were places for socialising. Whereas houses were intended for family life, a factory to work and a church to pray, these locations existed for people to enjoy their time together.

Their abandonment leaves a sad mark. Their failure was not the failure of an individual, but the failure of a community as a whole. People no longer gathered there, and in the end, there was nowhere left to meet. We can only imagine the joy that these places gave to their community and the sadness of their memories slowly fading away.

The reasons for these failures are numerous. New competition might have opened in the neighbourhood. Every business faces a cycle, one day it's "the place to be", then next day your customers start frequenting the competition.

The appearance of new hobbies and the decline of other activities are other factors. With time, populations and their habits change, and old forms of leisure become outmoded. There's the slow migration of people from small villages to bigger cities. Bad administration, natural disasters or just the passing of time, all aid in the decline of these places before they eventually close their doors.

The aesthetics here are, to my eyes, more important than in other abandoned places because, as I said earlier, they were full of life and there to impress and attract people in discovering new pleasures. So, the decoration and the style had to be in harmony with this spirit and convey the right mood for the people visiting. And usually, this type of location had to use grandeur to attract the public.

Typically, these locations were where you would find and admire the most beautiful architecture (in casinos or swimming pools), paintings and ornaments (houses or theaters), or furniture (hotels or ballrooms). Moreover, we can easily see how unique they were and how they are no longer built in such an impressive way.

Photographing these places was like trying to recapture the spirit of someone's broken childhood dreams. Every time you entered a room, you had to imagine those ghosts on the dance floor in the nightclub in front of you or the screams of children playing in a theme park. It's a part of someone's youth collapsed in front of you. It's everybody's failure we are facing here, the failure of our own selves. We never forget the happy moments and nothing is worse than seeing a place which used to be full of happiness getting forgotten, little by little.

When you search deep in your memory, you can find an example of a place like this. For me, it was the famous piscine "Molltor" in Paris. My mother used to go there when she was young and she once took me there before its closure in 1989. I have only blurred memories of this day, but sometimes images still flash through my mind from time to time when I pass by it.

In my head, this day at "Molitor" was incredible and my memories would take me back, to the time when I was a 6 year old child again. But watching the building being destroyed was very painful for me. I didn't understand how this could be abandoned and forgotten when it represented so much to so many people.

Our heritage, especially when it concerns our youth, is something sacred, even when we have grown up.

Now, "Molitor" has now been restored and has a new life as an opulent hotel. And that is exactly the fate I wish for all these amazing places that deserve to have a new generation visiting them and creating their own memories.

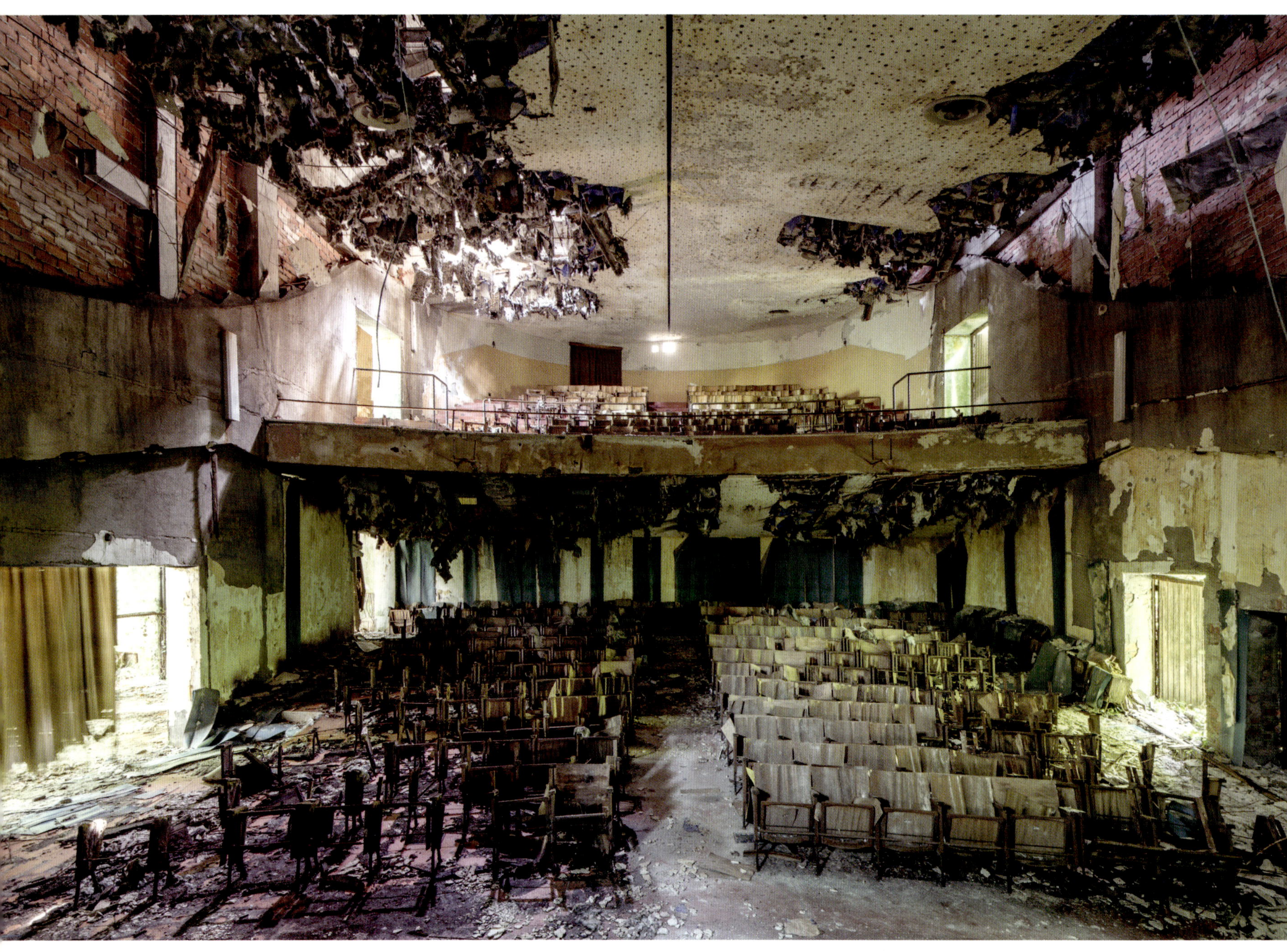

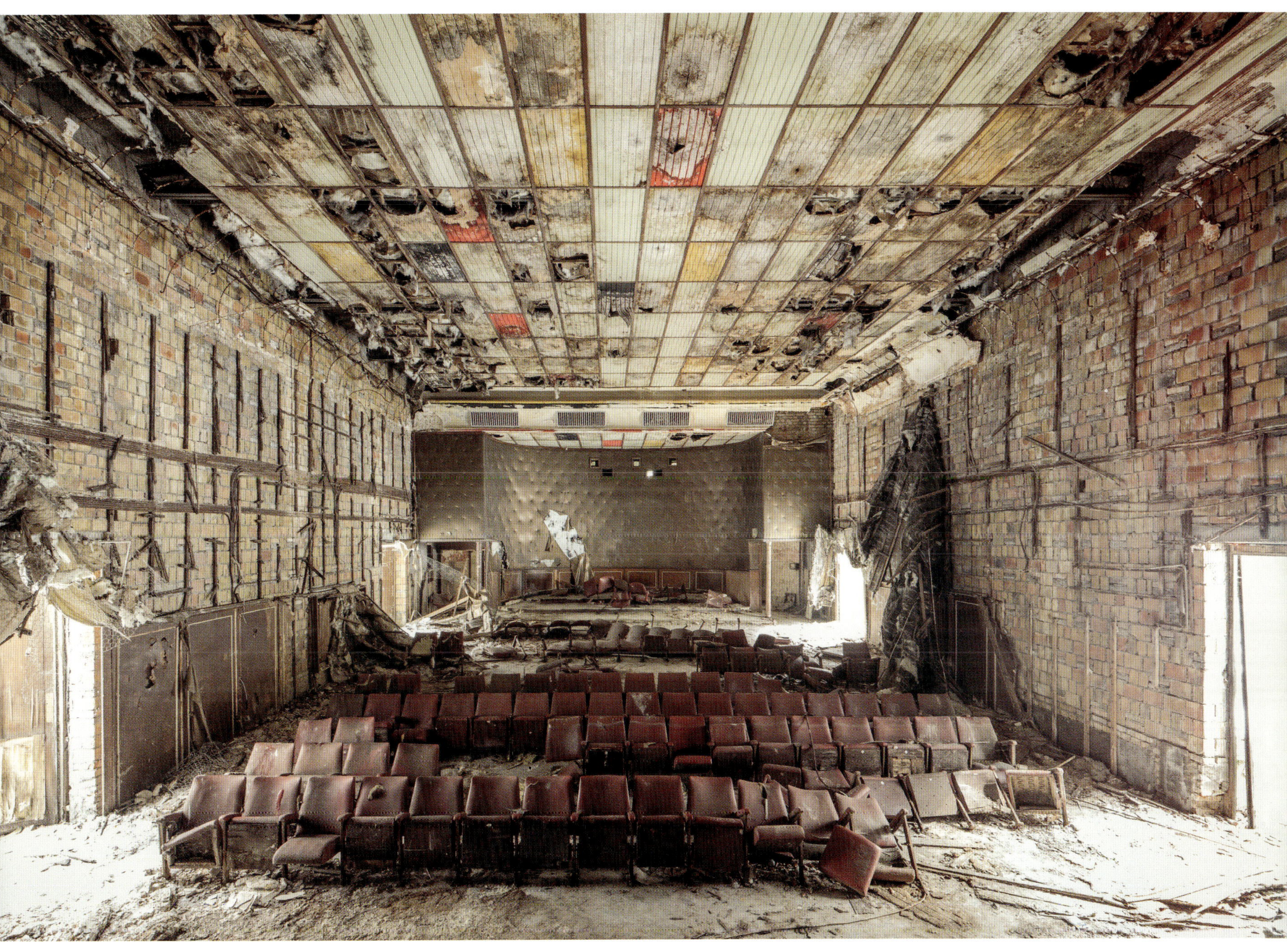

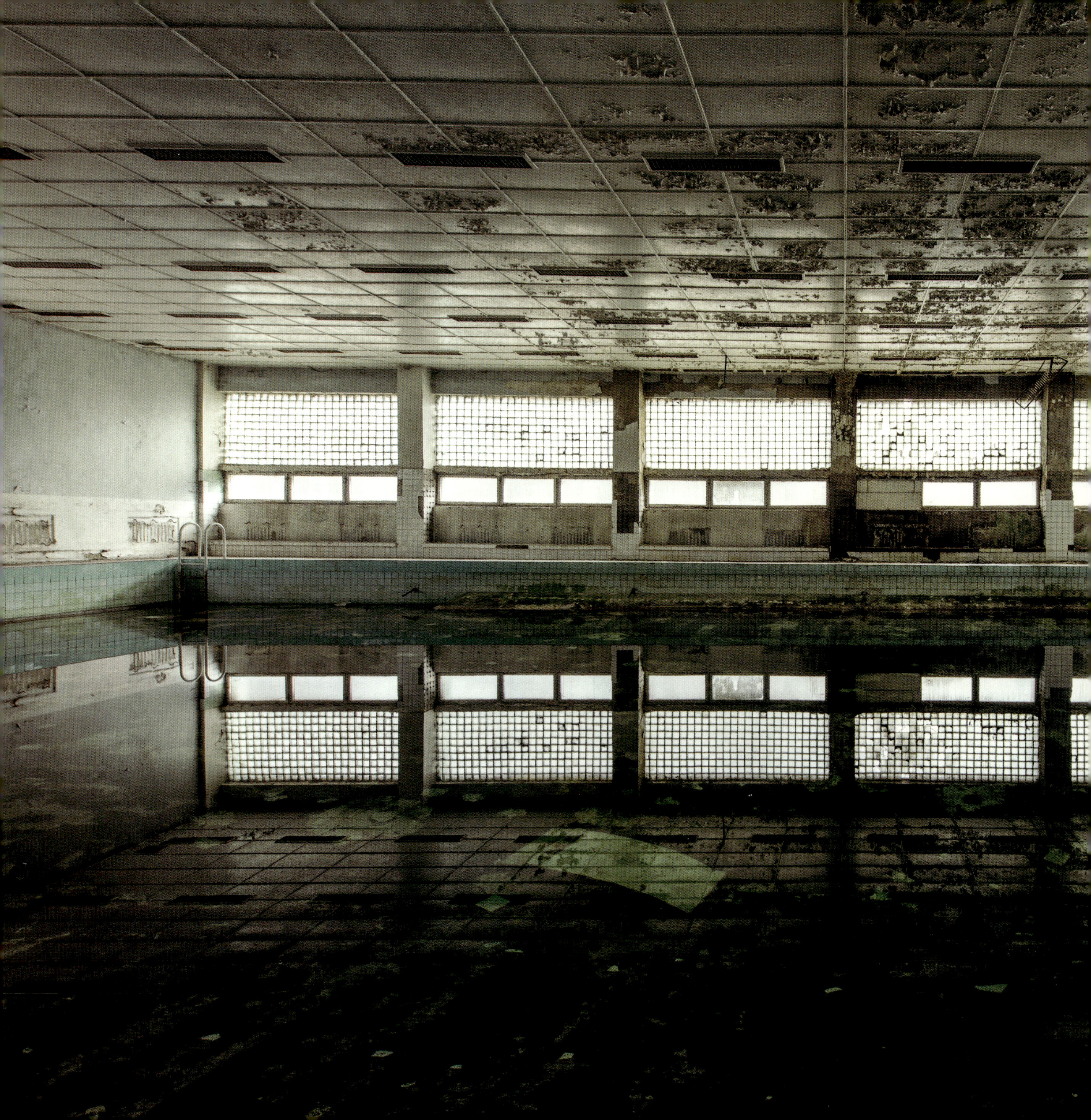

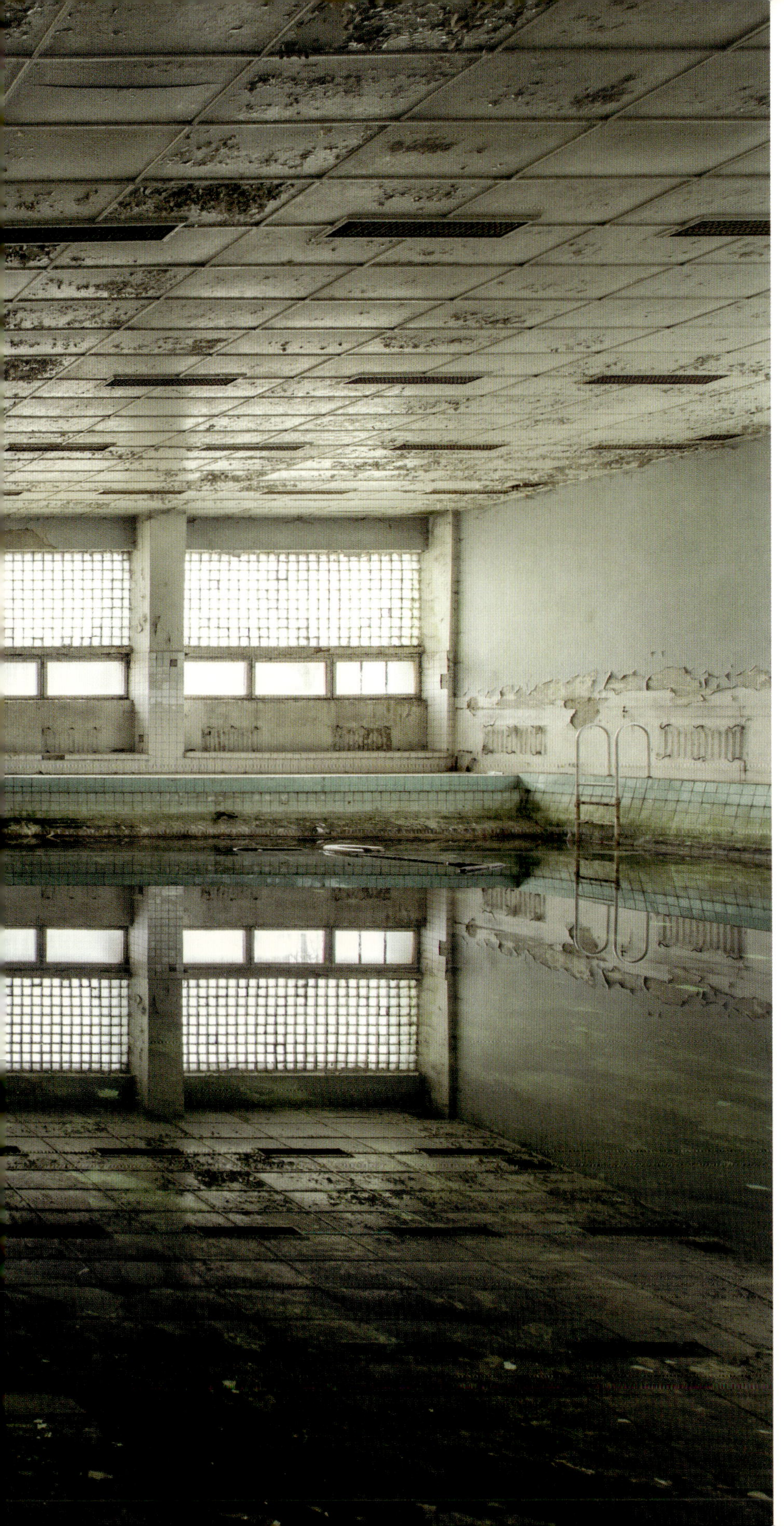

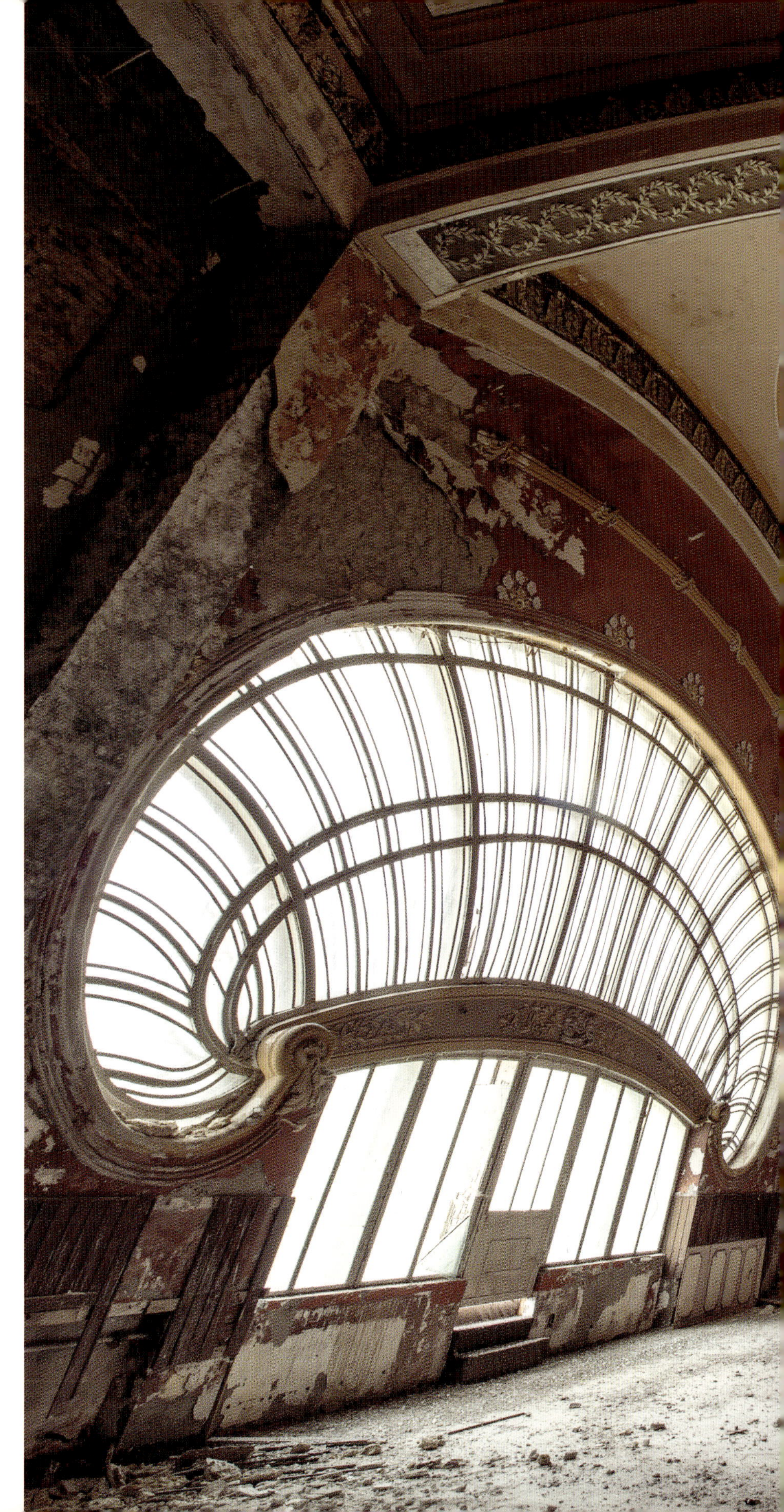

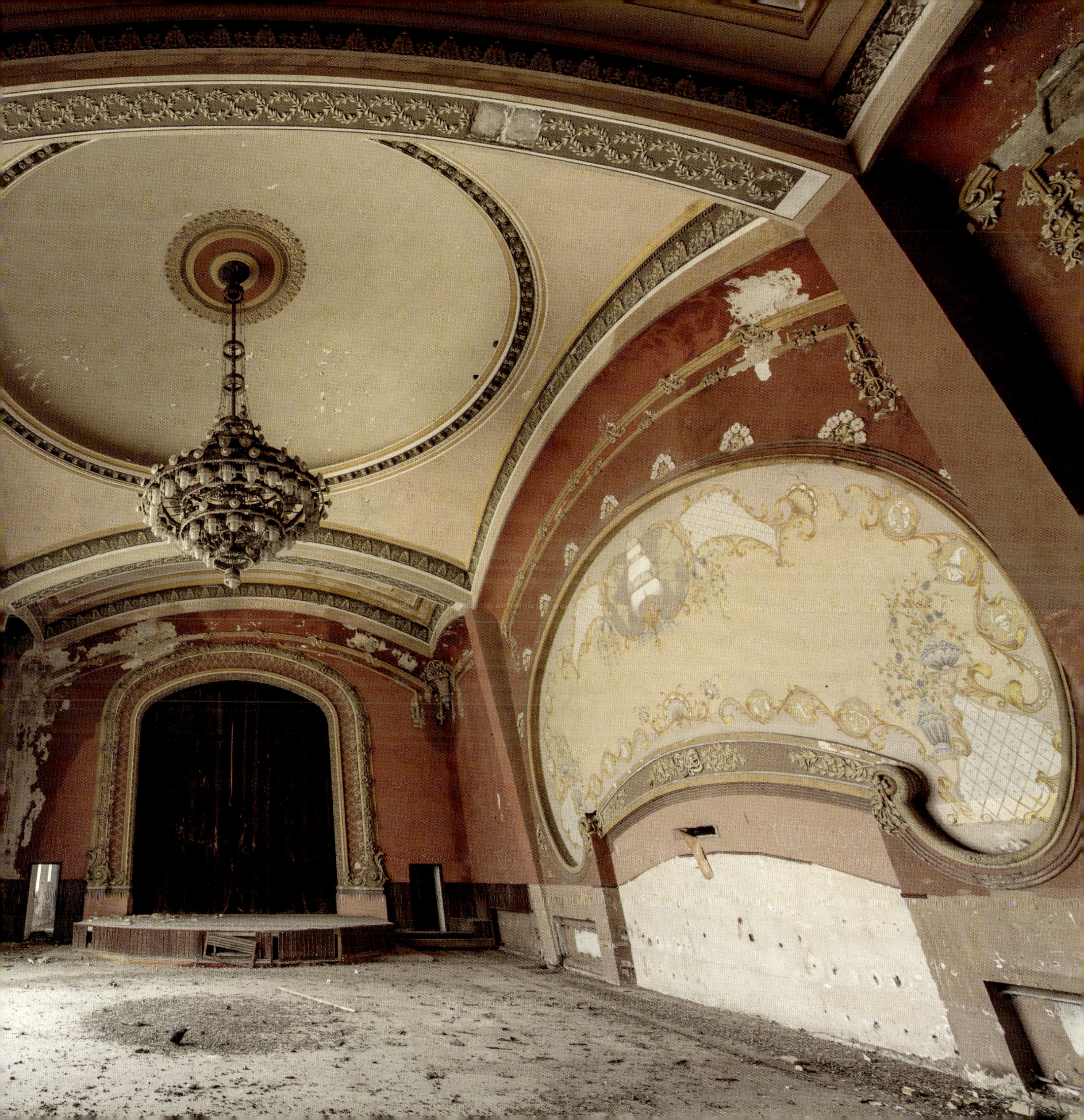

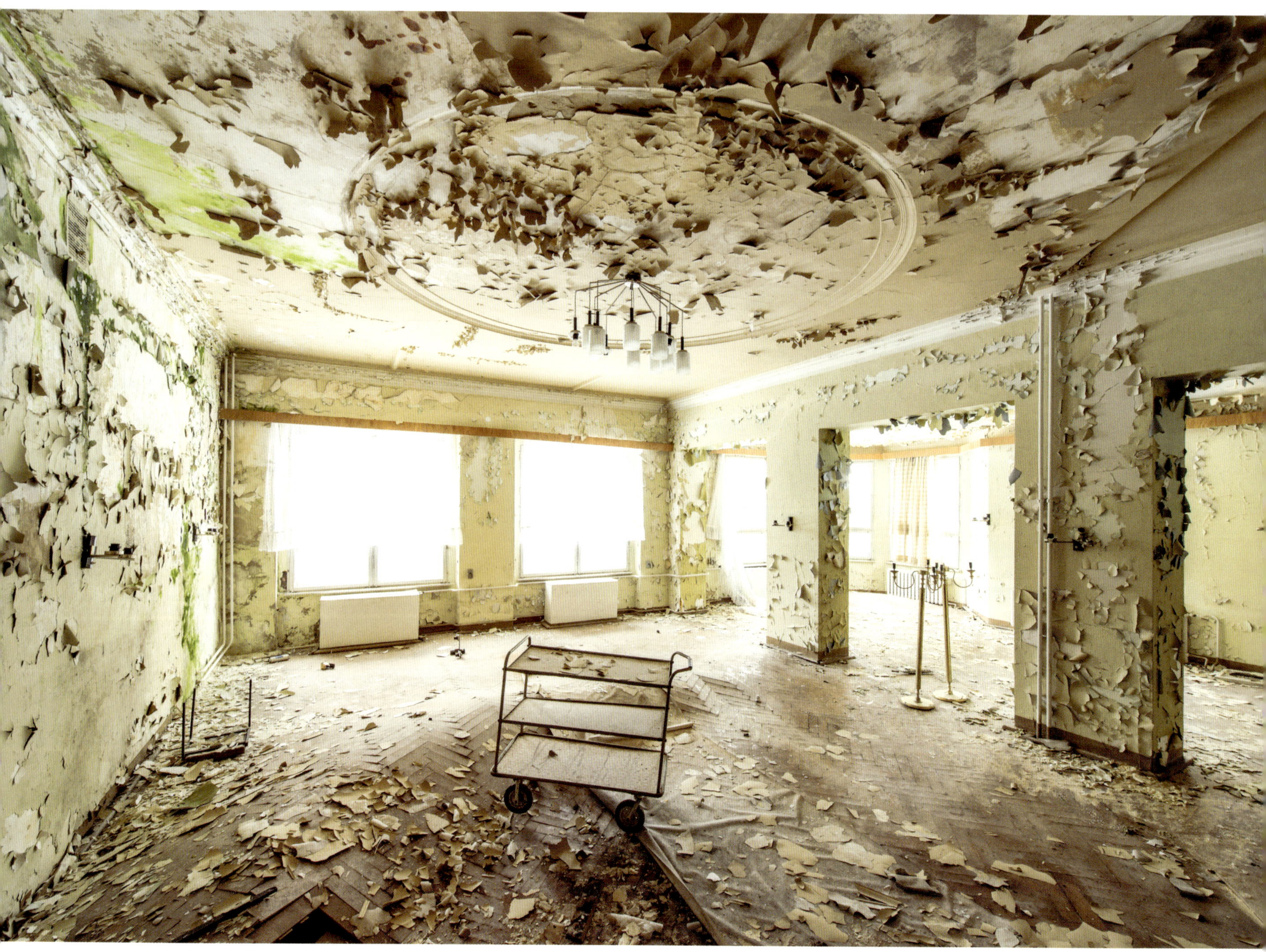

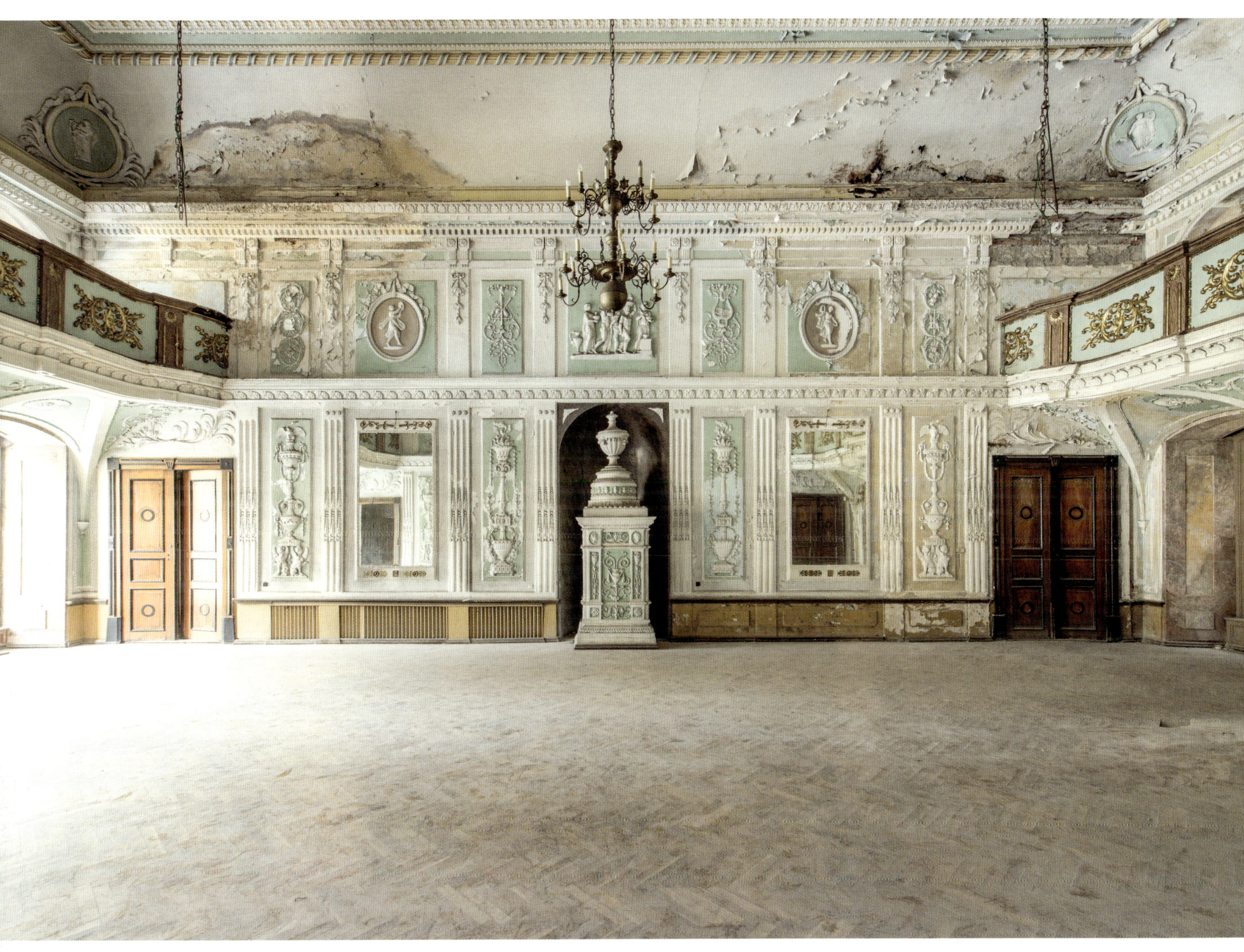

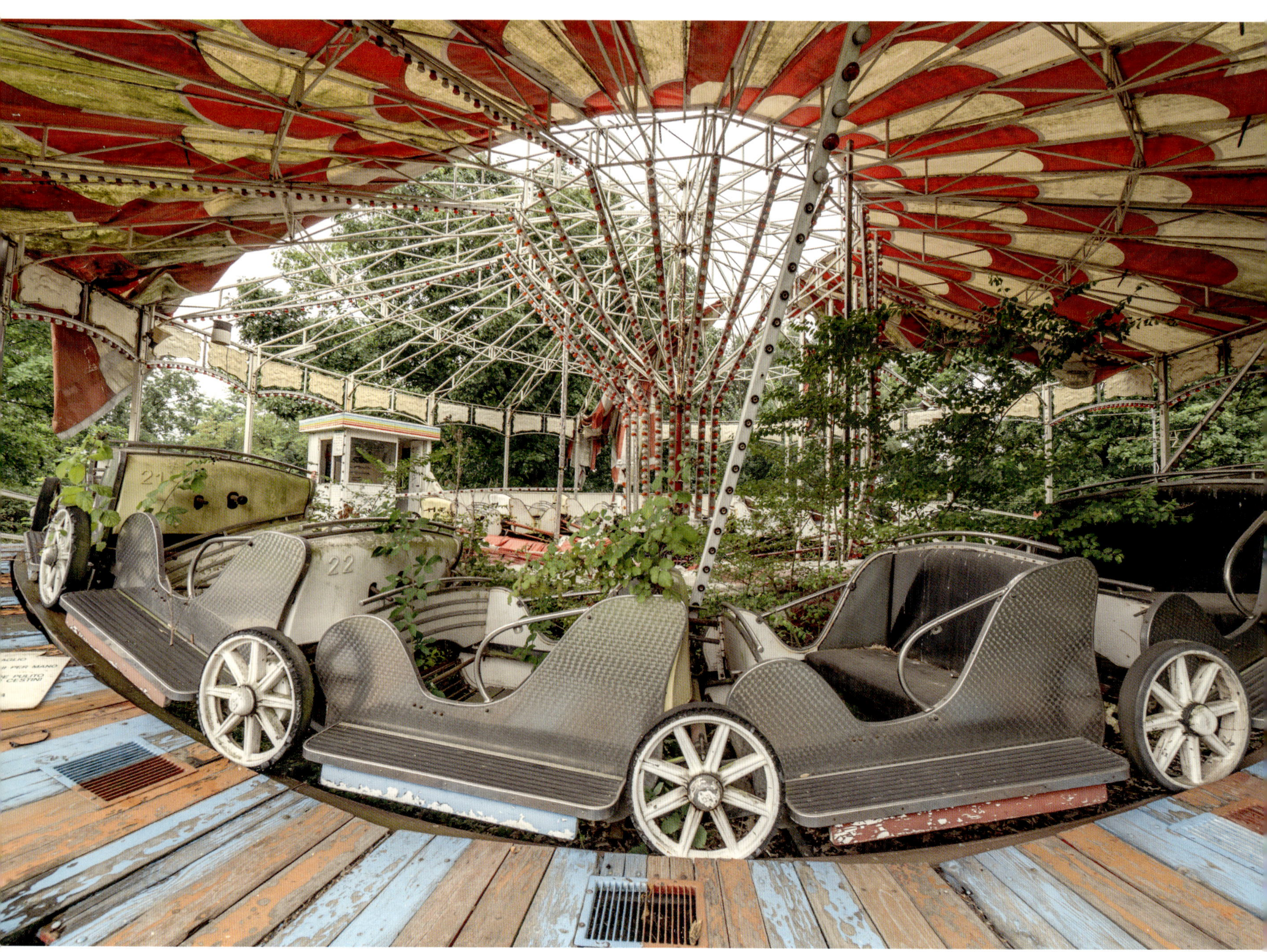

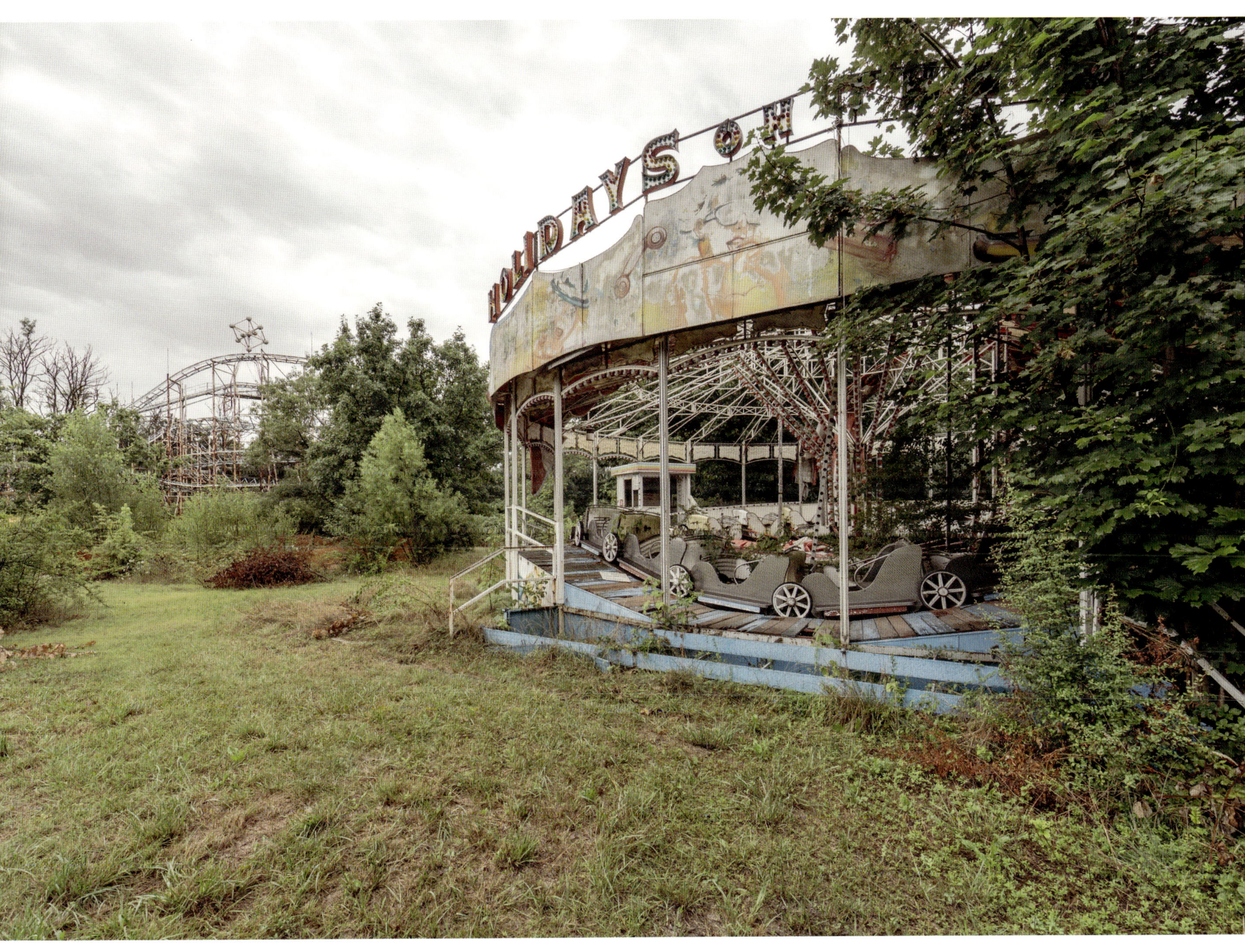
HOLIDAYS ON

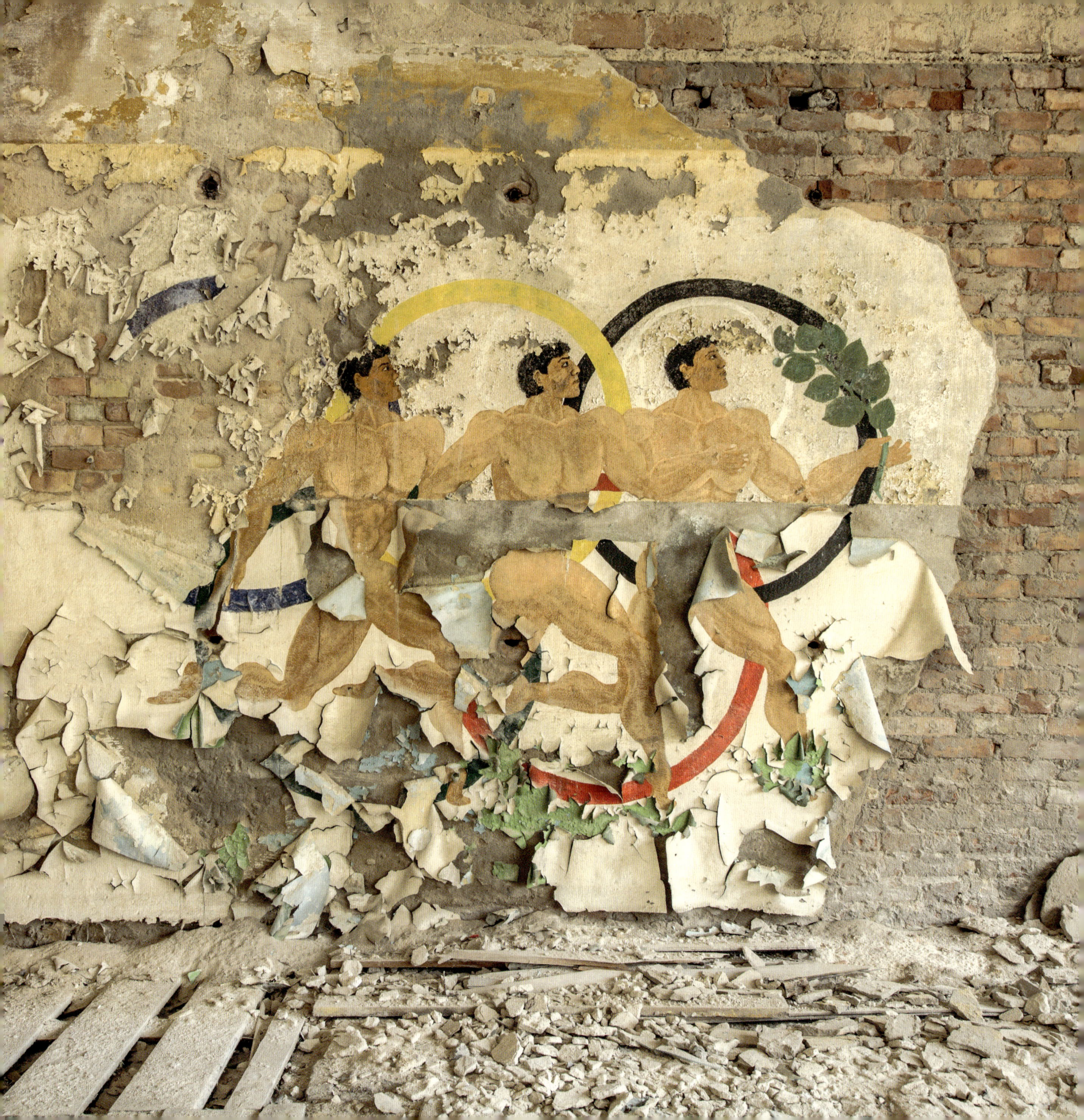

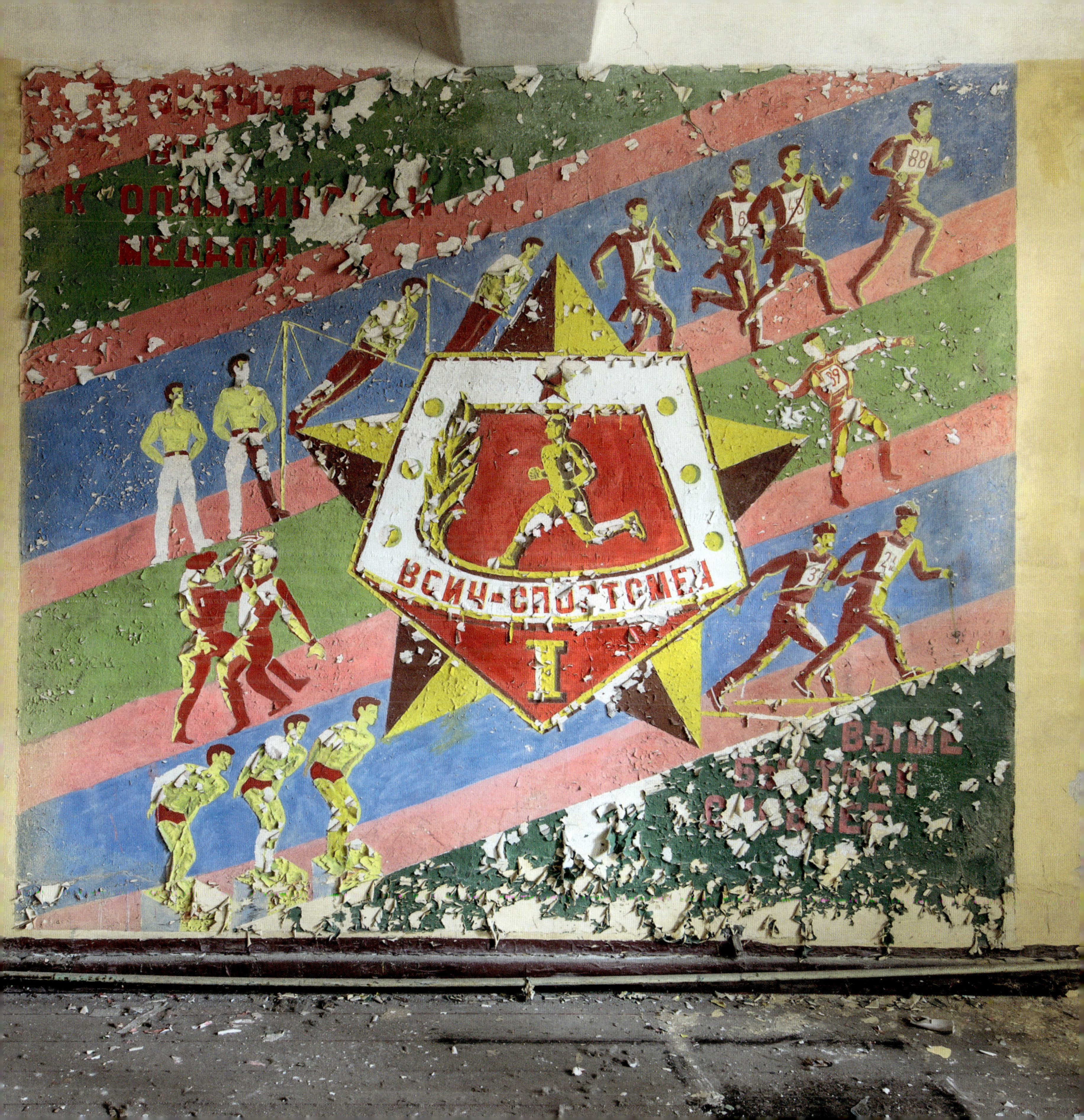
ВСИН-СПОРТСМЕН
I

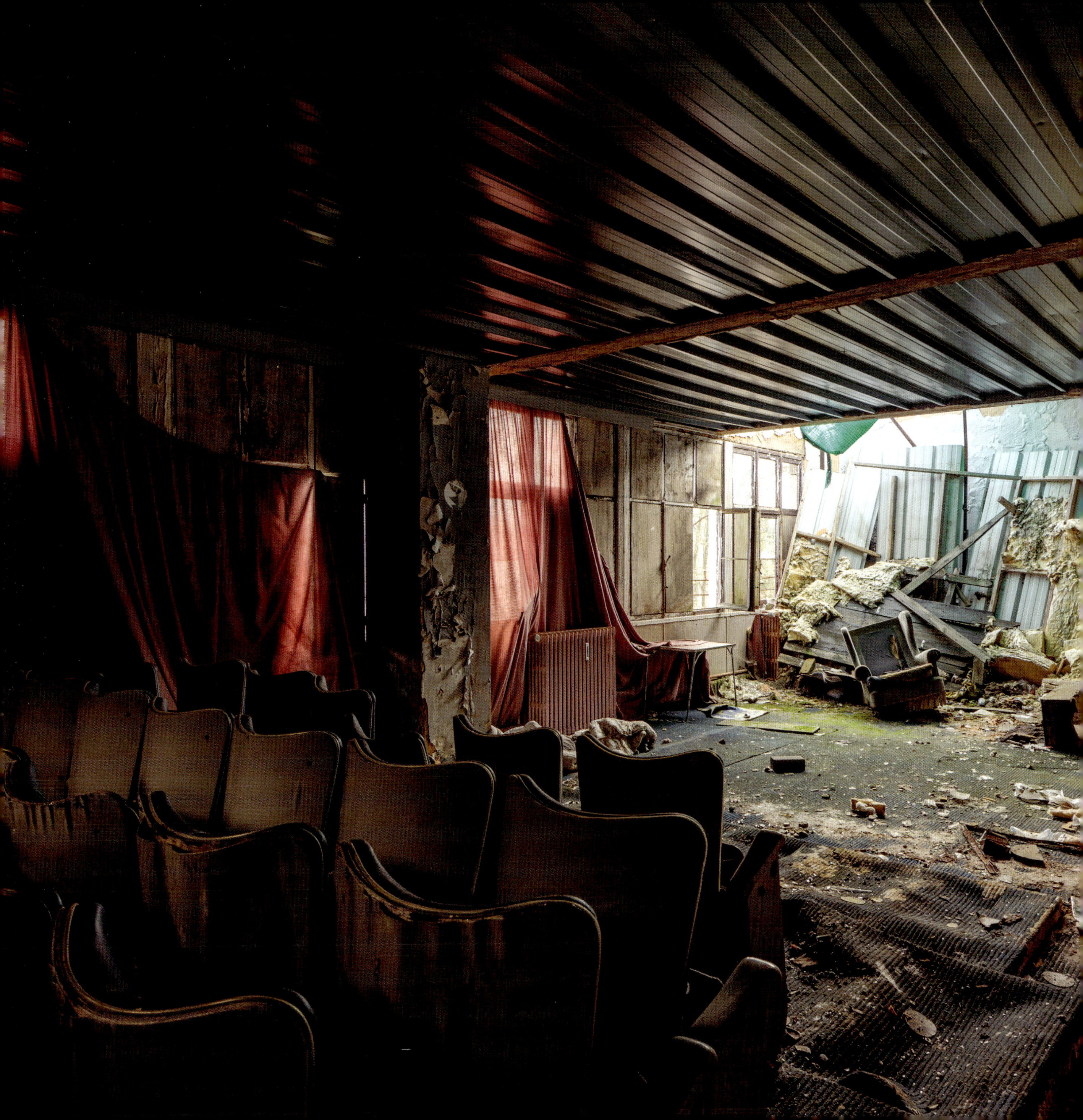

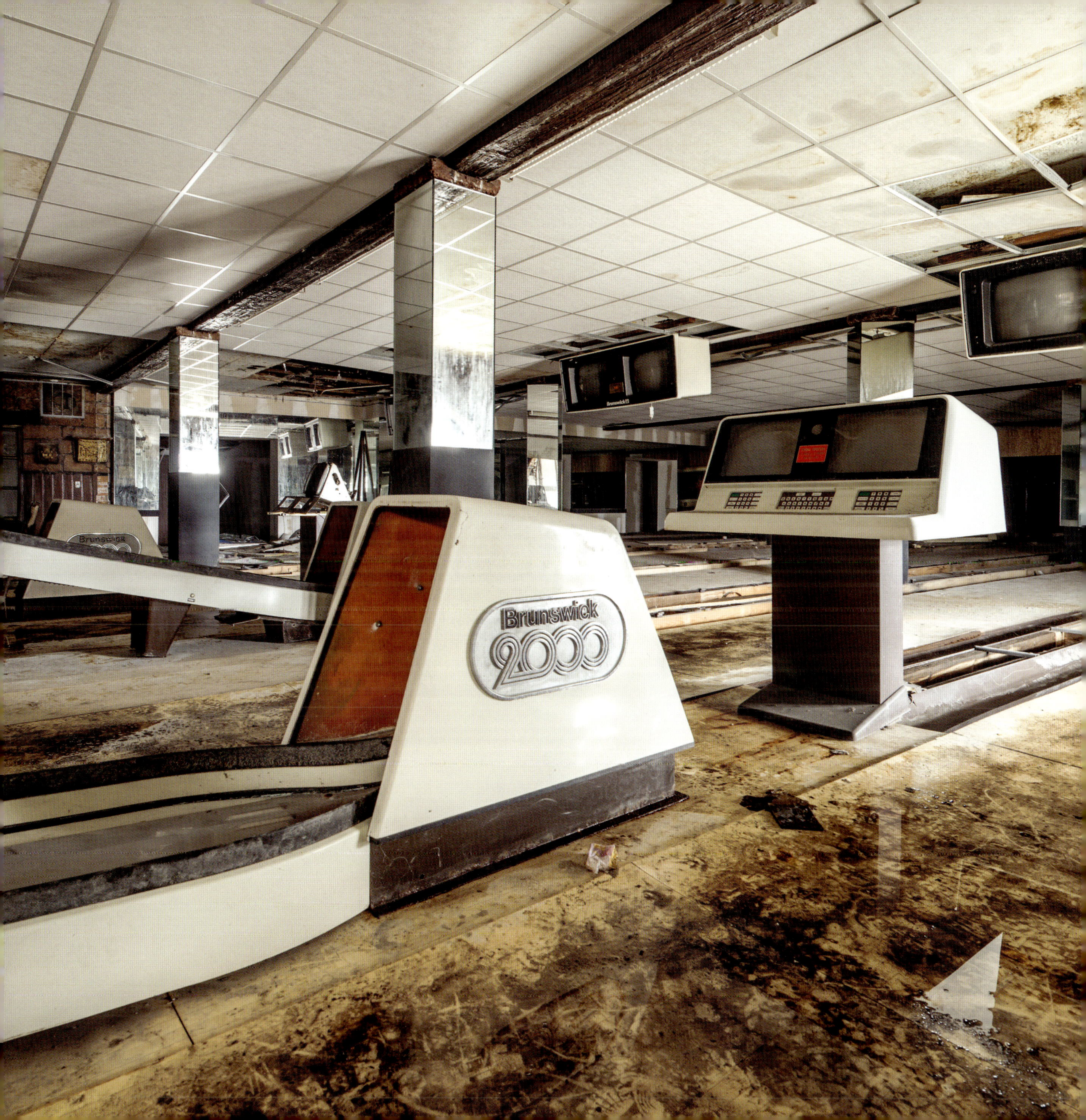
Brunswick
2000

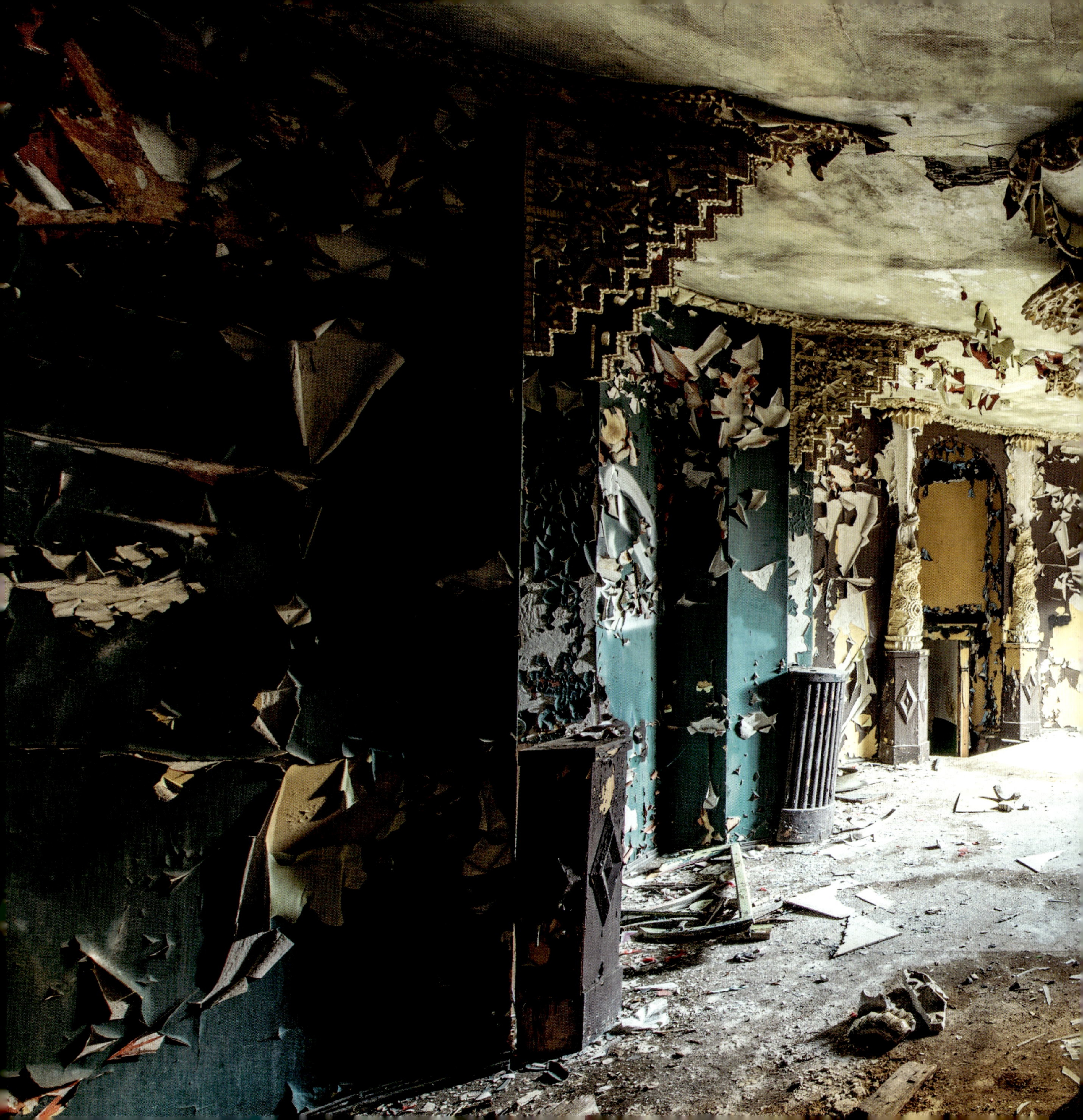

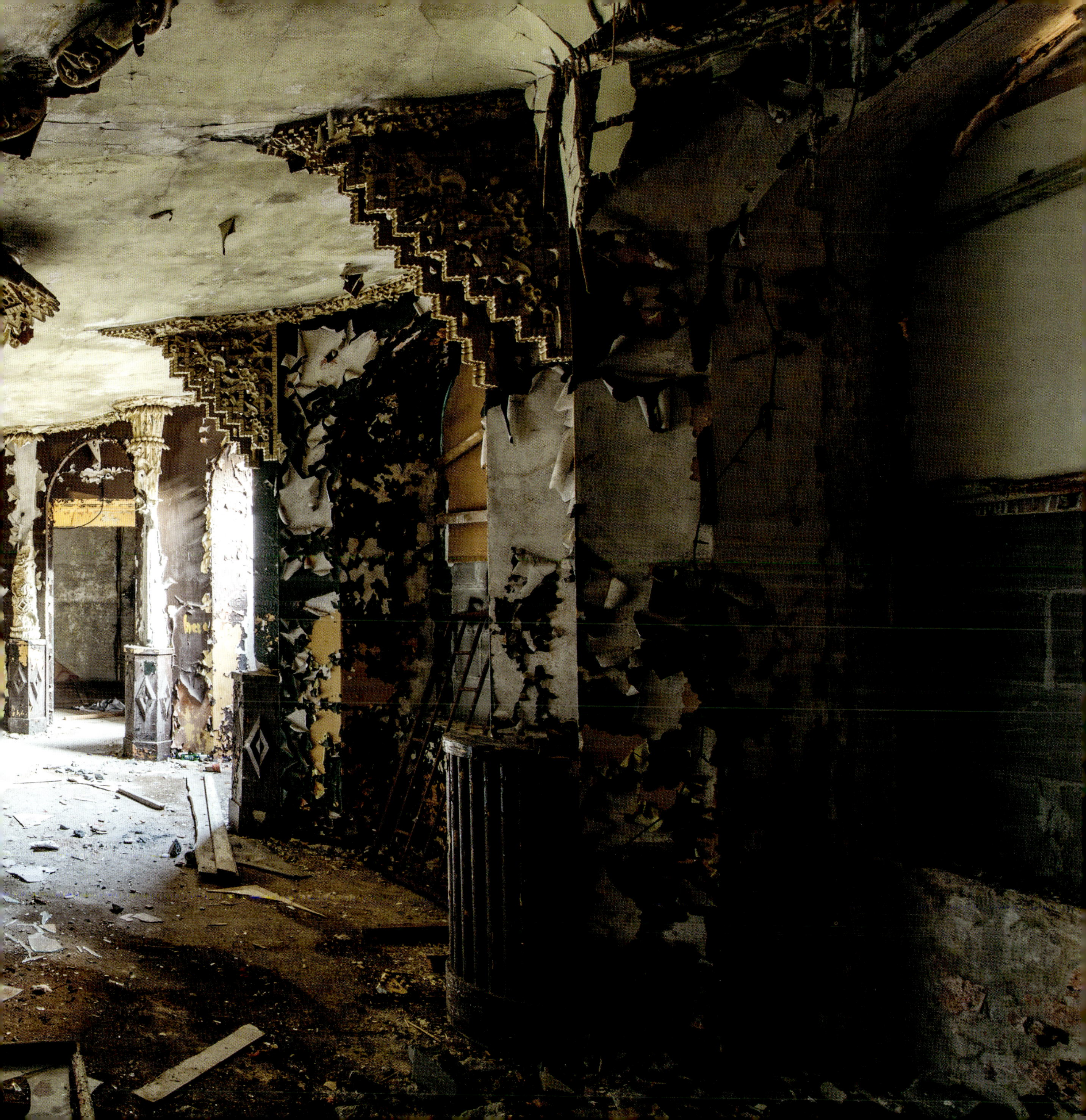

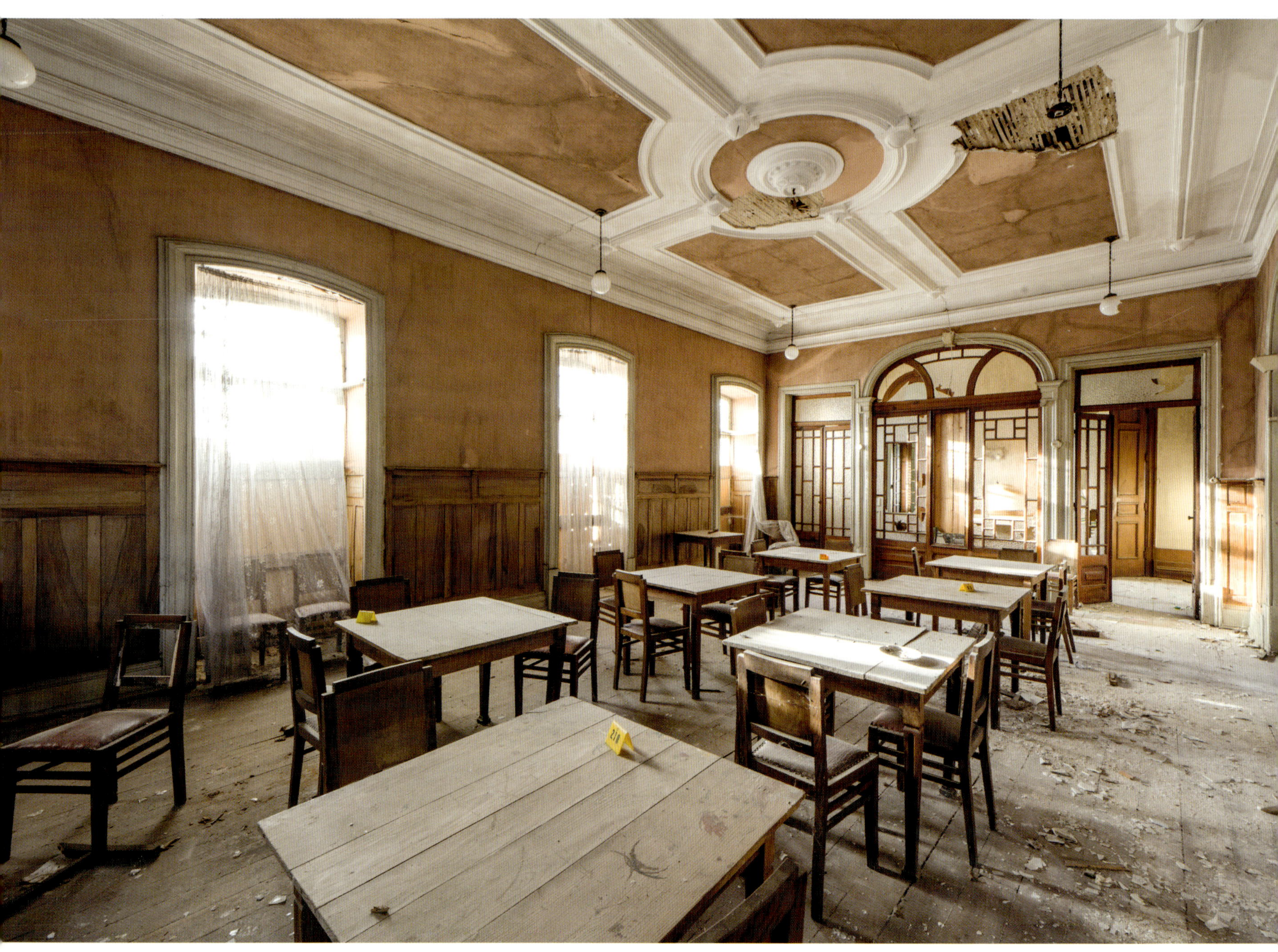

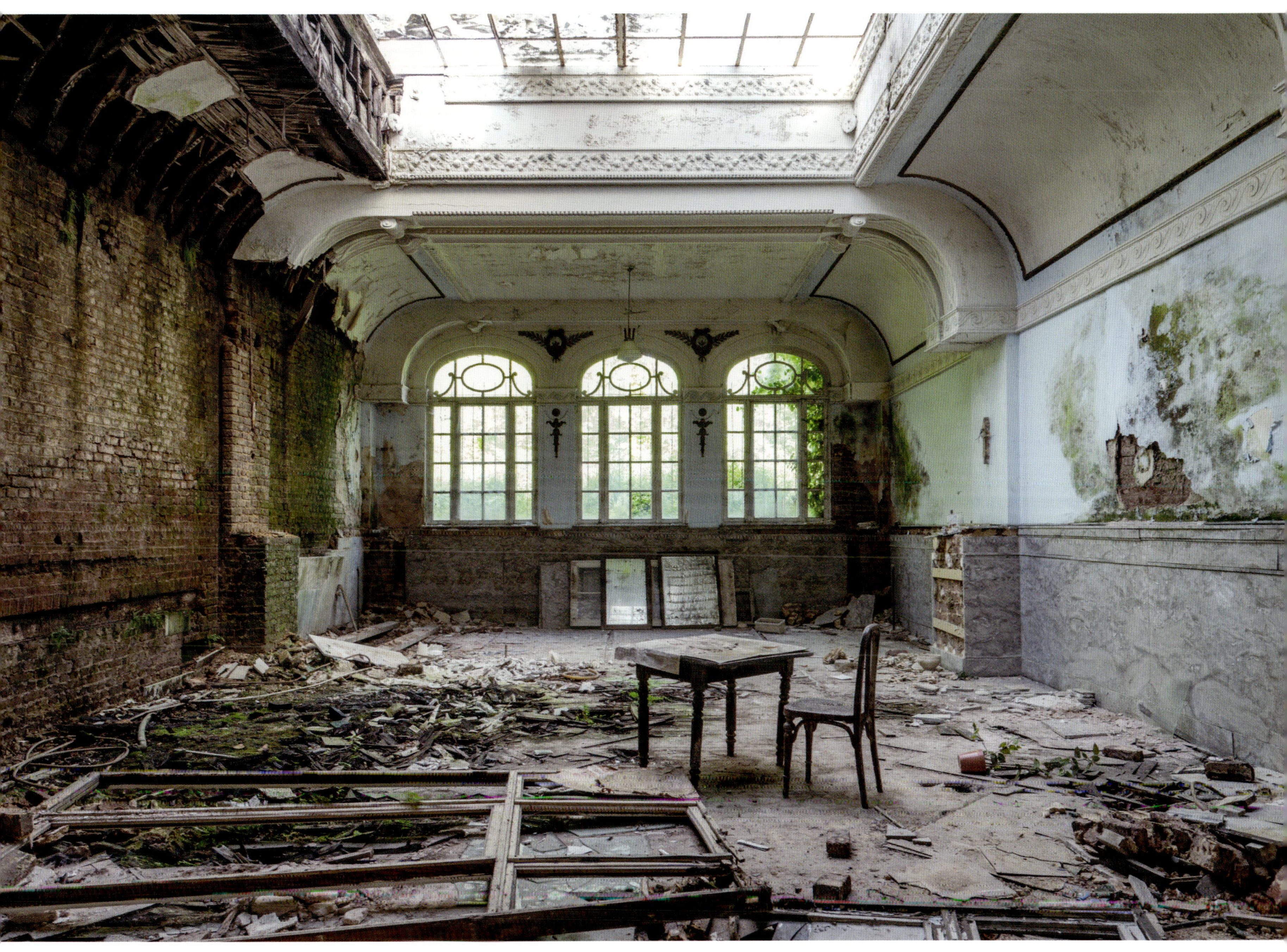

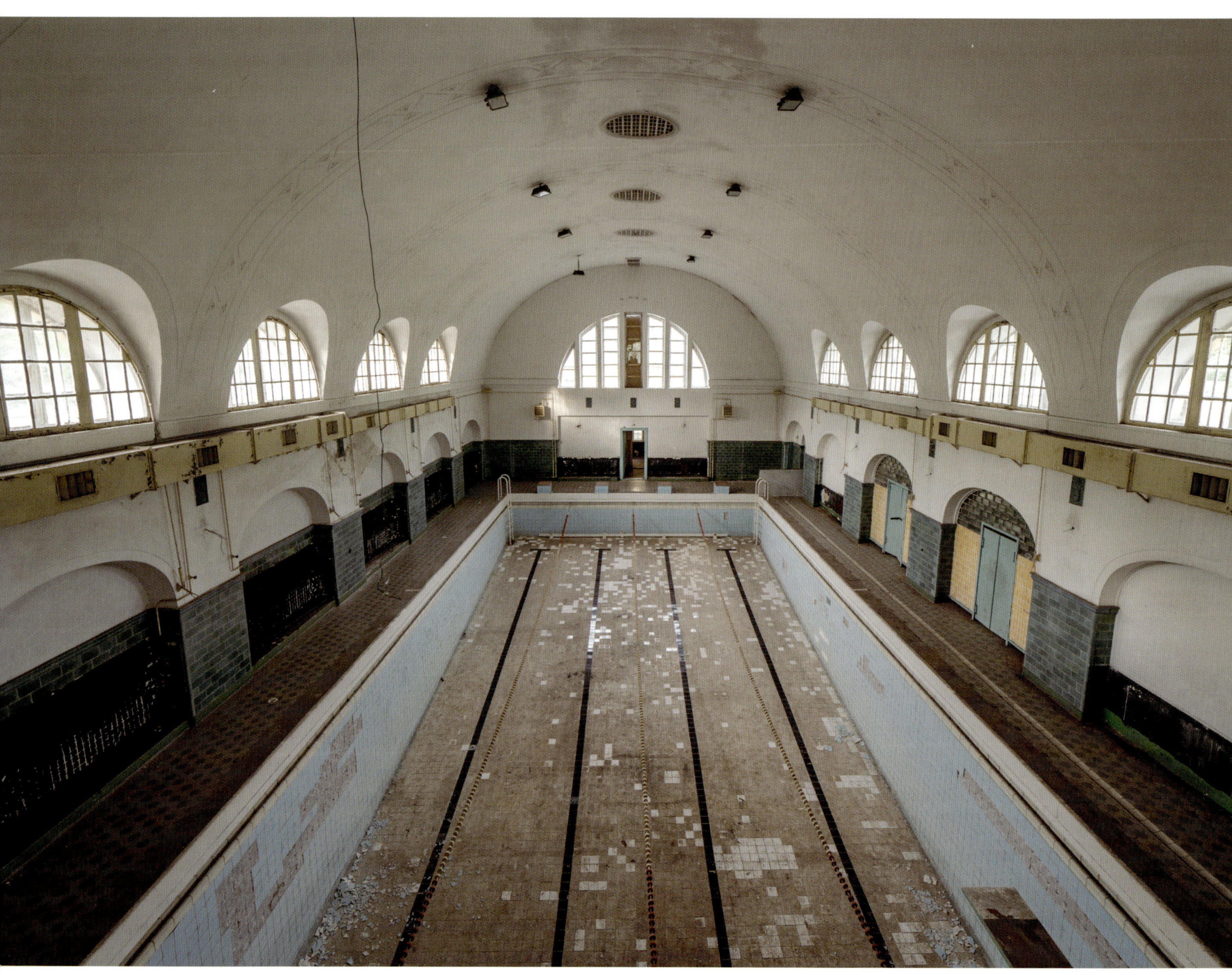

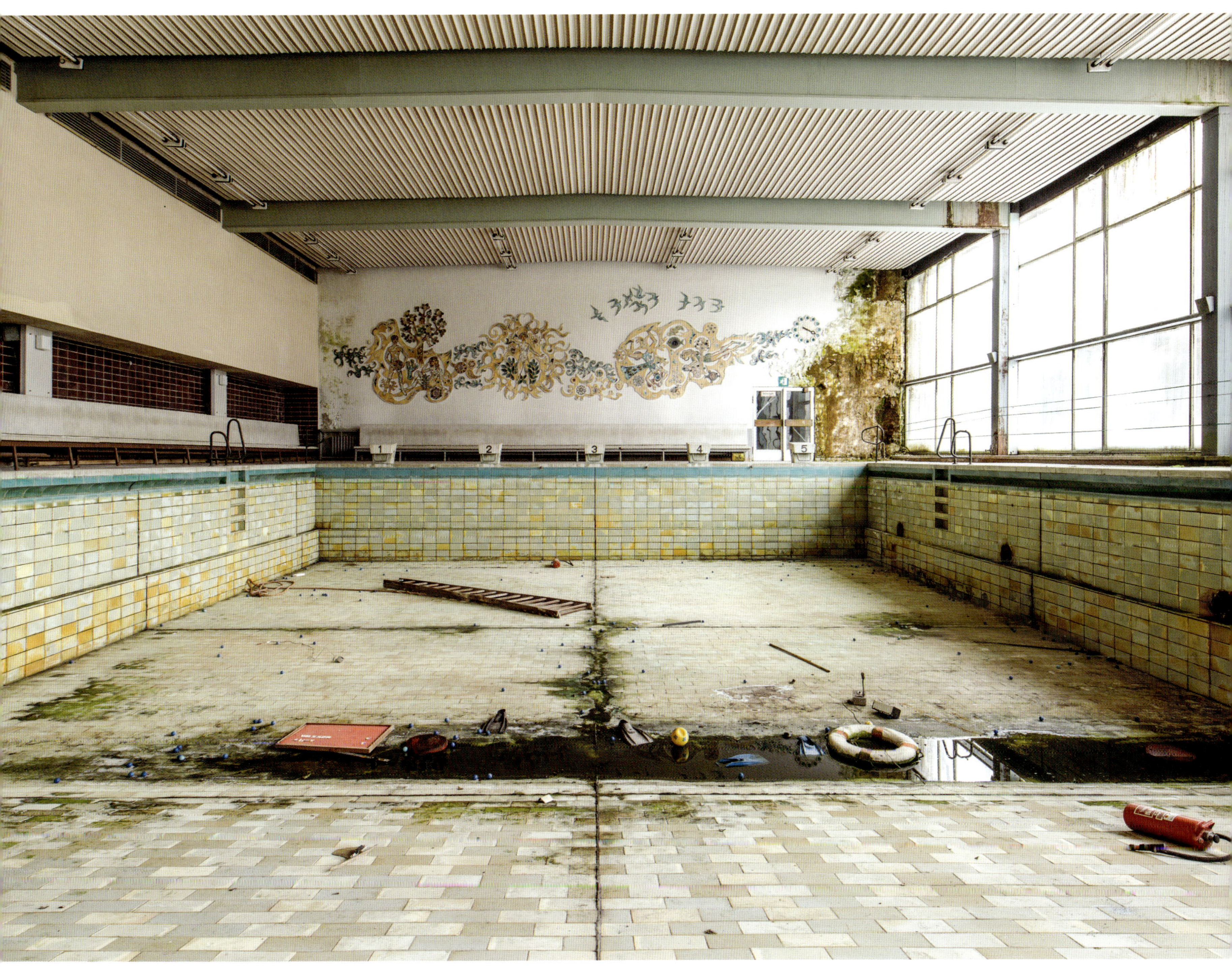

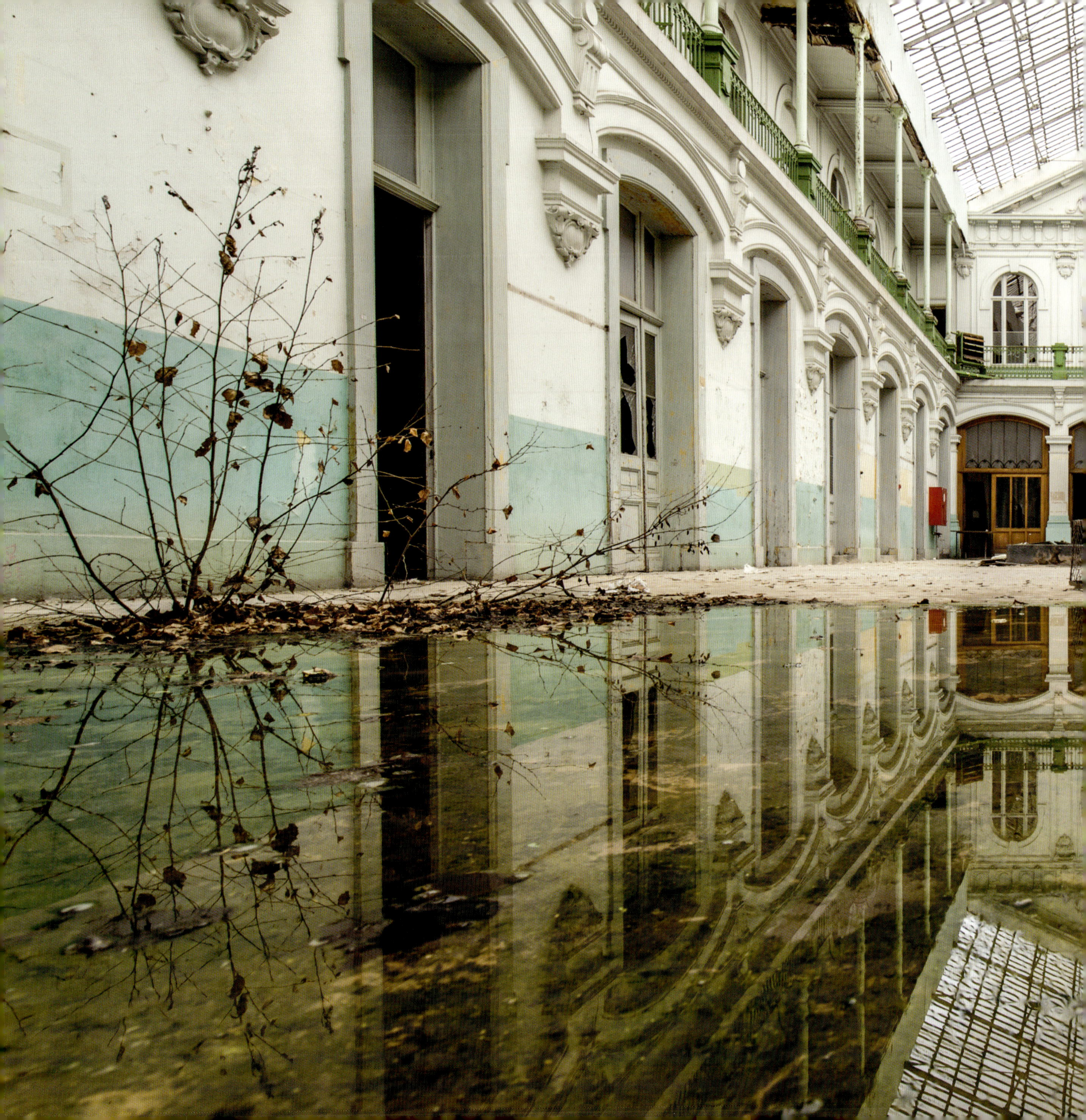

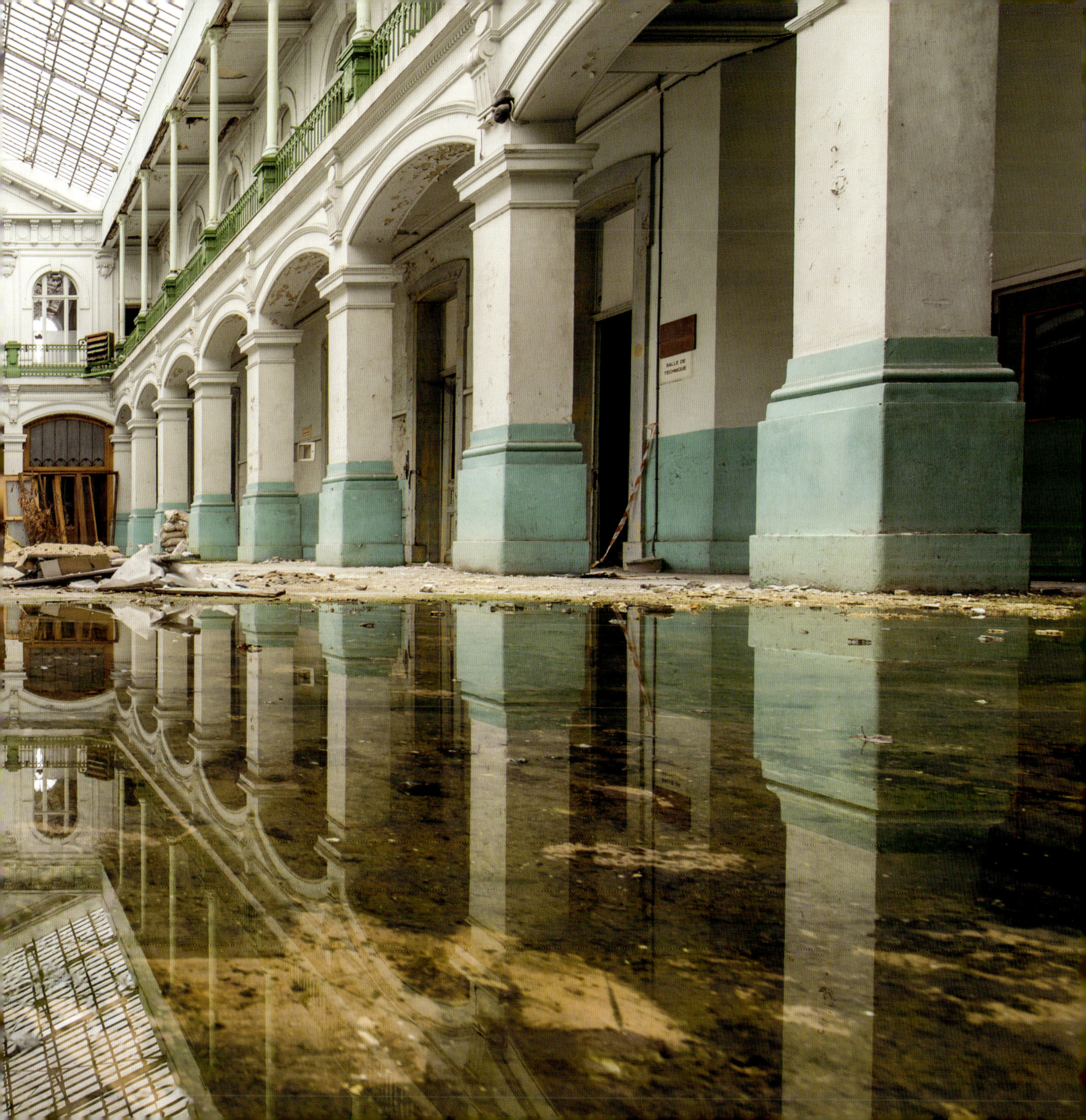
SALLE DE
TECHNIQUE

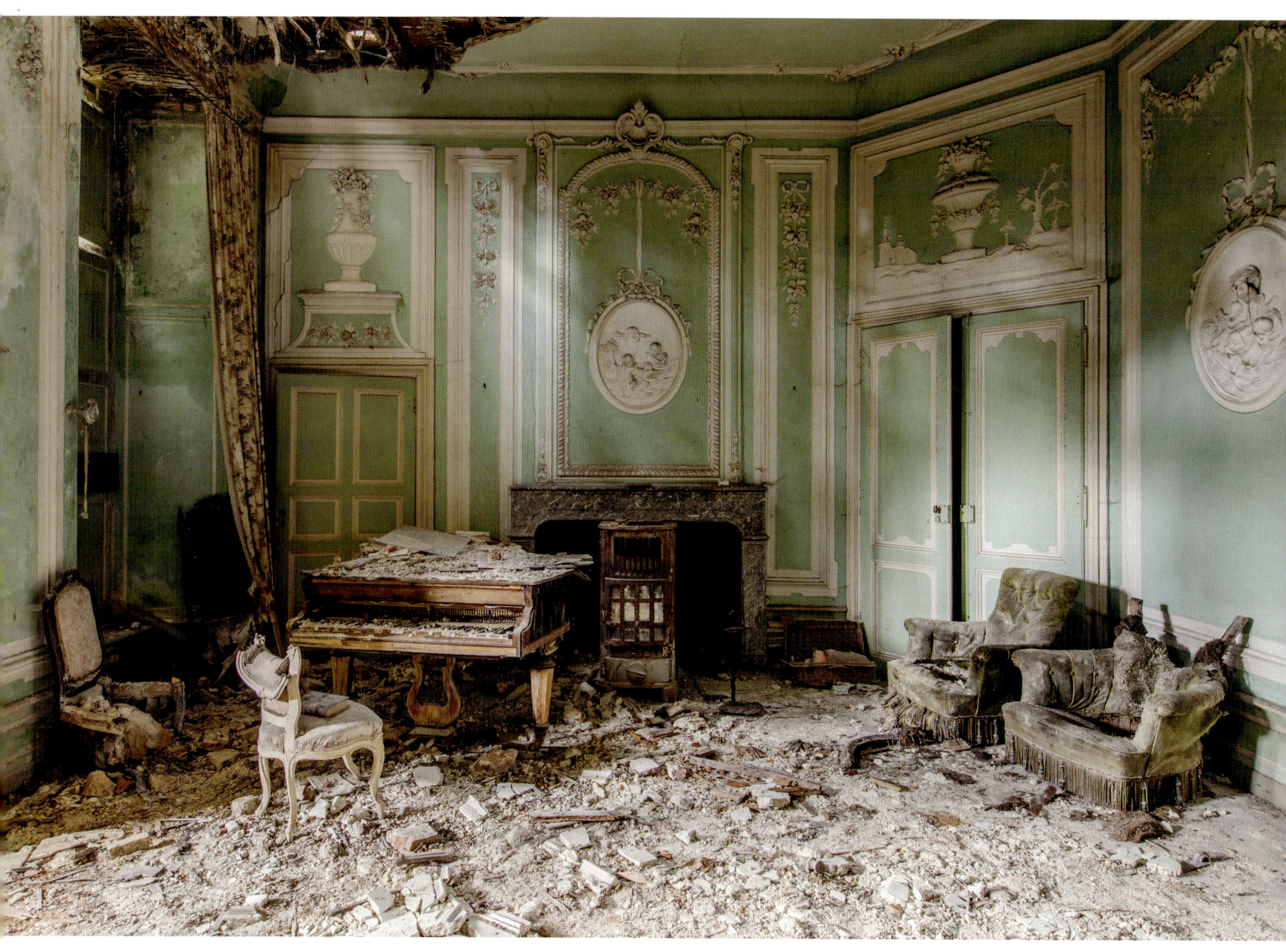

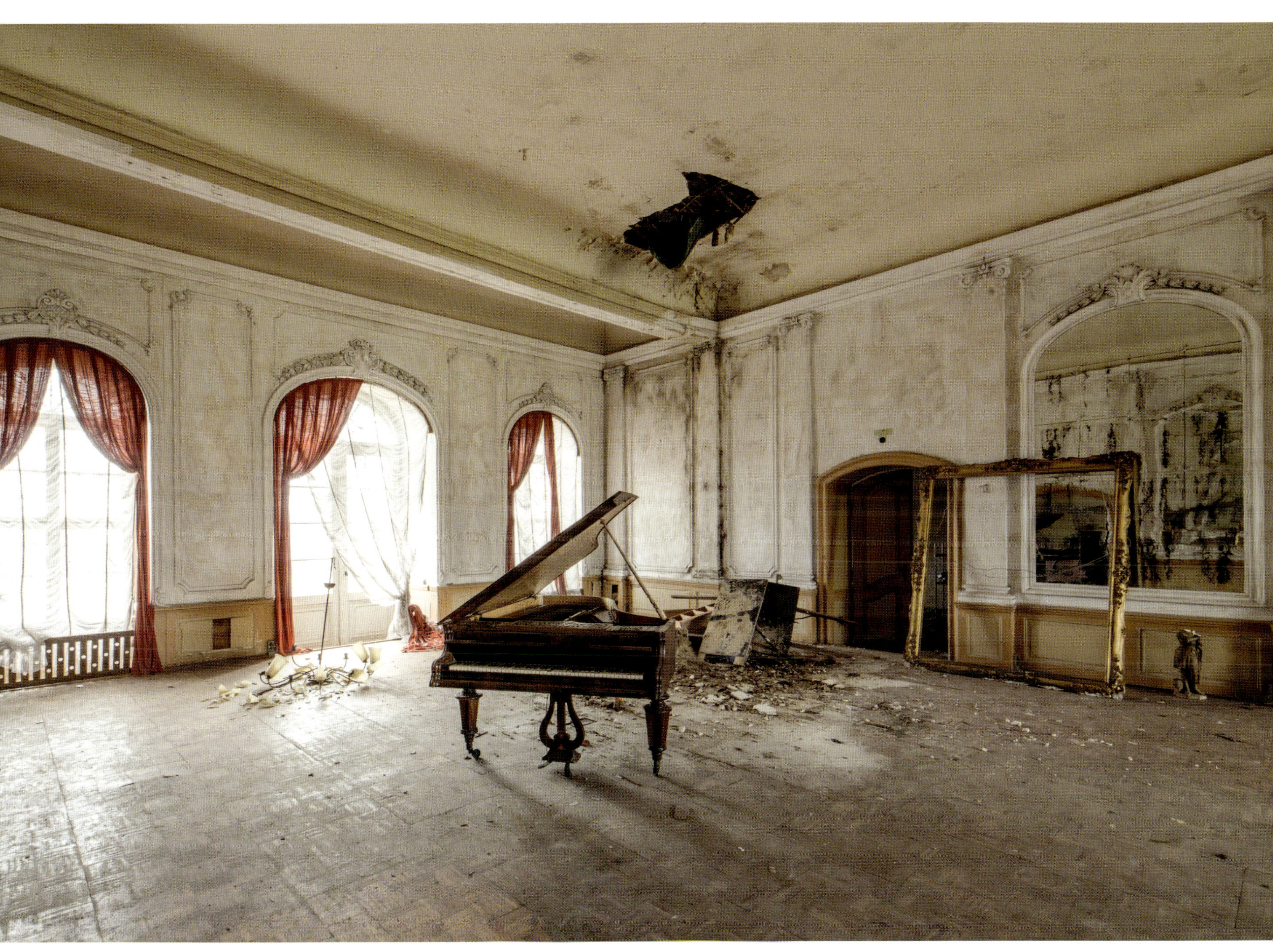

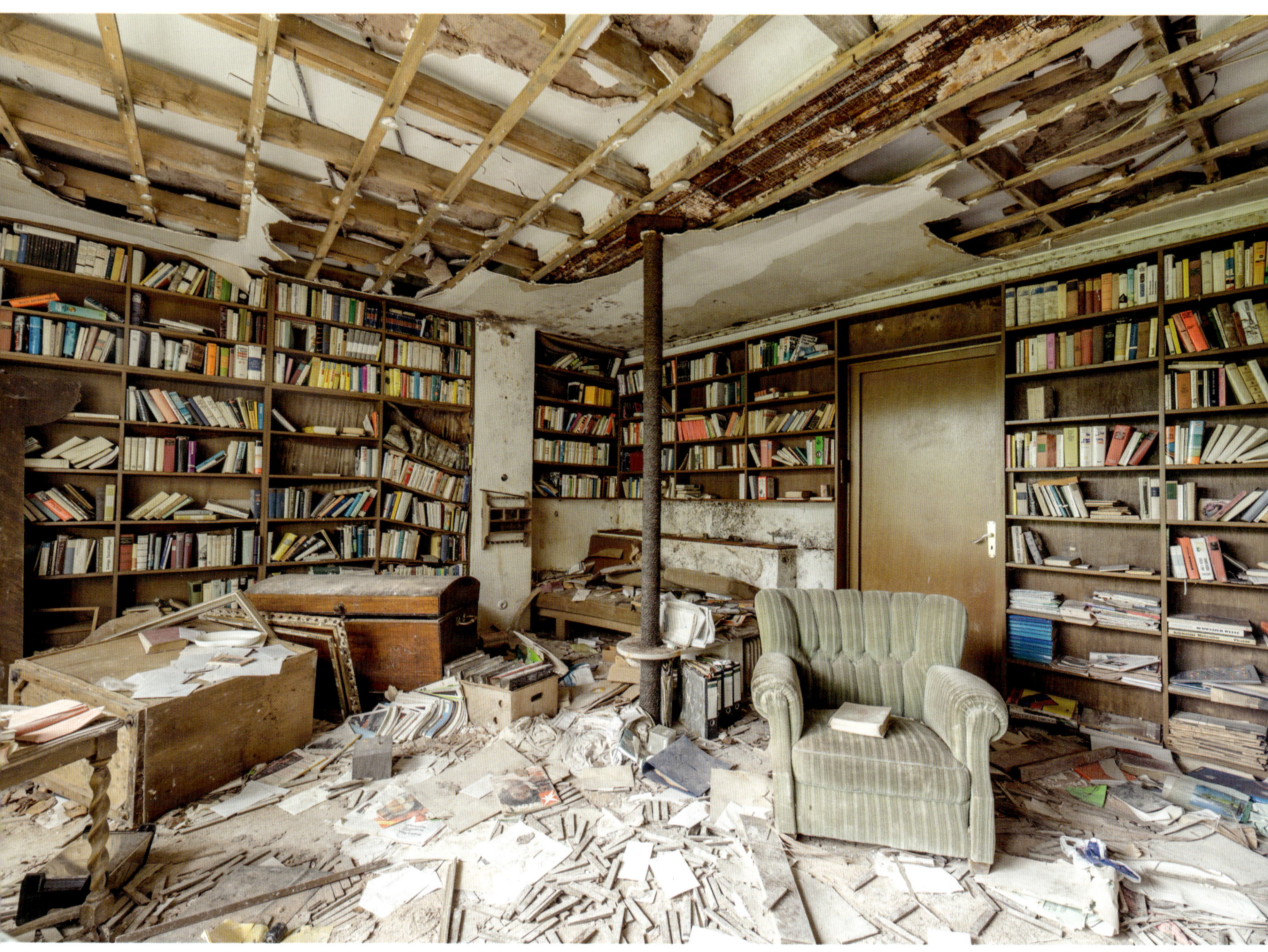

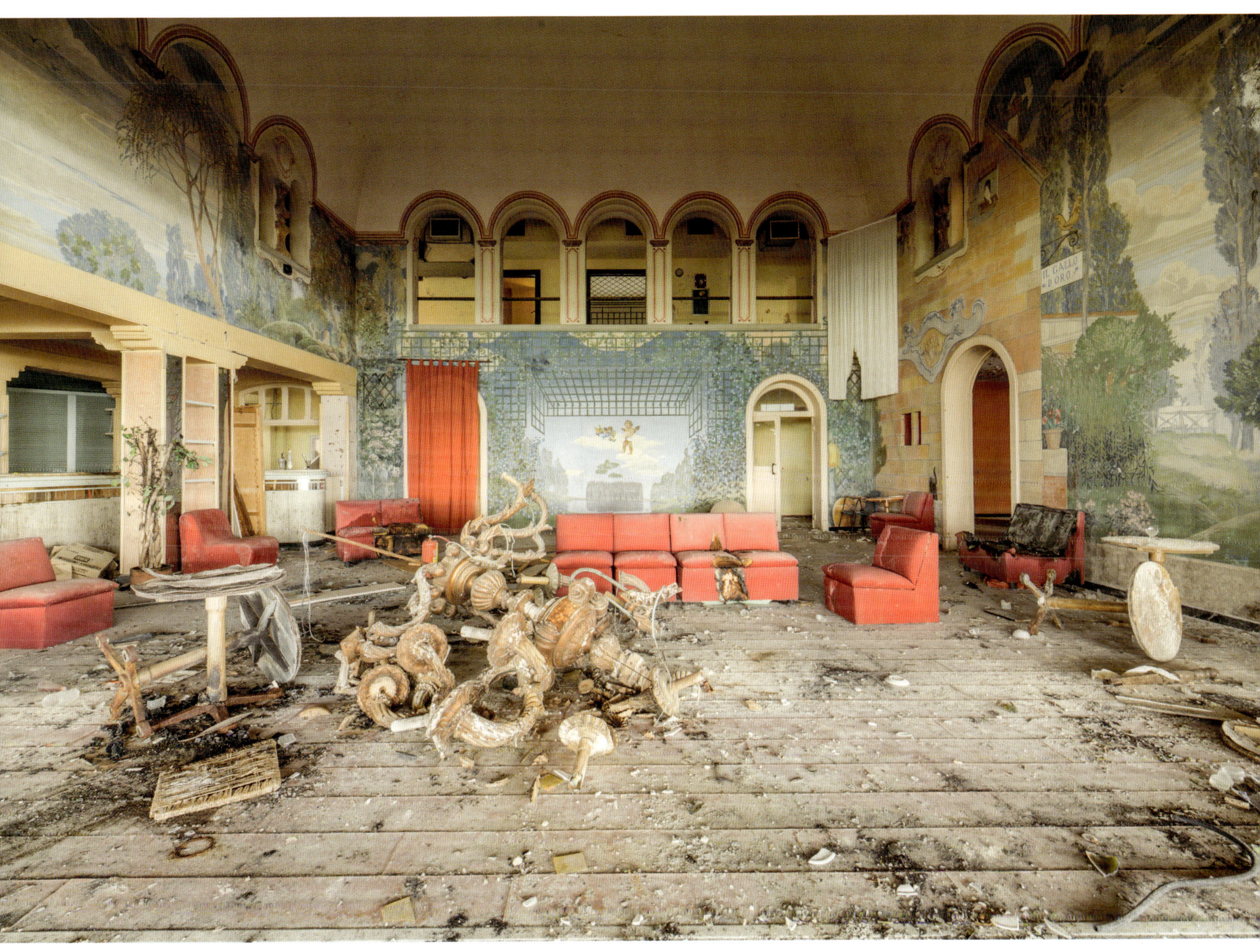

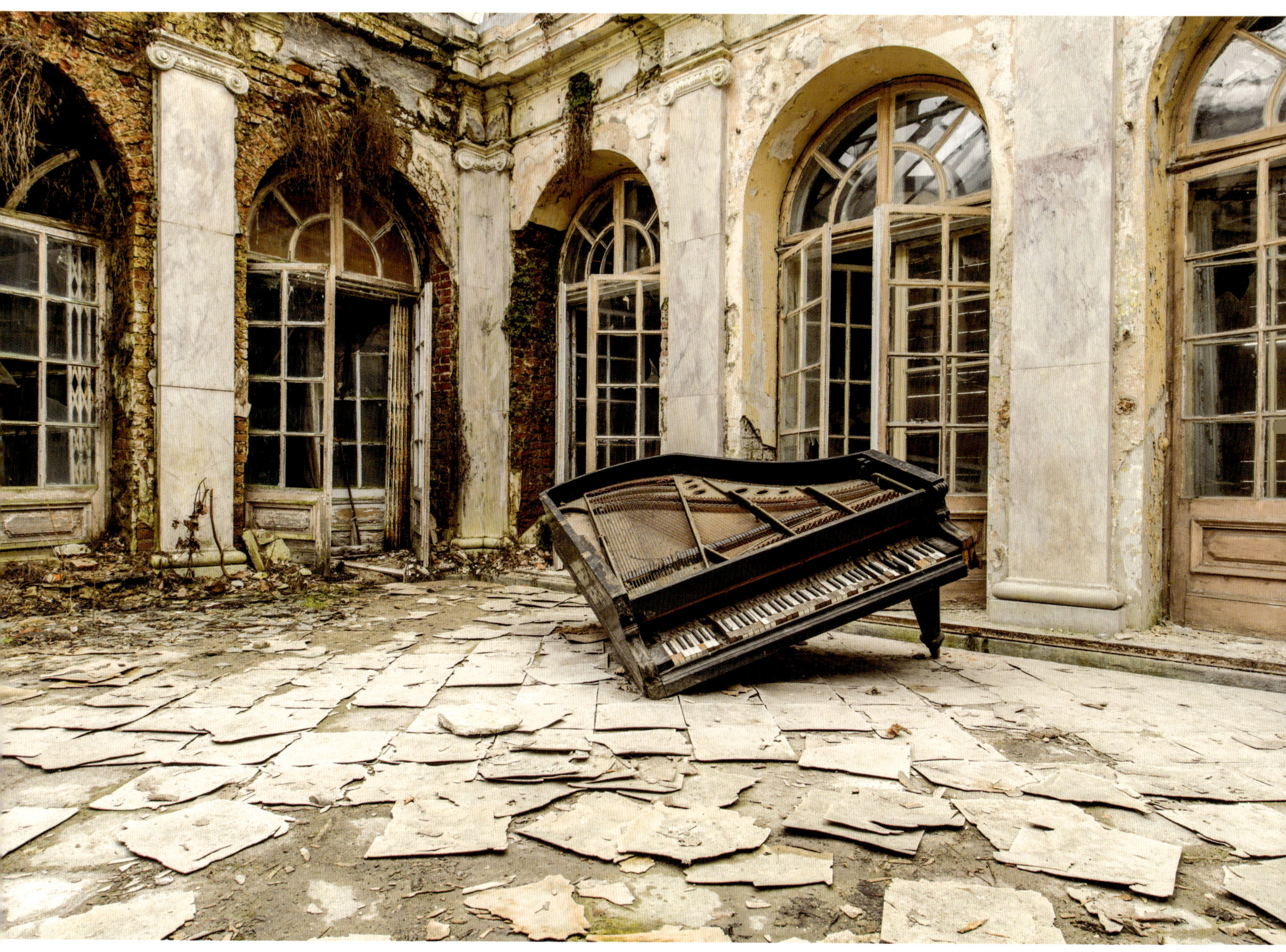

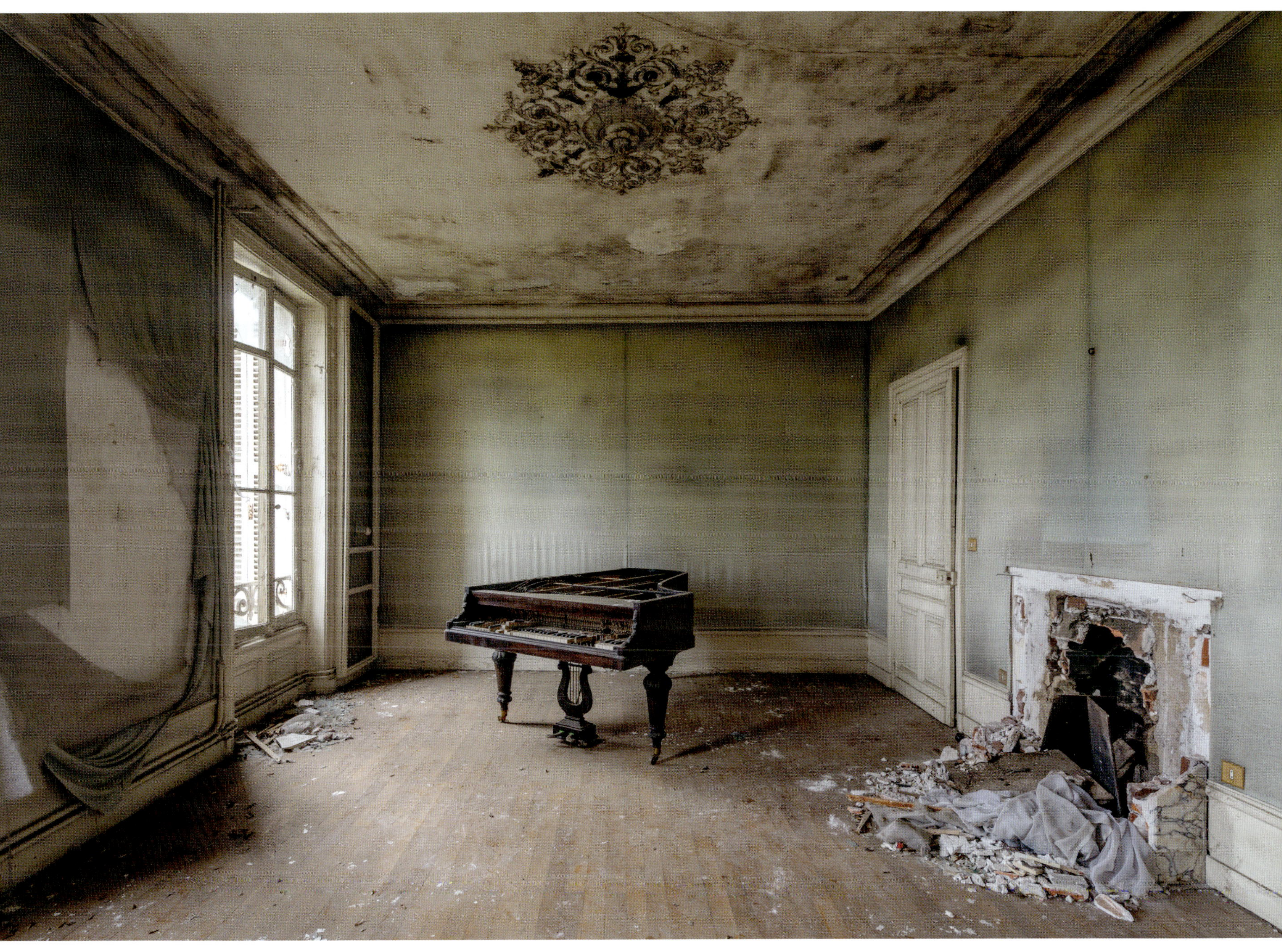

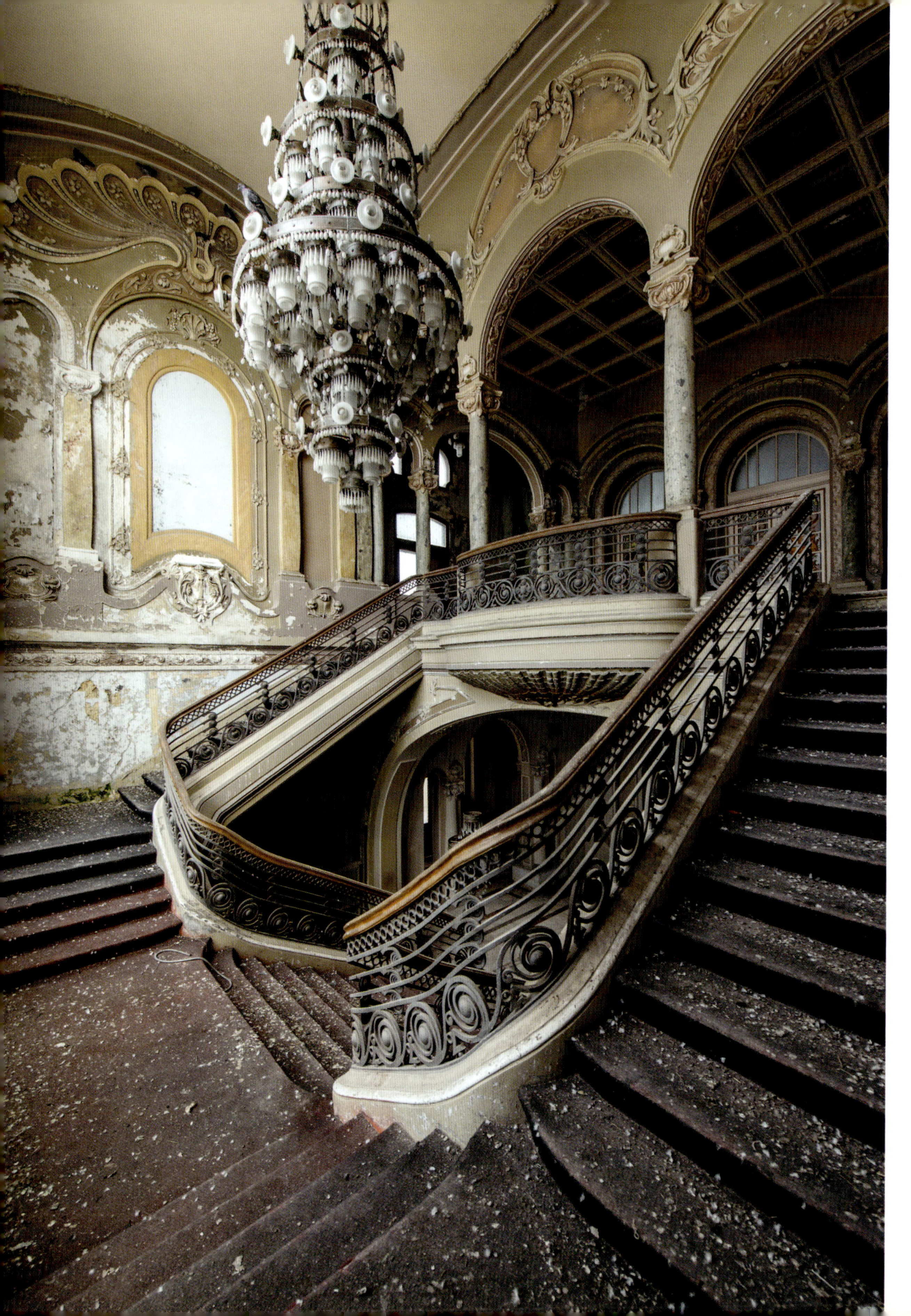

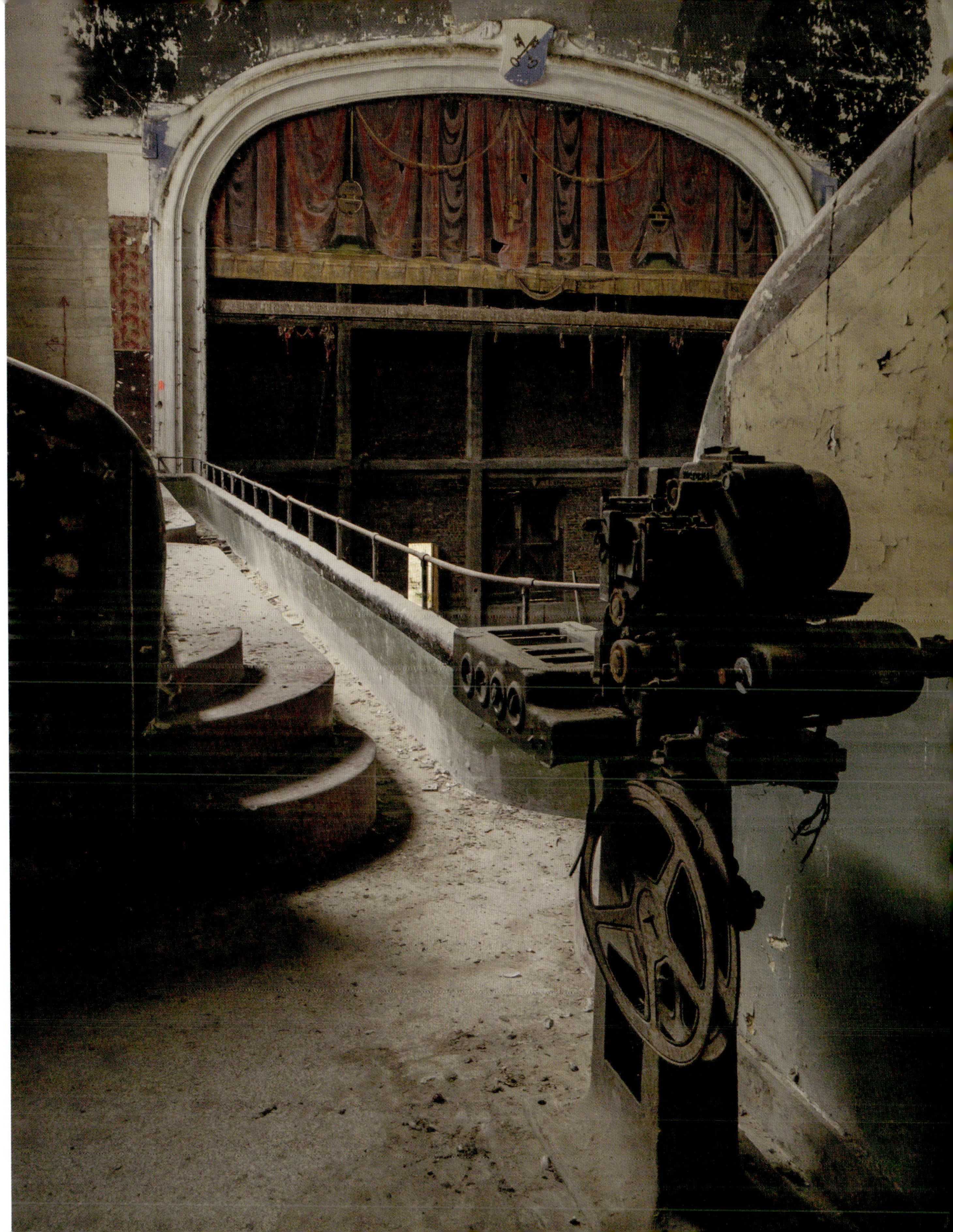

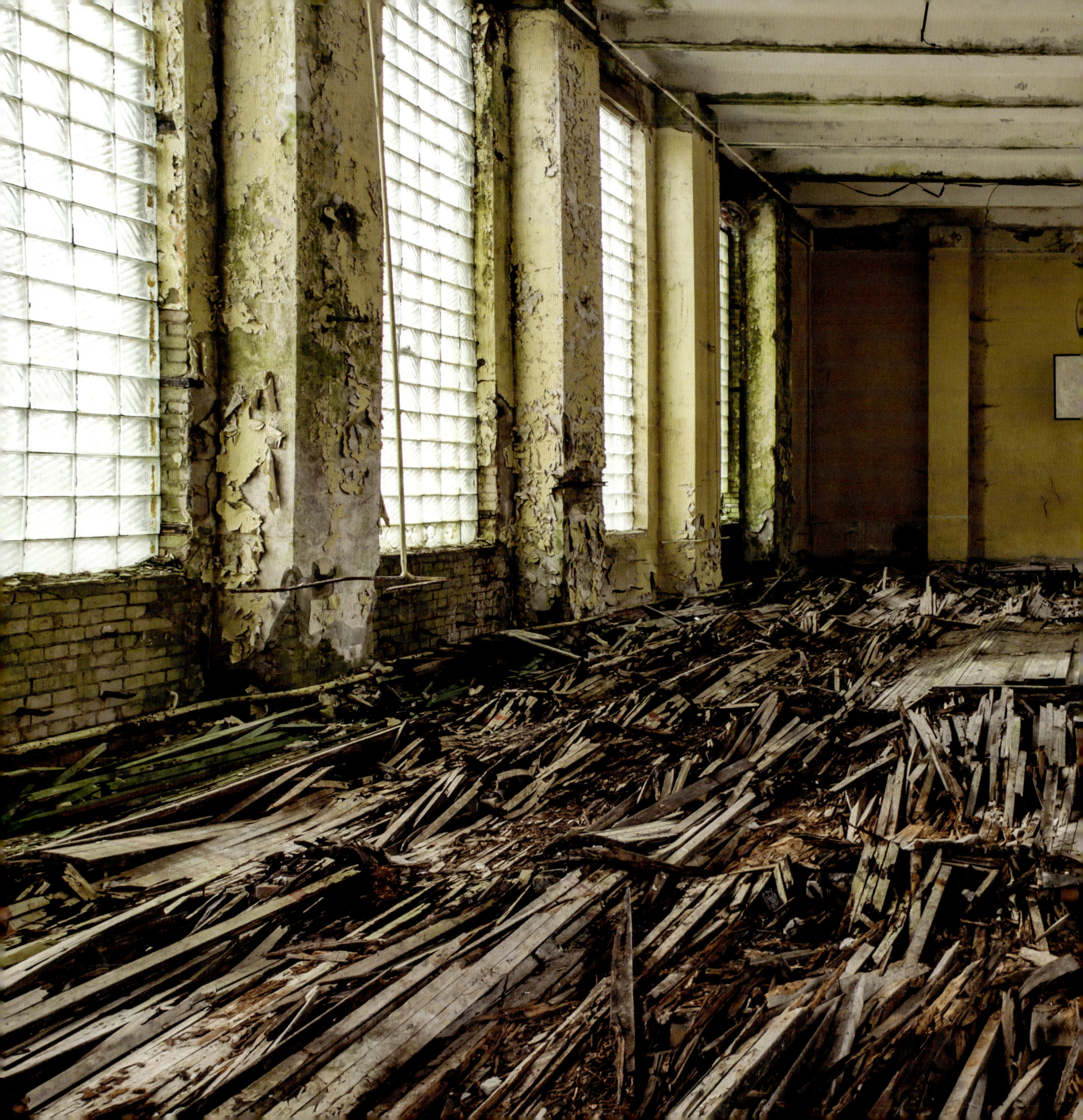

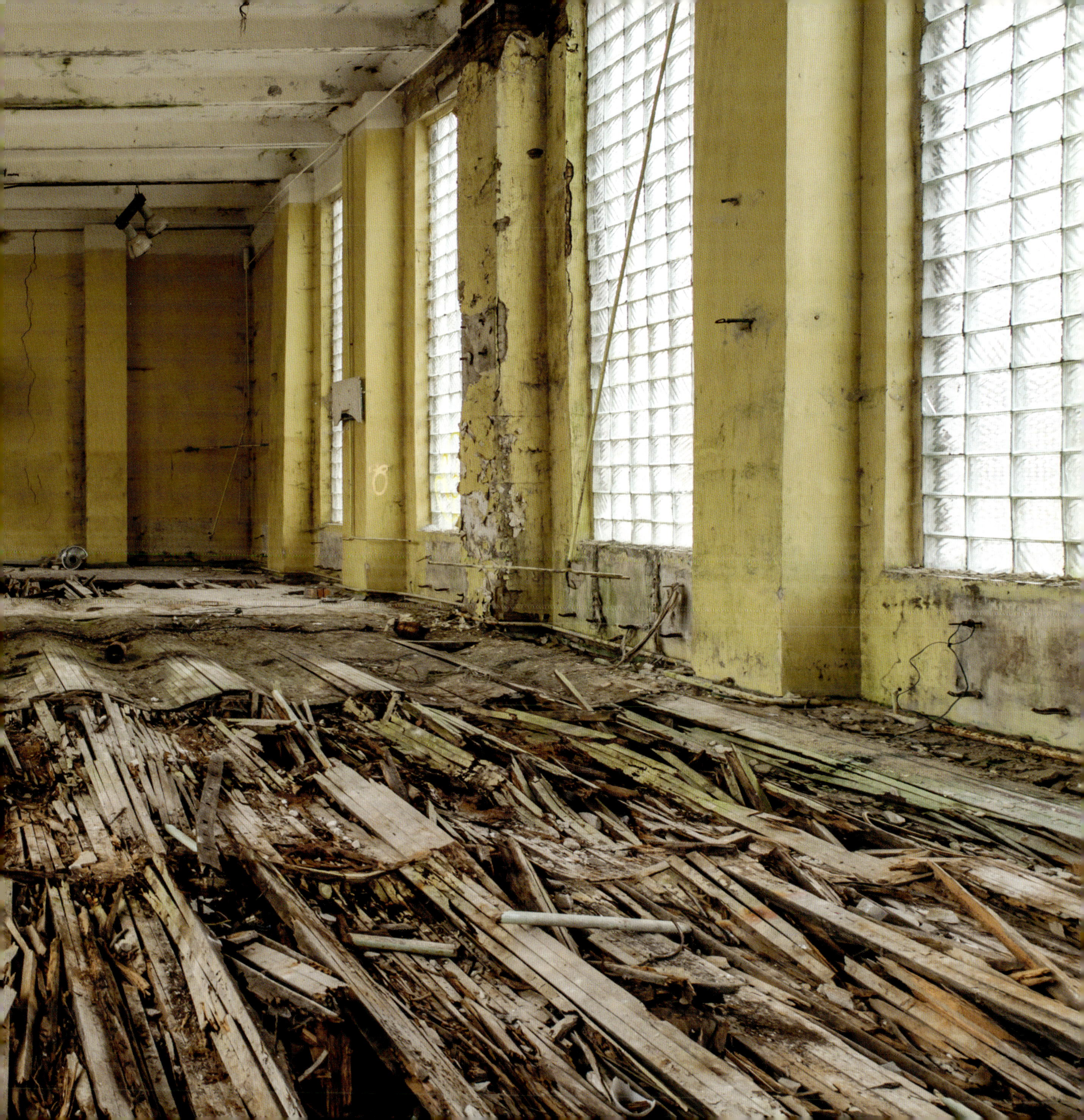

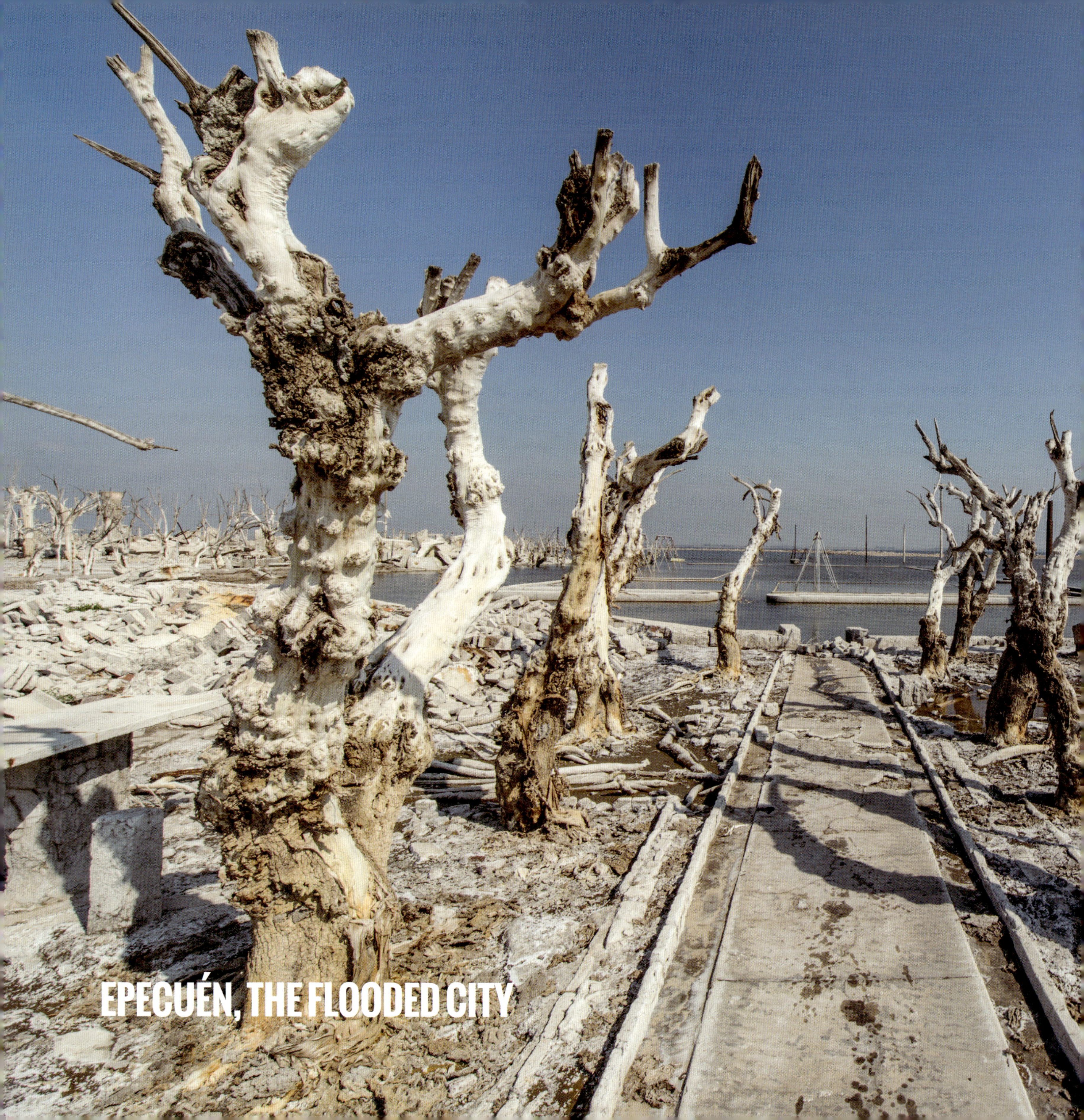

EPECUÉN, THE FLOODED CITY

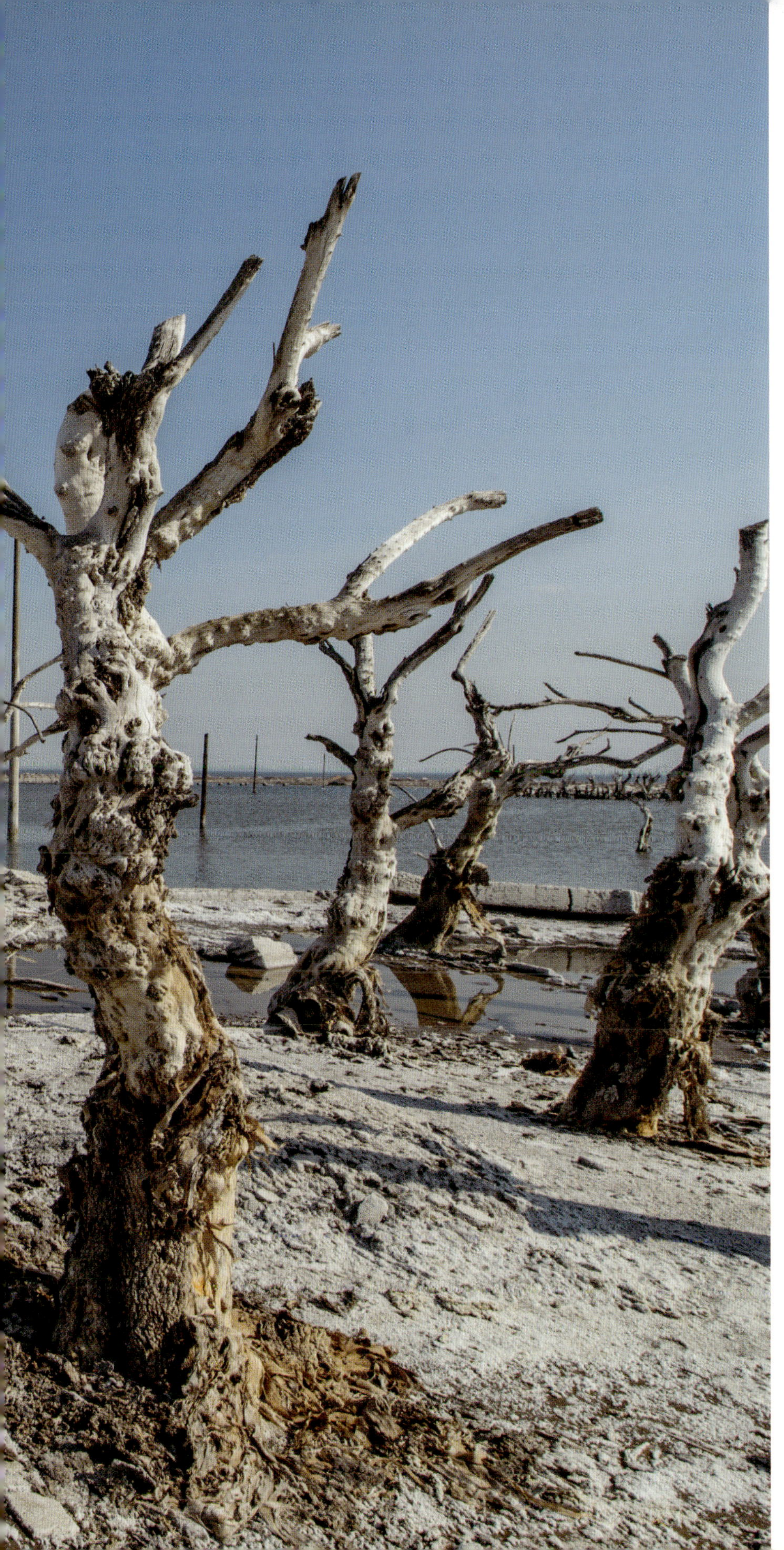

The destiny of the former spa resort
Epecuén was a tragic one. Located
approximately 500 kilometers south of
Buenos-Aires, Argentina, Epecuén was
founded in the early nineteen-twenties on
the margin of the eponymous lagoon.
Legend holds that the lake was formed by
the tears of a great chief crying for the pain
of his beloved.

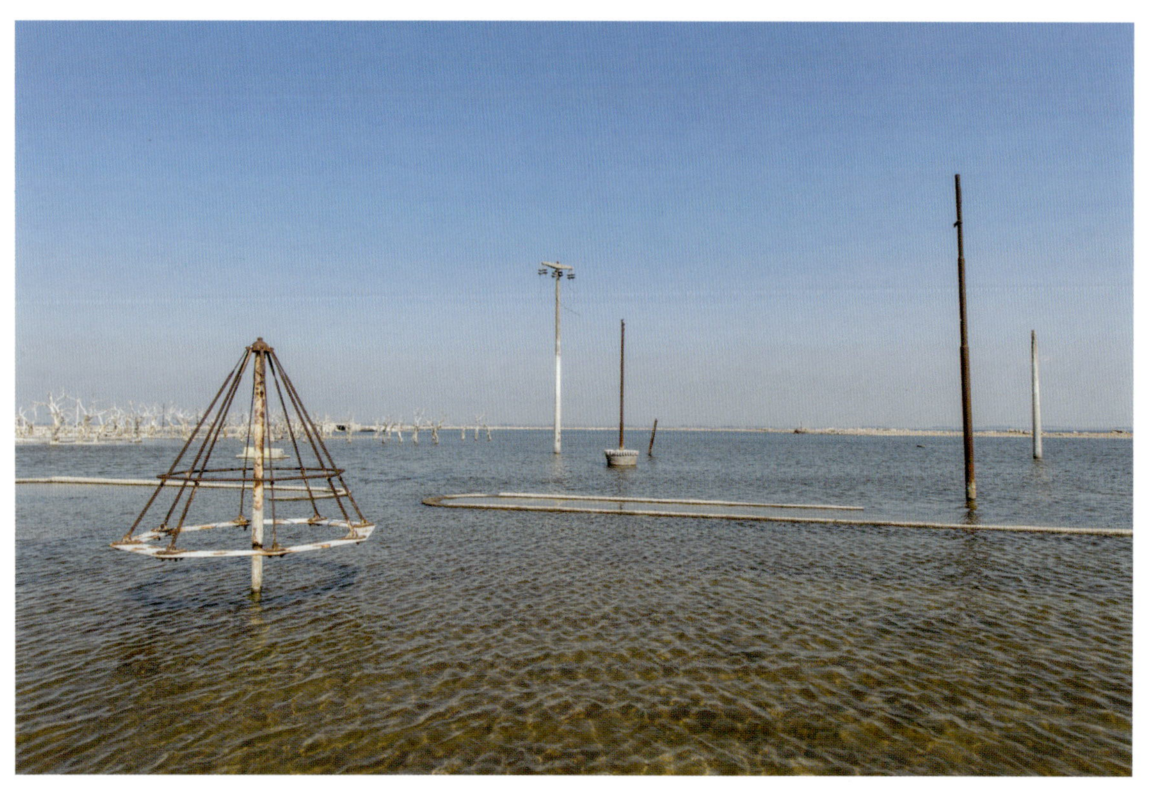

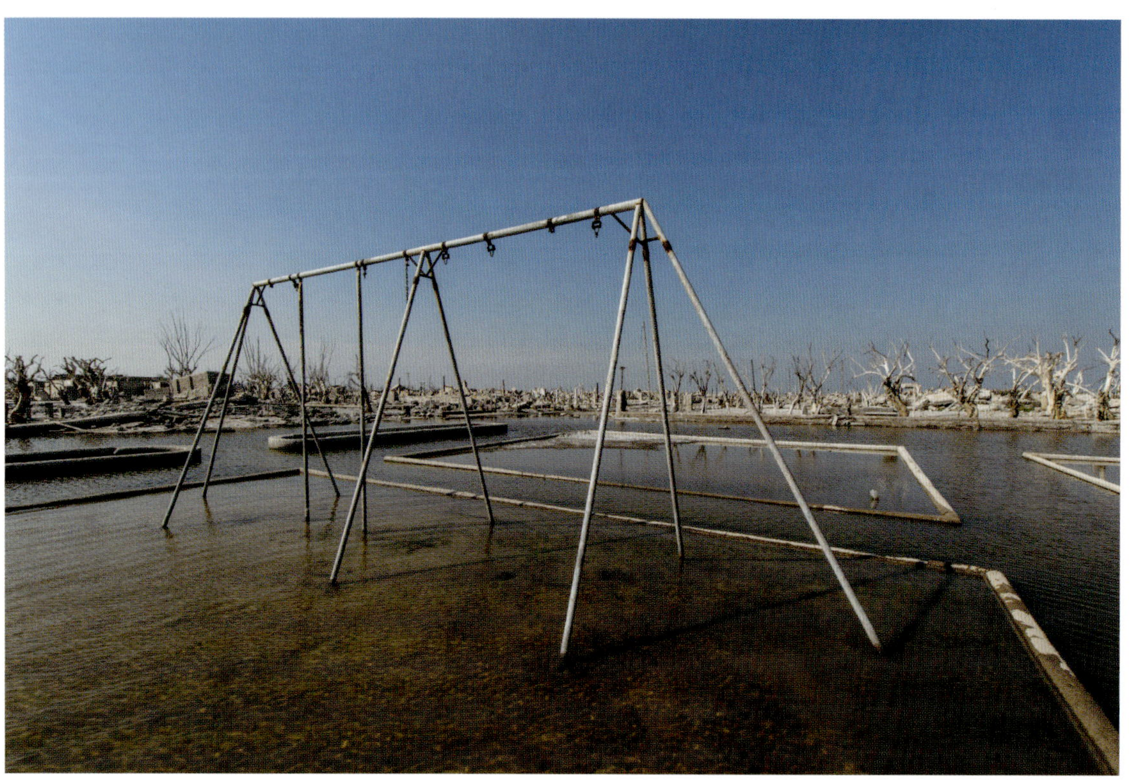

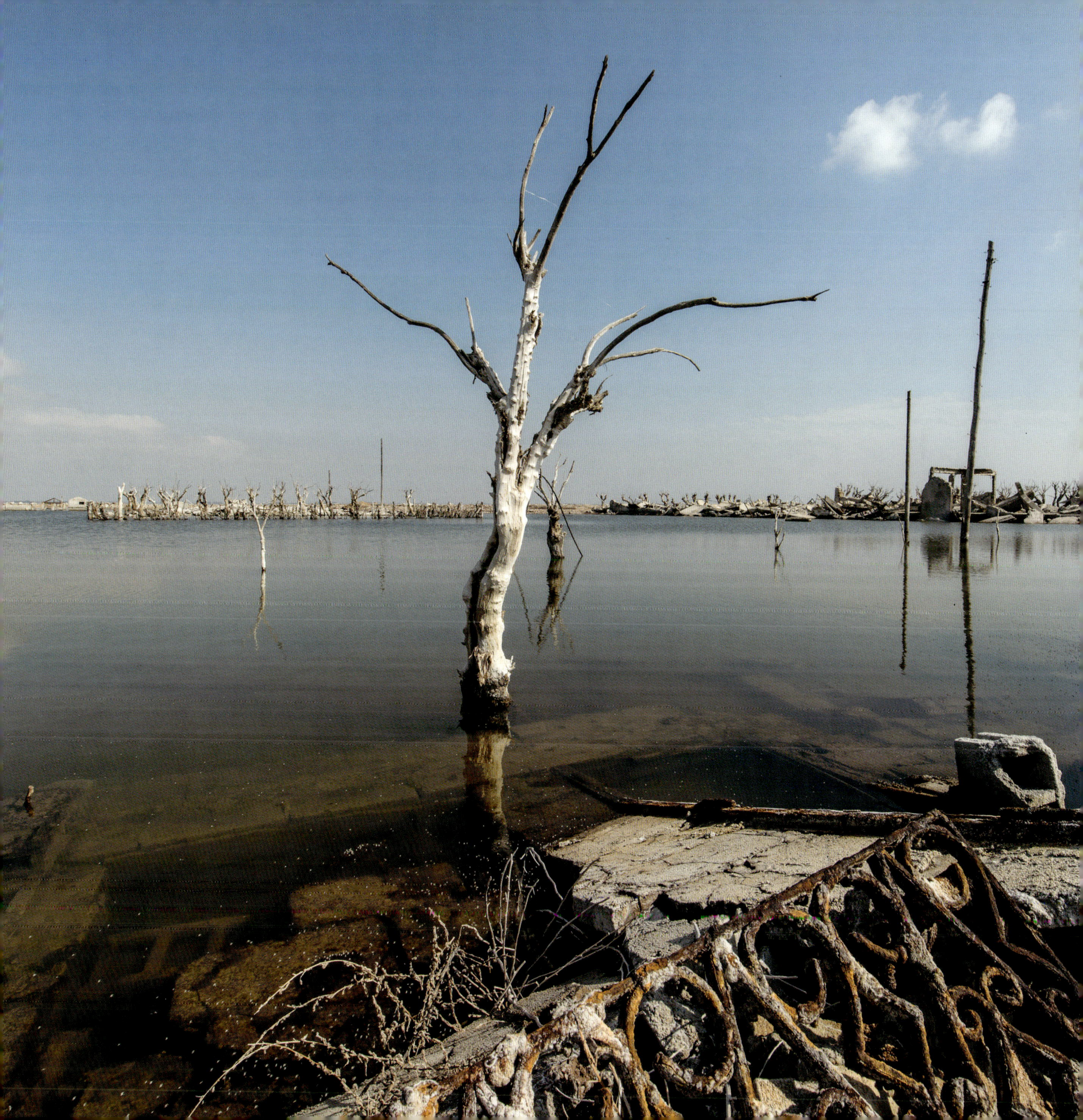

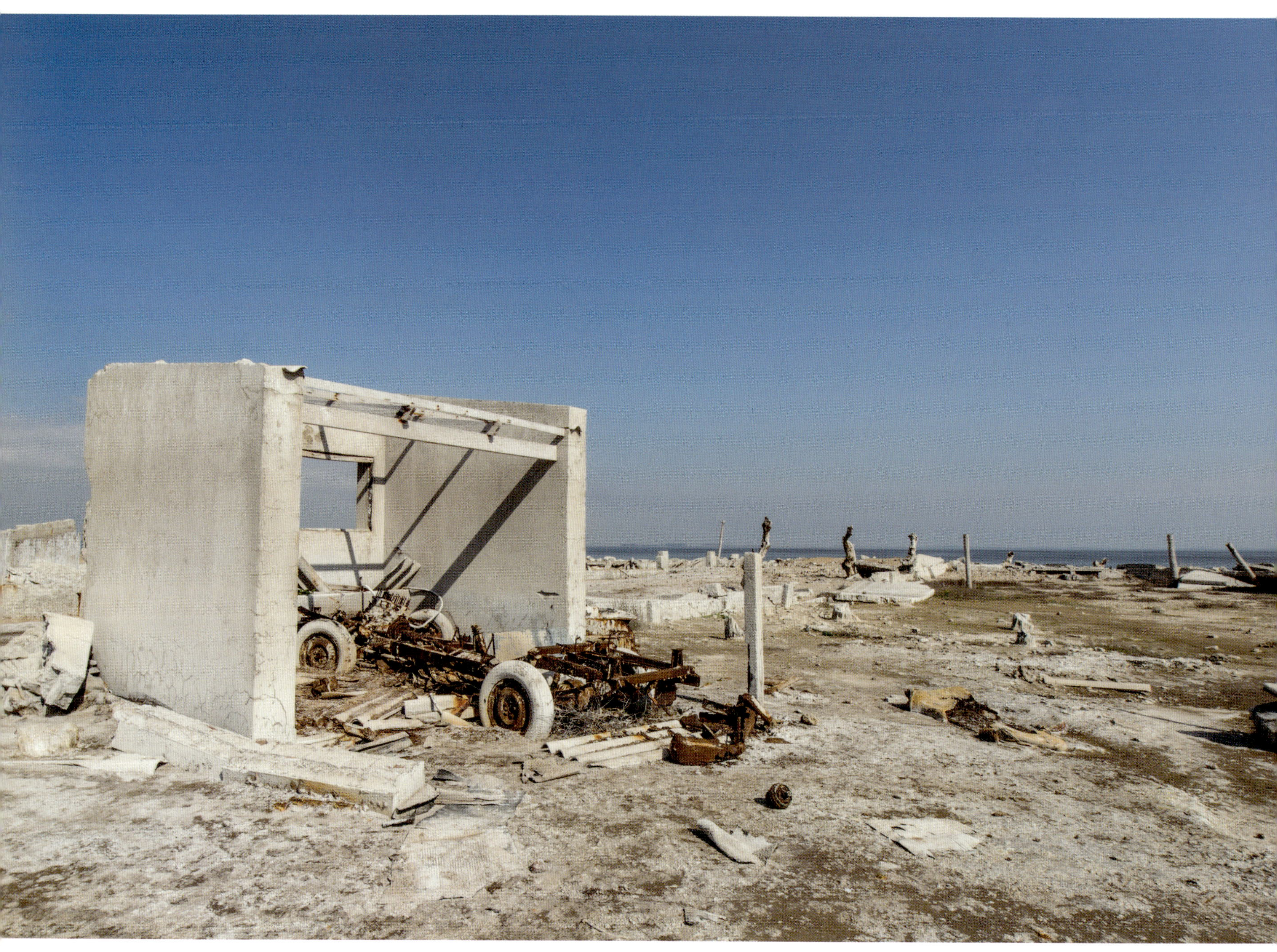

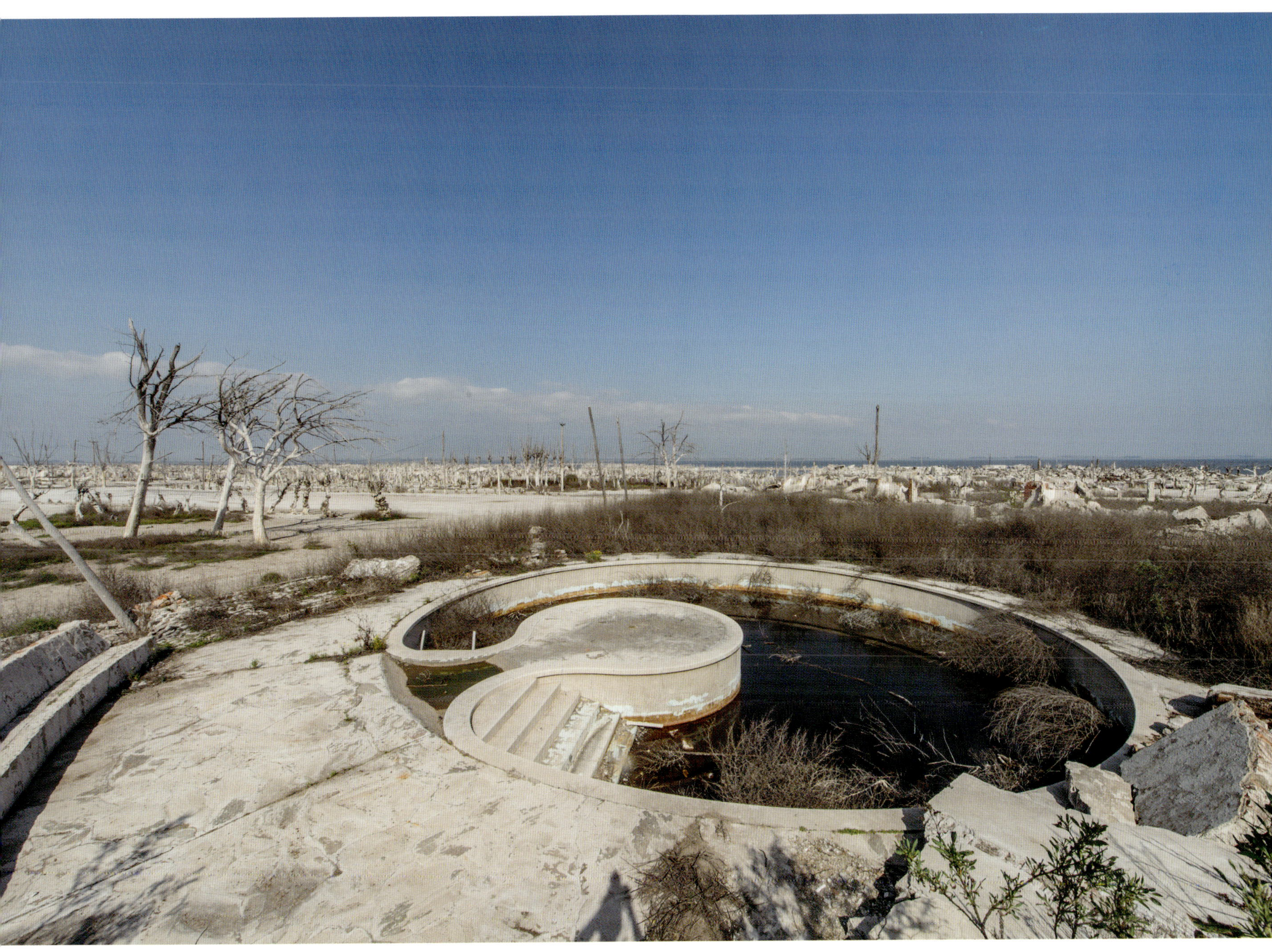

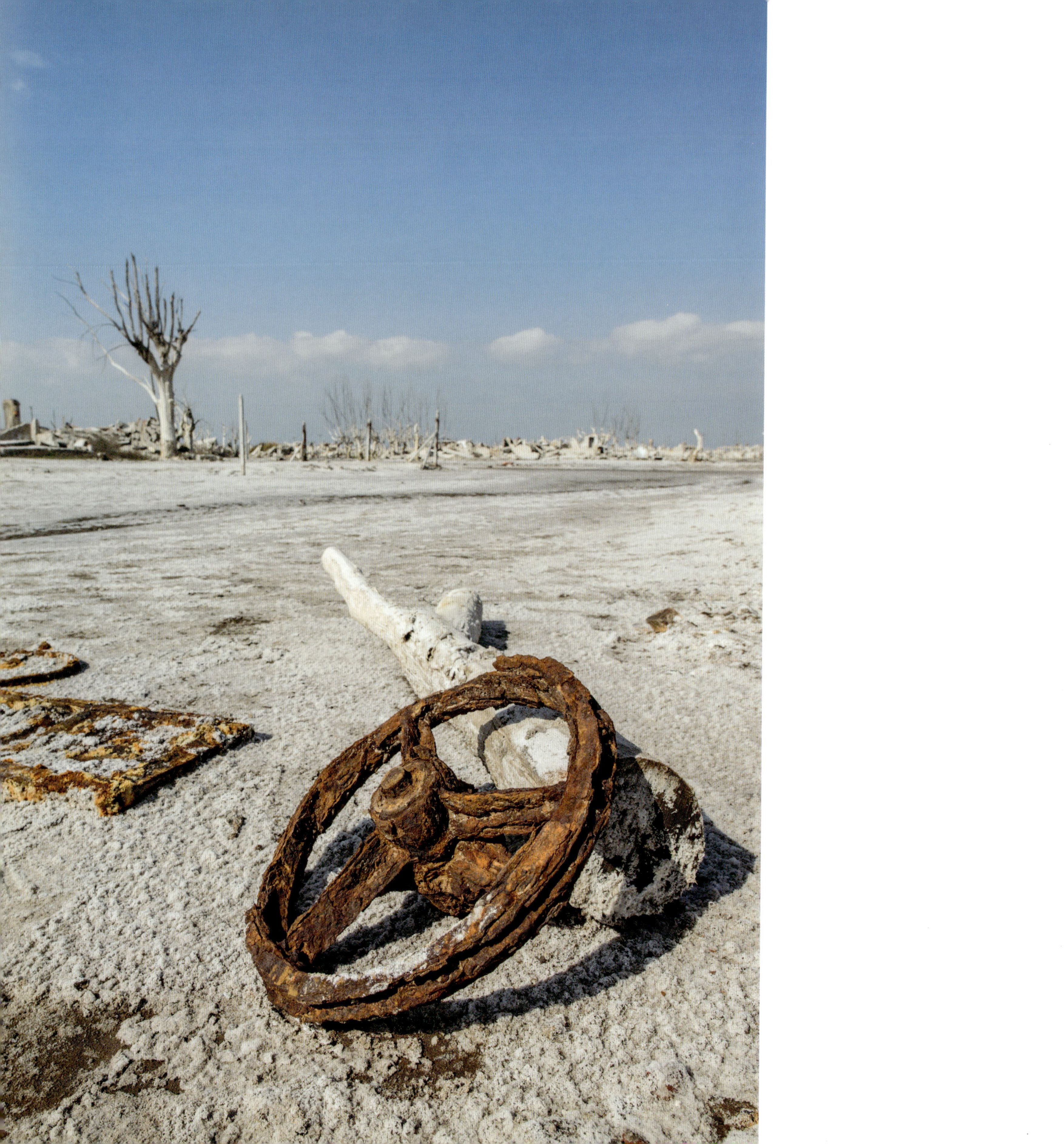

The lake was famous for its salinity. They say that it was as salty as the Dead Sea and ten times more than the oceans. Consequently, it used to attract a lot of Argentineans and other South American tourists looking to escape the city at the weekend while enjoying the curative properties of its salted water.

Very quickly, this 'holiday destination' became a big success attracting more than 20,000 tourists a year, with a local population of 1,500 (helped by the fact that Epecuén had a railway line built to link it to Buenos Aires). Several hotels were constructed to meet the growing demand; followed quickly by nightclubs, restaurants, clothes shops and even a real castle of French inspiration! Epecuén became one of the top destinations in Argentina.

Despite the growing success, the population of Epecuén already knew the seawalls weren't enough and needed more work to be effective. But the government didn't fund the necessary work. The day inevitably came when it was too late. Heavy rain fell in the area for a few weeks, and the dyke protecting the city from the lake that surrounded it, broke on the 10th of November 1985.

In a dozen days, the city was completely submerged under ten meters of water and its inhabitants were obliged to escape. Most of them had no choice but to flee to the closest city of Carhué; with only their essential belongings in a cart, leaving behind them their memories.

During the next 25 years, the water stagnated and Epecuén stayed submerged. Most of the inhabitants settled in the nearby city of Carhué, with some preferring to settle further away because the pain of staying just a few kilometers from their old house was too strong.

If at first, some of them thought it could be possible one day to return, their hopes vanished with time. They slowly began to forget how it was before, even if the scar was still there reminding them that a part of them had disappeared along with their town. It's enough to get lost for a few hours through the muddied streets of Epecuén to understand how hard it must have been to lose everything overnight and to have to start all over again in spite of it.

After 25 years passed, with Epecuén engulfed under the lake, the water started receding due to climate changes and shifting weather patterns. Dryness made Epecuén surface again, offering an incredible sight of desolation both terrifying and wonderful. Today, only a small part of the town is still a prisoner of the lake. And it's an apocalyptic landscape that rises in front of us as if an earthquake had destroyed everything.

Relics of the life of the former occupants resurfaced, petrified by the salt, each telling a different tale. Whether it be the wreck of an old car, a rusted bath, rotten wooden beds or old bottles, everything rises daily to the surface to remind us of the trauma that the locals experienced. Being able to photograph this amazing location is a photographer's dream. All the elements are there for both a reportage and aesthetic approach.

Only one resident went back there to live. Pablo Novak accomplishes his daily walk with his dog through his former city looking for memories or maybe just so as not to forget. When he was young, his father, a realist, told him that the water was there before and that it will come back. He was right. Pablo, is the complete opposite of former residents who prefer to forget the past, he still wants to tell the story of how life used to be. Before, he dreamt that it would be rebuilt and that he would be a part of it; but not anymore, somewhere along the way he lost hope. Now, he waits patiently with his dog to be the last one to die in the same place he was born and for whom he is the guardian.

The post-apocalyptic vista is completely unreal when you enter Epecuén. The bushes and vegetation at the

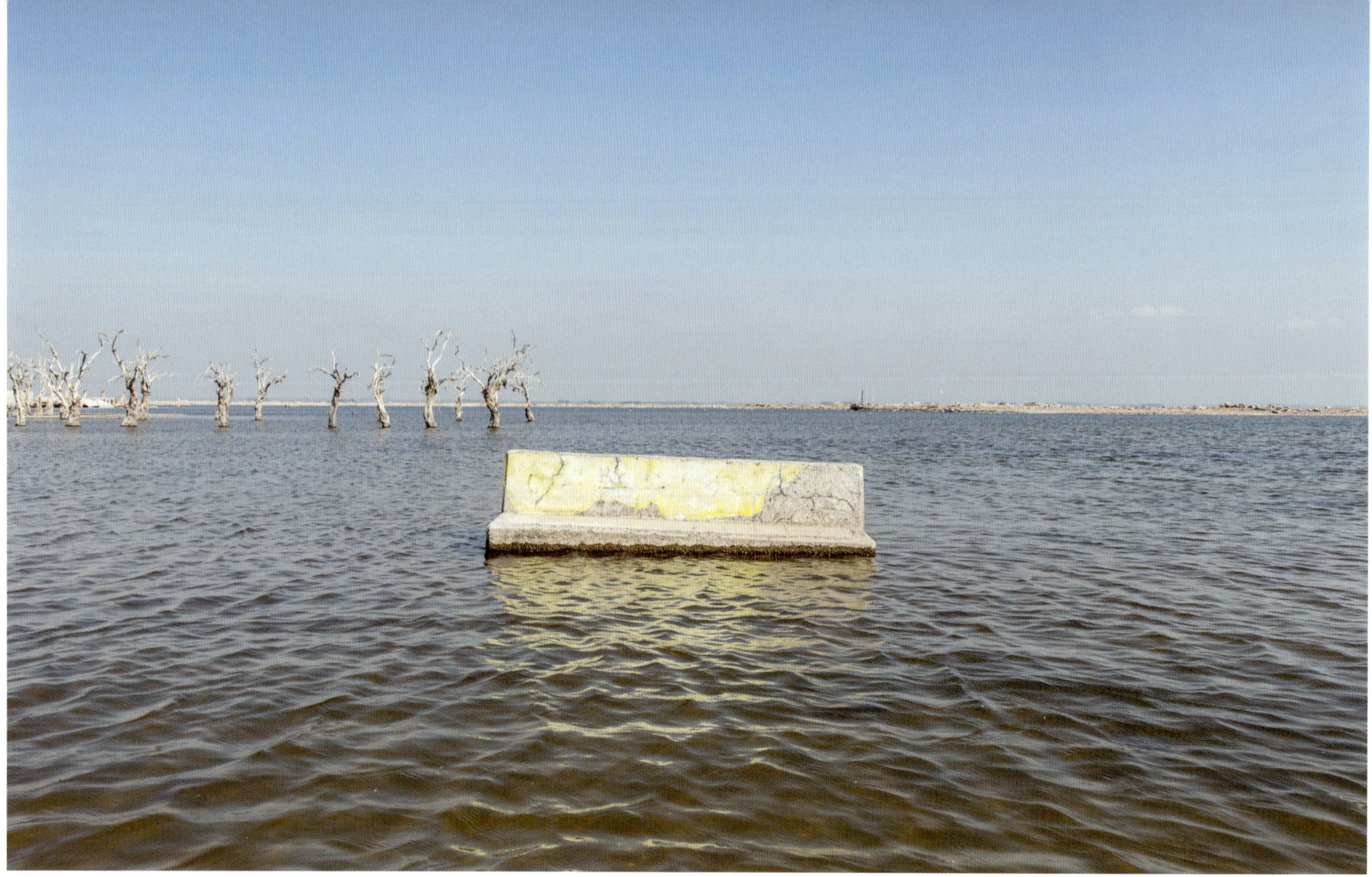

top of the city, which is elevated a little above the water level, disappear rapidly as you explore further.

Soon you realize the entire city has been petrified by salt, the trees, the walls, the doors and the cars. This incredible white against the backdrop of the blue of the sky and the lake makes you think you are on another planet where life has been gone for centuries.

When you observe closely, you start recognizing what was once a booming city. Small houses, the swimming pools of hotels, a door's frame bears last witness standing on a pile of remains, the garden tables, the sunken bathtubs which had travelled thanks to the water, to odd places, the still sunken children's playground or even the rusty hydraulic power station!

Each object is a clue to imagining how magnificent Epecuén was. Everything makes you feel like you are the last man on earth.

On the future of Epecuén, a second life has begun to arise in the last few years. More and more tourists are coming to see what is left of the city, to feel what it's like to walk in this surreal landscape.

Production companies also choose Epecuén for shoots as it is a unique location perfectly fitting for

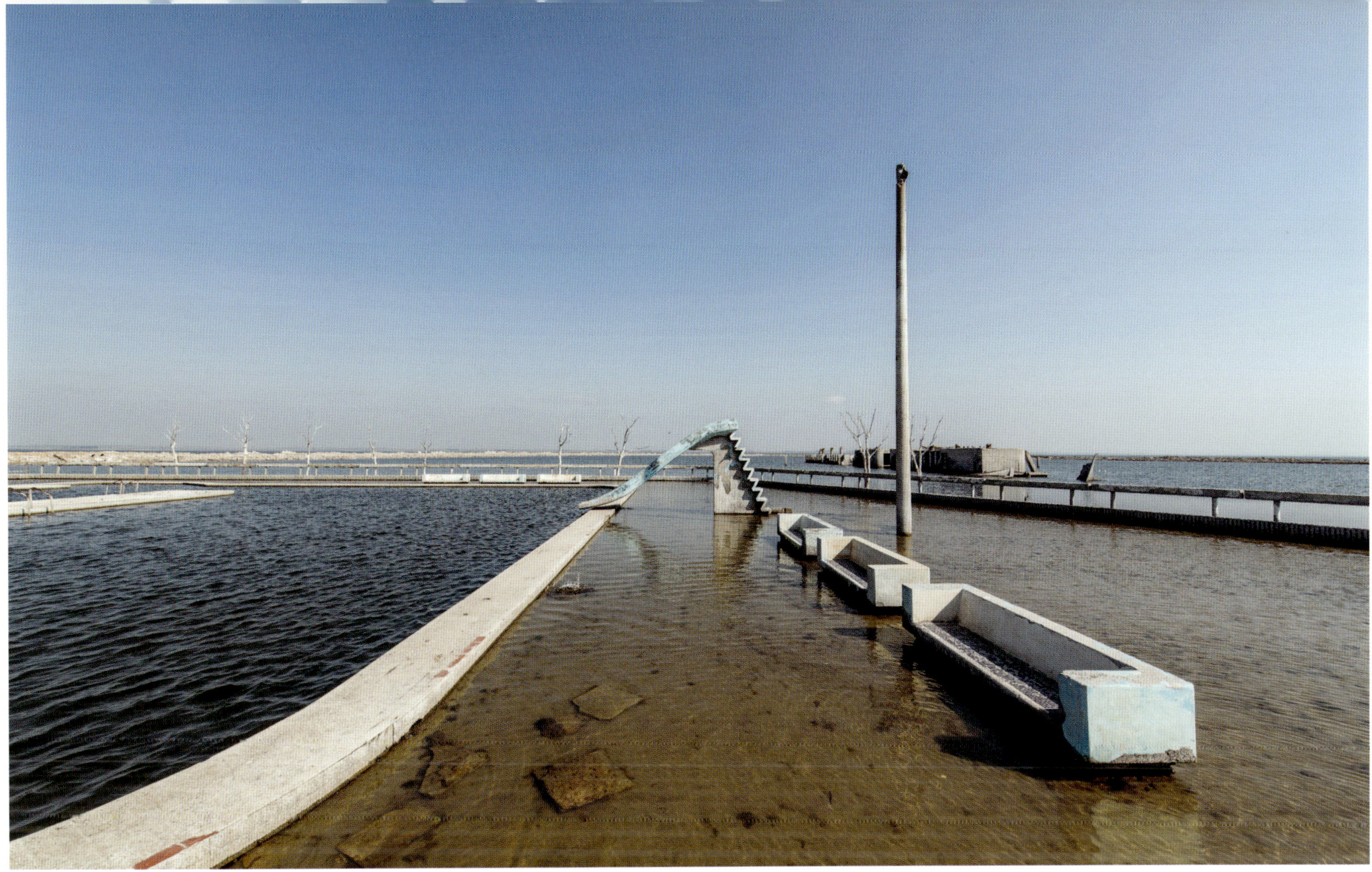

documentaries and movies such as "And Soon The Darkness".

Finally, Argentineans are starting to enjoy coming back here, since Epecuén has been advertised as a place to relax or just take a walk by the lake. All is not lost, and when the last drop of water is gone from Epecuén, guided tours will take place to explain what life was like back then and tell the story of this unique city.

But what if the water came back? What happened once could happen again with the weather patterns we are facing. Like the myth of Atlantis, Epecuén was flooded by water as if the gods were trying to send a message to mankind: We are nothing when the elements are unleashed.

Ruins reappearing act as a threat to our idea that we can bend nature to our will. The environmental change is the first consequence, but we should never forget the fate of Epecuén. We must change our ways of interacting with nature to avoid the same catastrophe.

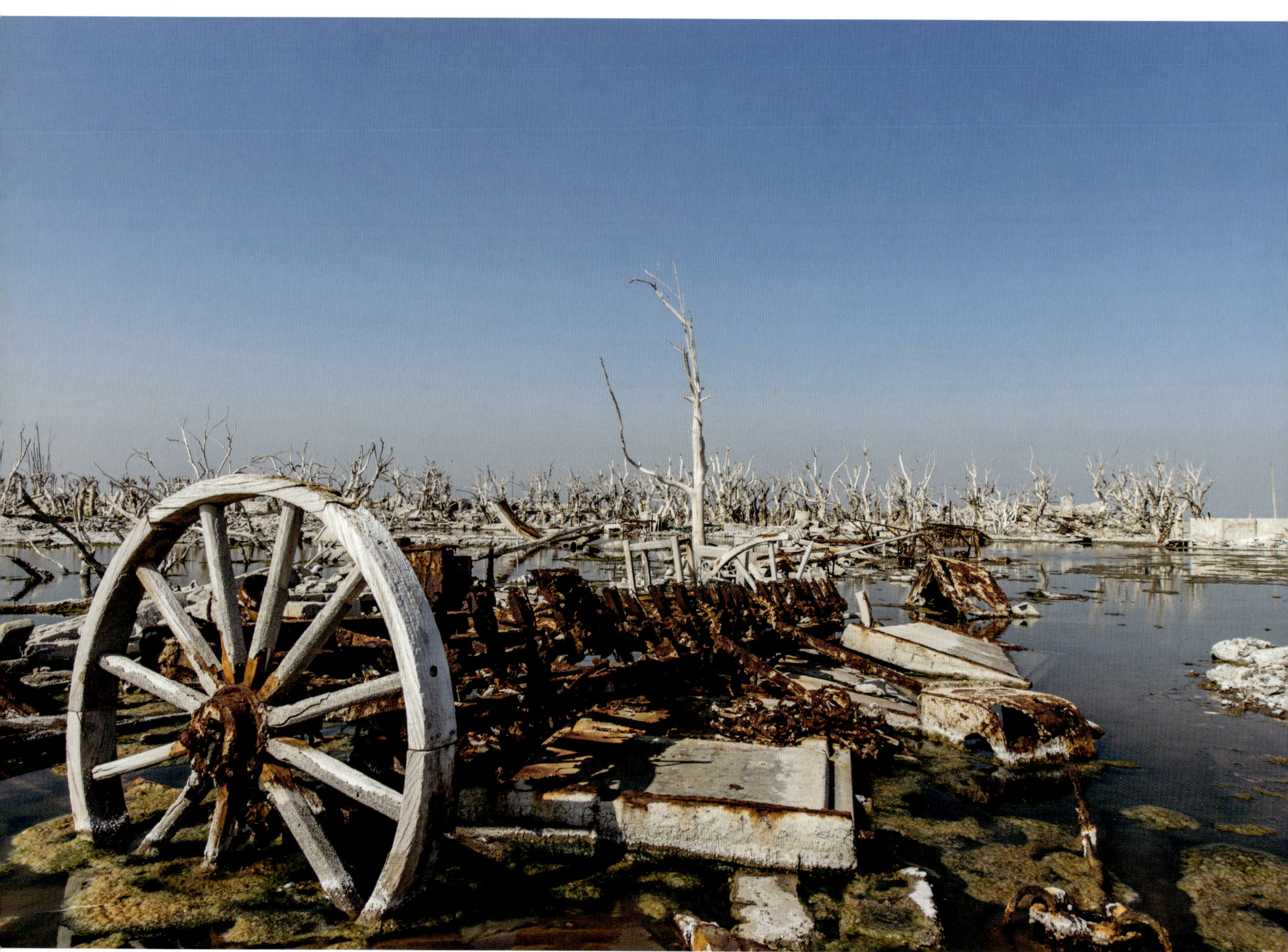

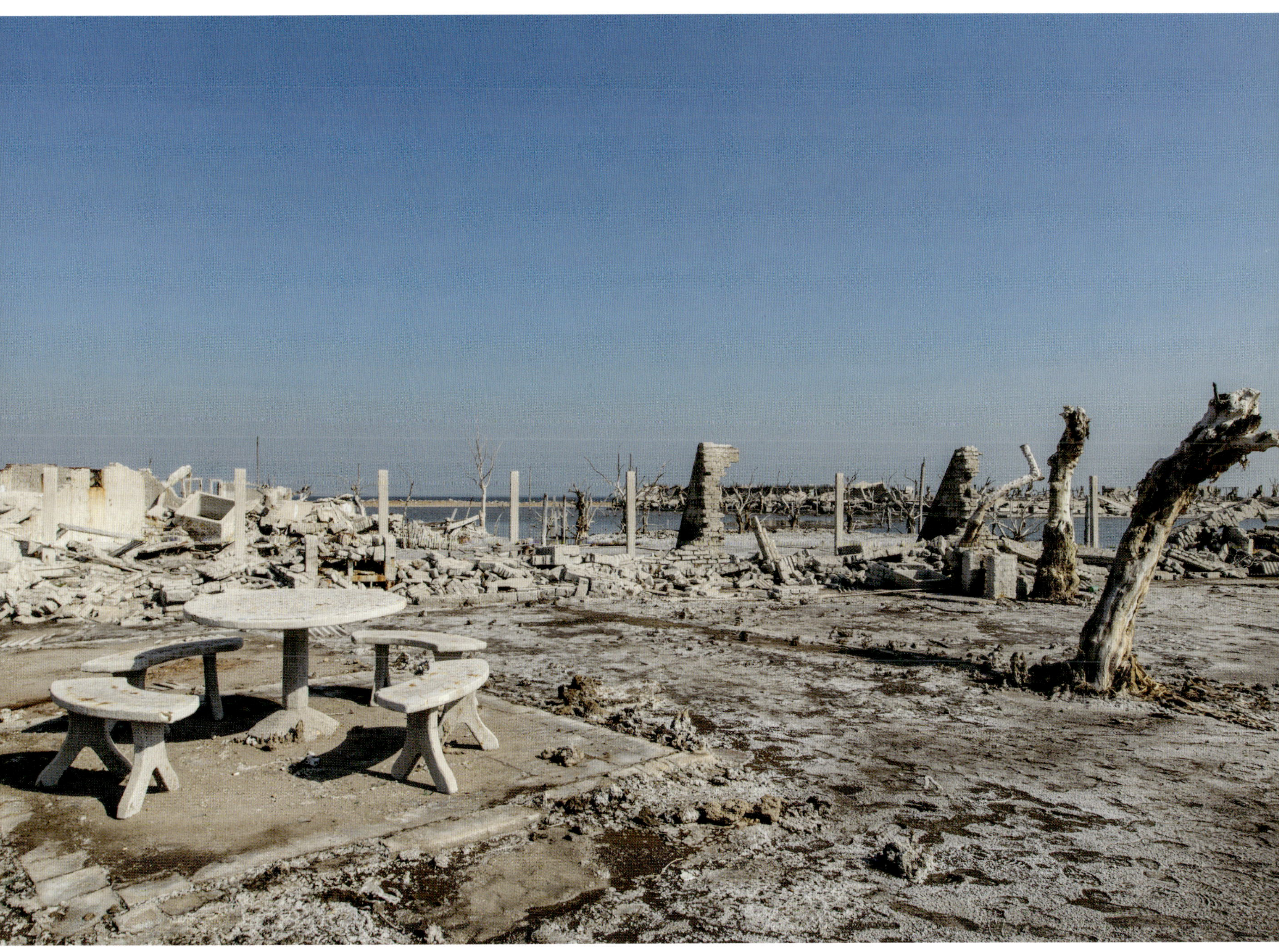

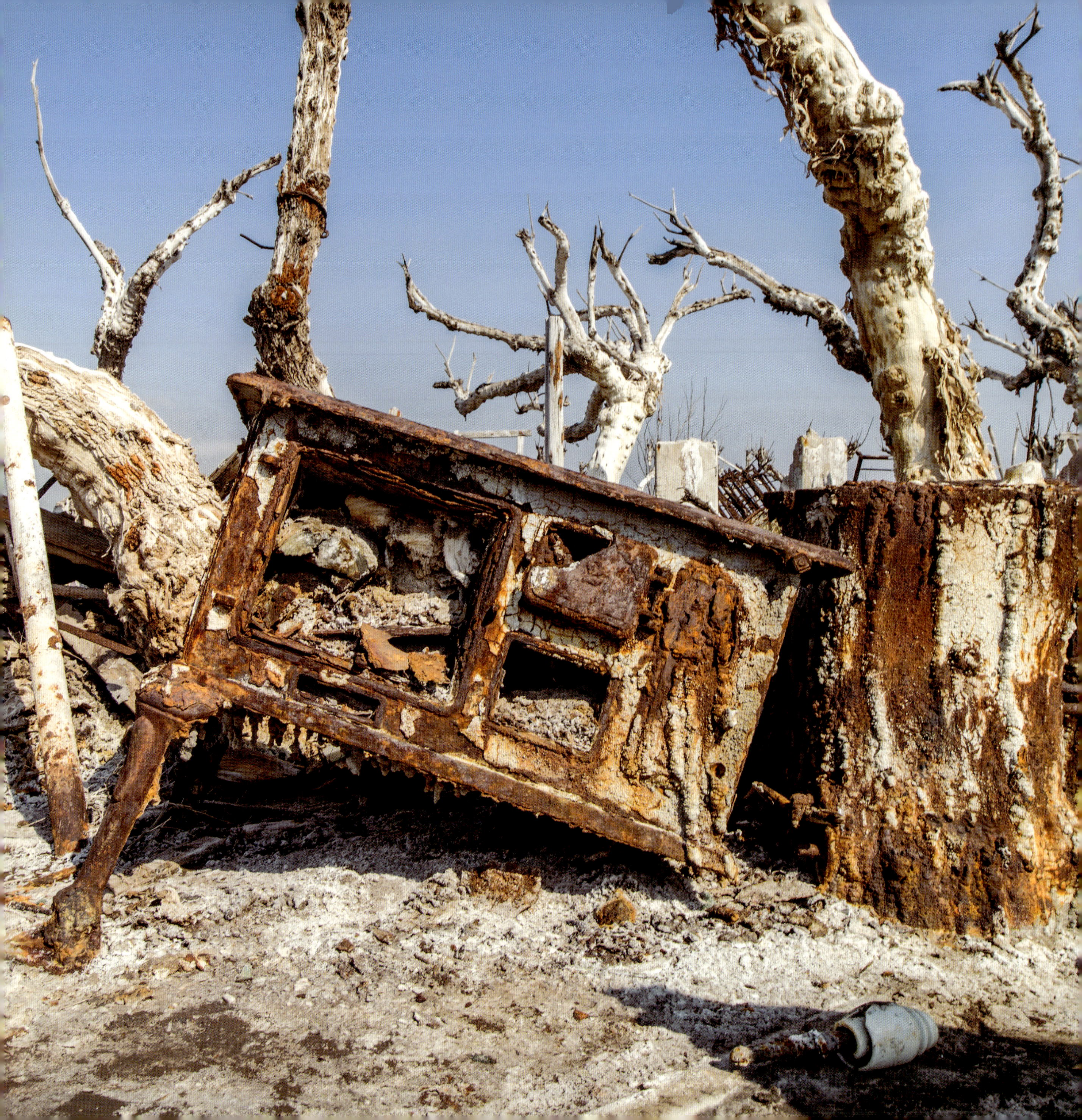

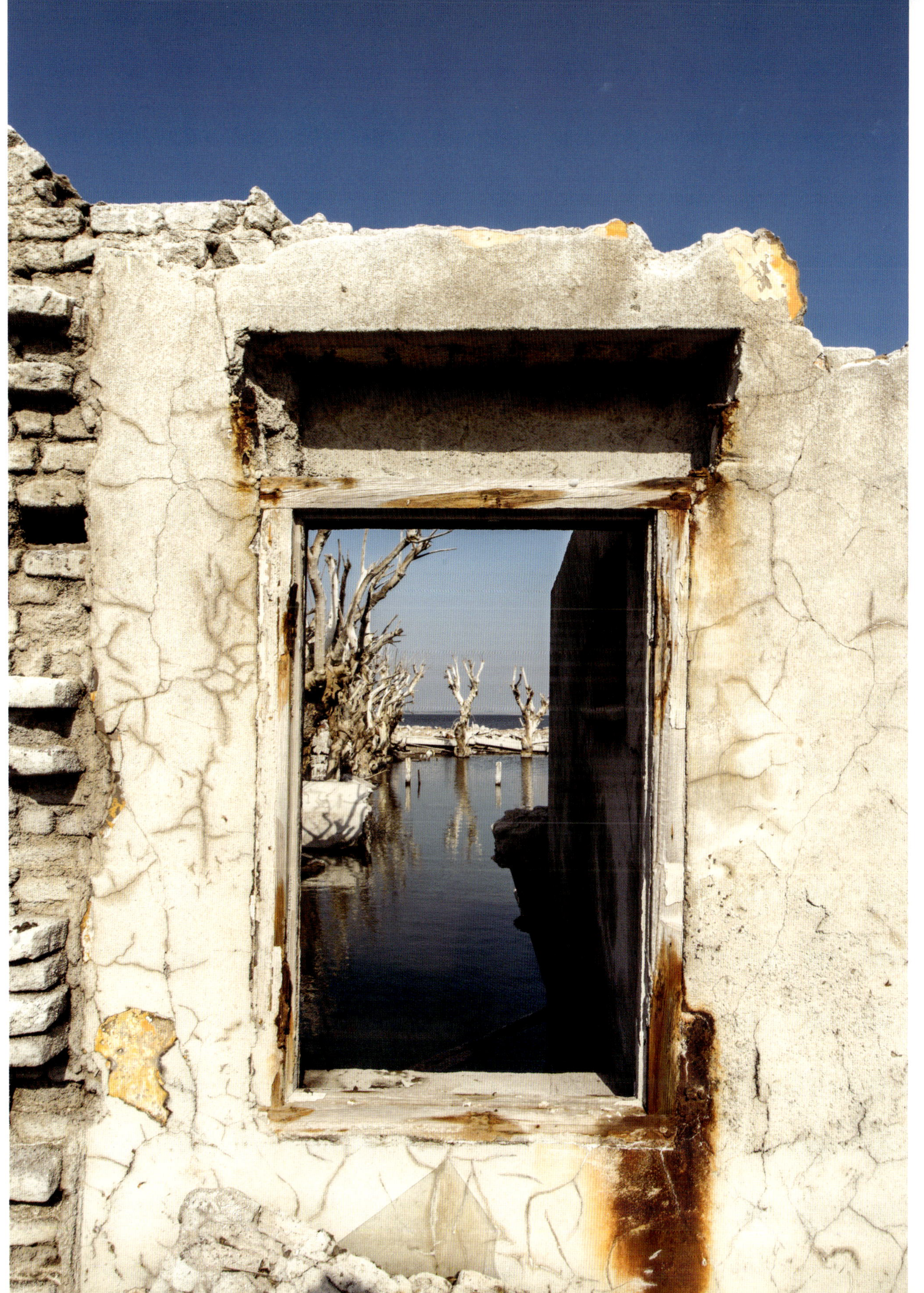

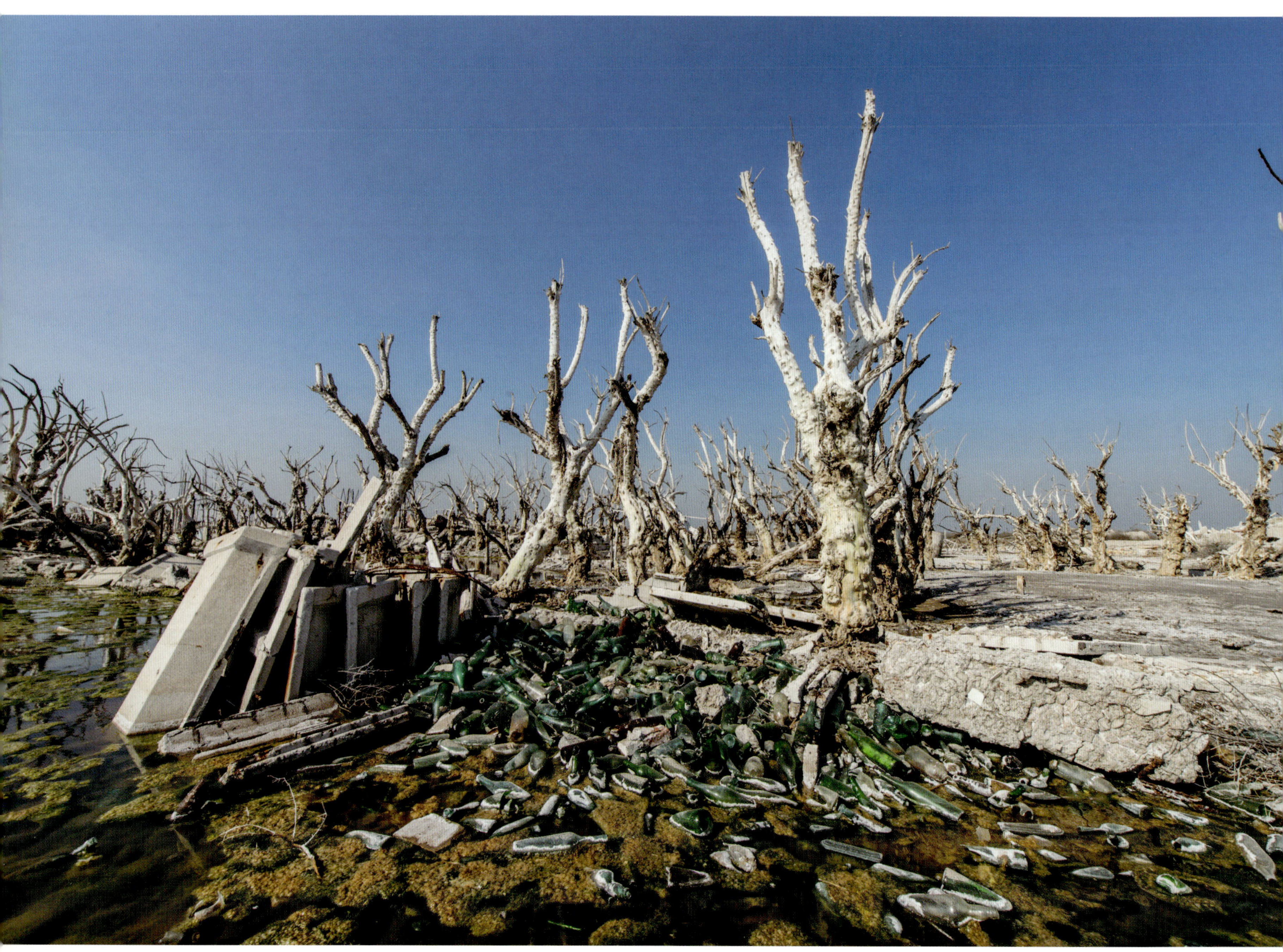

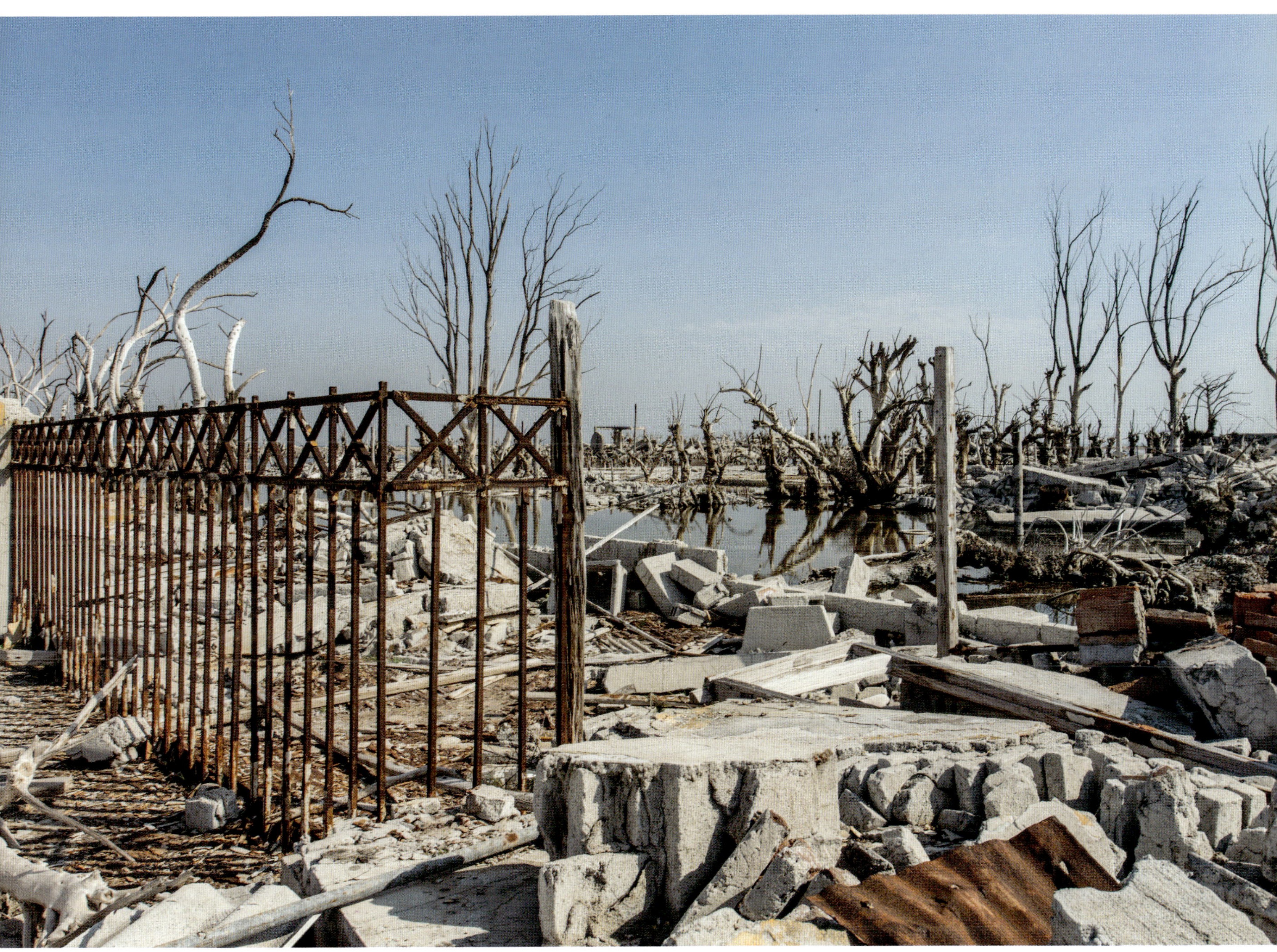

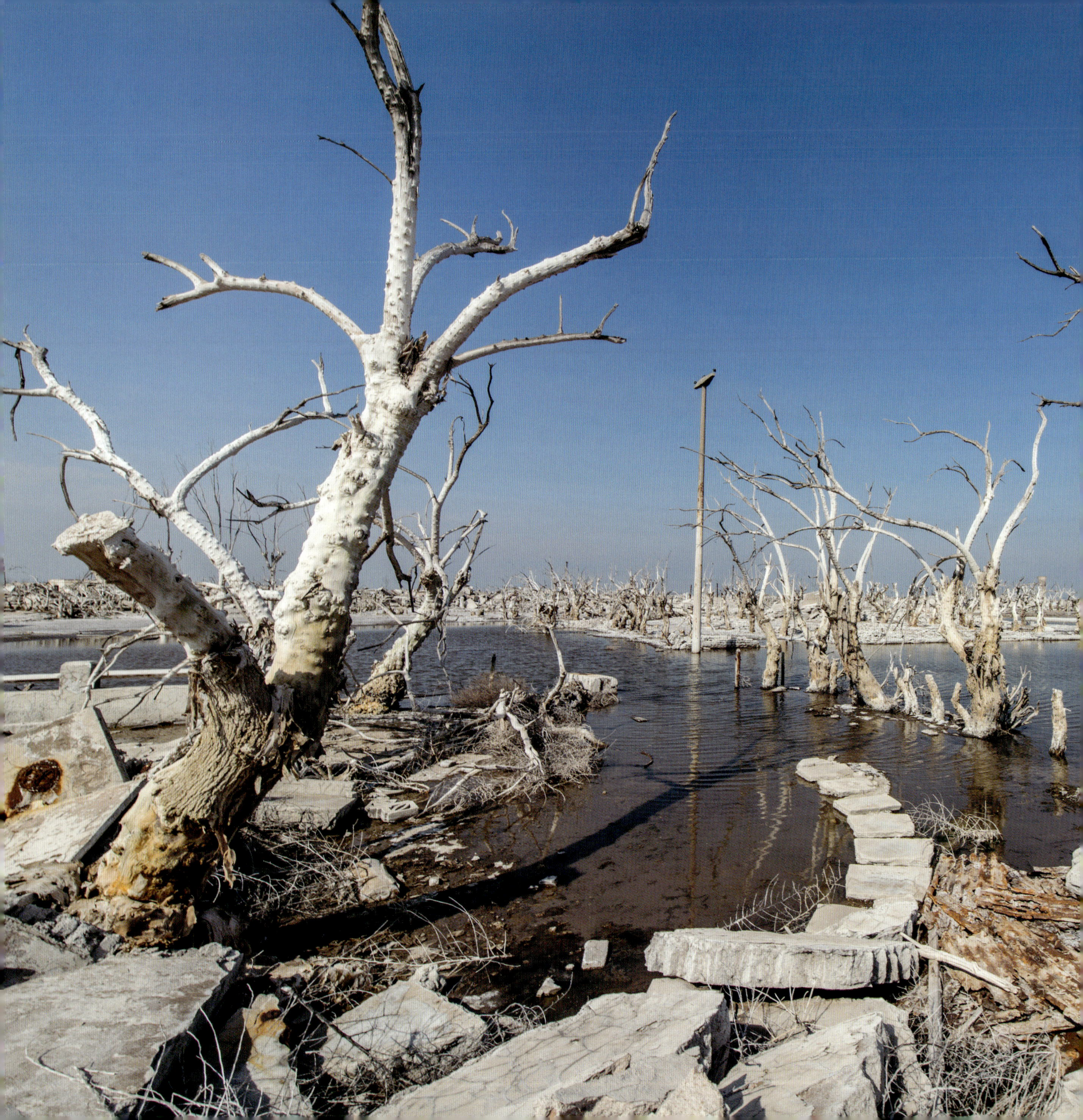

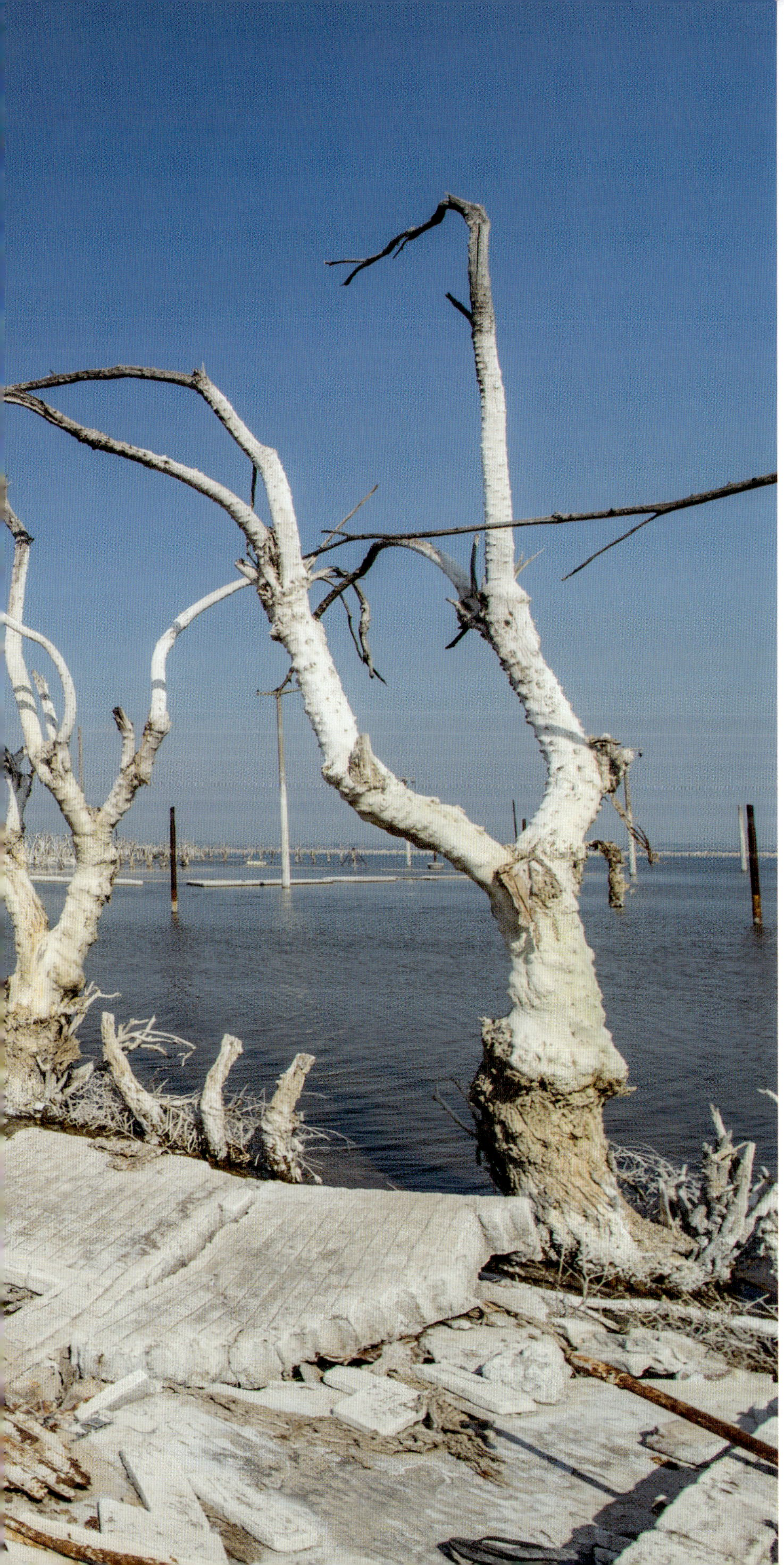

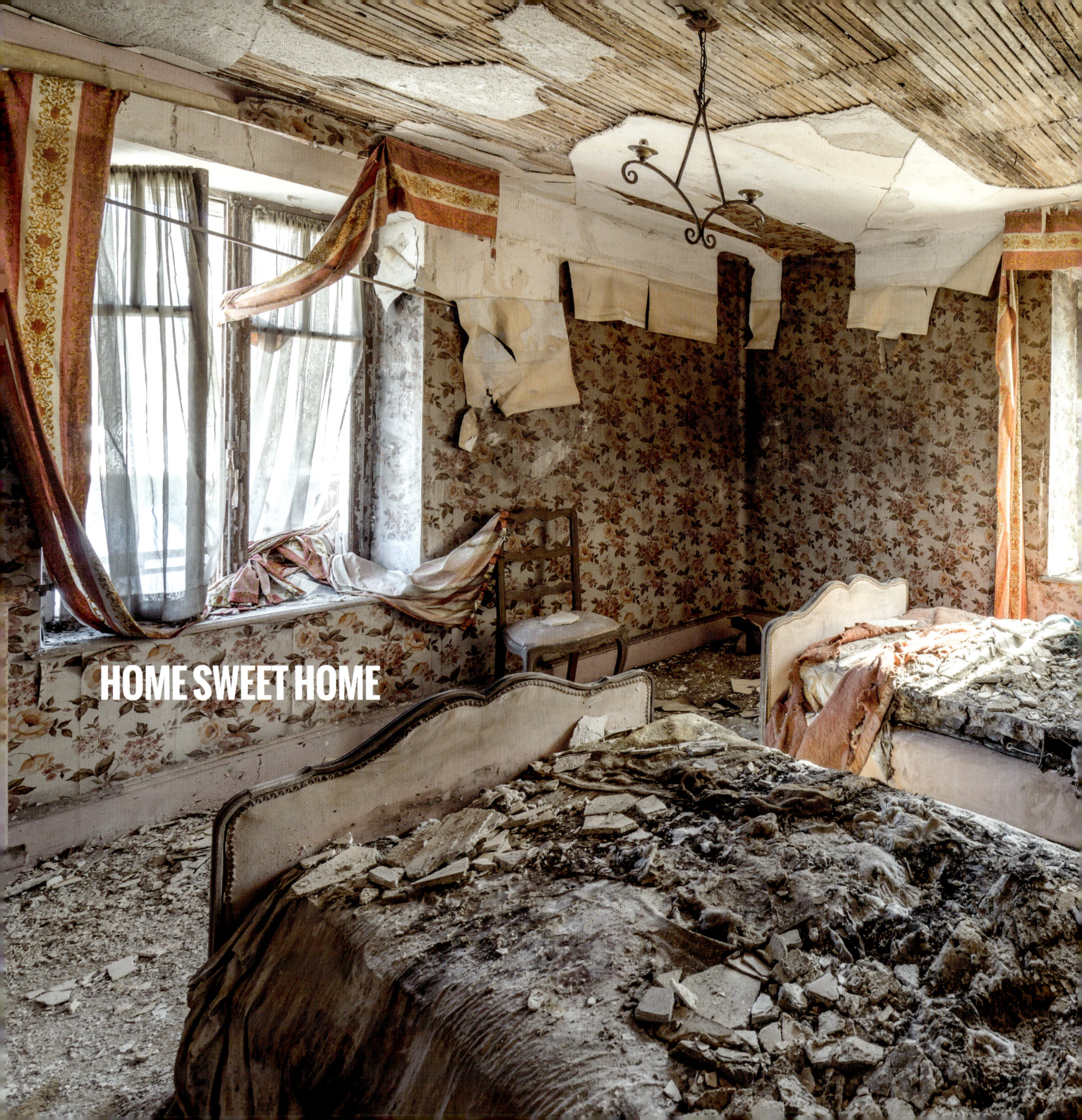

HOME SWEET HOME

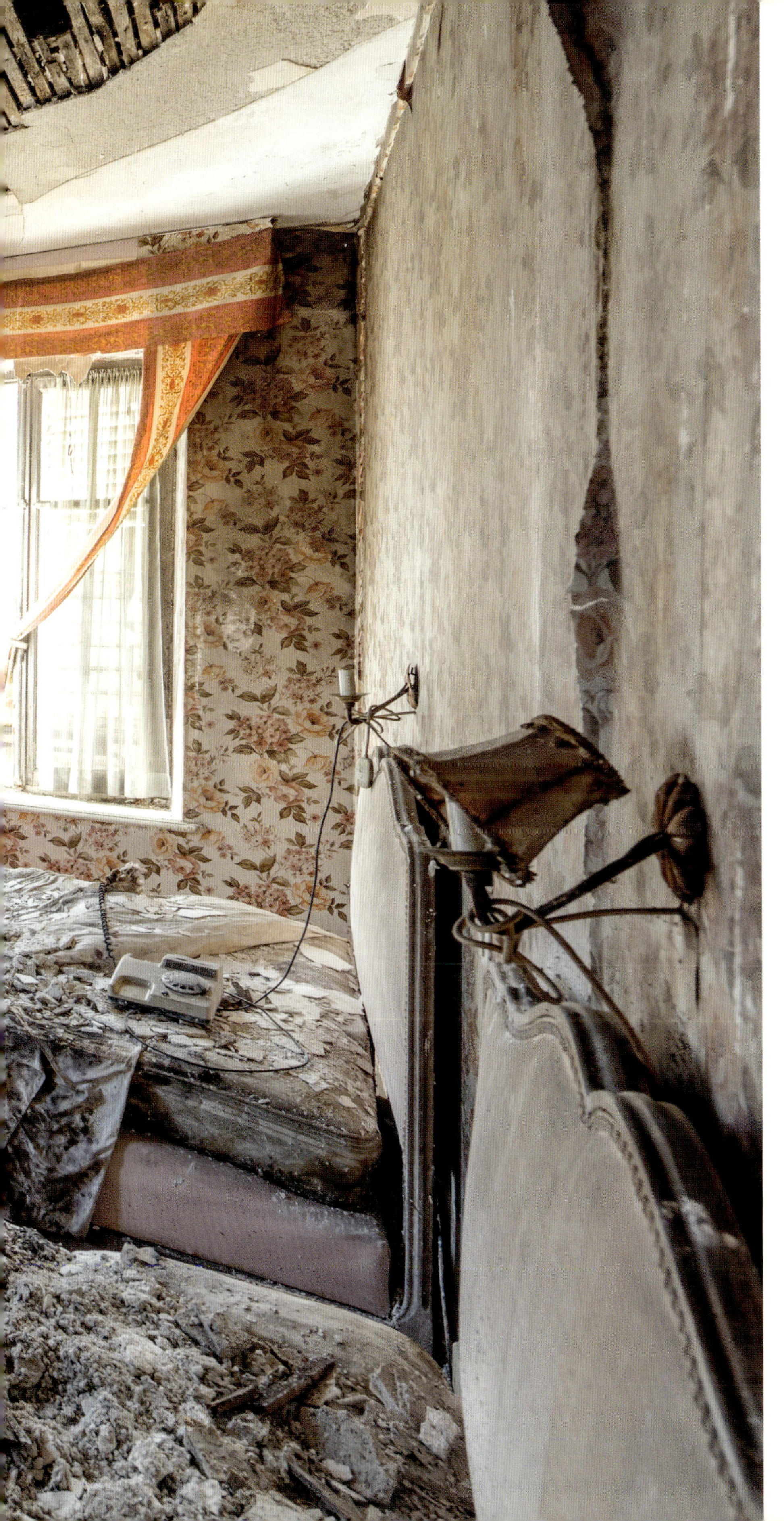

One of the questions I get asked the most
when I am talking about my work is:
"But why was it abandoned and what is
the story of this place". From my
experience when talking to people who are
interested, I know that the stories
embedded in these walls, fascinate
people as much as the photographs
themselves.

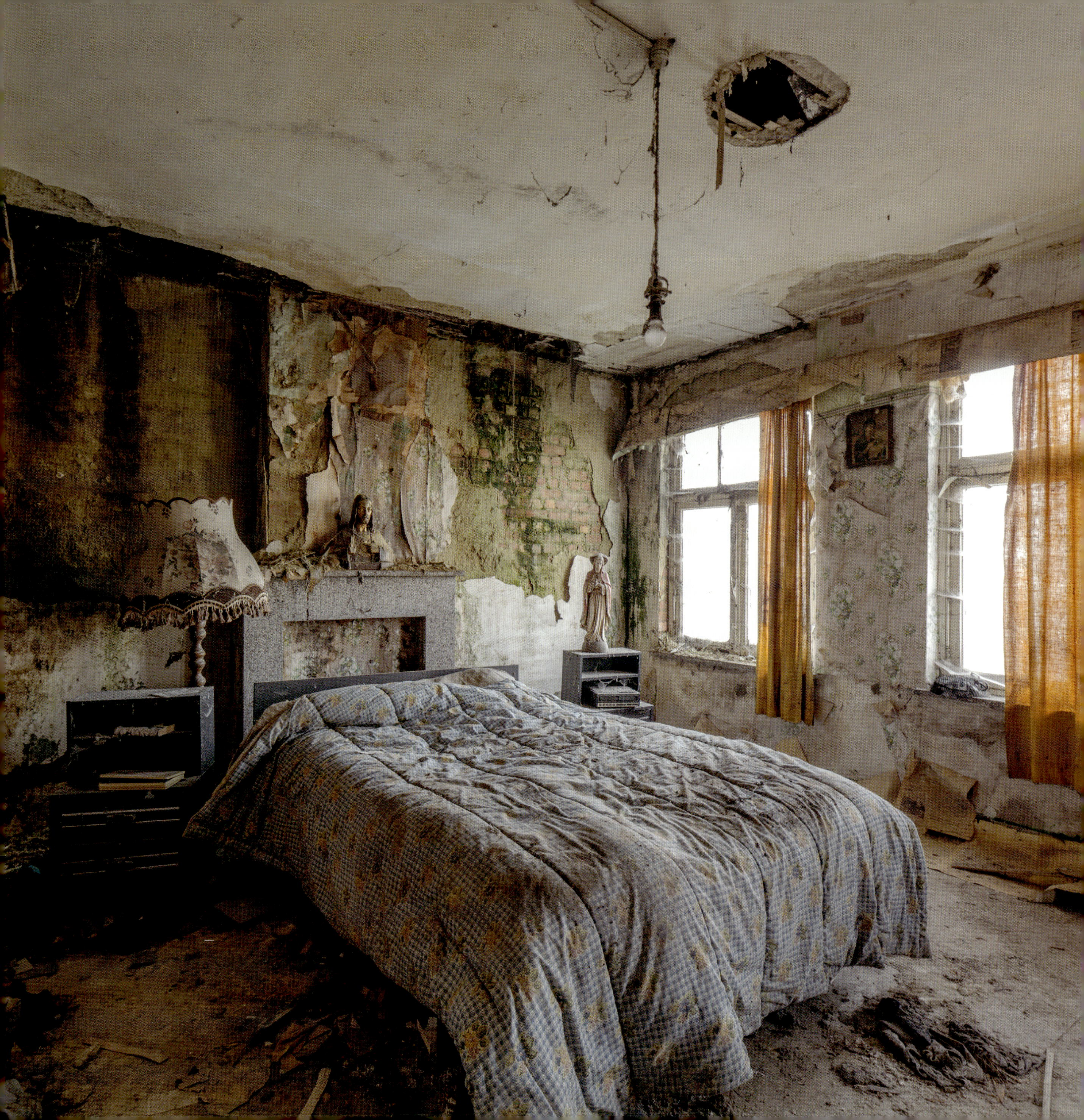

It is mainly when people are looking at the pictures of houses, villas and castles where you can find all kinds of different relics of people's lives. So why are we so captivated, especially by places that were households?

I guess it is because the viewer sees a reflection of their own home, or perhaps their grandmother's where they used to go for vacation. They can identify their childhood memories with it. Everyone loves to imagine what stories hide behind an abandoned house and how it was when it was occupied.

People spend nearly a third of their life in their bed, and sometimes even more so in their own room. Maybe more than half of their life is used up by sleeping, watching TV, washing, eating or cleaning their own home.

Our home is a version of ourselves, a place we have made to the image we want it to be. For some, it will be about building a nest to feel safe and comfortable. For others, it will be a decorative way to express their creative minds. Or, it will just be the old family home where decades of personal history are stored and where past generation relics are mixed with present ones.

Every one of these rooms contain a part of history of a human being.

Thanks to the objects still present as witnesses of a forgotten time, people can play detective and imagine what could have been of the former life of these residents. A wedding photograph lying on the floor can express so much more feeling than words can describe. The rooms themselves are witness of the past: The table where everyone had dinner, the marital bed, the old family library full of books or the magnificent staircase we used to climb to escape the arguments of our parents. All of these pictures are an invitation to create our own stories of what might have happened there.

It is not only the objects in the rooms. It can be a mural on the wall, the view from the window or just a feeling in the atmosphere. Every little clue of the past inspires us to travel in a world of our own creation.

The reasons why these buildings are abandoned are various; there is not a simple answer. Each of them has a unique story and it's not always possible to know the tale of their dereliction. Of course, a common reason is the death of the inhabitant. When there are heirs, it is common for disputes over dividing the inheritance to last years, with the building left to rot alone.

Areas with a struggling economy (mining industries in the north of France for example) where the population has left to find jobs in bigger cities, are also a place where you can find a lot of abandoned houses. Fewer people want to live there and with time, decay has done its job.

Natural disasters like earthquakes or environmental catastrophes (like the pollution of the ground), isolation in a tough region, war or civil conflicts are other reasons that can push people to leave what used to be their nest behind them.

That's why I believe that contemplating a picture of an abandoned room is closer to reading a book than other types of photography. To my mind, it is a perfect combination: You build a universe and a story where you include the characters you like and make them do whatever you want, inspired by a photograph. In a book you already have the characters and the script but you have to imagine them in the universe the writer has chosen. As you gaze at these images, however, you have thousands of possibilities in front of you and

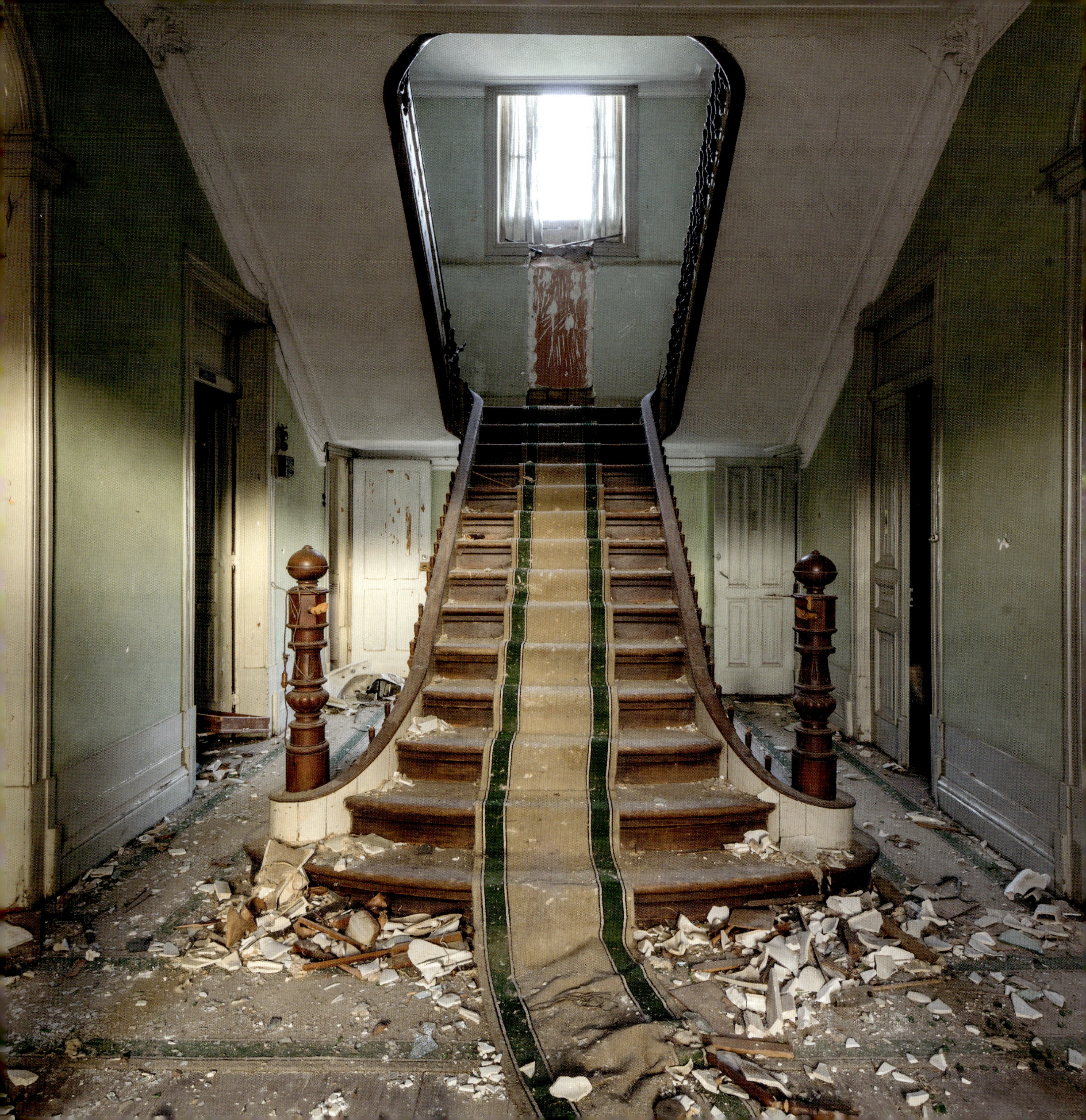

your story will be what you choose it to be: sad, happy, funny, magical…

But talking about forgotten time often leads to sorrow.

If sadness is always around when we speak of abandoned places, it comes more often when we are discussing someone's home. It's not difficult to understand why. These places mostly represented happiness for people. For others, safety, childhood or family. Only a few of them may hold memories of sadness or fear.

And when life decided to leave, we have to decide if it was a place full of happiness or if it was a horror house full of nightmares. We have all heard during our youth the story (or a close alternative one) where the old witch died alone in her isolated house that is now haunted by her ghost. Children always bet the other won't dare to go there at night.

One other thing we can observe when we look at these pictures is the different kind of lives people lived. There is so much difference between daily routine and family wealth, whether it's in Belgium, Germany, France, Italy or Portugal.

It is also an excellent way of discovering differences in countries and cultures. When in Italy, you can admire frescos on nearly every wall. You can focus on the very religious and simple constructions of Belgian houses or the grandeur and renaissance style of French castles. Every building you are able to visit tells you a story and shows you what life at a particular place was like at a particular time. This travelling in time is for me like an immersion in a history book.

"Time capsule" is a common expression to define these unique places because as we have seen, time seems to have been frozen and we can travel in time by simply entering and wandering there. And everything we notice leads to that: some surreal walk inside our imagination searching for a new adventure. As a combination of reading a book, watching a movie or playing a video game, exploring these places gives us the opportunity to create our own story where we could be the hero and decide everything.

Photography is just a way to describe what we feel inside them and how we want the public to see it from our point of view. The atmosphere will depend on the way we have chosen to depict those locations. And here I have tried to use light as much as I could to fill the emptiness created by the absence of man. As if life was slowly coming back for an instant. That is also why there are some magical and eerie moods when you look at them, as it all feels quite unreal.

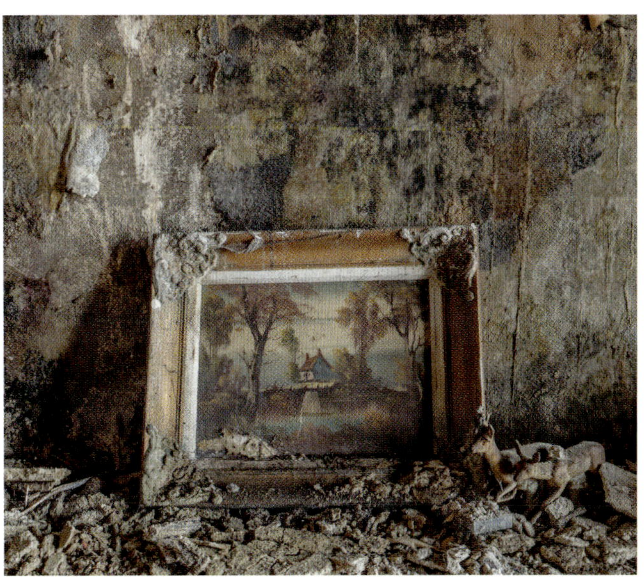

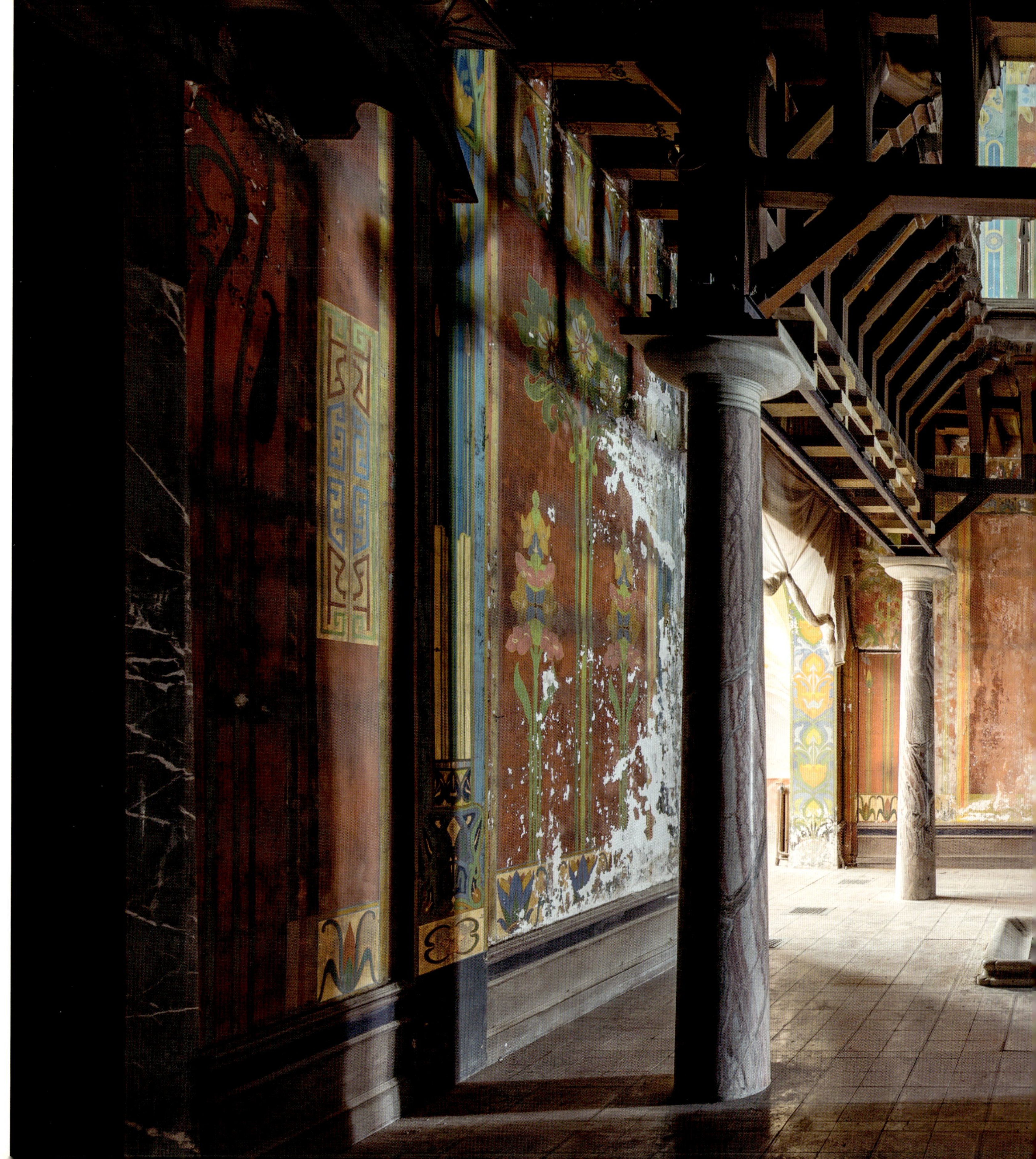

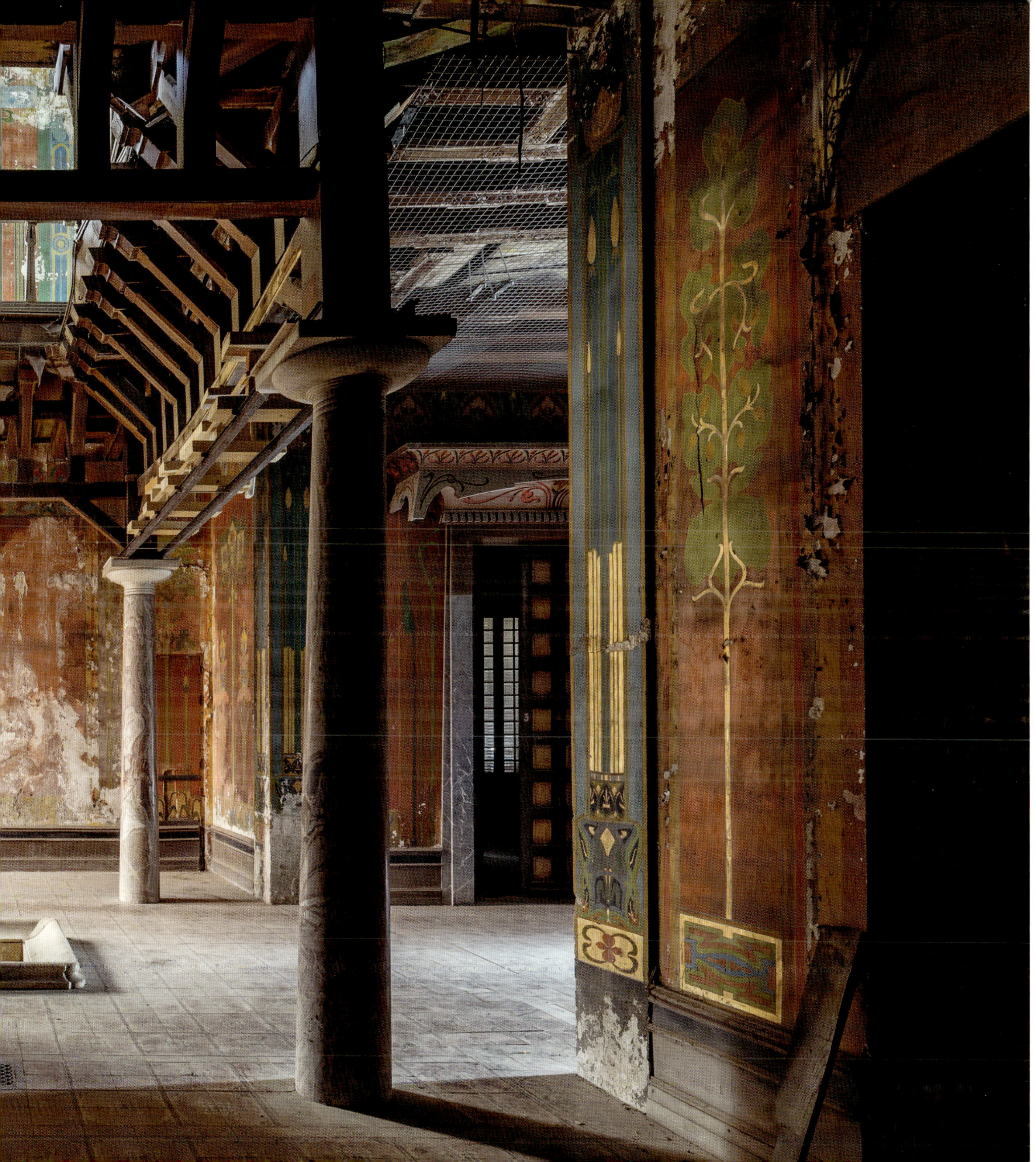

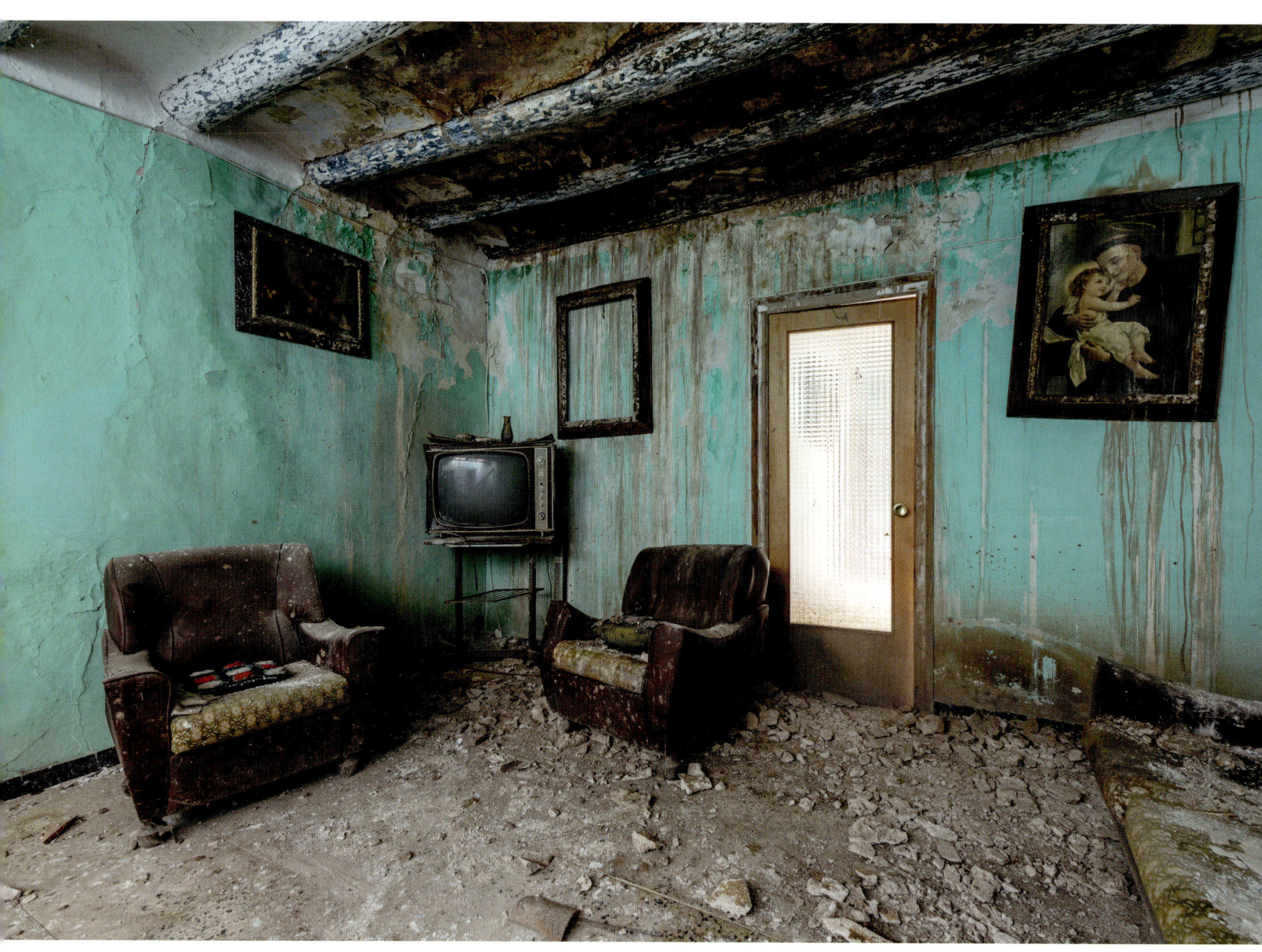

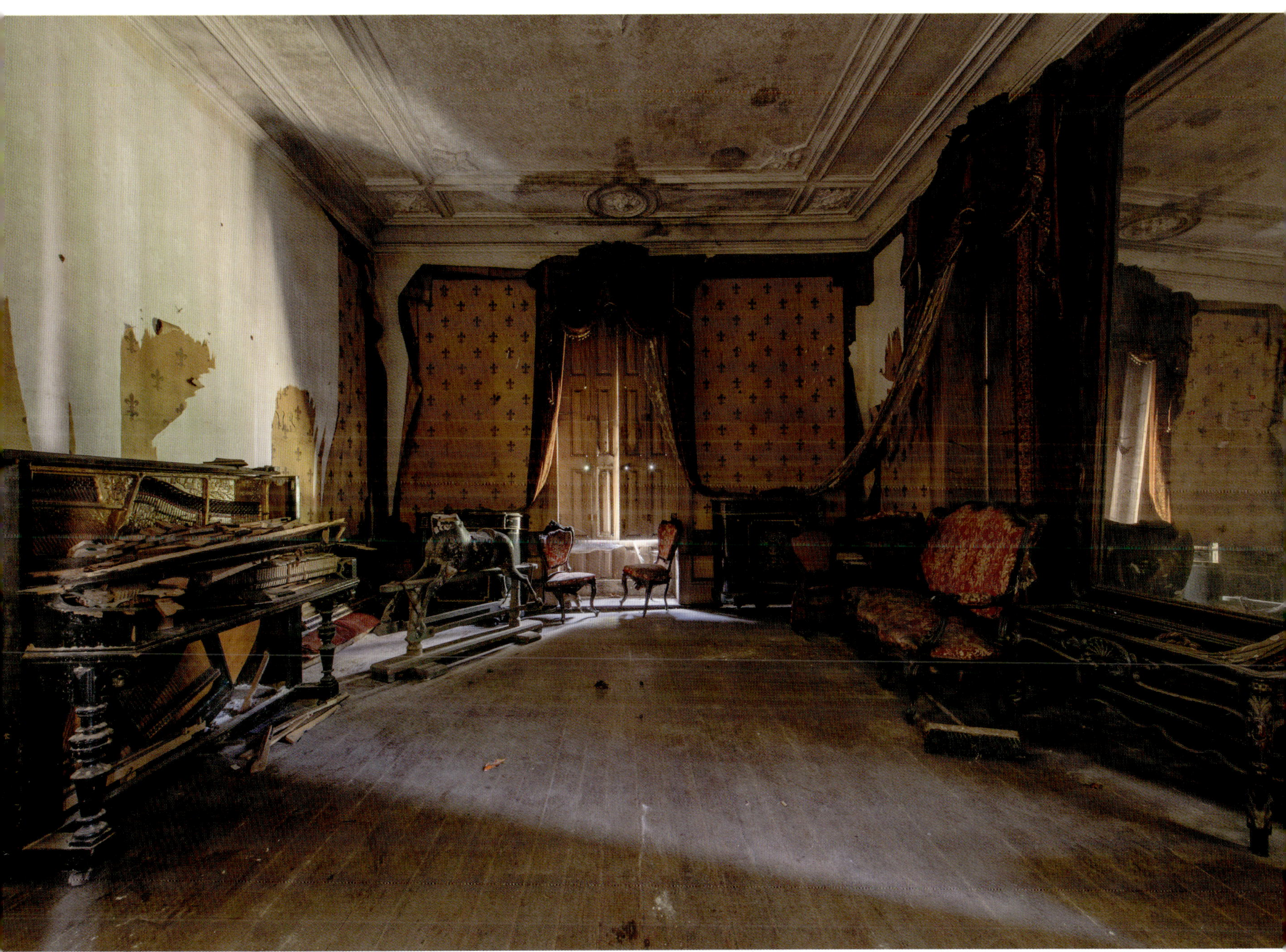

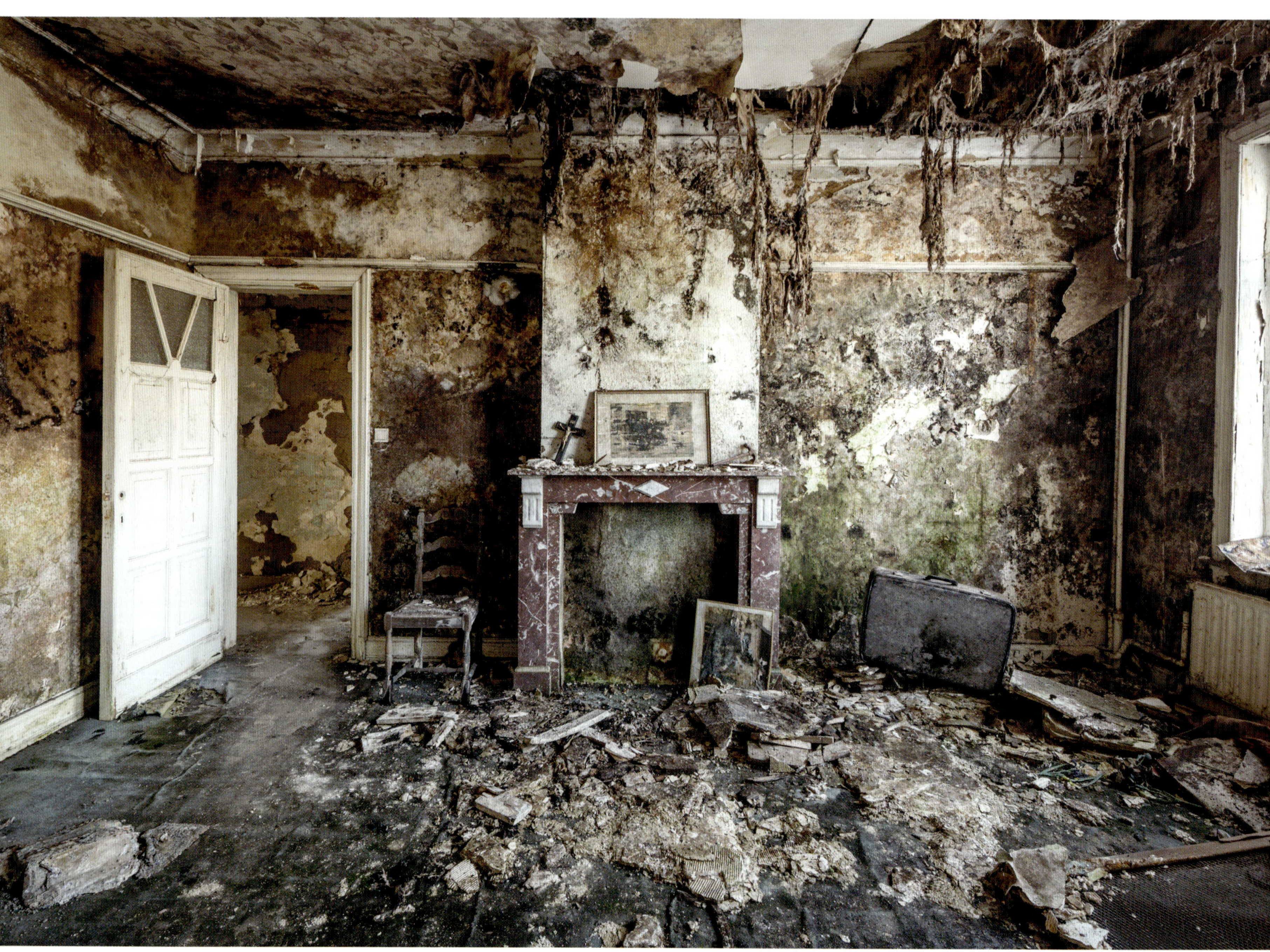

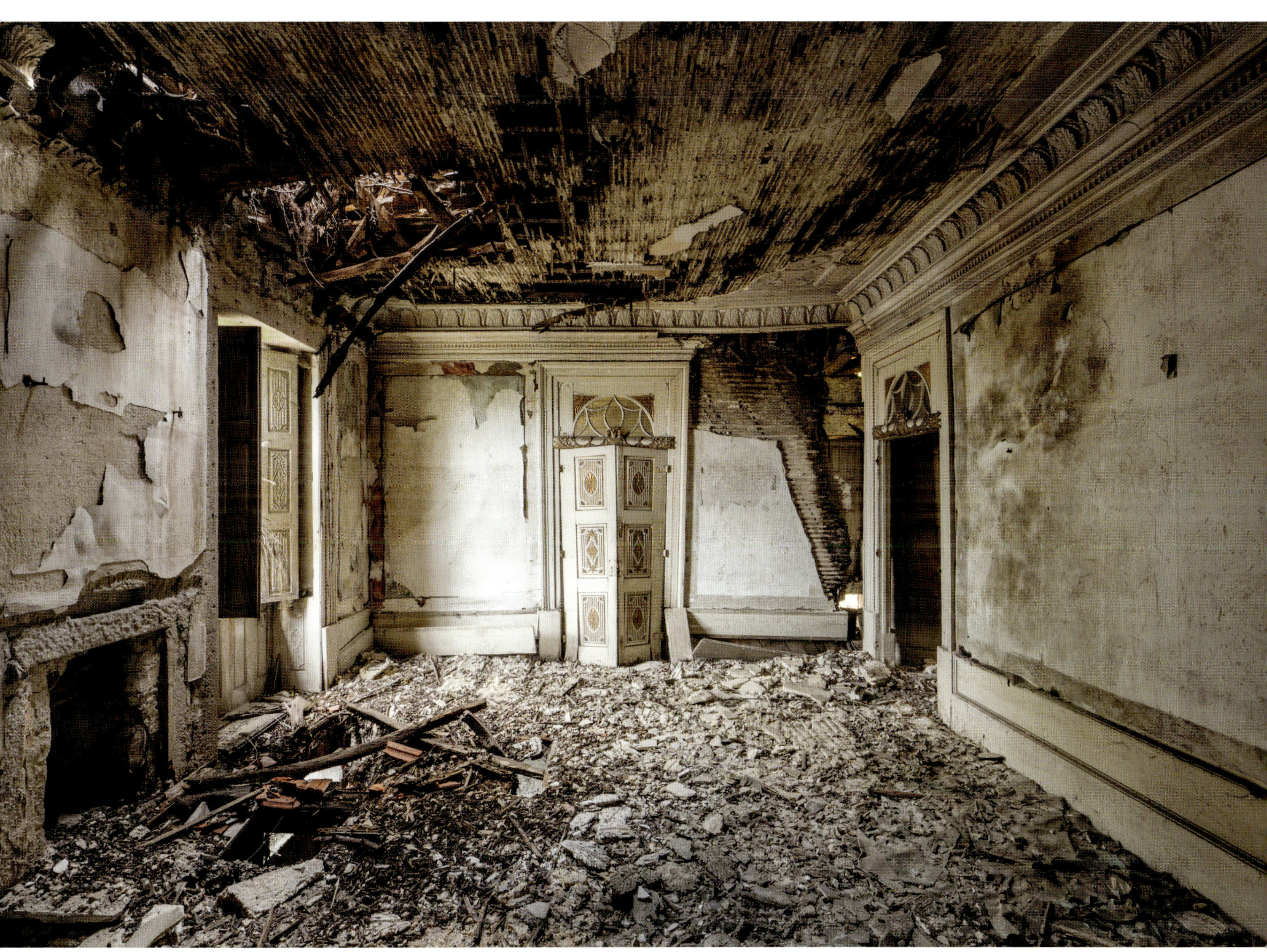

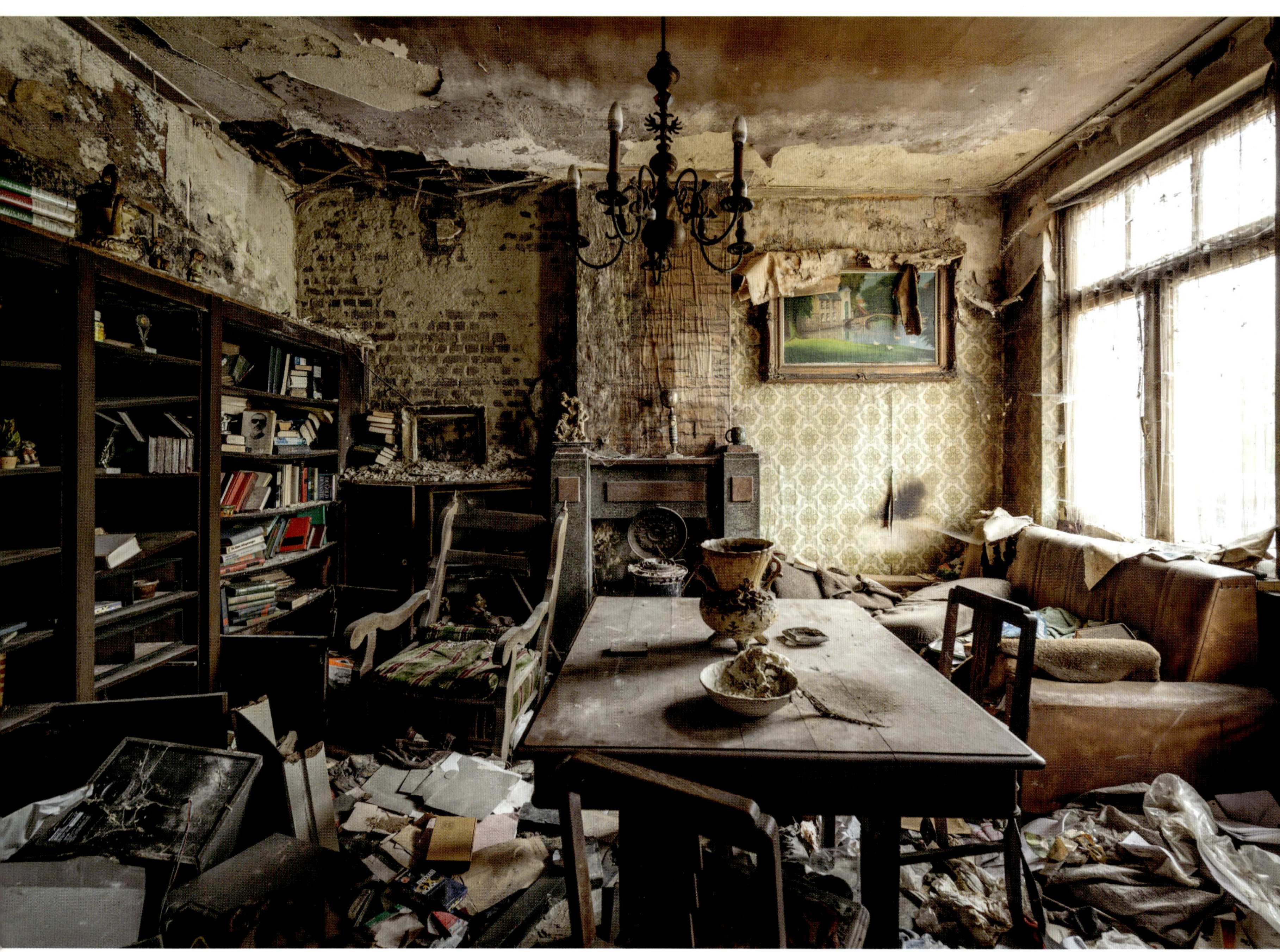

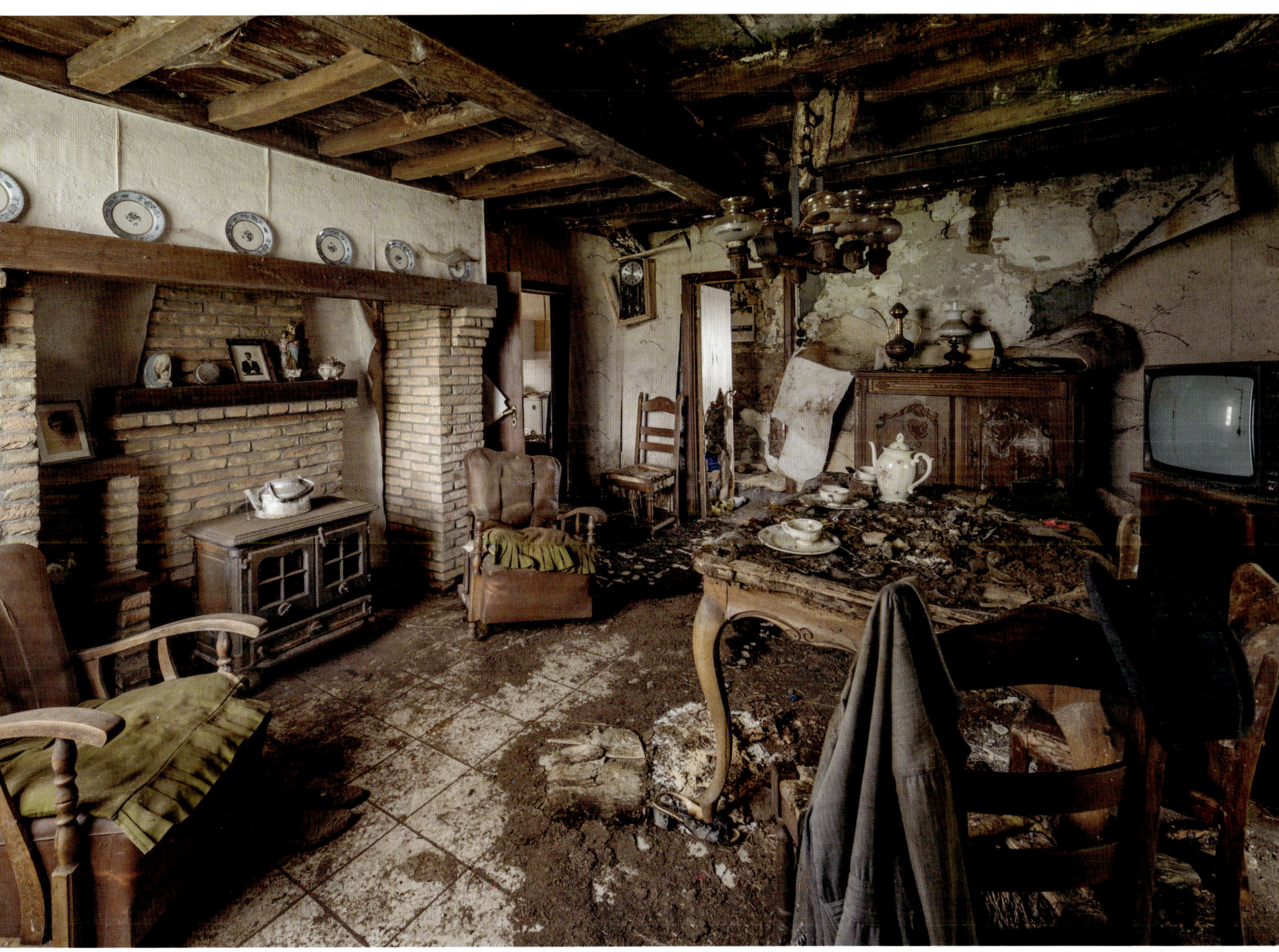

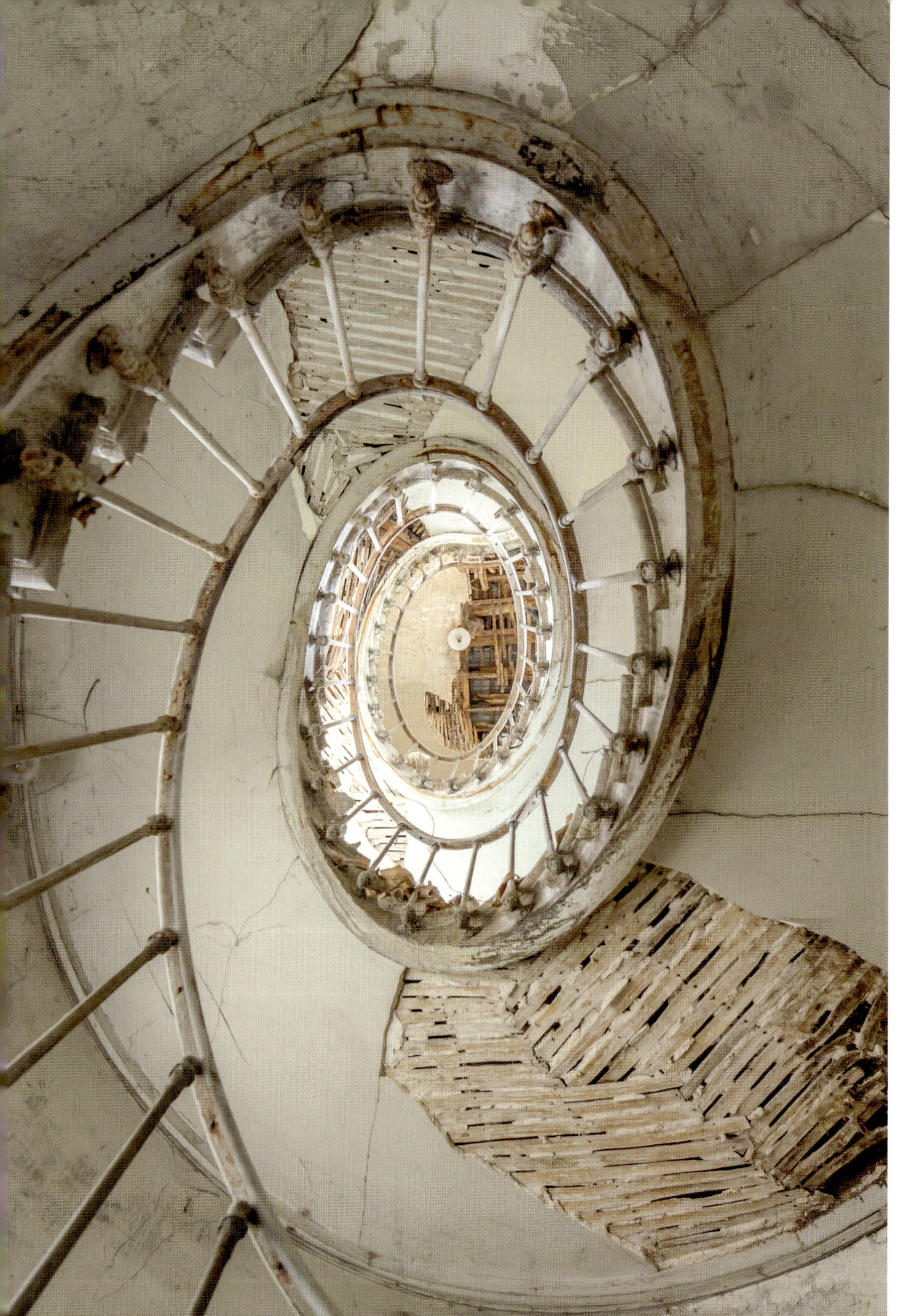

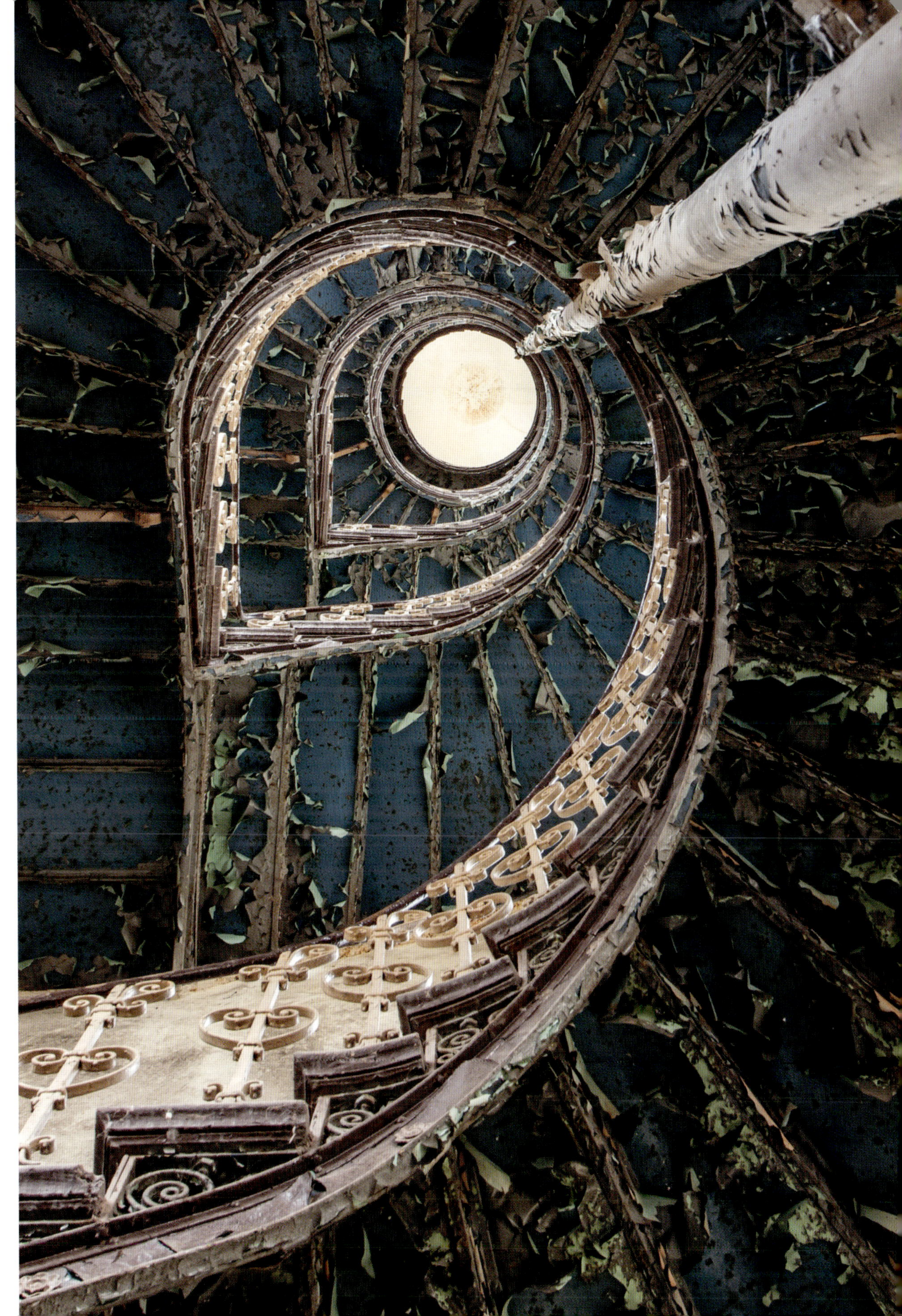

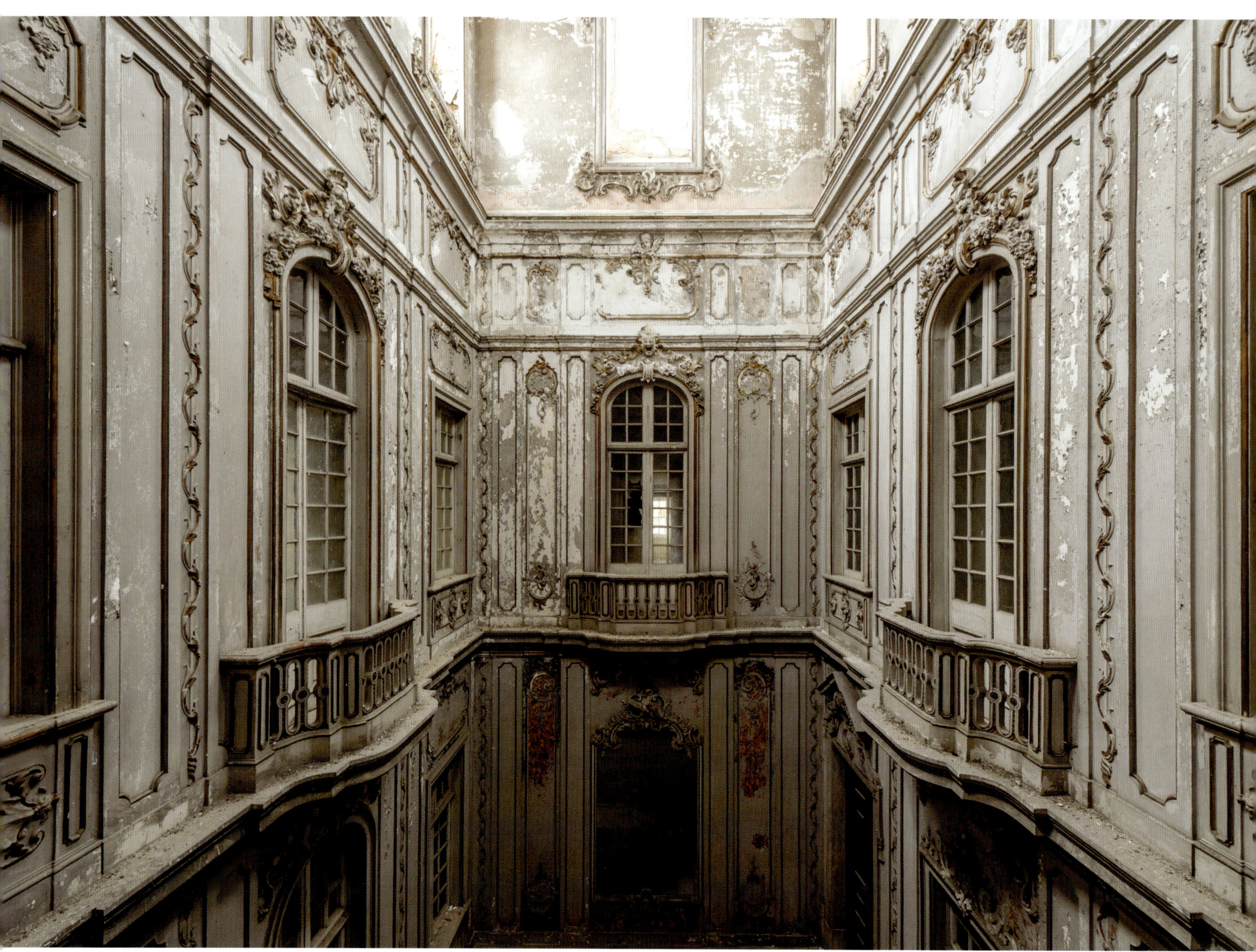

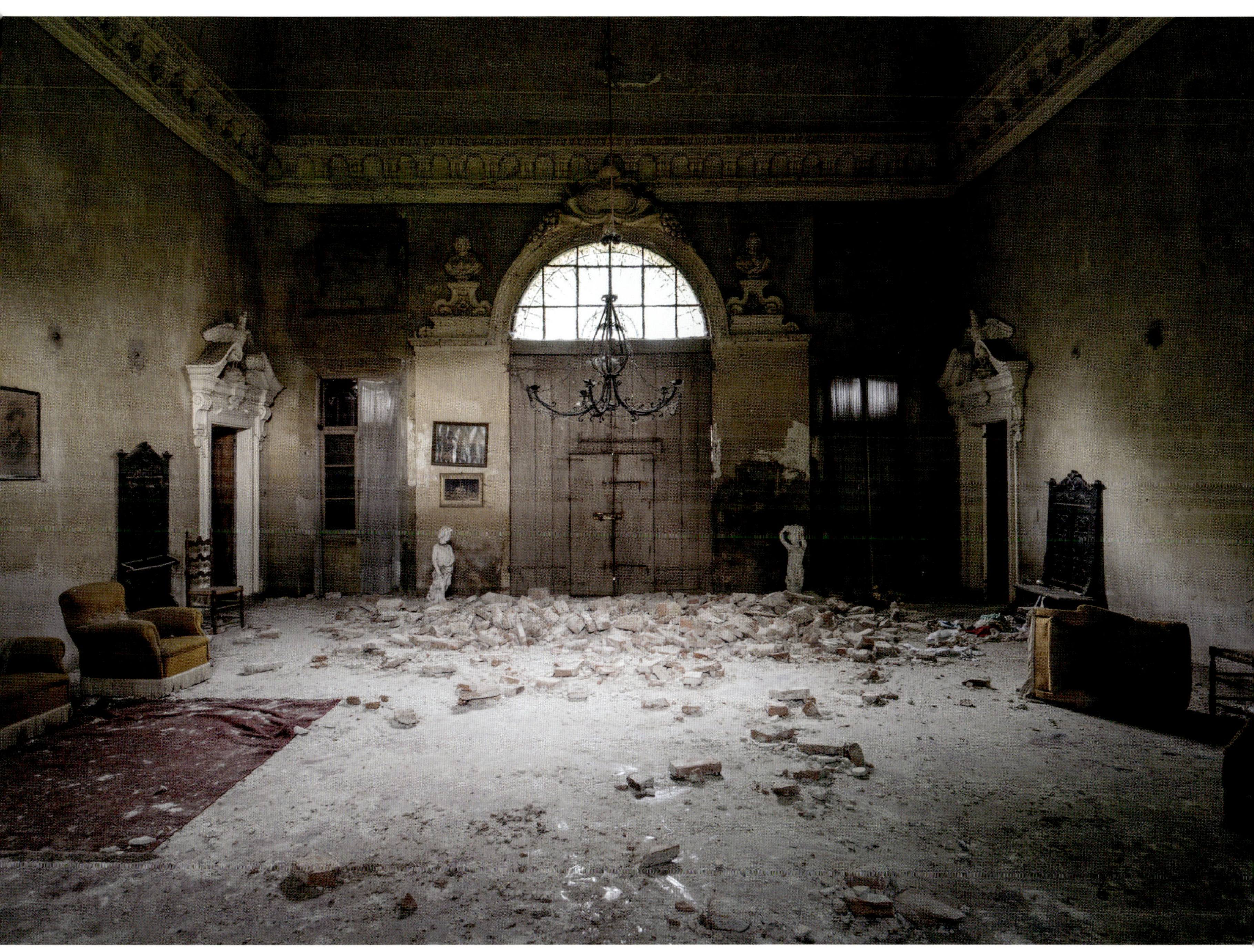

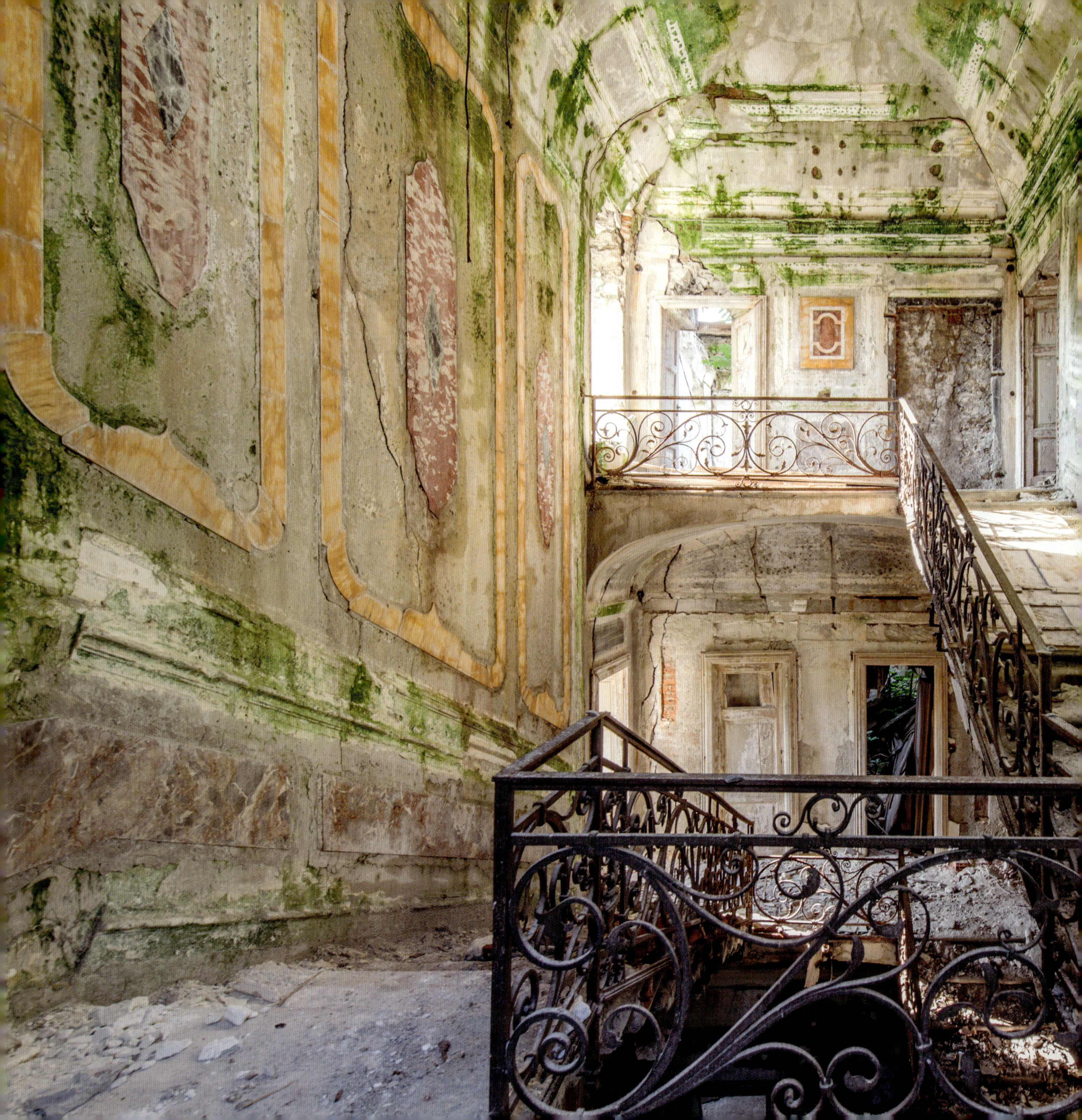

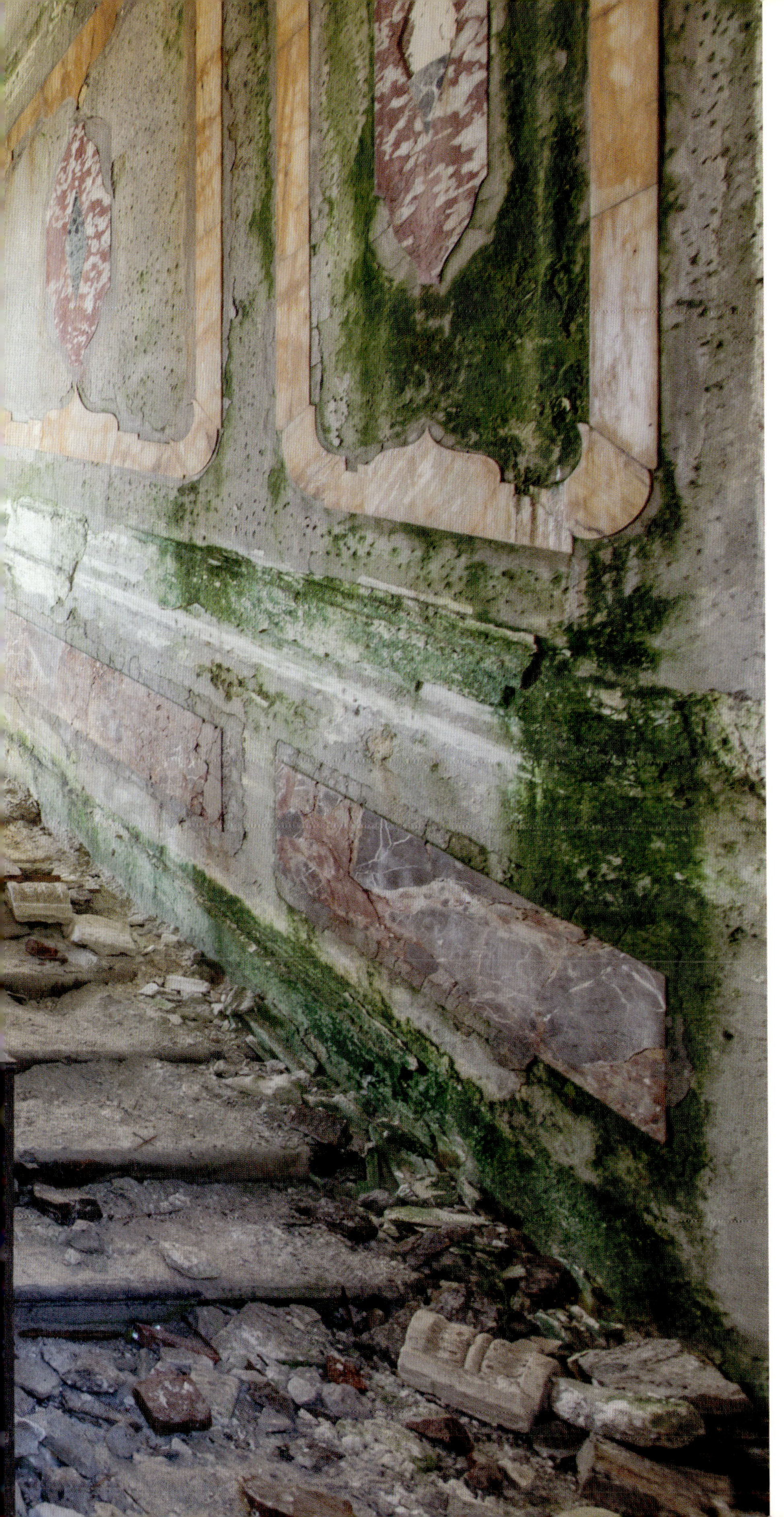

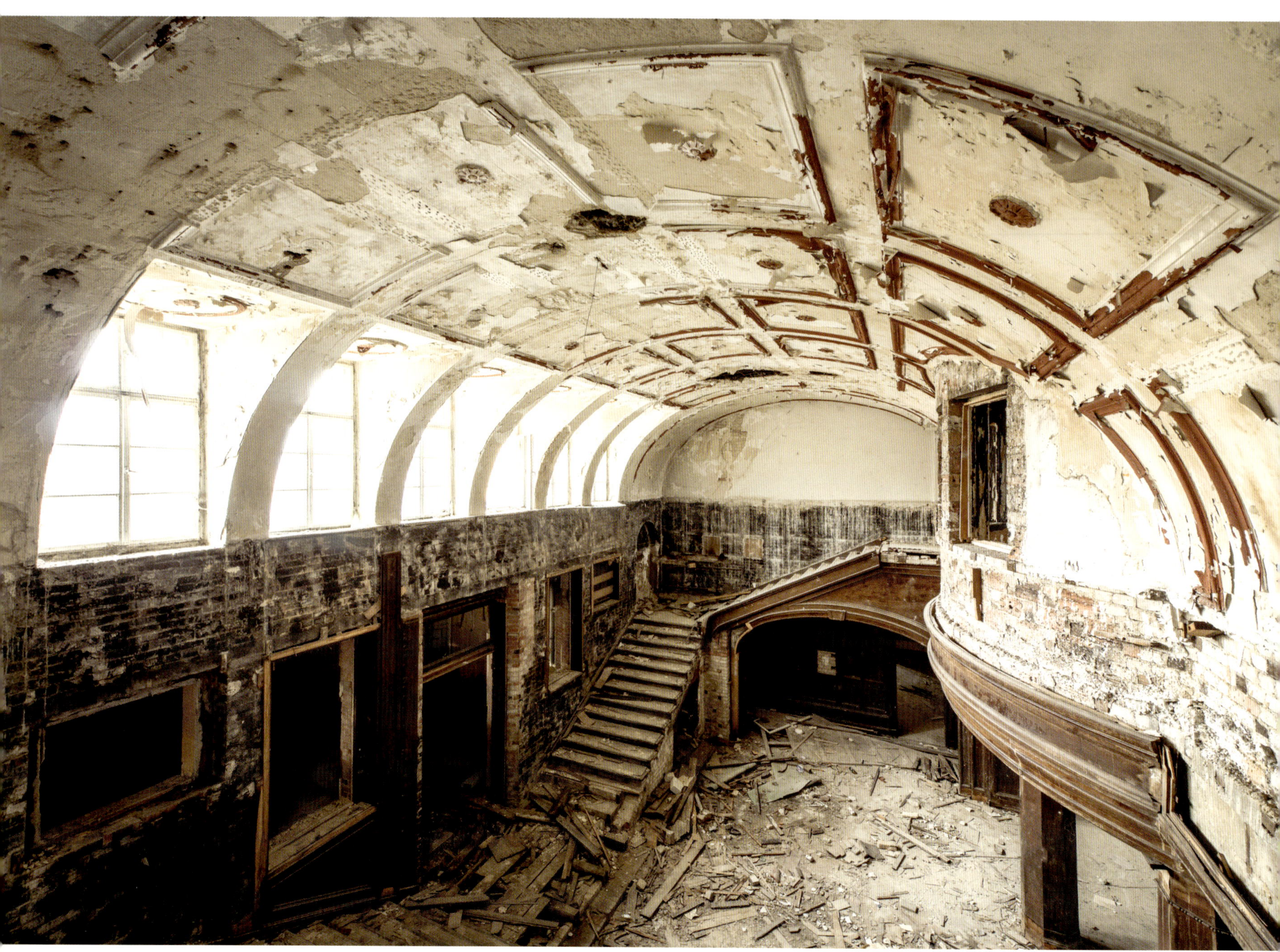

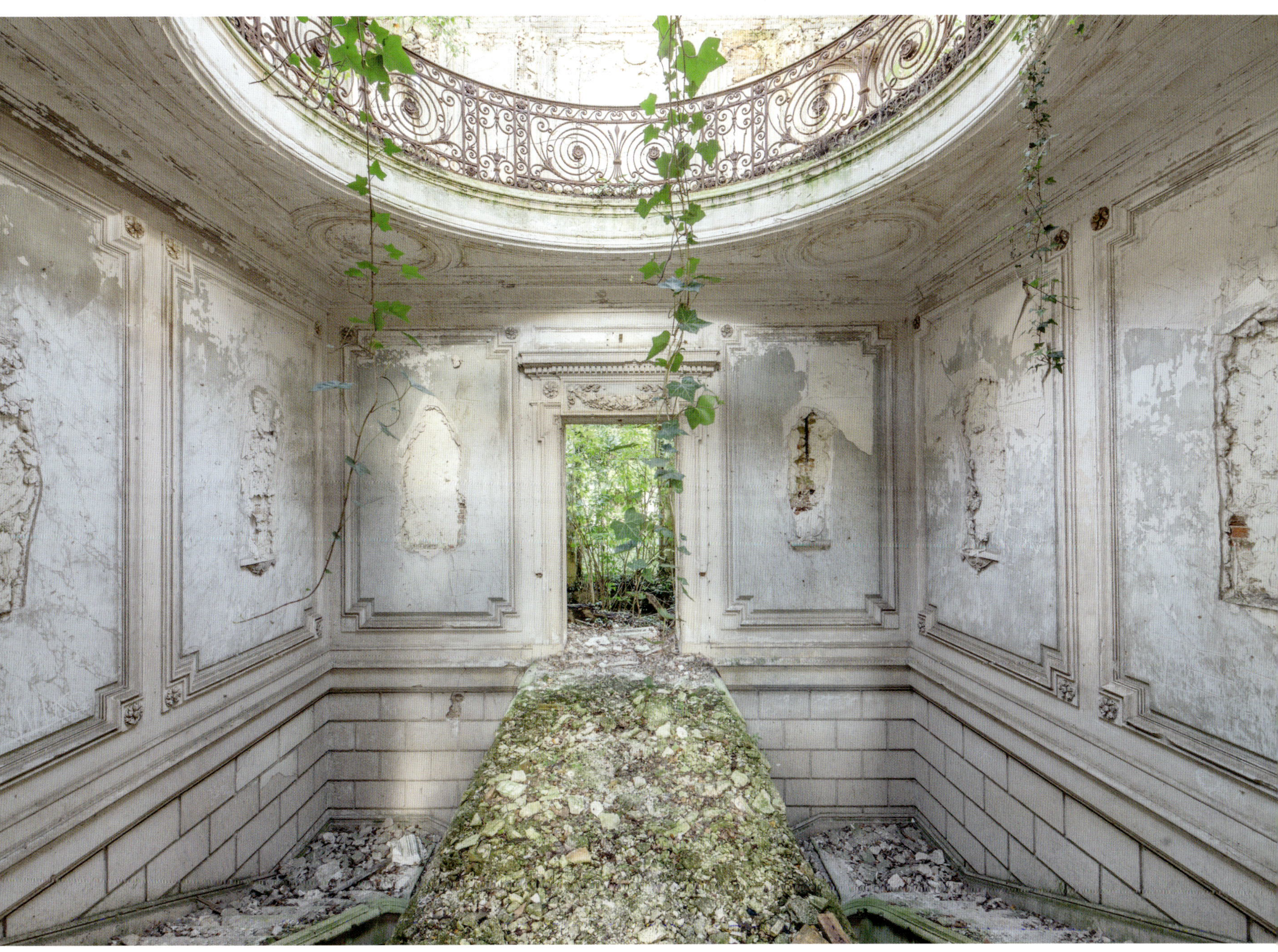

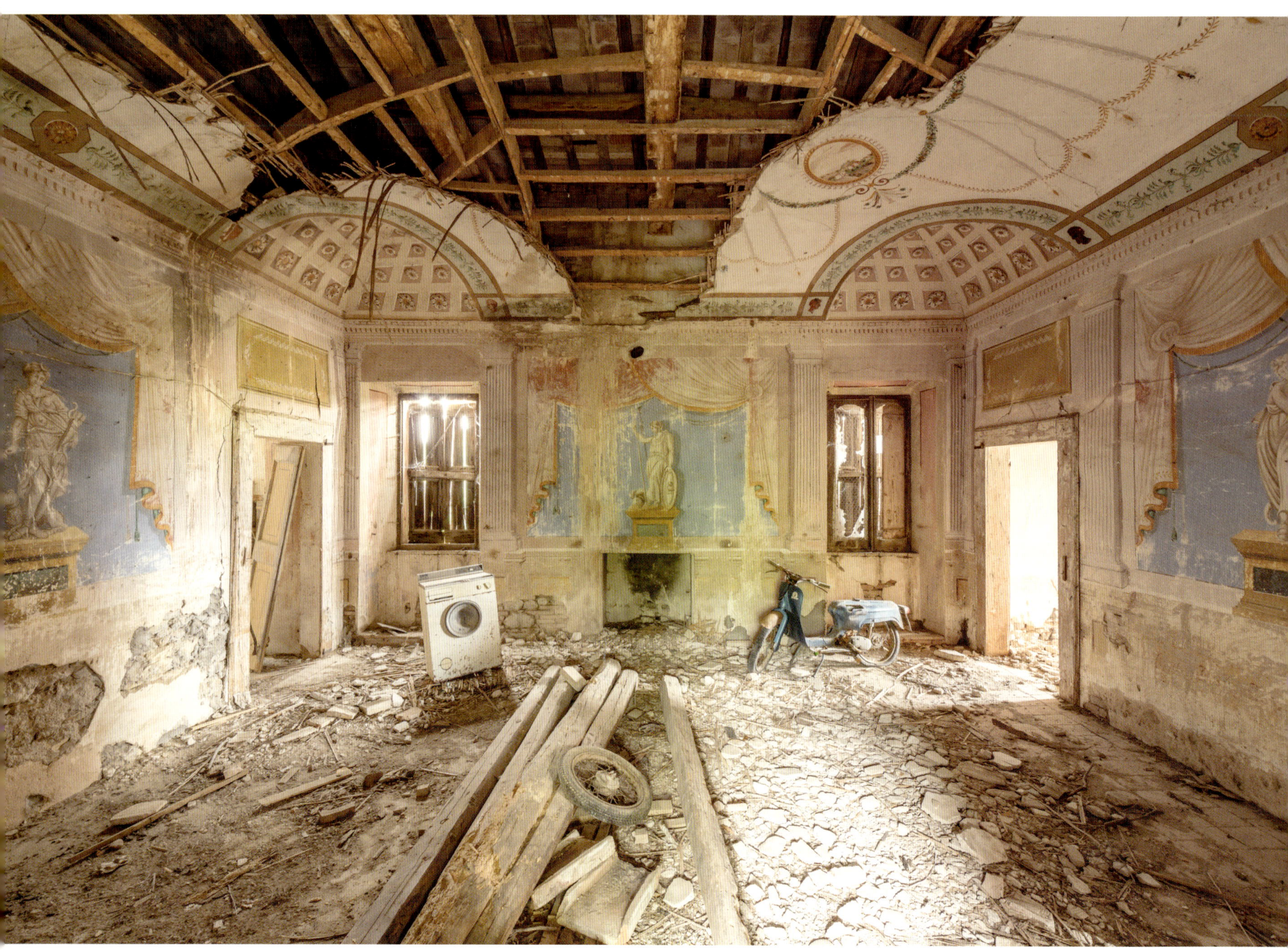

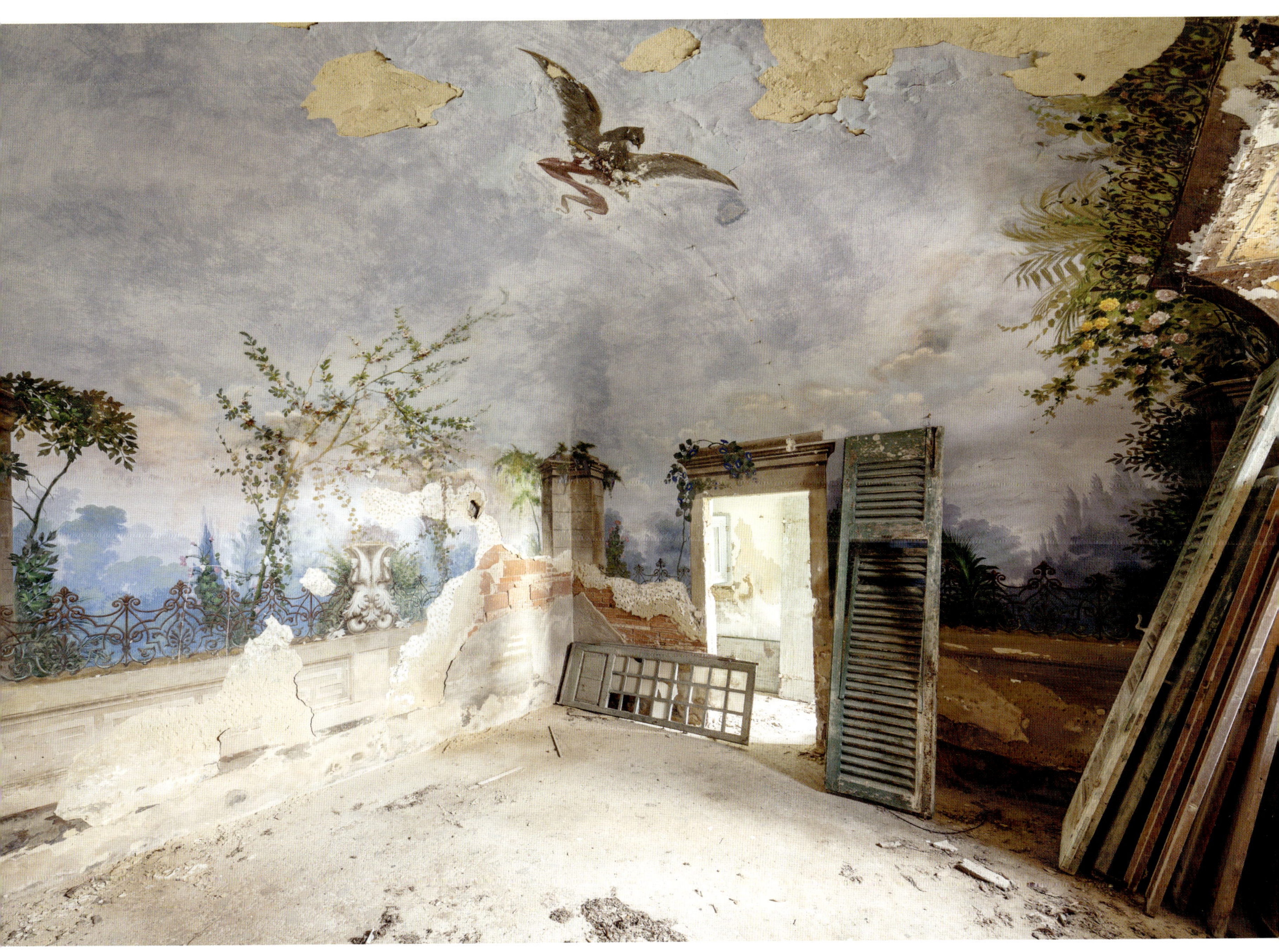

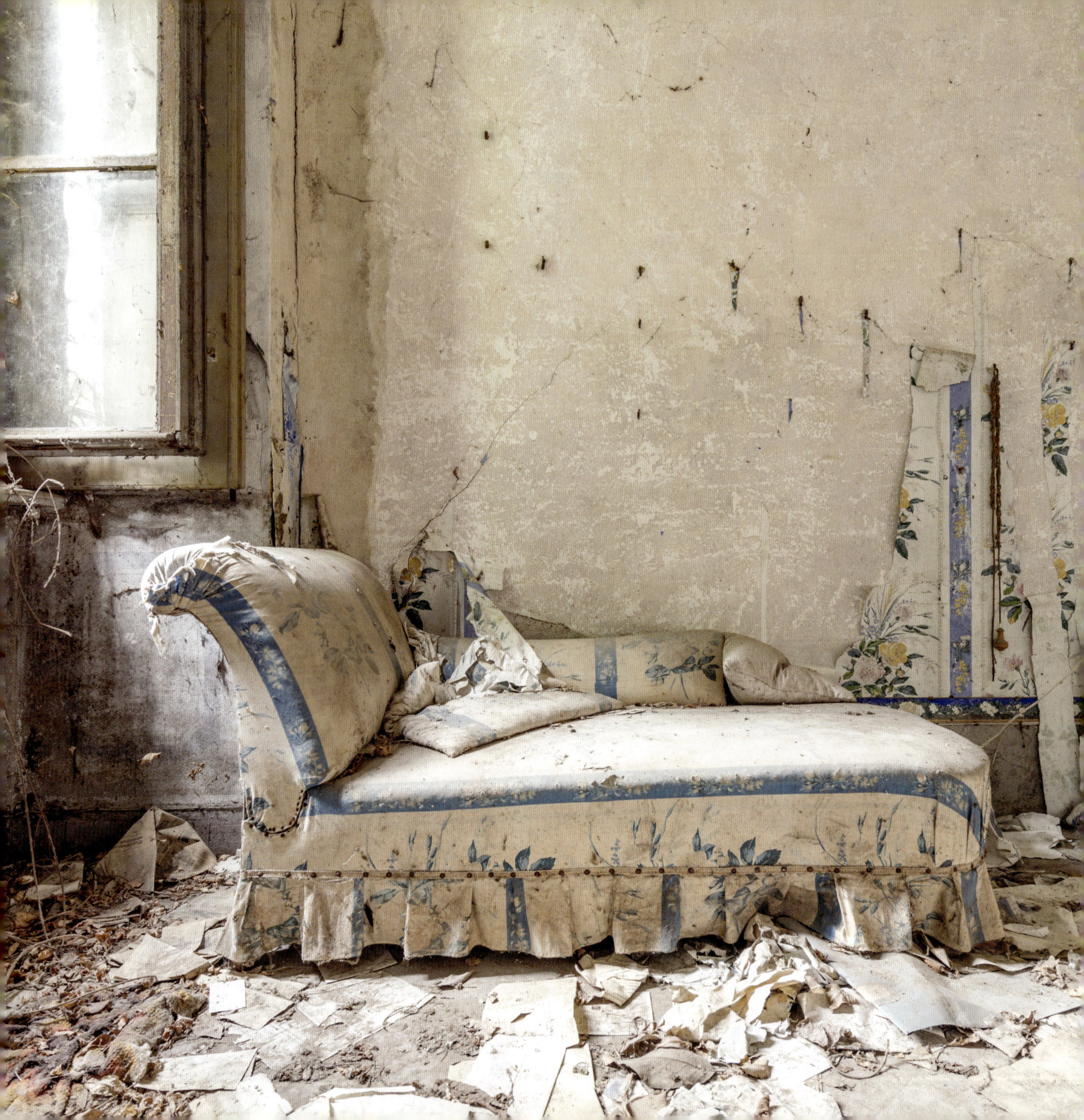

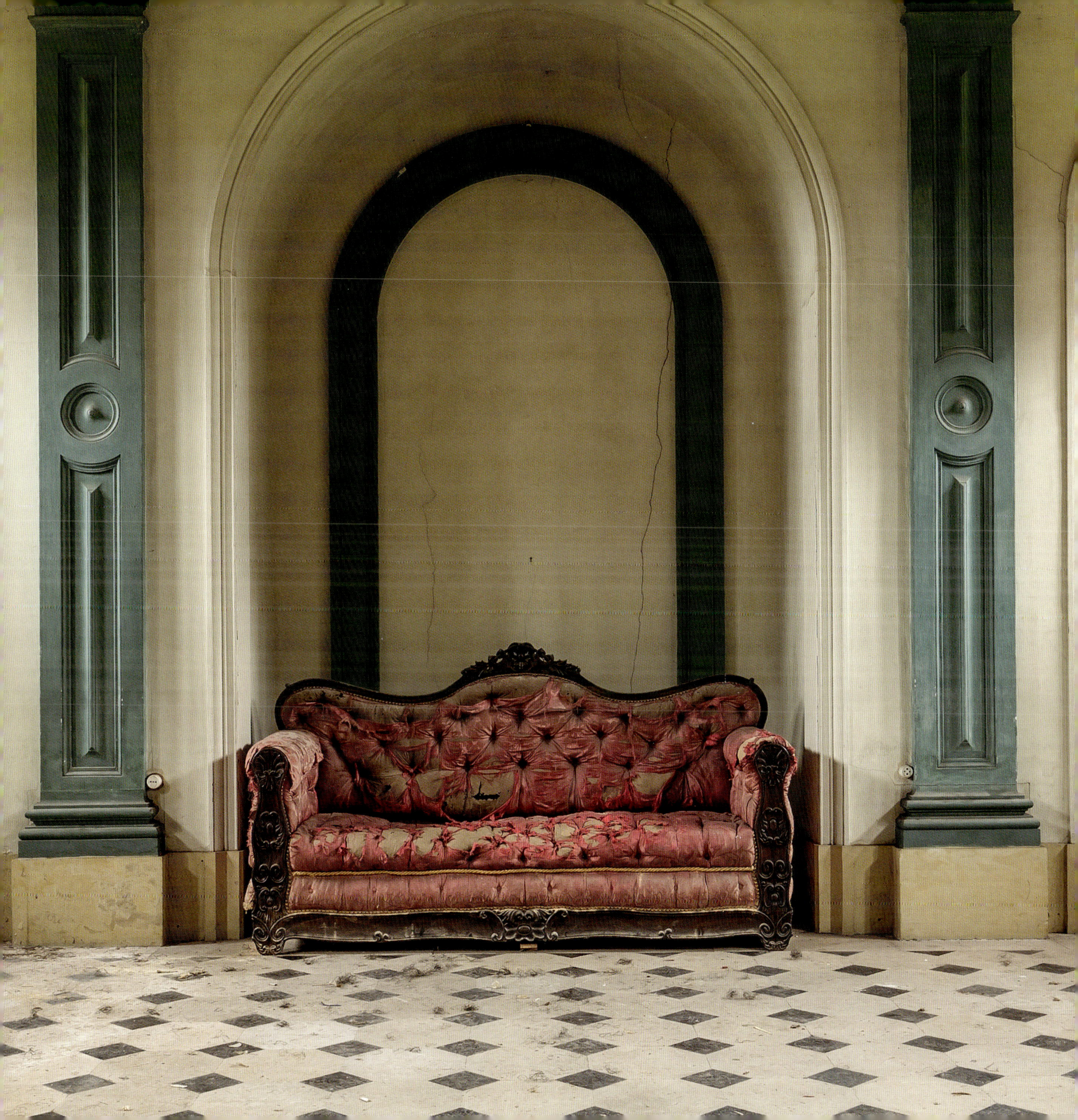

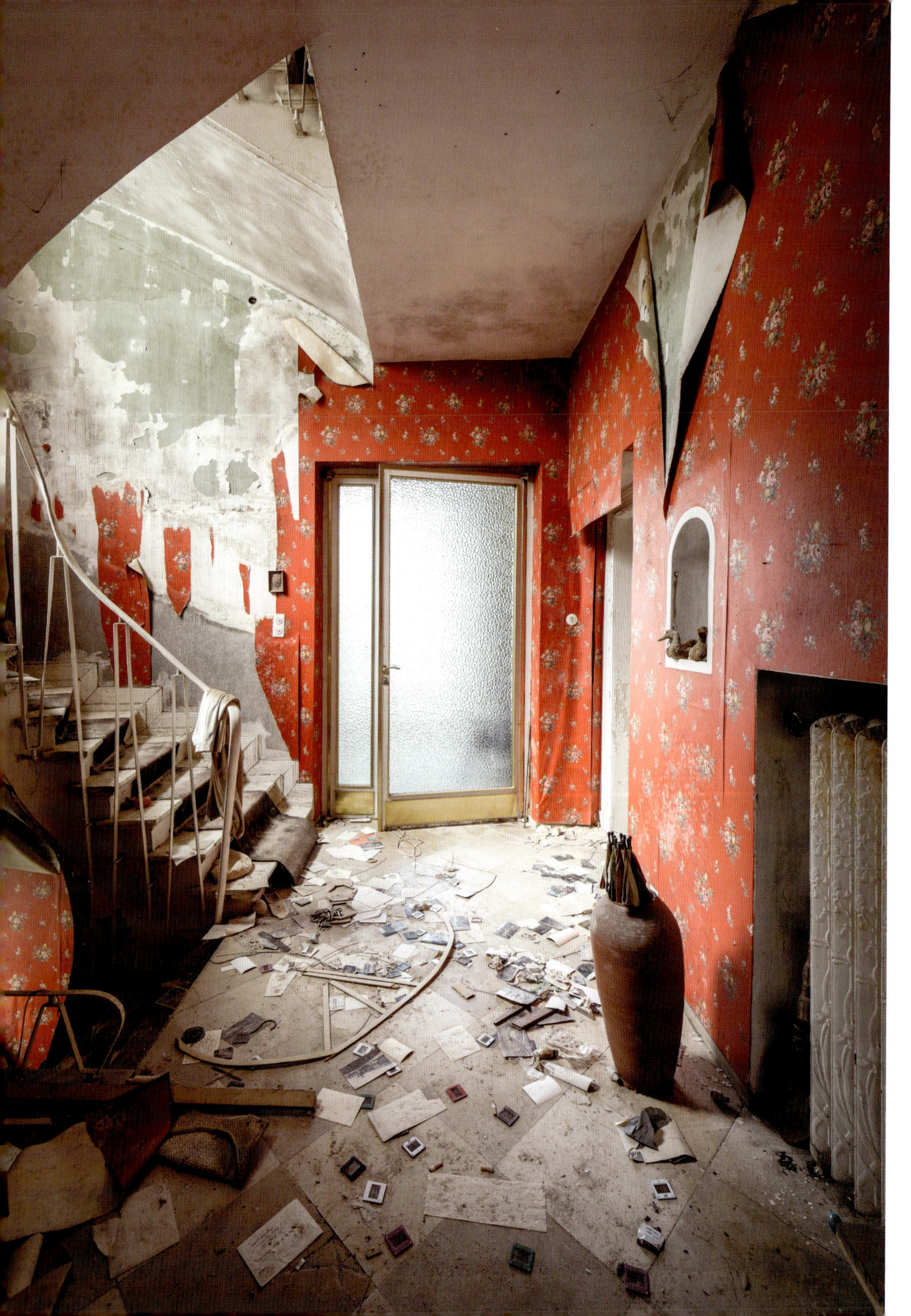

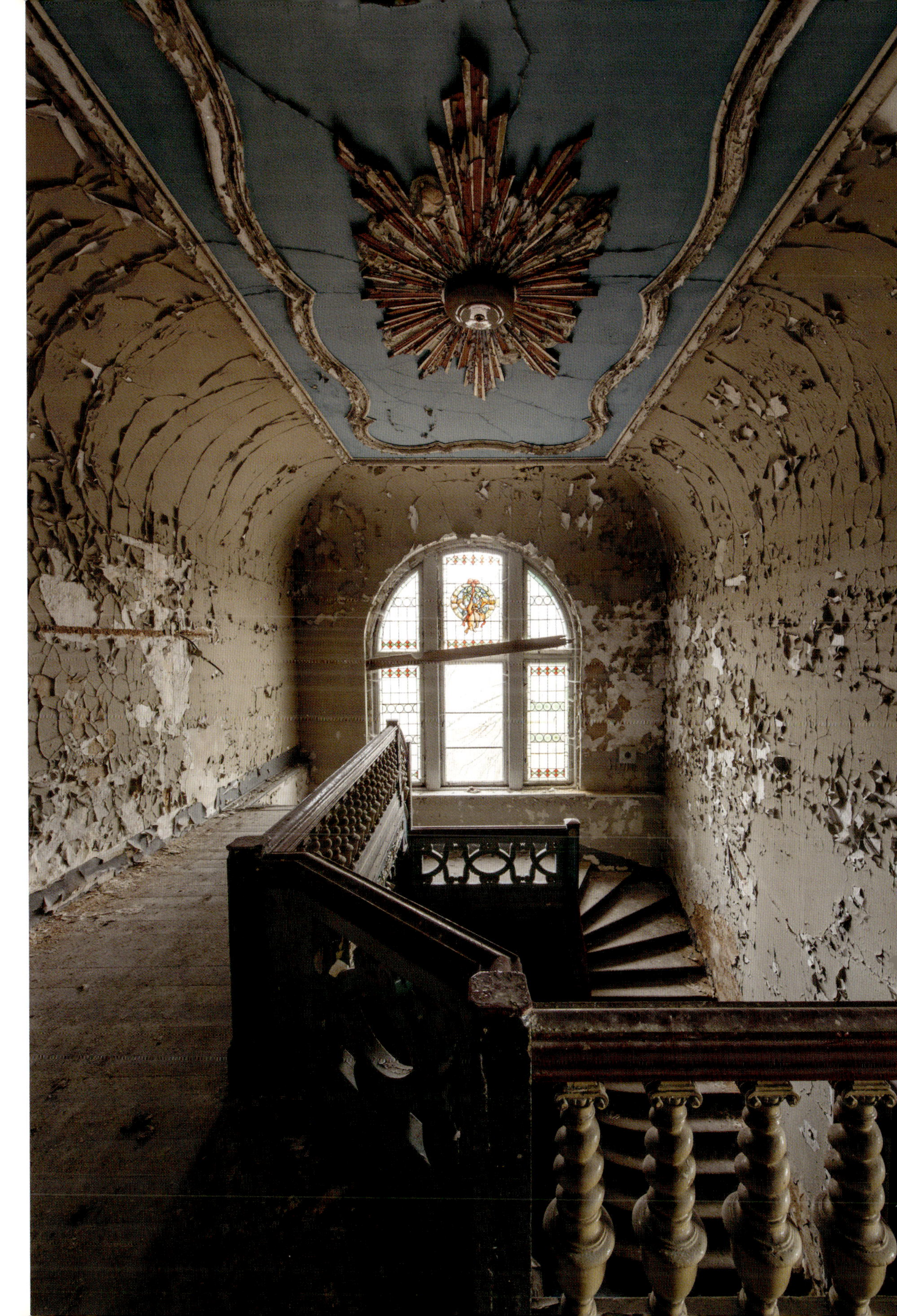

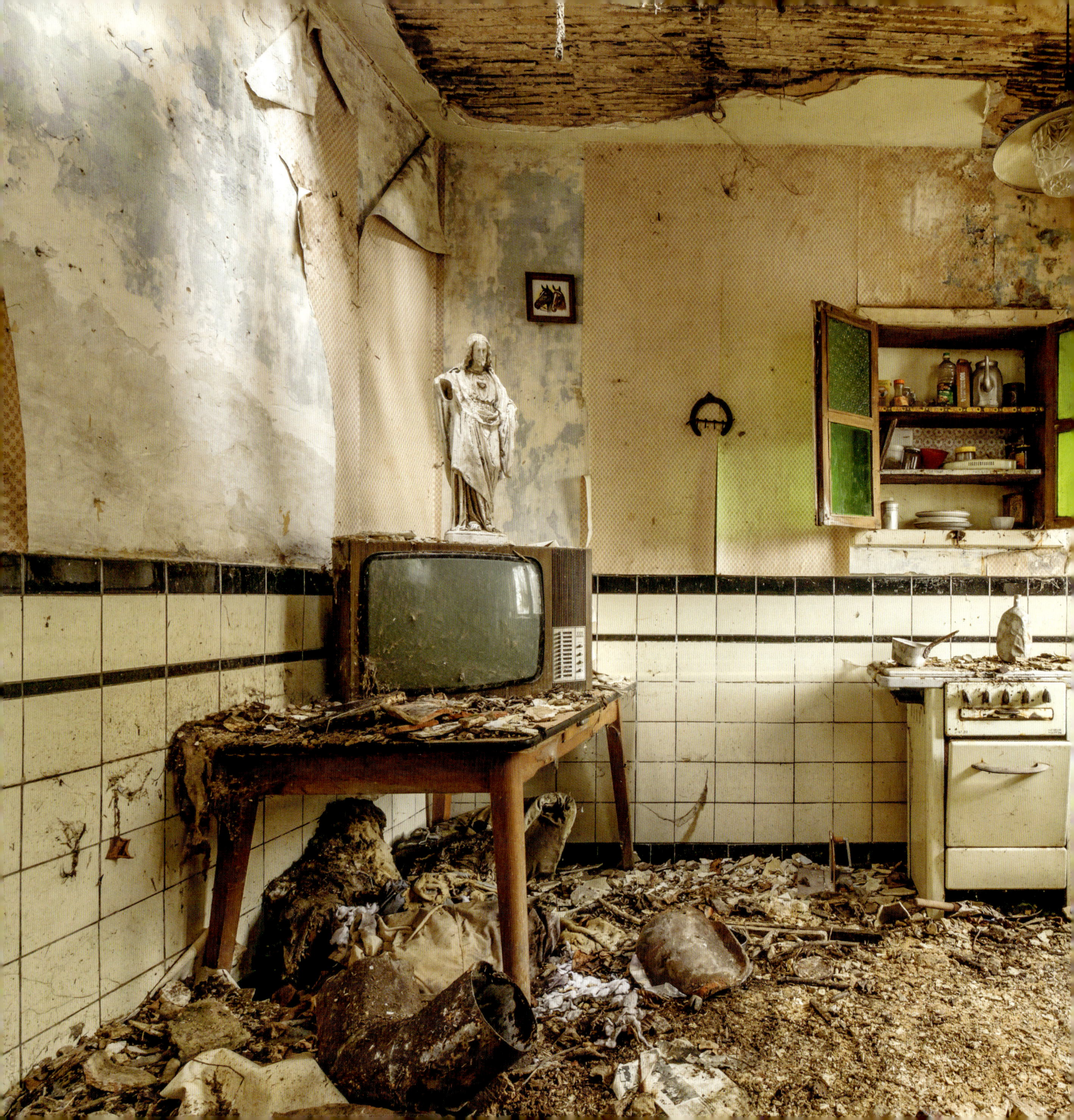

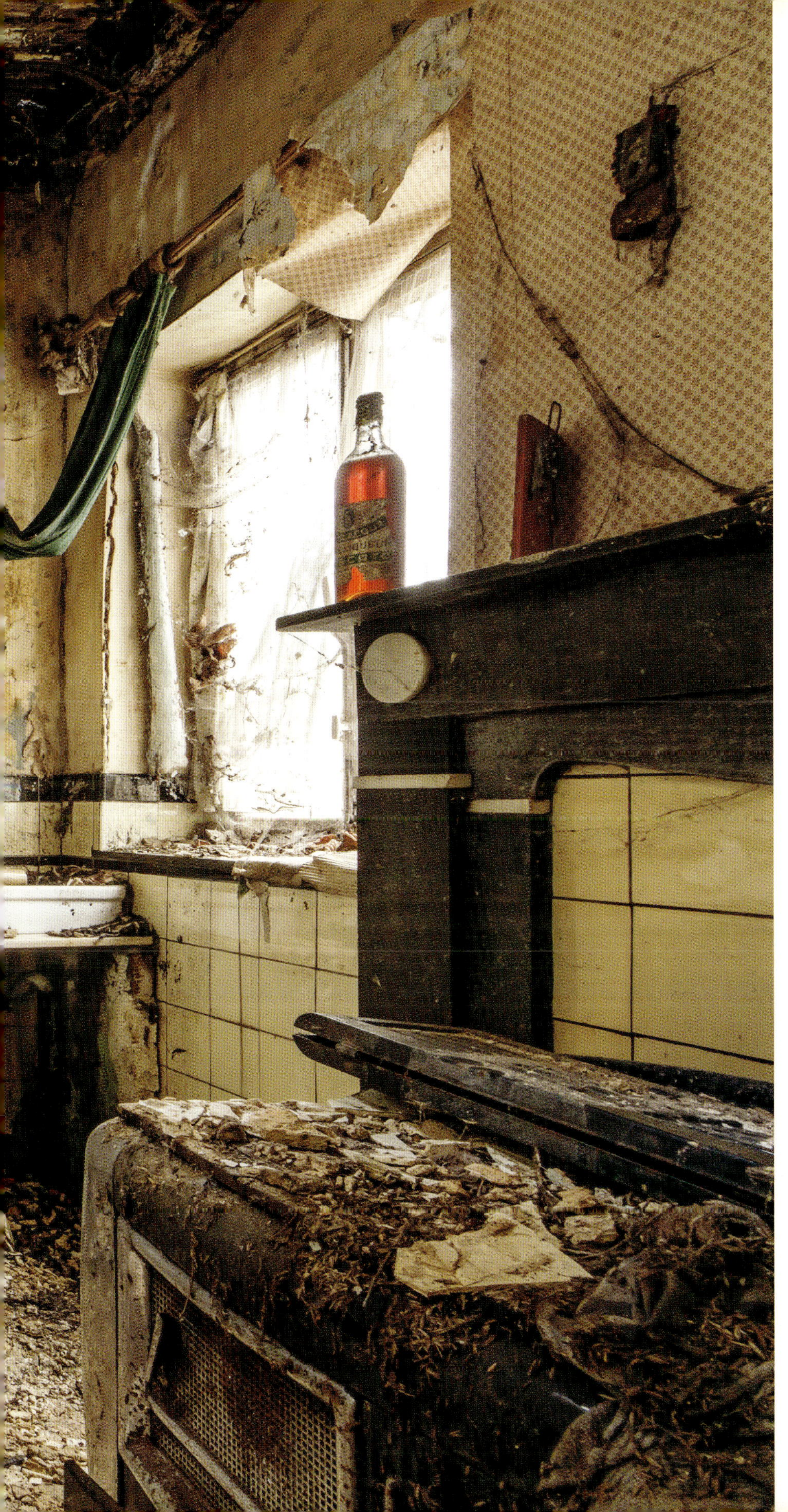

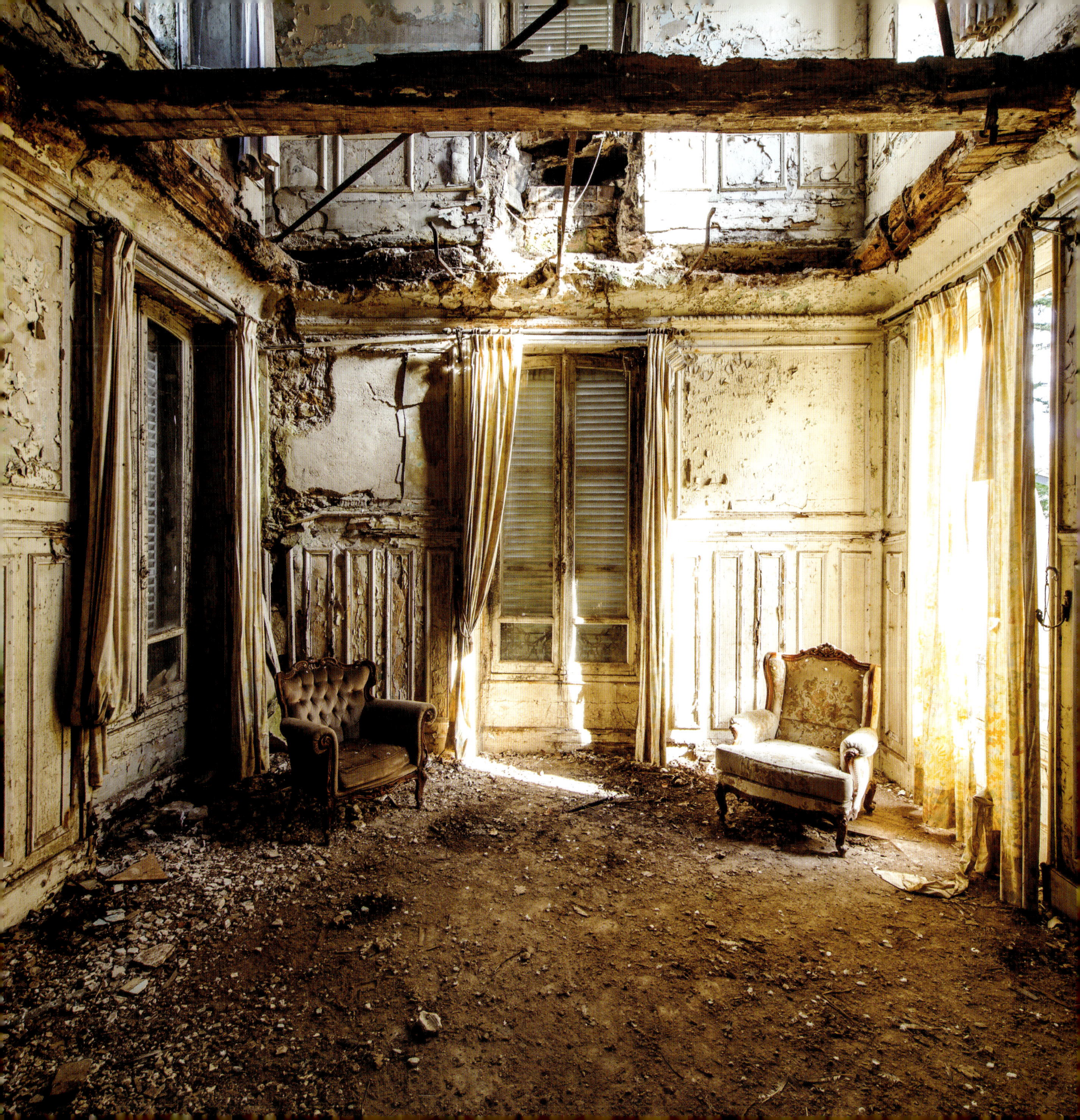

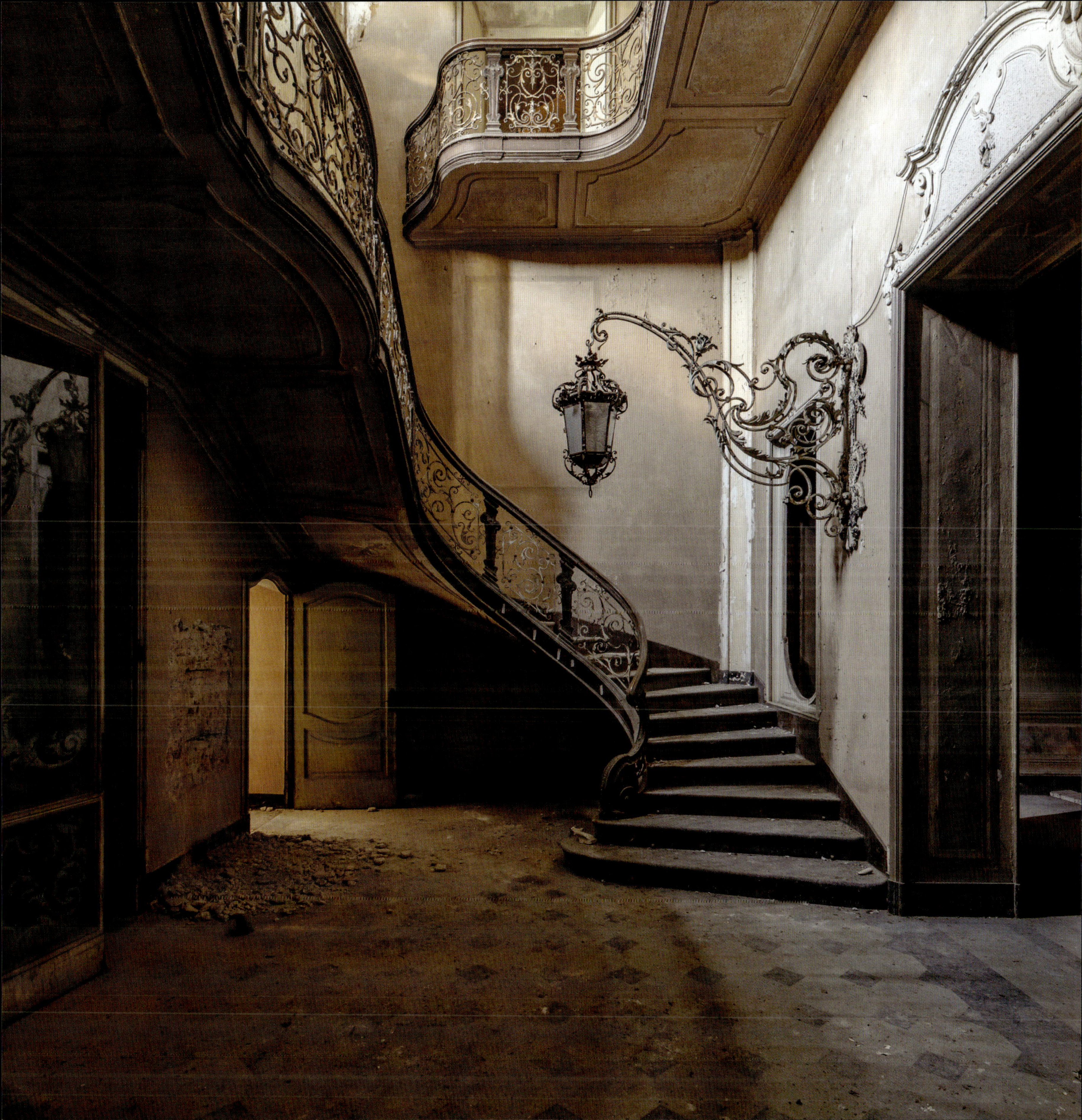

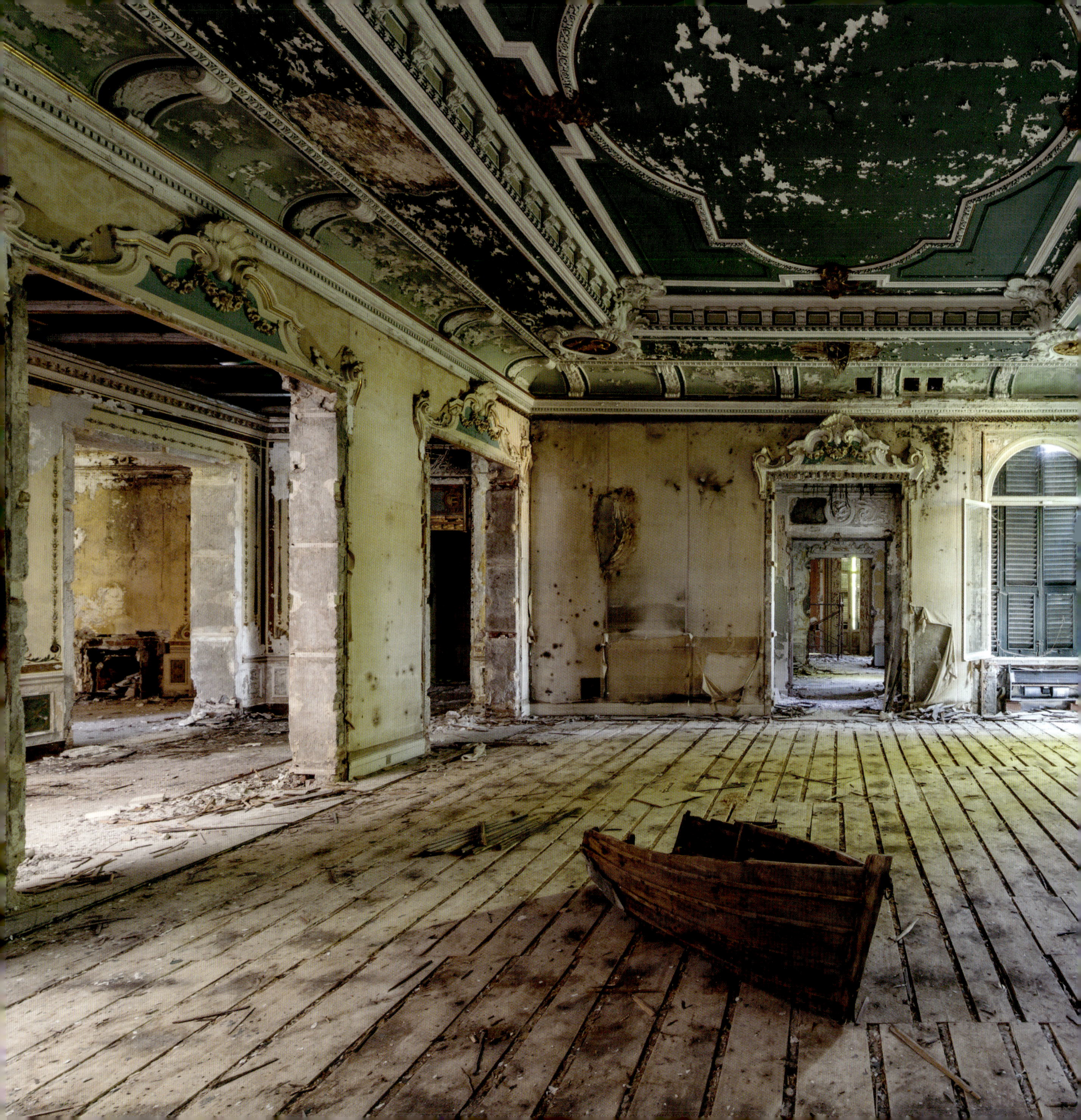

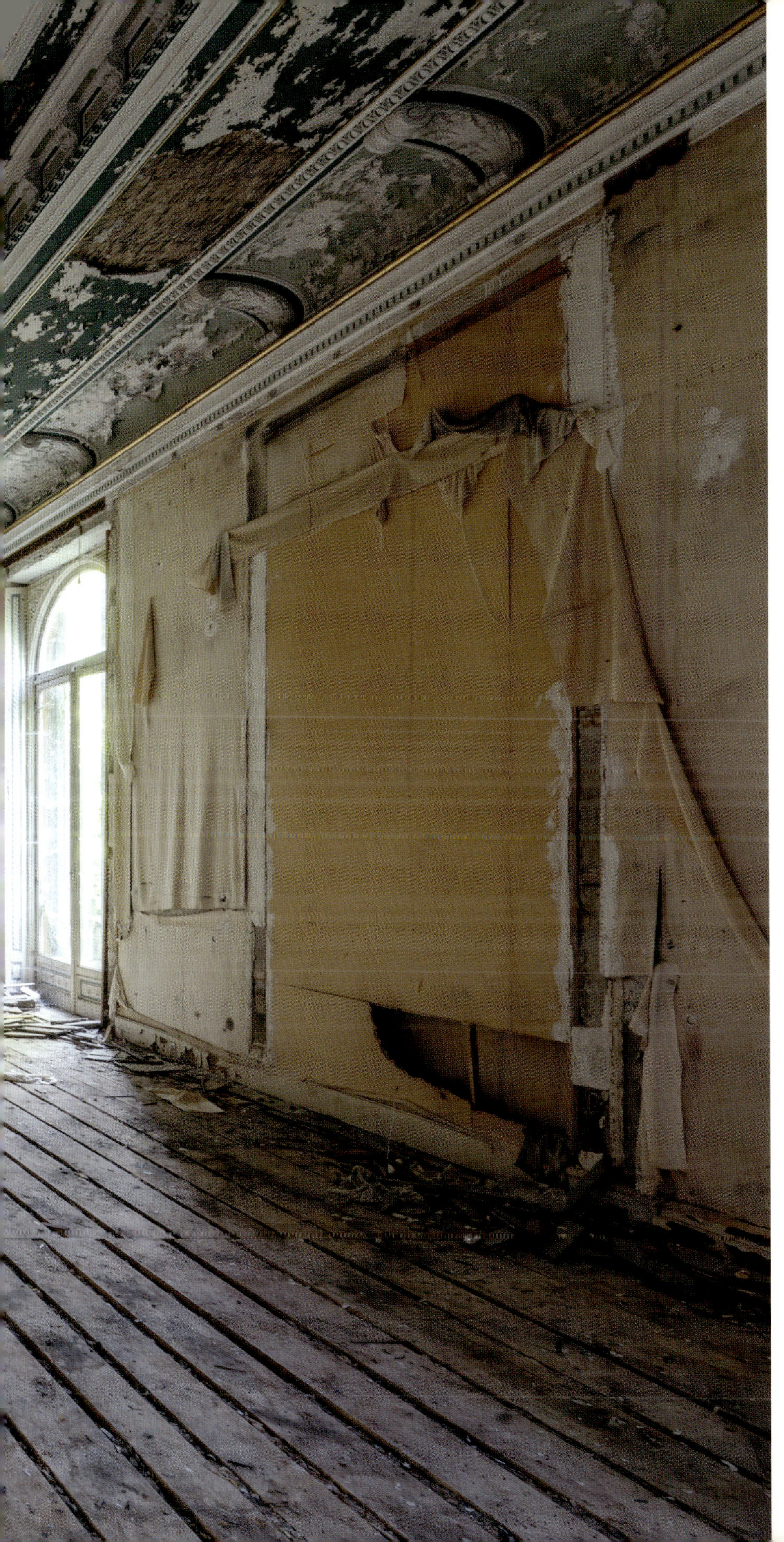

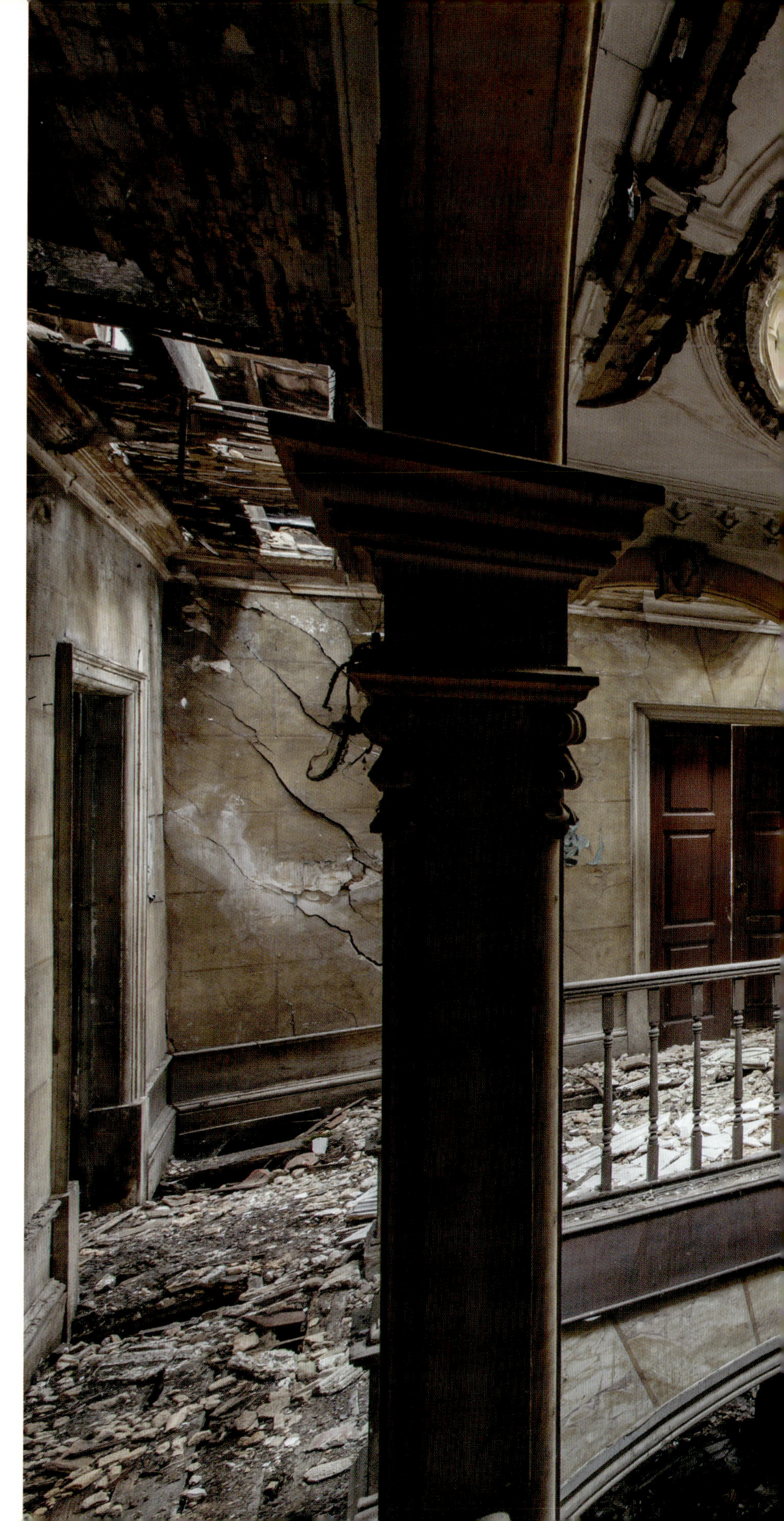

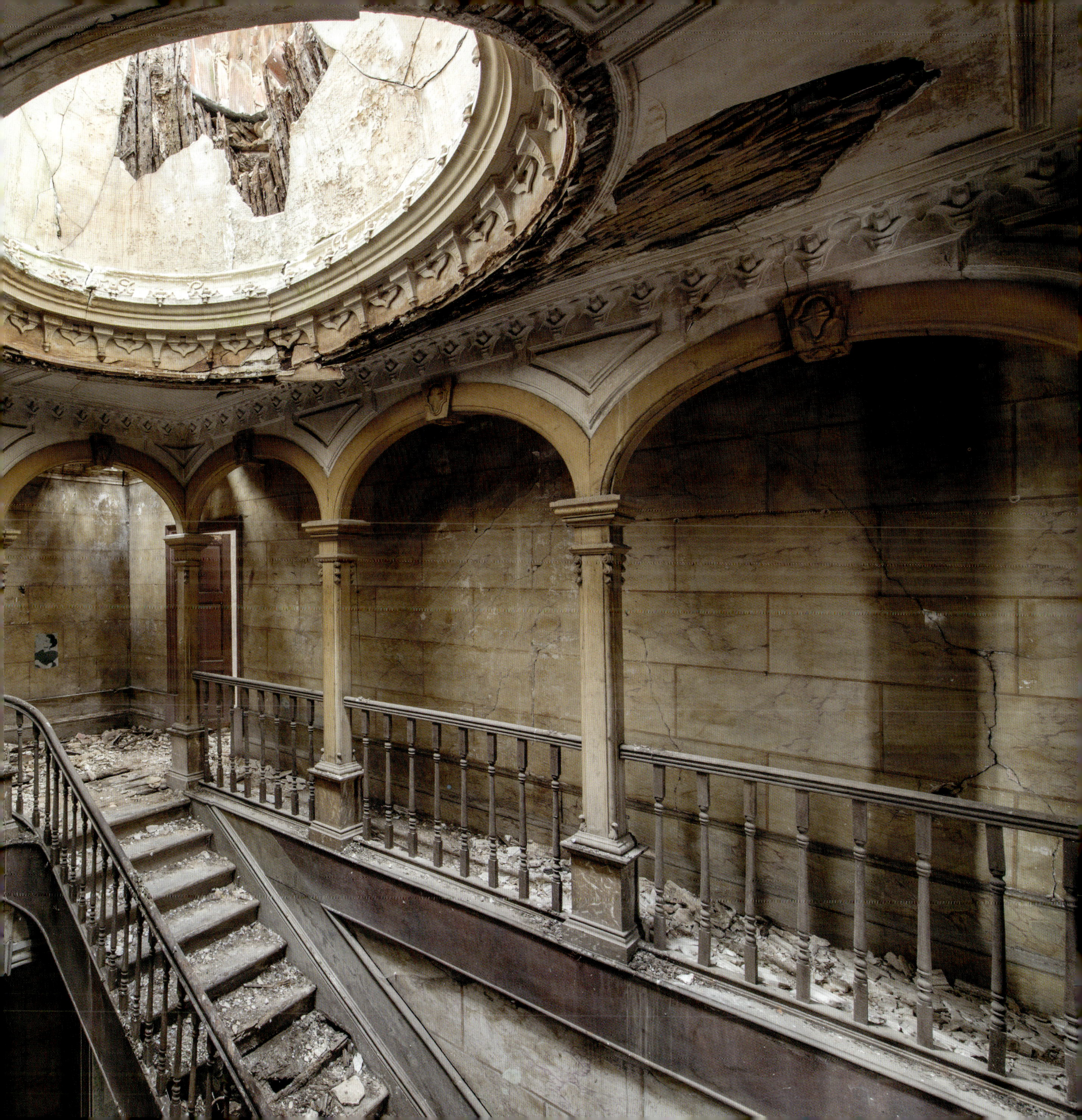

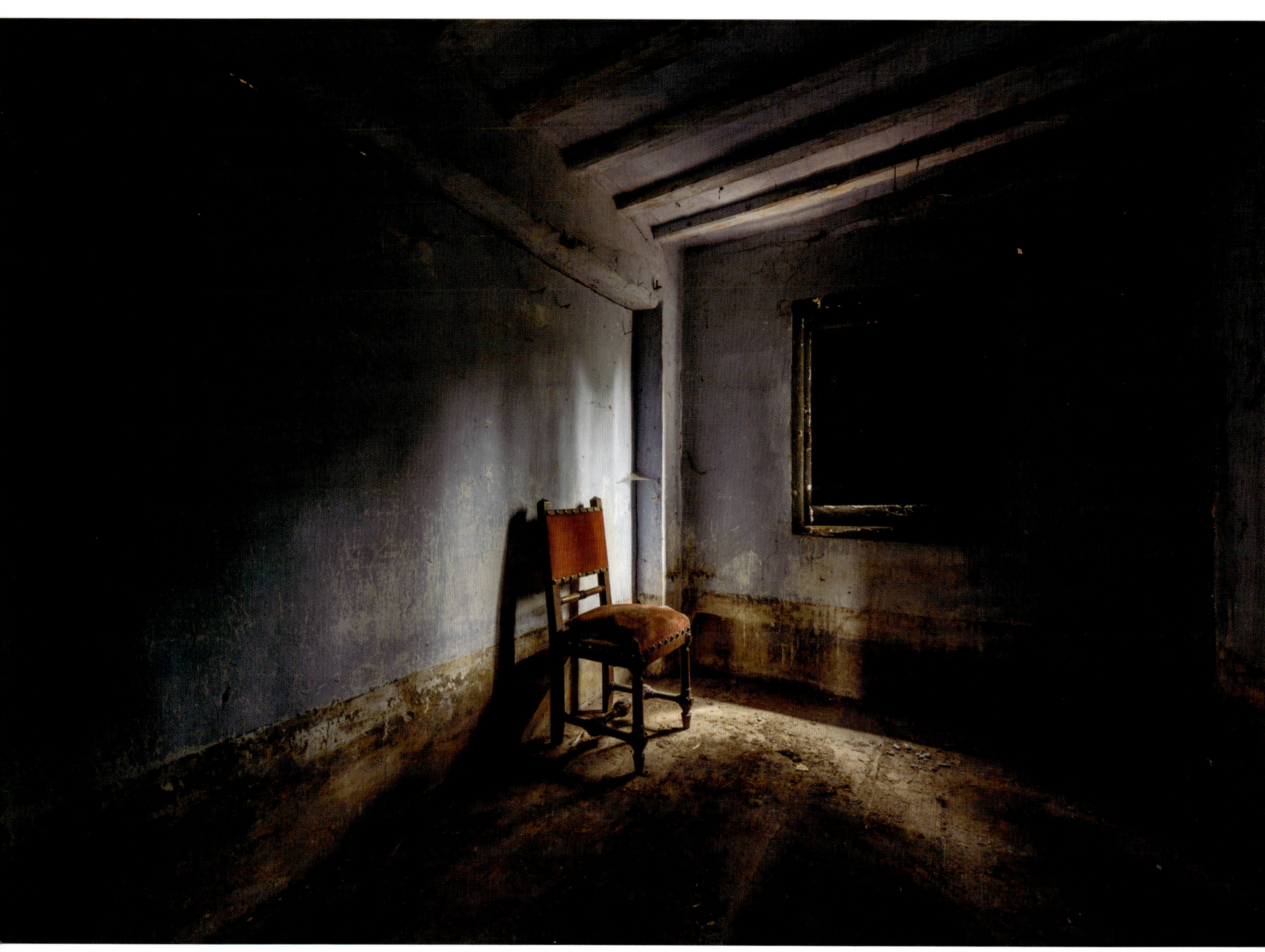

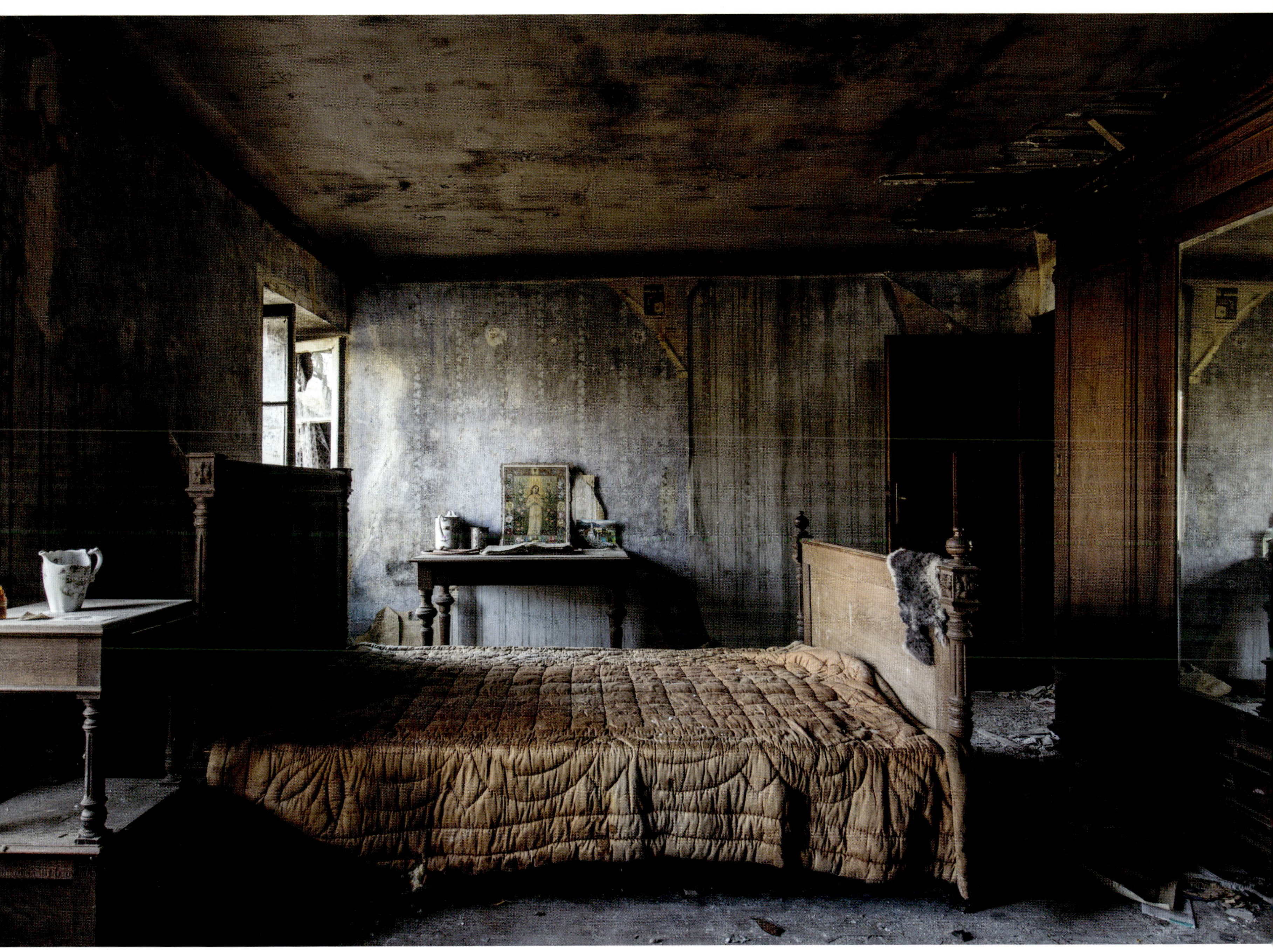

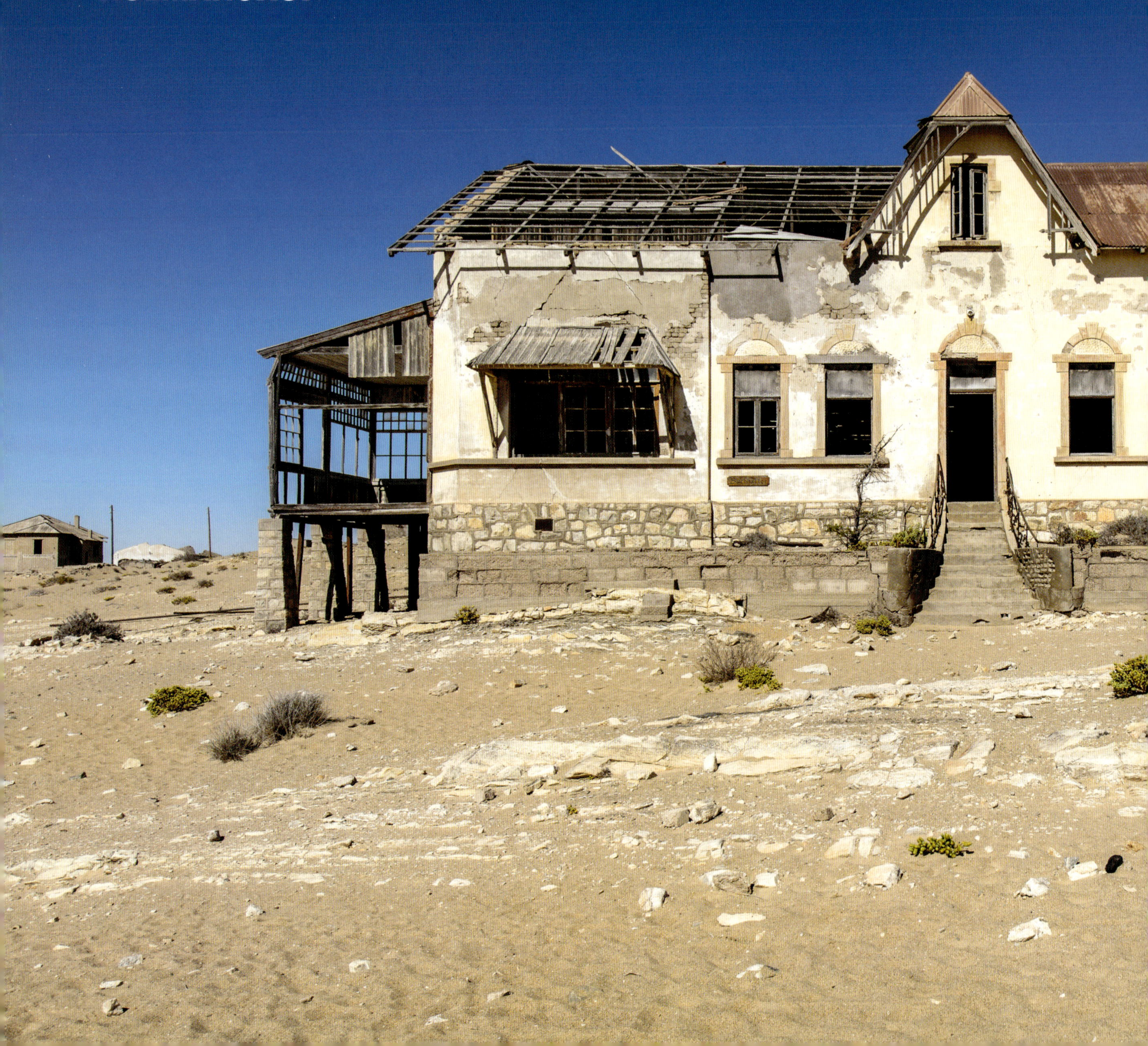
KOLMANSKOP

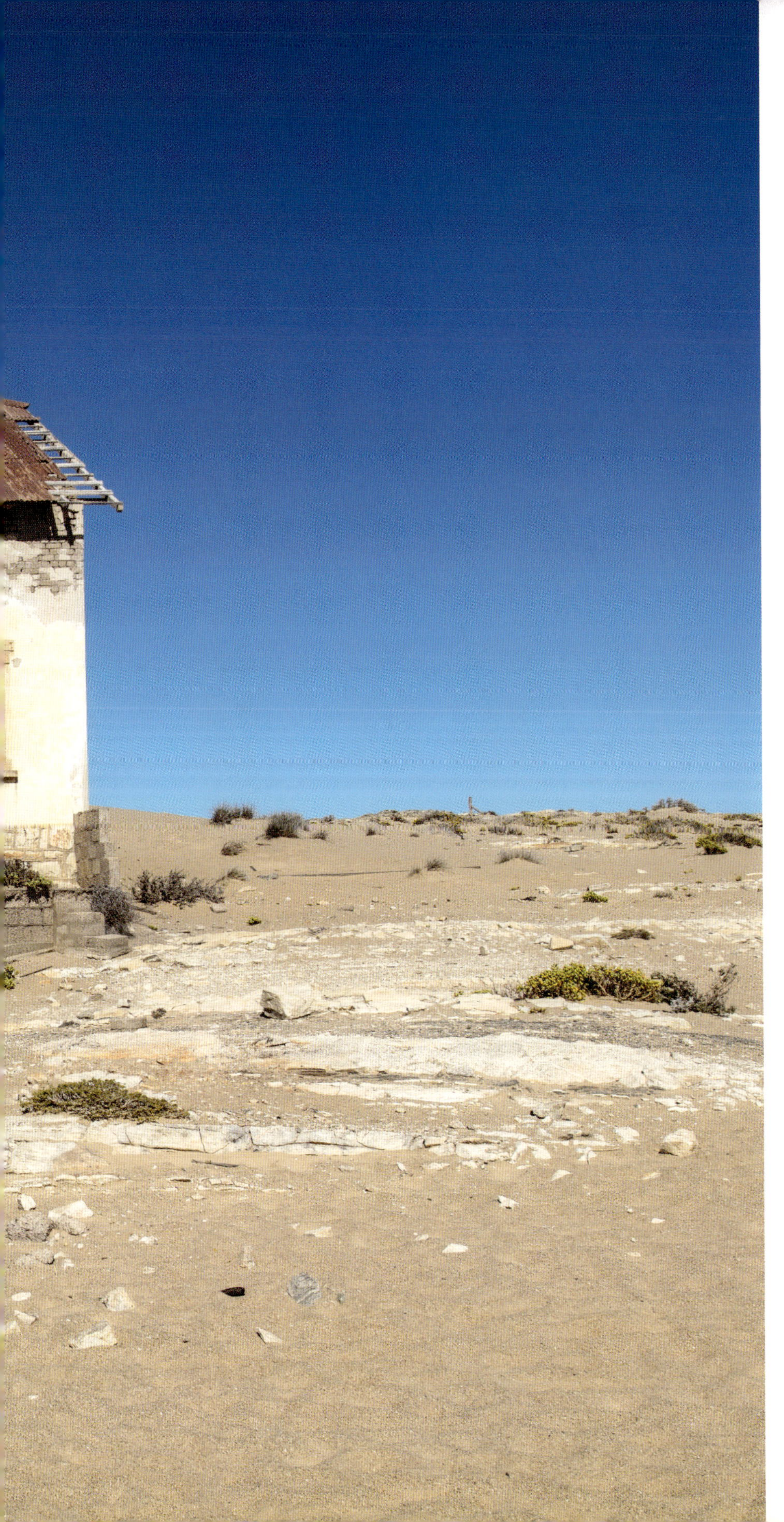

"One day Kolmanskop's sand clearing squad failed to turn up, the ice man stayed away, and the school bell stopped ringing."

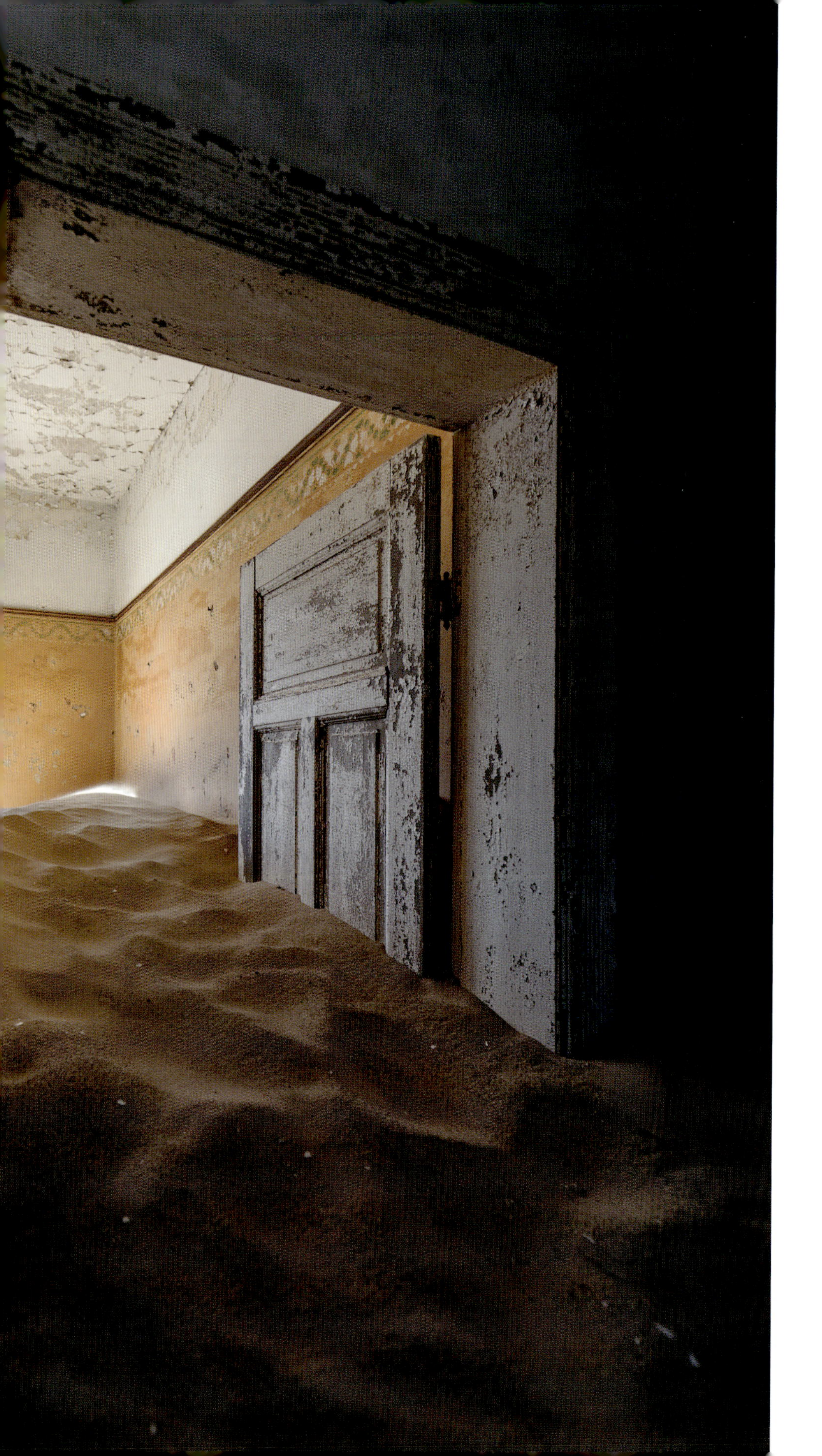

Once rich and opulent, Kolmanskop is now, and will be forevermore, a ghost town invaded by sand, lost in the middle of the desert on the southern Atlantic seaboard. But its history remains as surprising as it is short. In 1908, Namibia was still under German control. A railroad worker named Zacharias Lewala found a diamond while working on the construction of new train tracks between Keetmanshoop and Lüderitz. Initially, the rumors of miners finding diamonds were received with great skepticism; but soon the gossip spread that diamonds were sold daily and that a geologist had confirmed the discovery. Kolmanskop was born.

Diamond fever erupted and Kolmanskop went through a real rush, rapidly becoming the nerve center of the area later called "Sperrgebiet" due to its rich deposits of diamonds. The legend says that even by night, you only had to go down on your hands and knees to find diamonds in the sand, thanks to the light of the moon.

Kolmanskop emerged from the earth very quickly, as new immigrants settled in the city, becoming a prosperous and fully functioning little town. Built from an architectural German inspiration, there was a hospital, a butcher shop, a bakery, an ice factory, bowling lanes, a casino, a ballroom, a school and a power plant.

So, Kolmanskop lived through a striking prosperity that attracted many adventurers, fortune hunters, miners and other prospectors; prosperity symbolized by the fact that the inhabitants of Kolmanskop used to get their clean water from Cape Town in South Africa over 1,000 kilometers away, received a daily delivery of ice. They even imported their Champagne from Reims in France! At its zenith, Kolmanskop welcomed more than 1,200 people and 700 families.

While Kolmanskop was booming and the diamonds were still abundant, the town owners decided to build the most surprising construction you could find in the middle of an arid desert: a swimming pool! The inhabitants and miners could relax there after a hard day of labour in the heat. For that, they had to build 28 kilometers of pipelines in the desert to reach the sea near the frontier! Yes, it was a saltwater pool of course. Clean water (mostly coming from South Africa) was too precious to be wasted.

If the town's population were pleased by the arrival of this new recreation, the swimming pool soon became the new novelty of the town's miners who used it to clean the diamonds they had found during the working day.

Concerning the hospital, it is very interesting to note that it received the first x-ray machine of the entire African continent; but unfortunately this machine was mostly used to verify that the miners hadn't swallowed a precious diamond. The hospital also had a maternity ward, an operating theater and its own wine cellar! (One of the resident doctors believed wine and champagne aided a faster recovery)

But after the First World War, the town started to decline because of the drop in the price of diamonds and the recession of the German economy. And of course, the surrender of the German army to South Africa that lead to the dispossession of the diamond concerns.

Little by little, the inhabitants abandoned the town leaving behind them their homes and their belongings.

In 1980, the Namibian government realized the potential for developing the ghost town as a tourist attraction. They renovated a few buildings, protected some others and organized tours and events in Kolmanskop. But even with that, the dunes inevitably pushed the structures over and buried them with the remains of former residents' lives. Nowadays, Kolmanskop is visited by only a handful of tourists or

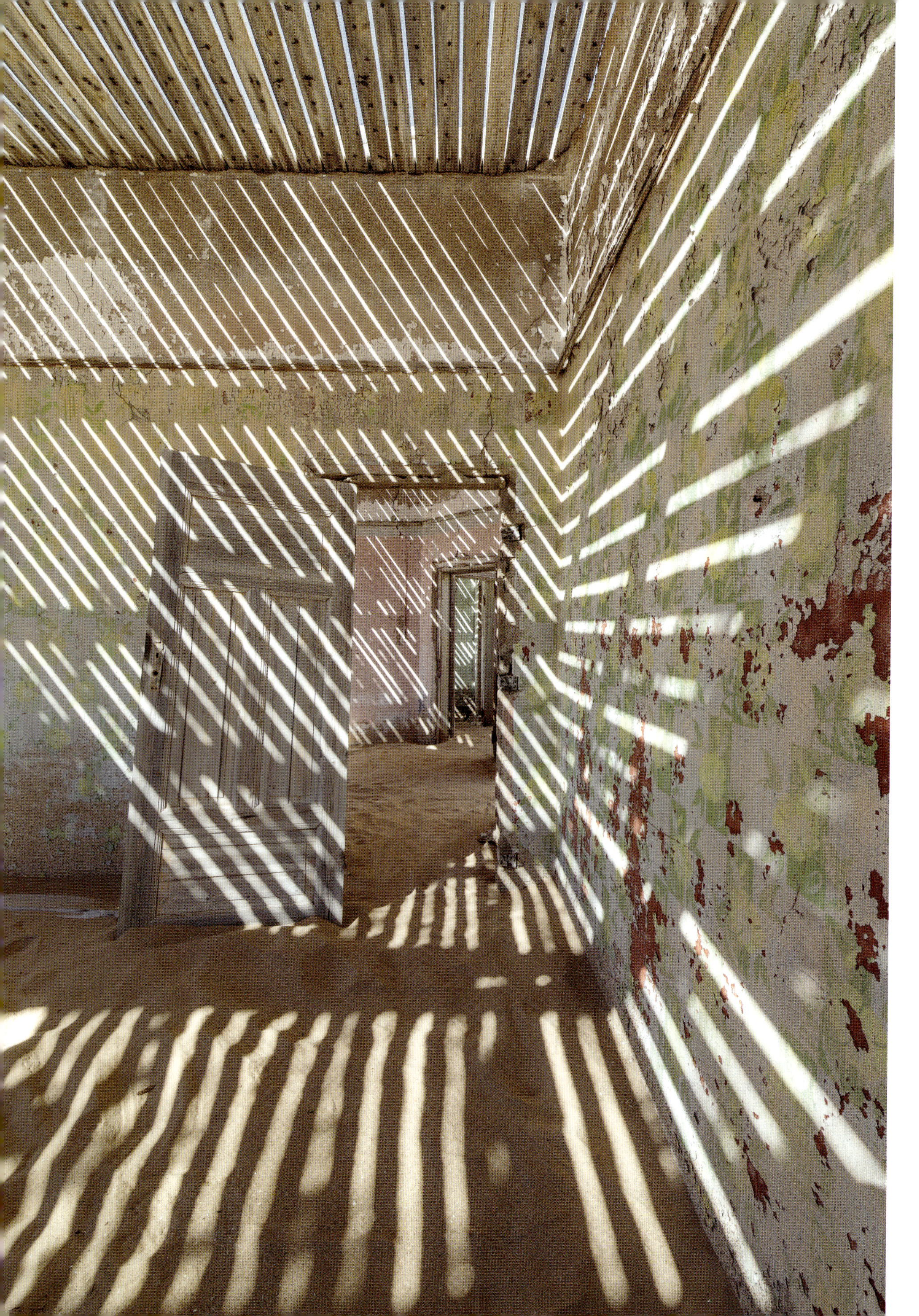

curious people that venture to this isolated area to imagine for a few hours what life used to be like for the former diamond miners.

With this set of photographs, I wanted to immerse the audience in a journey with me and pay tribute to this particular and extraordinary place and its glorious past. And for that, I have decided to underline the strength of nature that always takes back what's hers, but also the ephemeral aspect of human constructions; symbolized here by the progress of sand and dunes through what remains of the city.

We can imagine what it was like to live in such a hostile environment where sandstorms and heat assaulted you every day. The population had to be courageous and hardworking if they wanted to survive and continue with normal life, while having to fight the elements. These silted doors are for me the symbol of this fight and the inevitable passing of time that remind us that soon Kolmanskop won't exist anymore and to enjoy it while it lasts. As a memento mori, it reflects our human condition and reminds us of the importance of making the most of the time ahead of us.

Light illuminating the buildings is also essential to me because it brings an almost timeless atmosphere and a magical sensation as if it were unreal. Due to the constant presence of the sun, light is changing all day long through the windows and the holes in the ceiling, and you discover a new way of seeing the place every hour. Being there at the perfect time demands a lot of work; but when you have it, you can gaze at a masterpiece painting reinforced by the strength of the sun in such a place.

Along with the light, colours are also fundamental. As there are nearly no remains or objects from the past, walls and paintings are the only witness of that time. Each room has different wallpaper whose shiny colours reflect perfectly with the sand and illuminate some of the past life. We can still notice the switches on the walls that remind us how inventive and stubborn these men were when diamonds changed their hearts and made them build a town from nothing in one of the least inhospitable places on earth.

Life itself is always changing. Even today, these buildings seem to whisper the hopes and dreams of all those pioneers that were part of the creation and history of Kolmanskop. It's your turn to get lost in the desert looking for the ghosts of an ancient time and try to figure out what incredible stories must have taken place there, which desires were forgotten and which came true.

As for everything, life goes on and we can imagine there will be a future for Kolmanskop. In a few decades, the city will be buried under the sand, but one day these dunes will continue their travel and once again we will rediscover the city. It will be a new Kolmanskop, the state will be different but the stories will remain the same as we will uncover new parts and buildings of the town we thought had disappeared forever. New stories will have to be written!

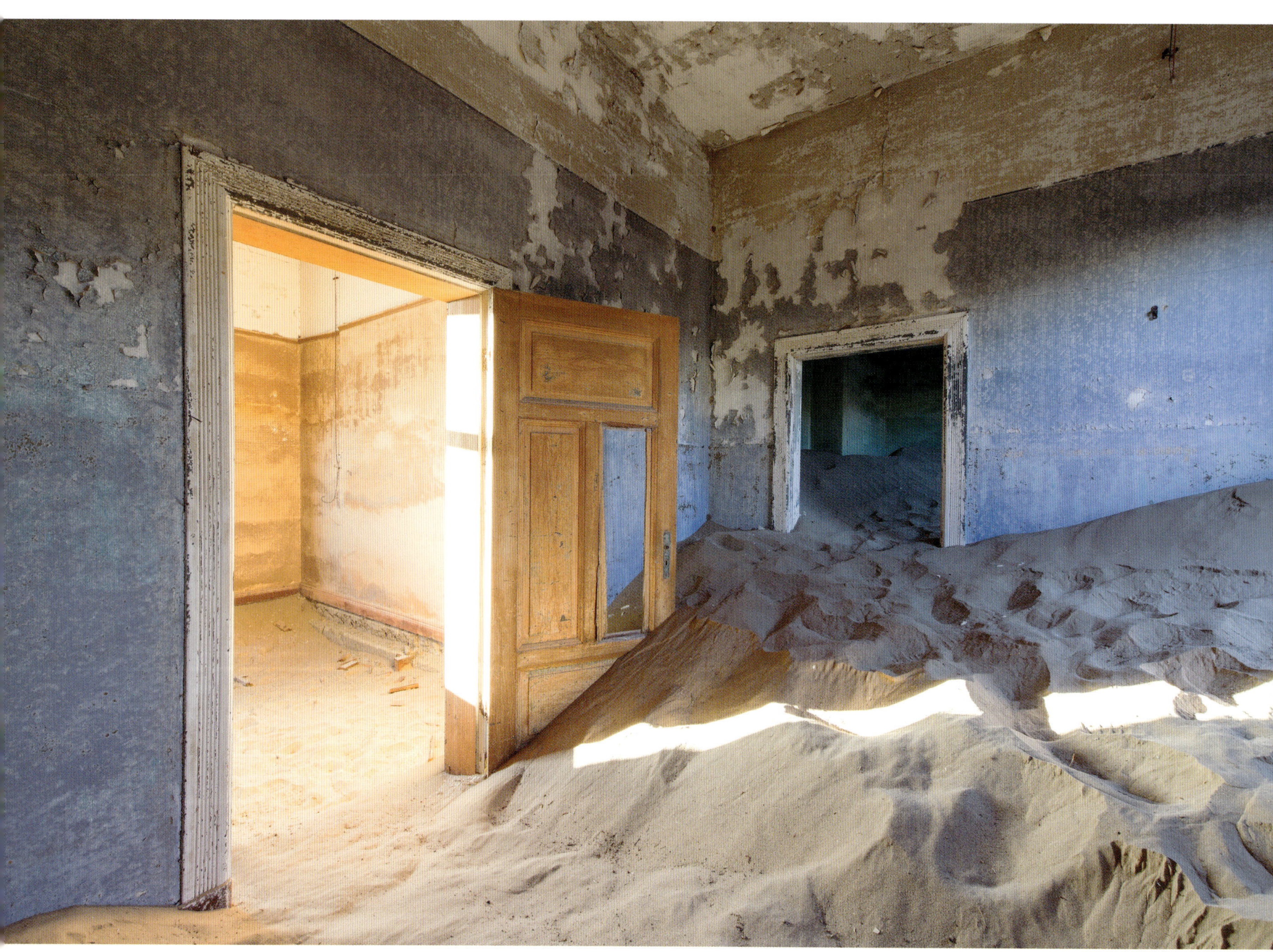

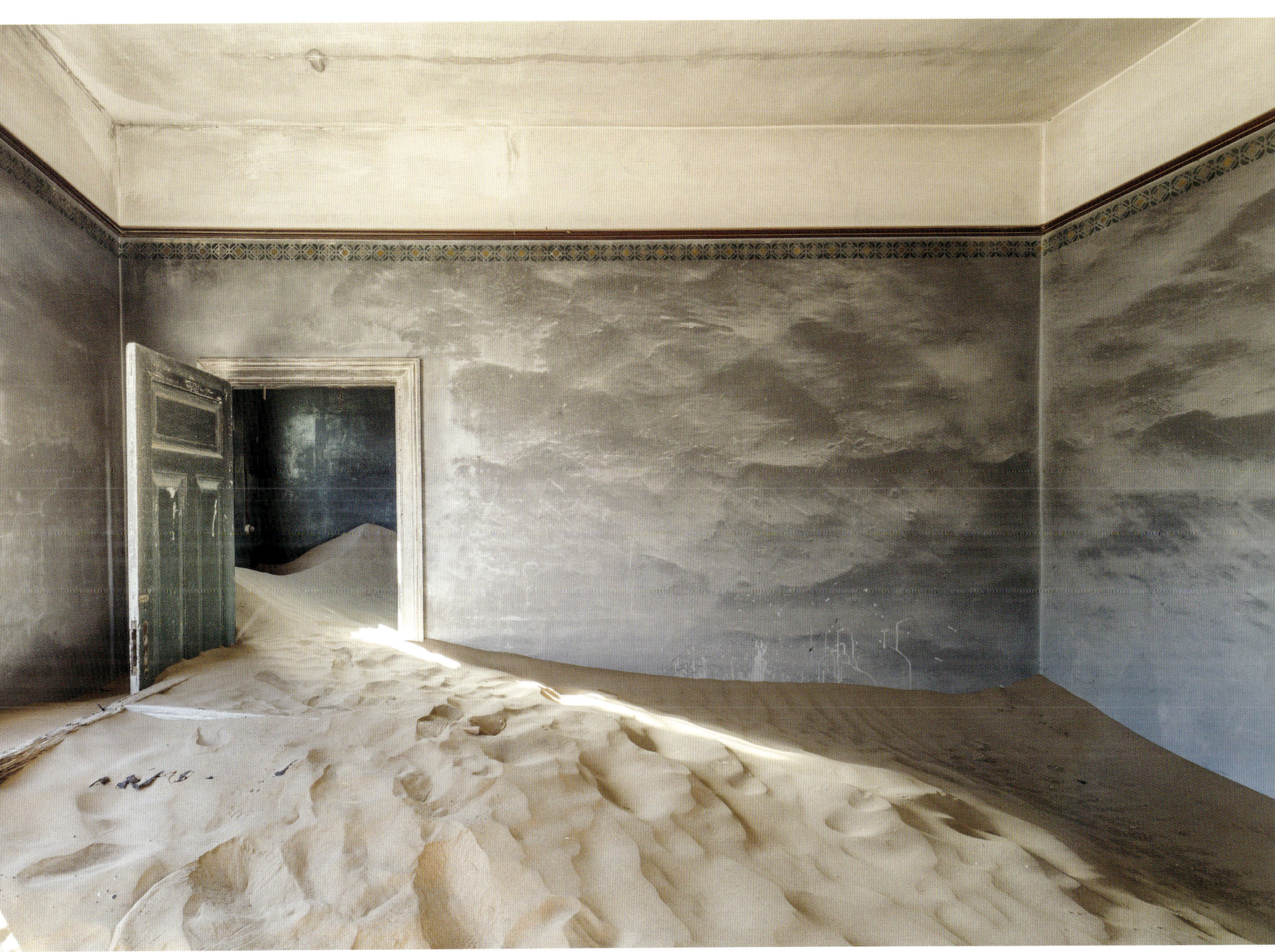

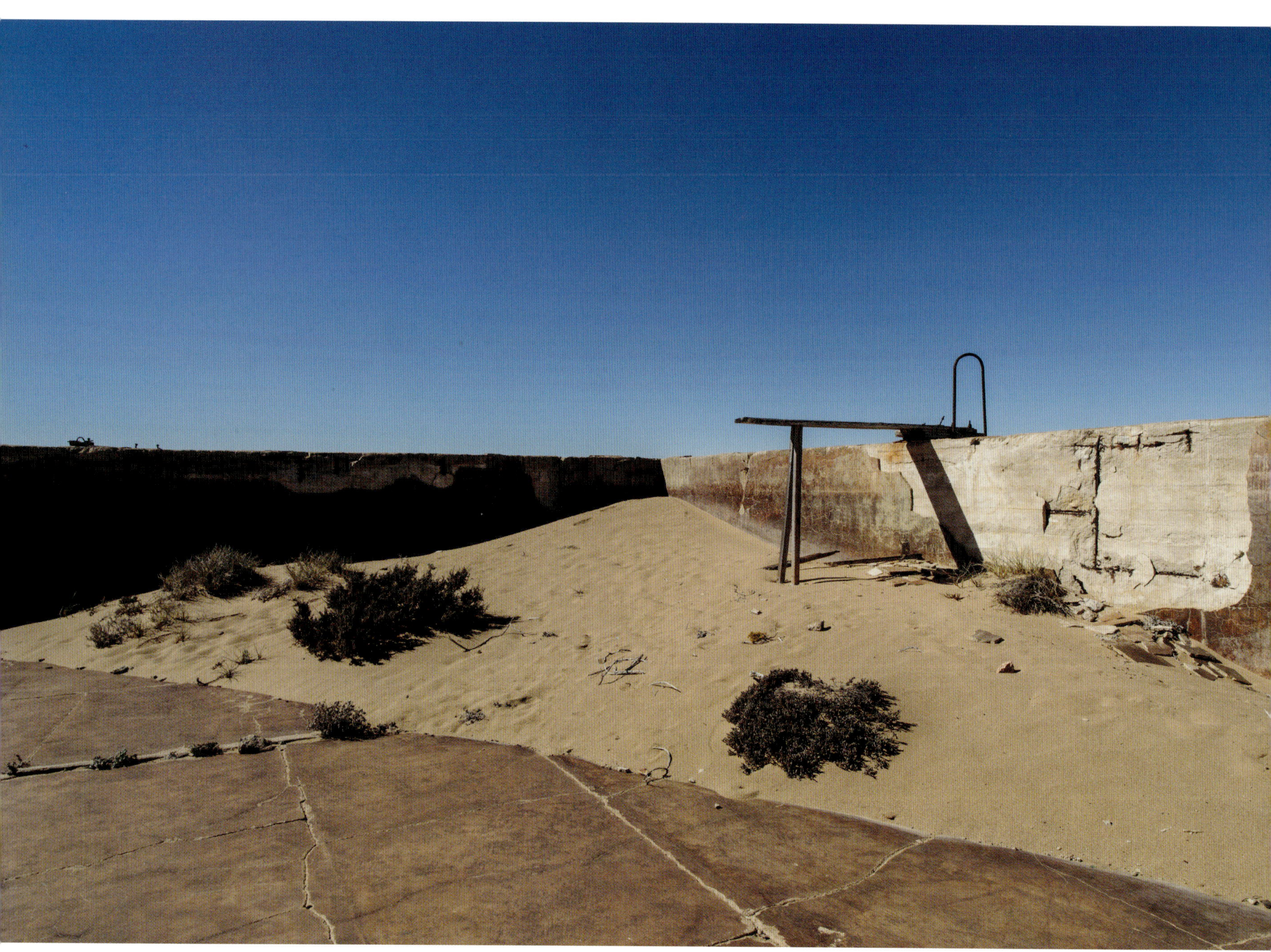

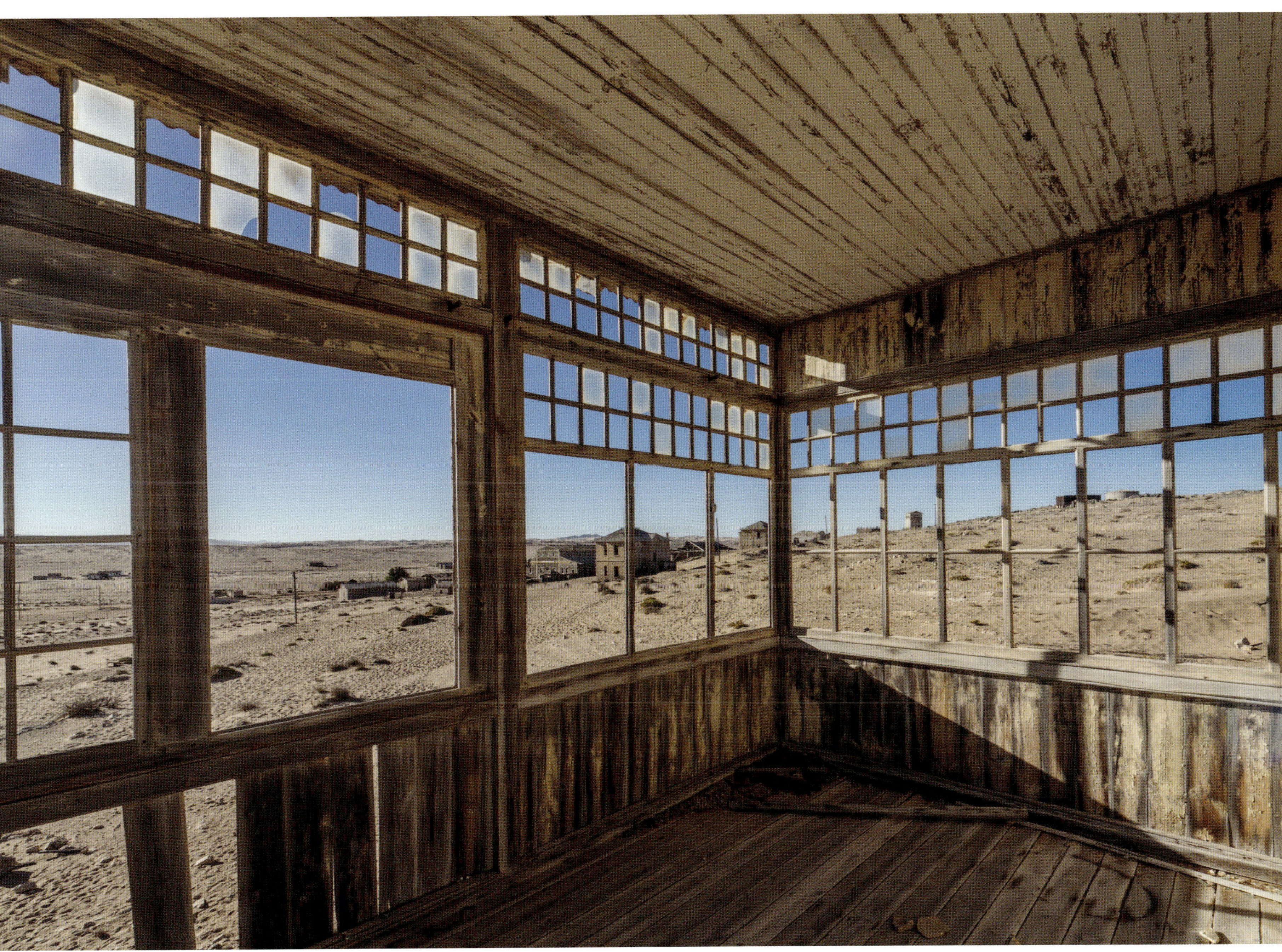

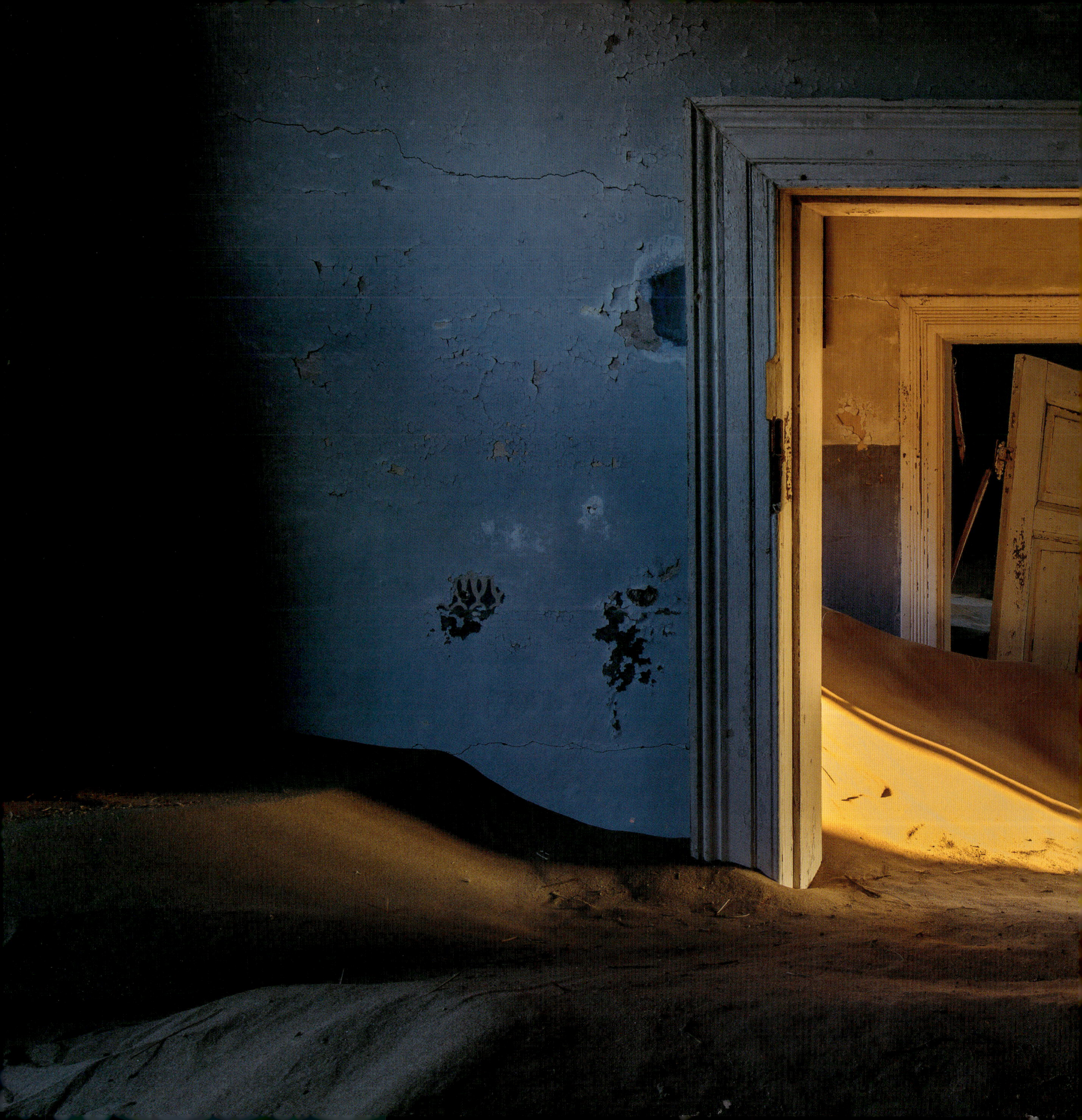

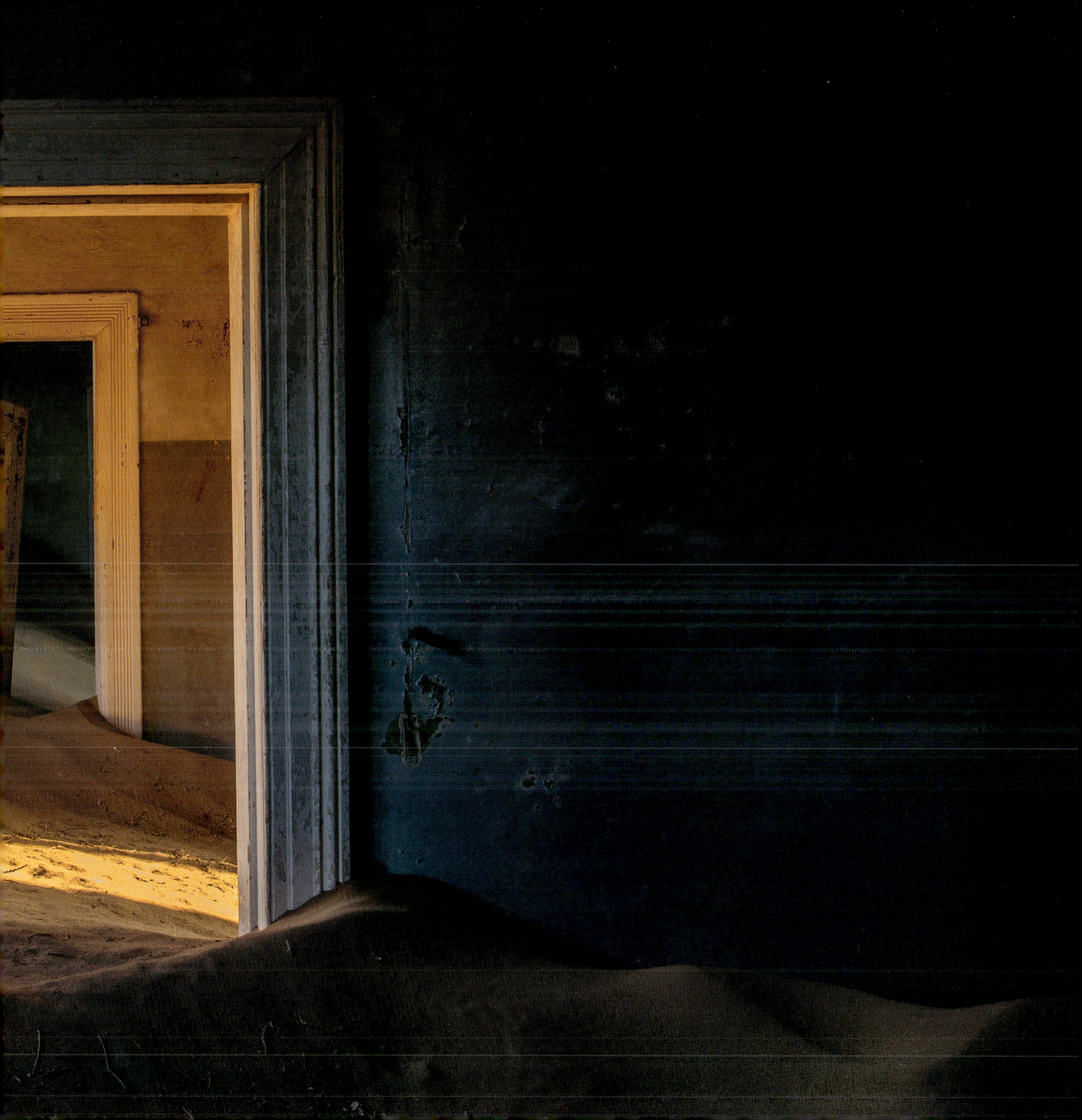

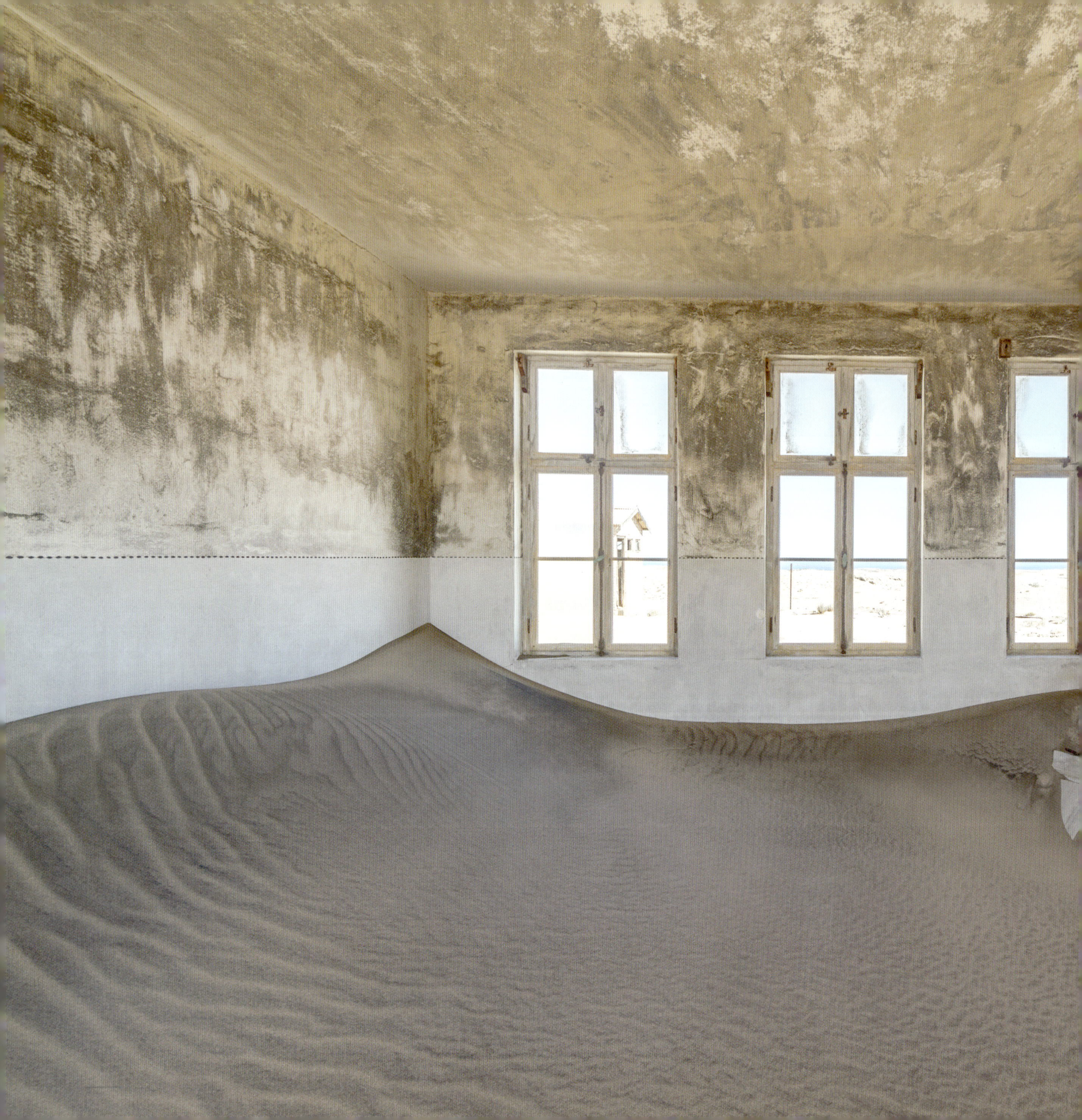

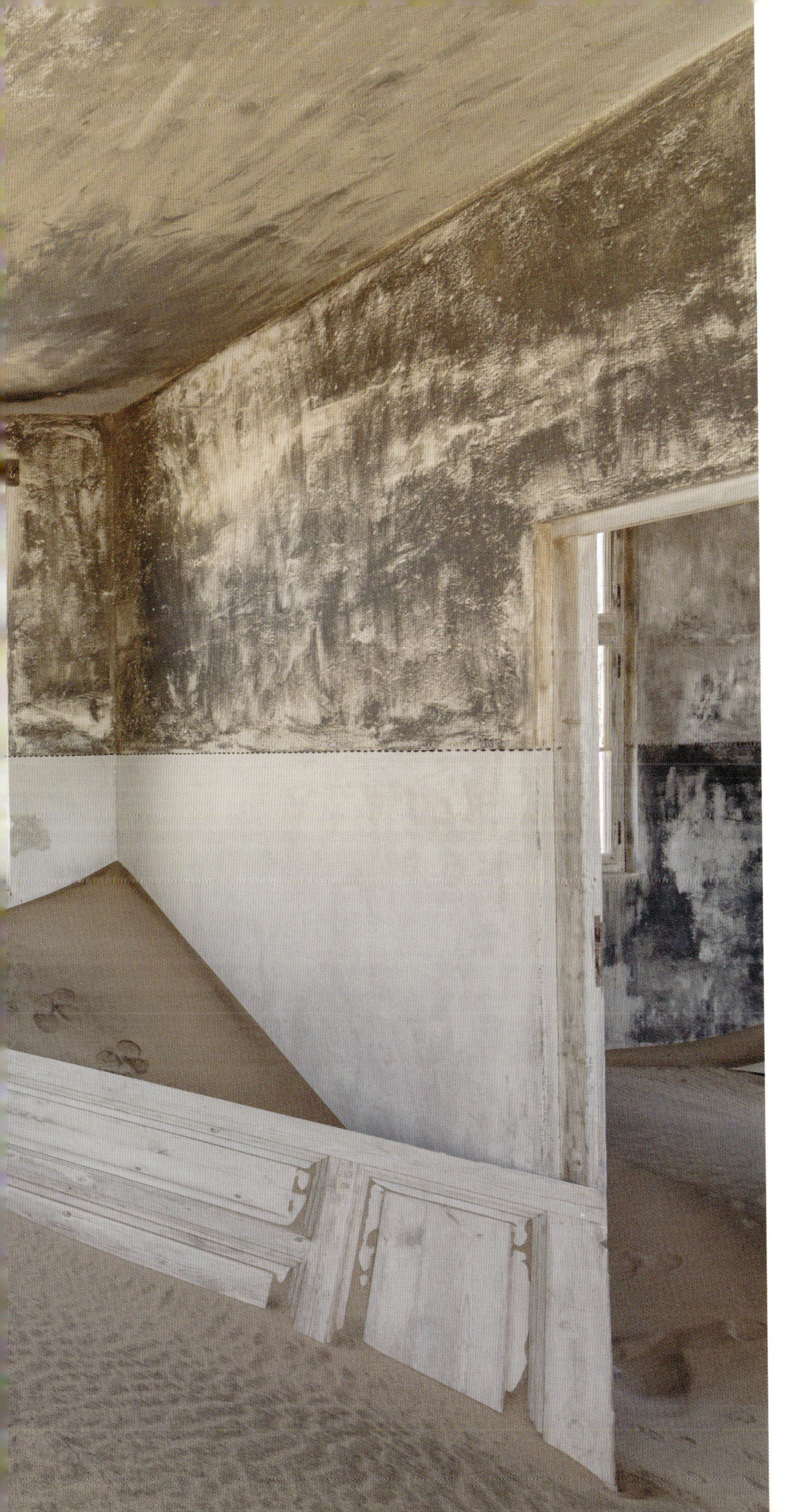

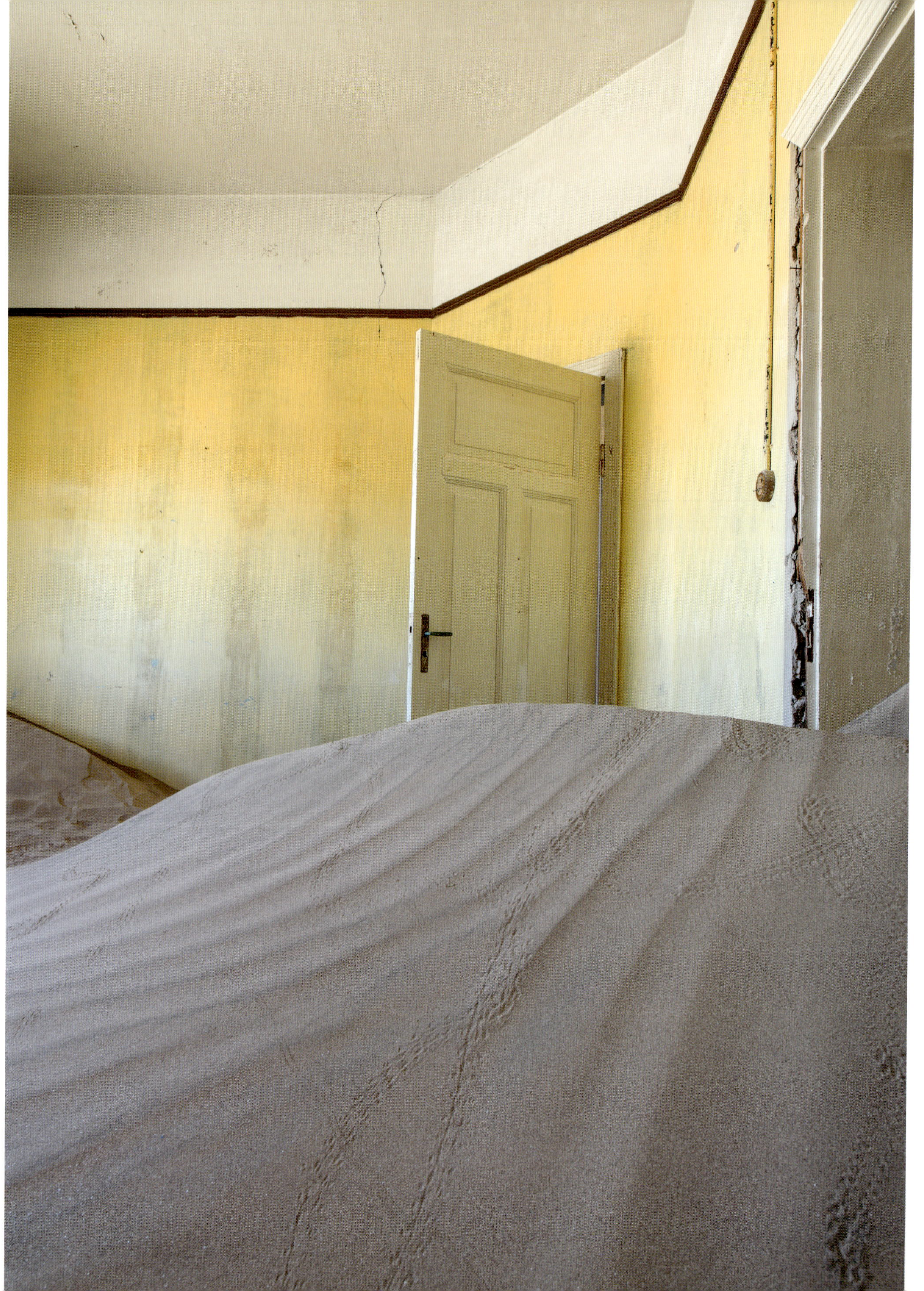

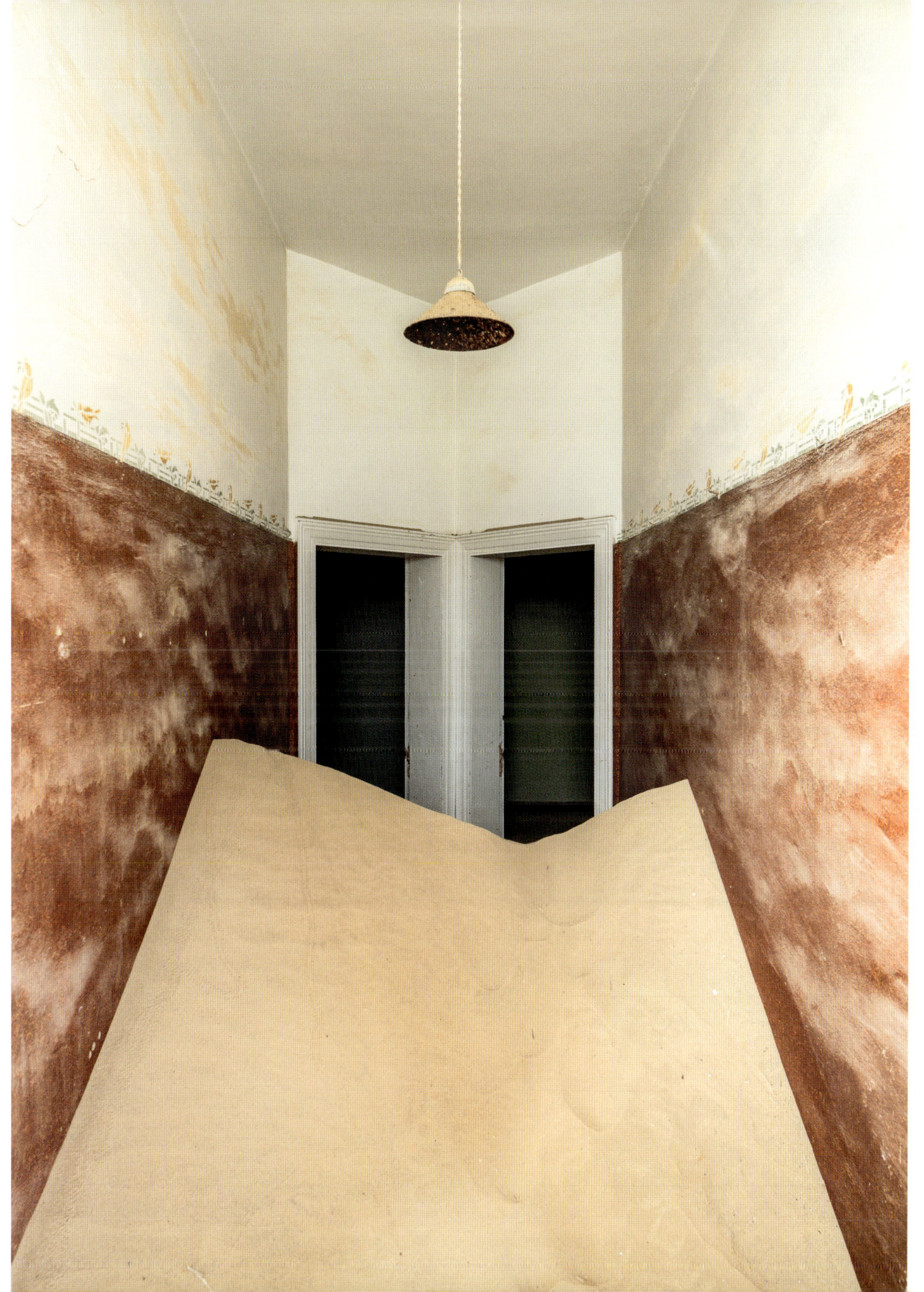

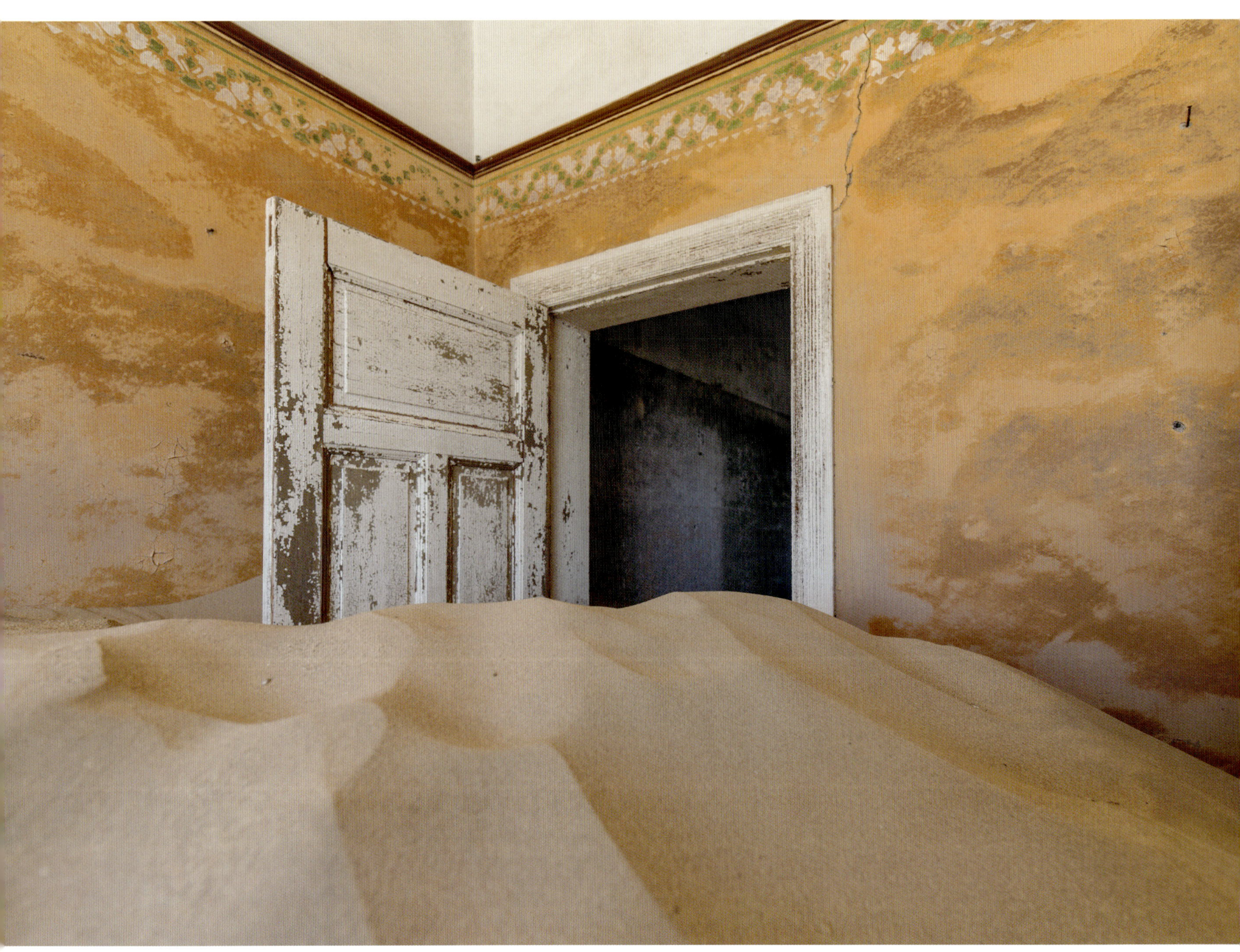

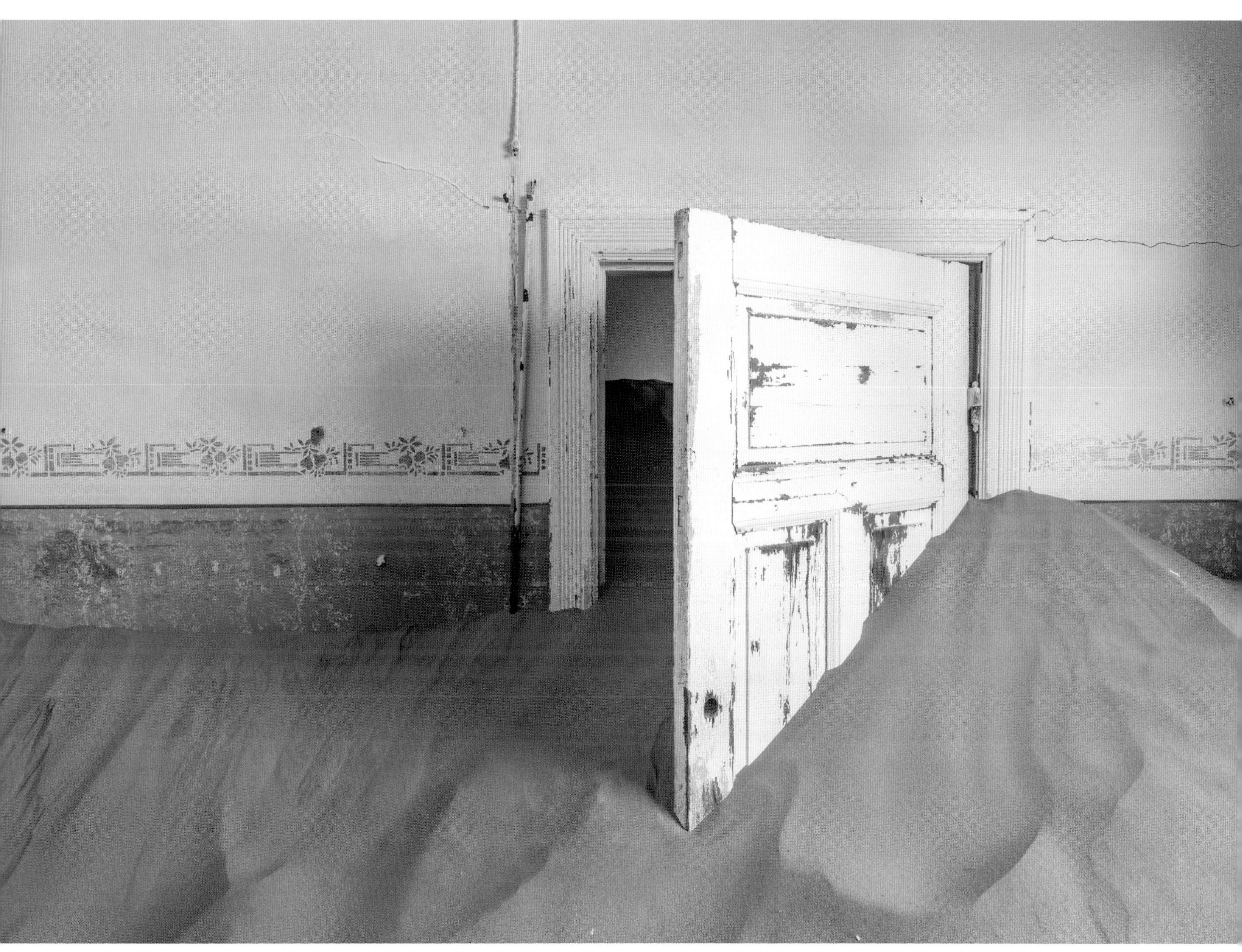

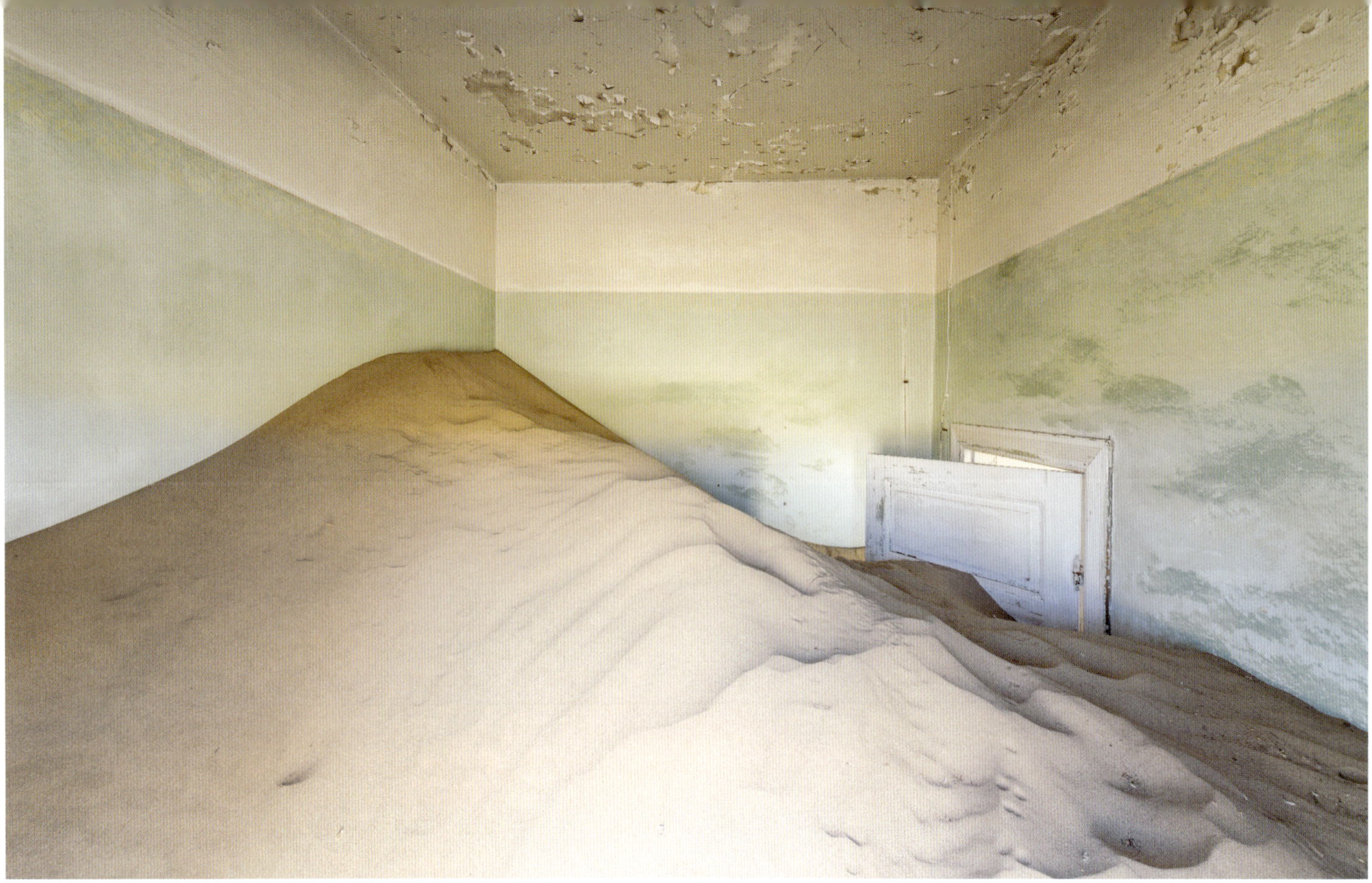

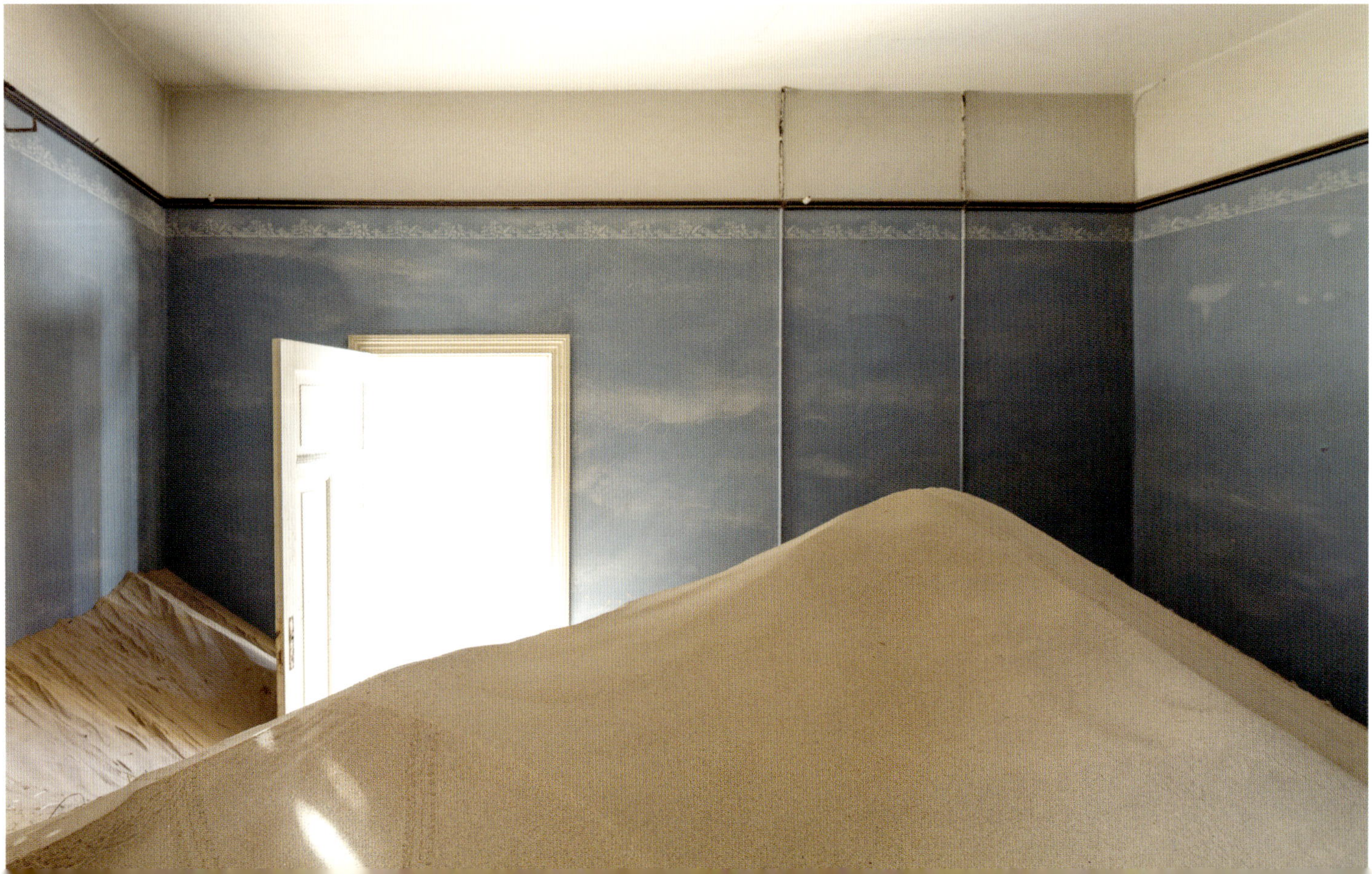

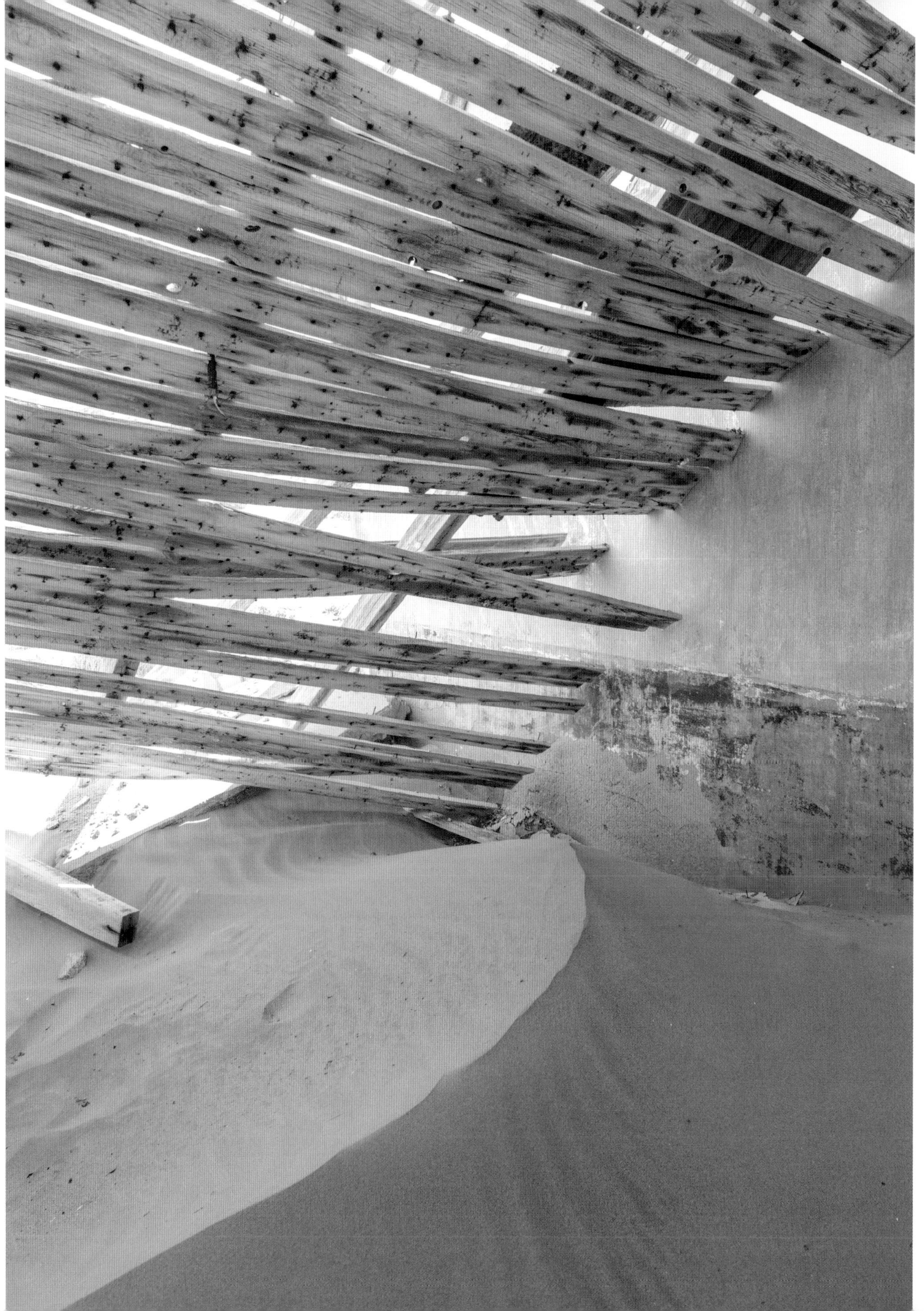

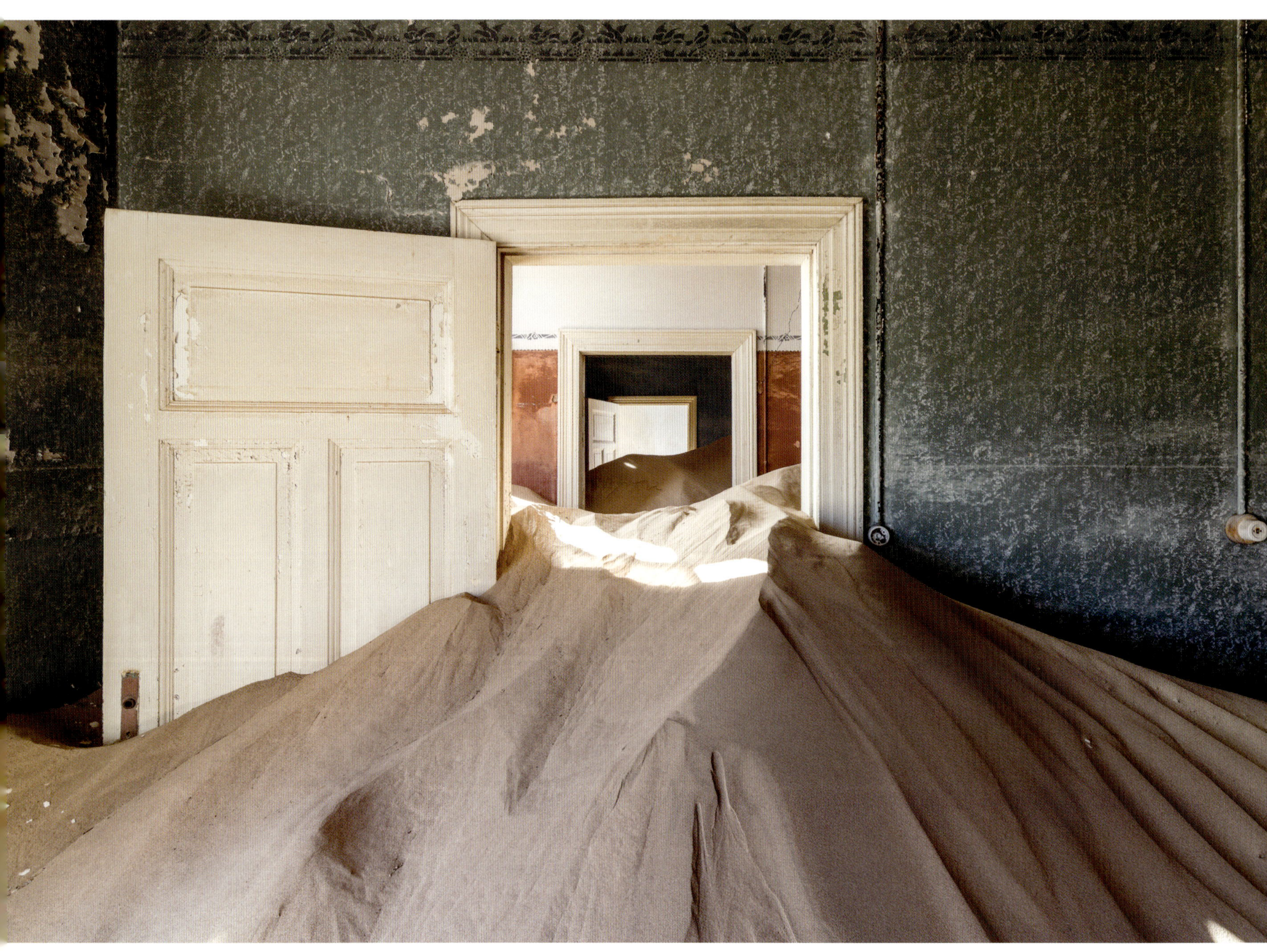

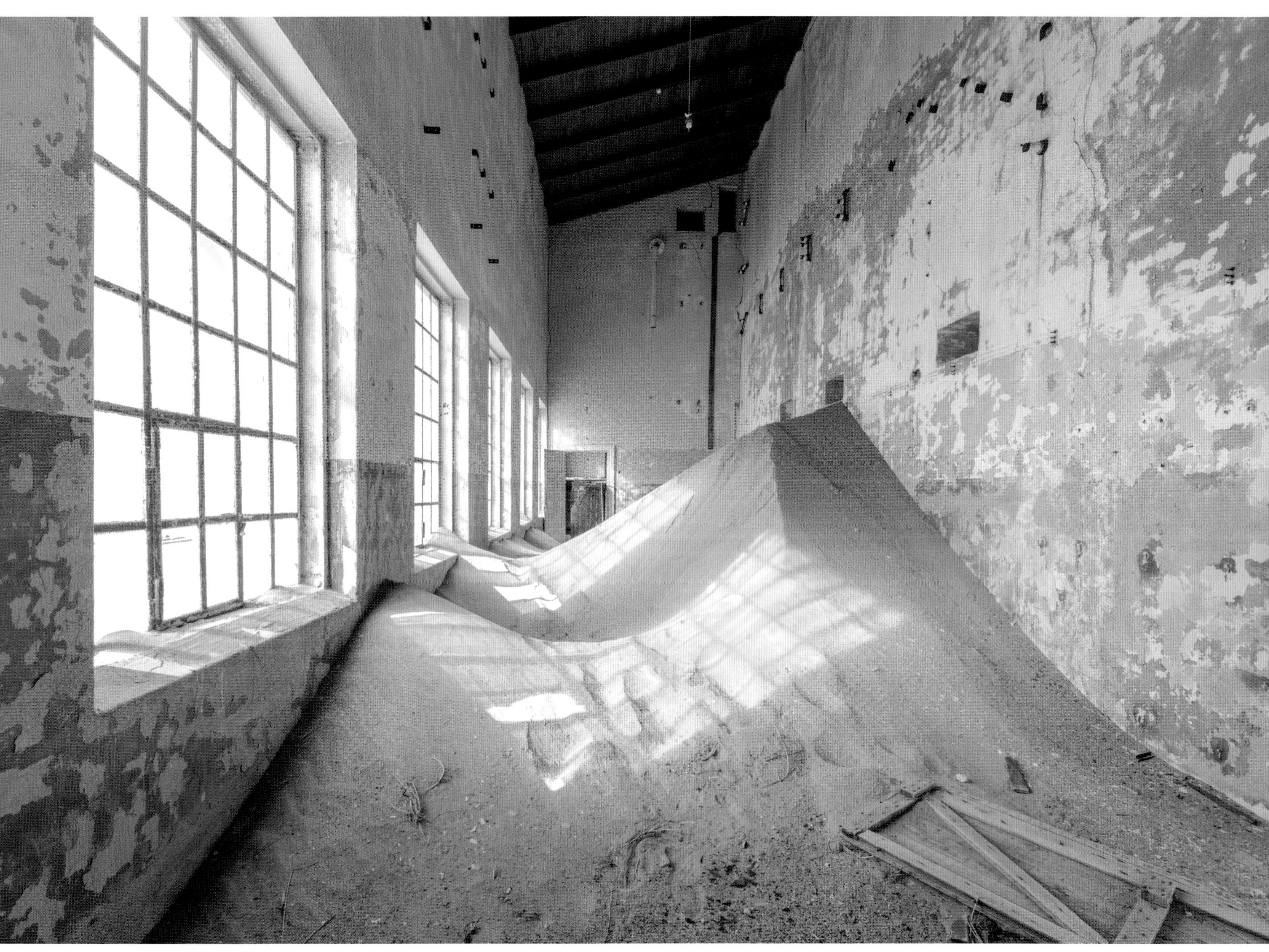

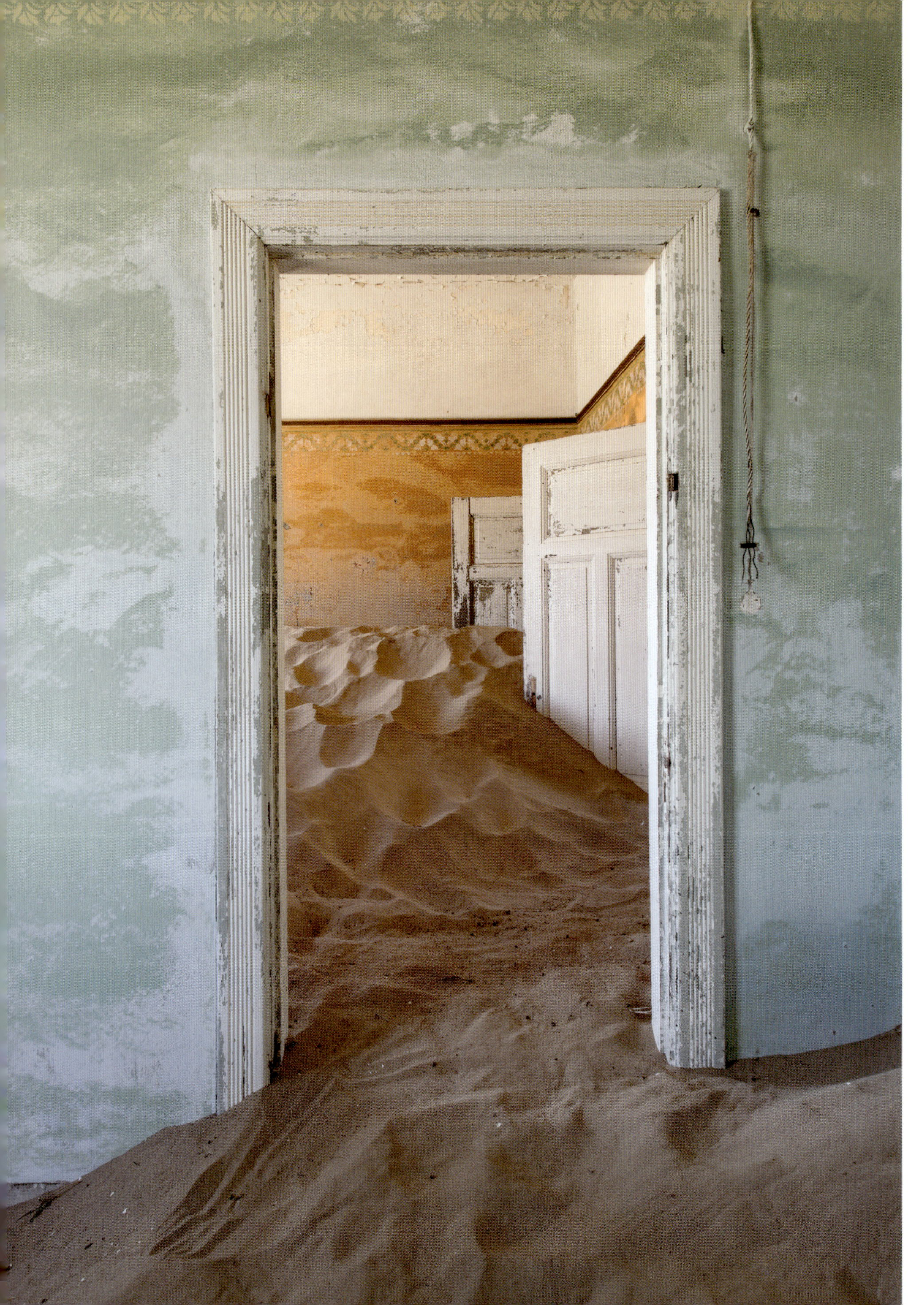

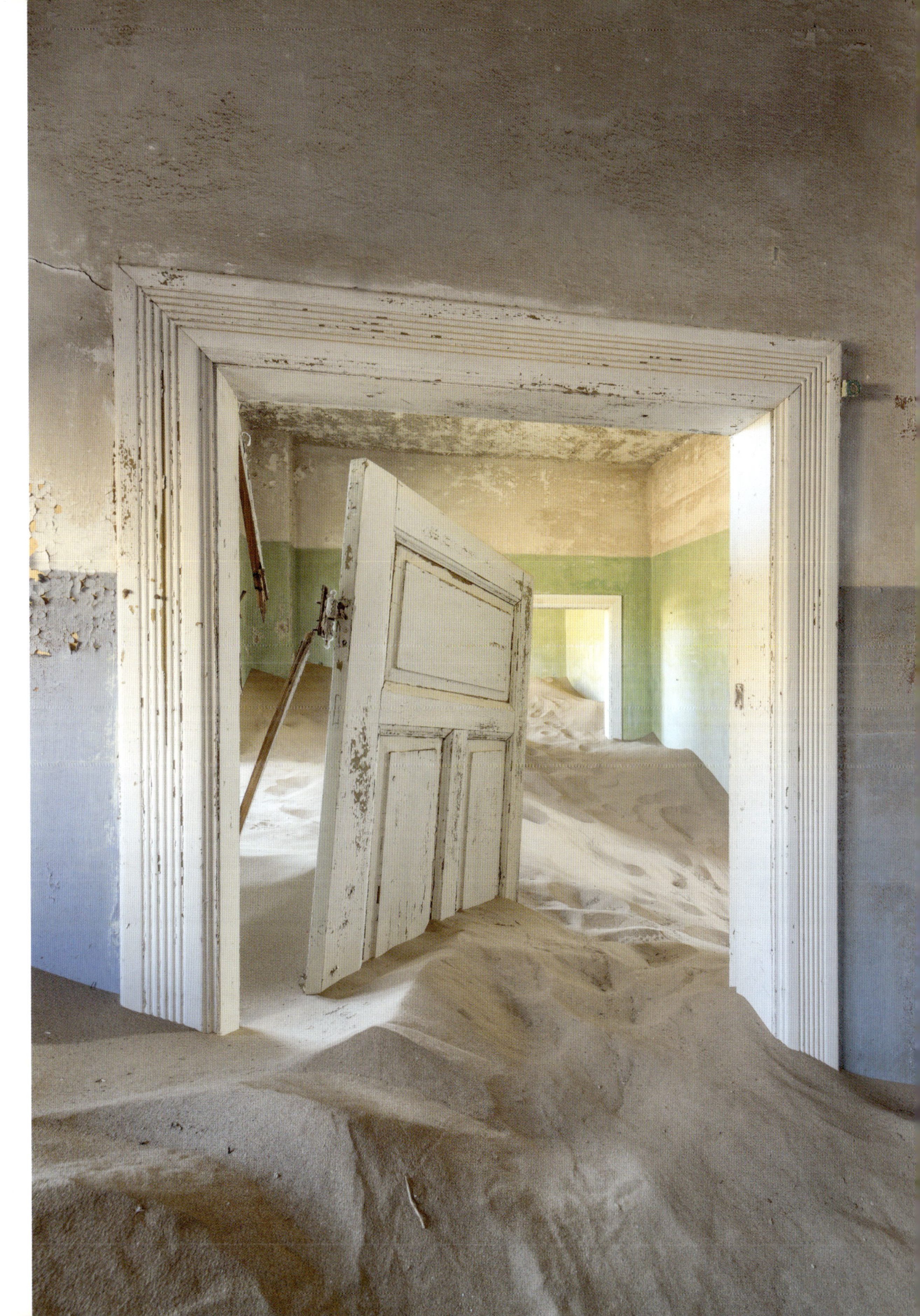

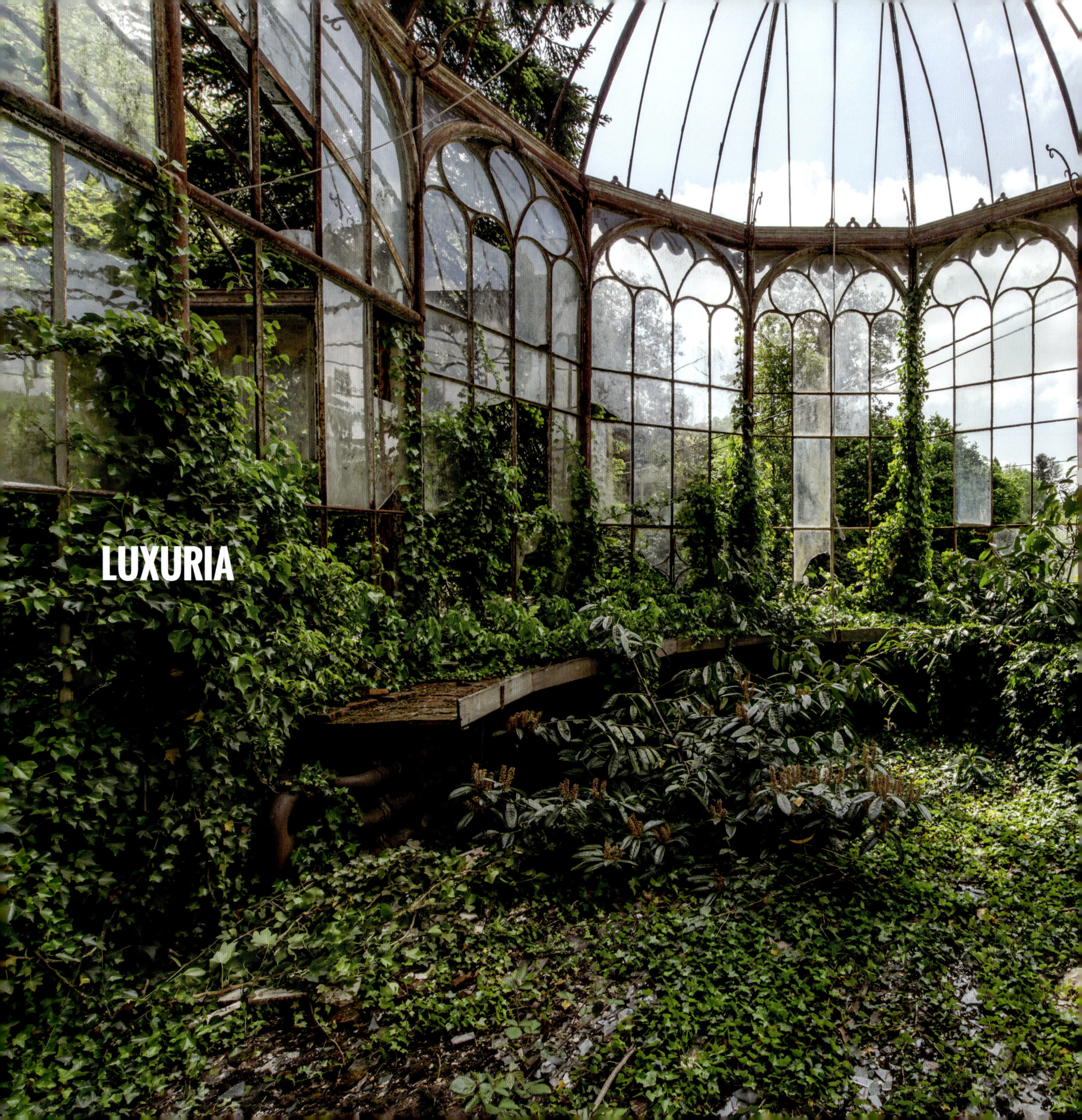
LUXURIA

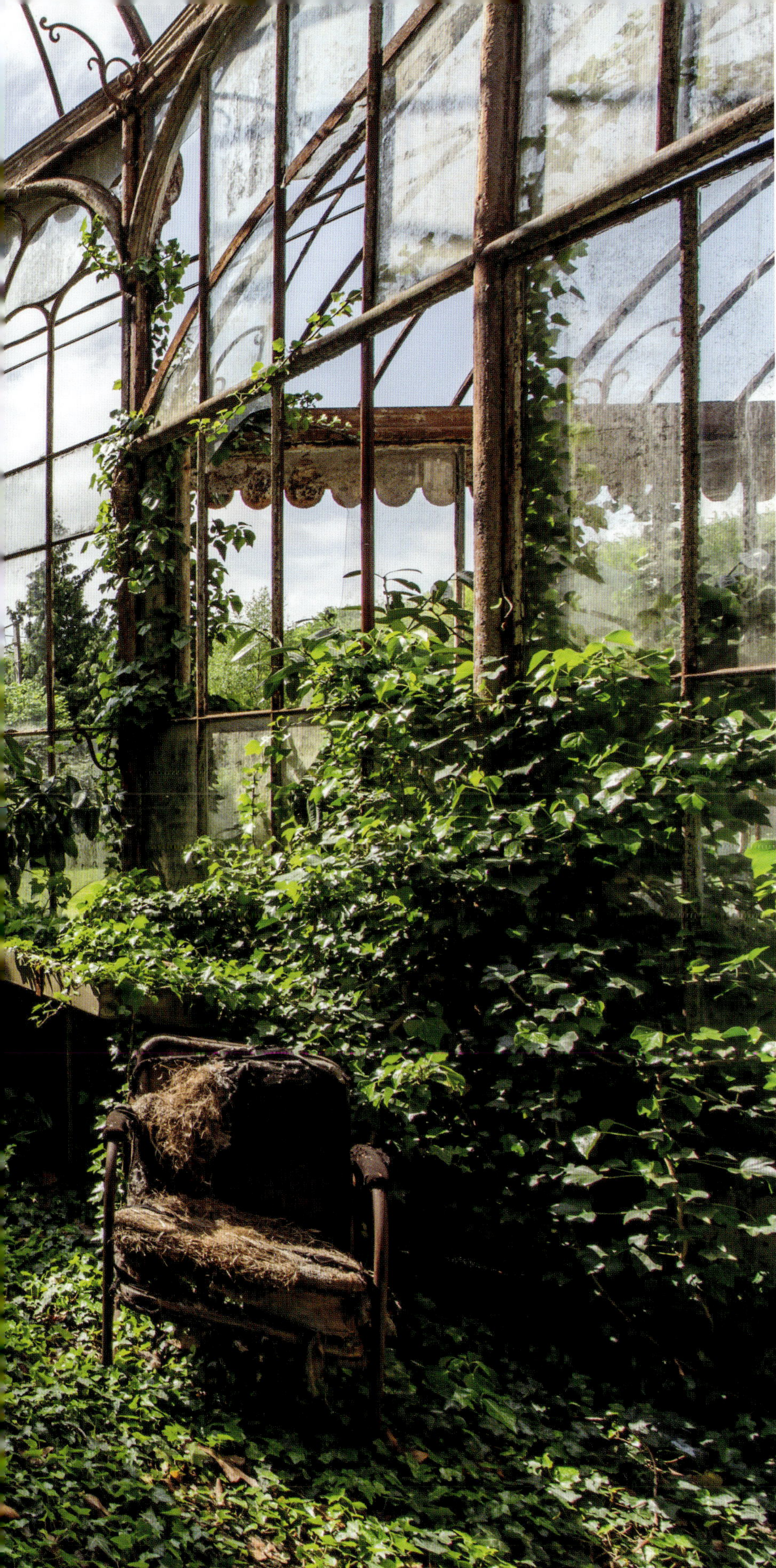

What would happen to the earth if all human life disappeared?

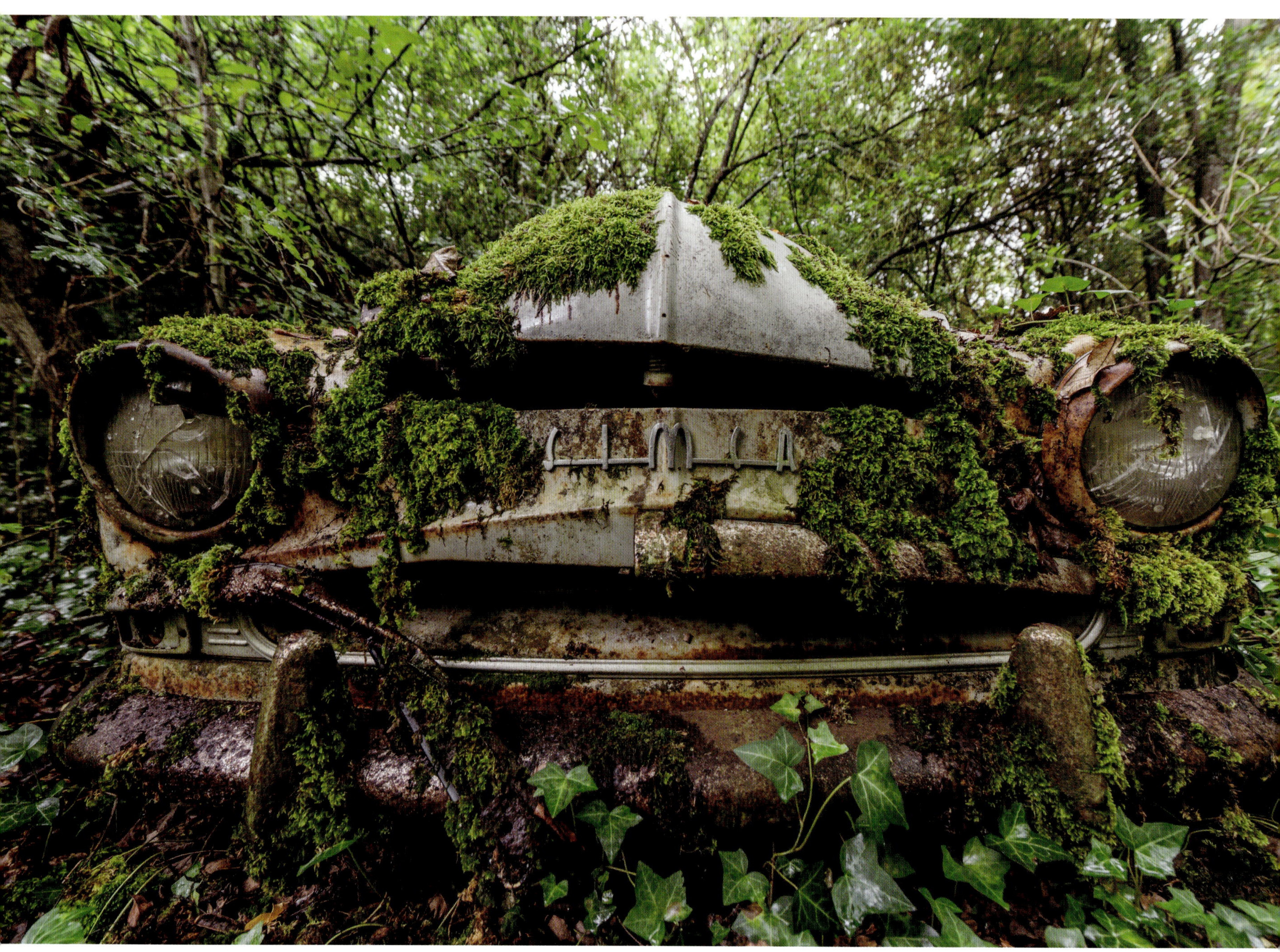

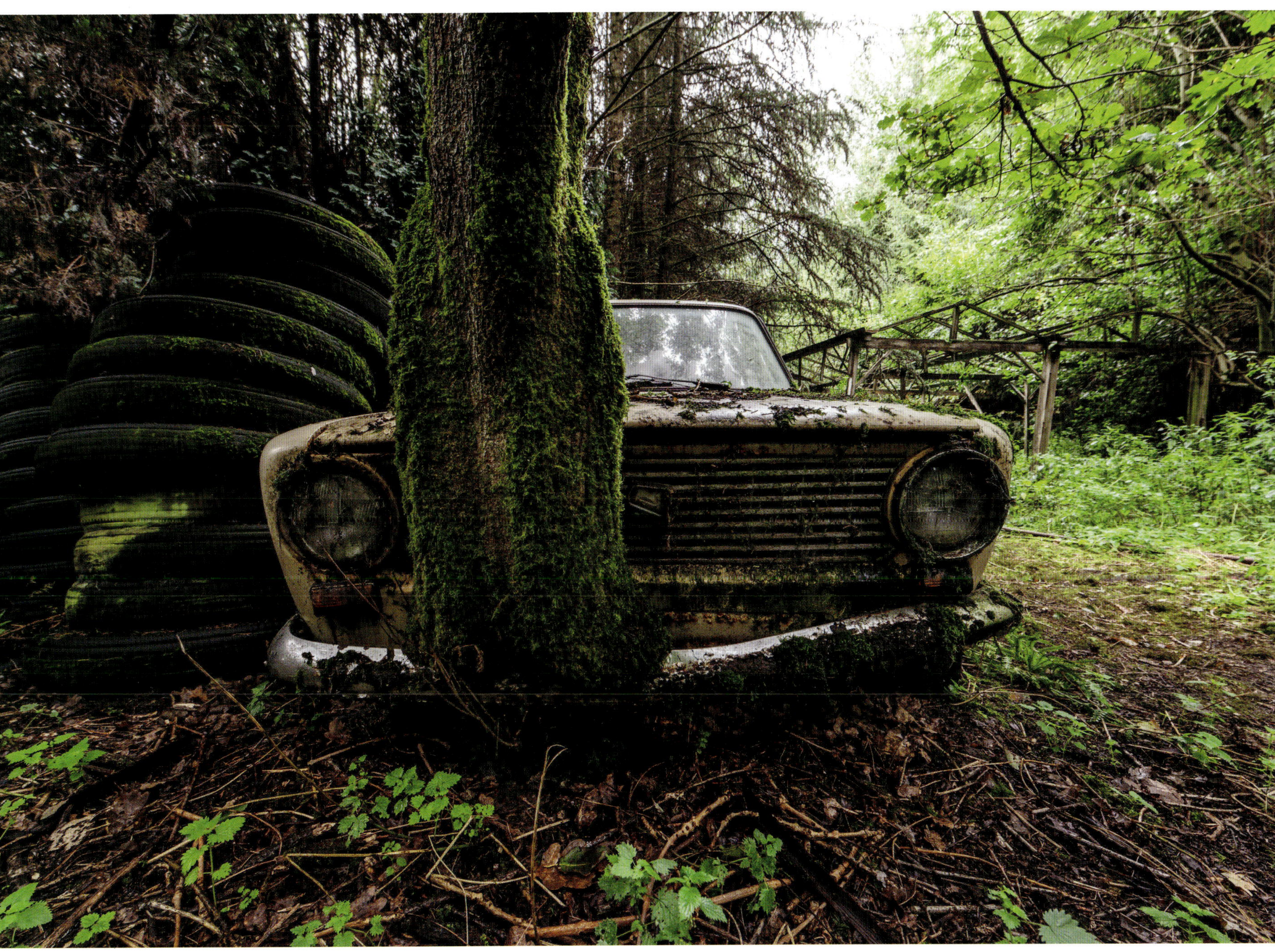

Trying to imagine what the answer might be has fascinated people since the beginning of time. What is interesting is that the answers change as society evolves. The first change that comes to mind is vegetation will simply grow over all human constructions. One of the most impressive and surreal changes of abandonment can best be illustrated by an old castle covered by moss and ivy.

Since the dawn of time mankind has had a huge impact on the planet; from remodeling the face of the earth, to the changing chemistry of the atmosphere. So, what would happen if man disappeared at exactly the same moment? Let's try to make a chronology of the facts.

We can imagine that with nobody controlling or providing fuel the electricity runs out and power plants shut down. Millions of buildings fall into darkness. Billions of animals will escape to find food. Dogs and cats will also become wild, and crave for food, they will evolve from domestic pets to wild animals.

Animals like chicken or cows will become extinct, soon eaten by predators. Insects and vermin are dependent of human life and will become extinct without them. On the other hand, species of fish will rapidly make a full recovery without humans. Animals will spread and reclaim land quickly. The sad example of Chernobyl proves that nature will fill the void within a few decades and is now an extraordinary wildlife sanctuary.

Major catastrophes will happen and fire will rage uncontrollably destroying cities worldwide. A single fire will spread to entire towns and will destroy everything (helped by the papers and boxes left behind by humans). What remains will be eaten by termites and other decomposers.

In a hundred years, wooden buildings will be gone and the ones made of steel and iron, such as bridges, cars or buildings will follow the same path. Without people to maintain them, paint and coatings will corrode; iron will react with oxygen in the atmosphere and will rust. Over time, all these structures will slowly fall to pieces.

Nuclear facilities will be a great cause of catastrophe, without any electricity to maintain the correct temperature in the pools where the radioactive fuel is stored. Without any electricity to cool them down, they will soon start overheating.

It may take time but every great city will be overcome by the wilderness.

While these buildings are slowly collapsing, nature will reclaim its heritage. Without human activity, the climate will be colder, enabling ice and flooding to do more damage to what's left of our built environment. Even cement will become degraded by the freezing action. Without maintenance, cracks will soon appear, allowing plants to take root and widen the fractures further.

Electric water pumps will cease function anymore. Subways and underground parking will completely fill with water, as well as a large number of the streets and boulevards. Weeds, vines, trees and vegetation will soon reappear and rapidly create a jungle of the city. Natural ecosystems will regenerate shortly after the disappearance of people.

Ultimately, it is still unclear how long animals will have to suffer the consequences of human creation. Over the centuries, plants will absorb concentrated heavy metals, recycle, redeposit, and gradually dilute them. But this won't be possible for nuclear waste. The example of Chernobyl we spoke about earlier or Johnston atoll in the Pacific Ocean, (where the American government detonated 12 thermonuclear warheads and incinerated various chemical weapons during the cold war), show us how life can extraordinarily recover. Imagine, in 500 years, forests will go back to the state they were 10,000 years ago.

Painters like William Turner were the pioneers of depicting ruins in their art; and especially old abandoned abbeys and monasteries in the English countryside. They were already trying to illustrate the survival of mankind and ask questions about the future of their society and its legacy. Even the Nazi iconic architect, Albrecht Speer, had a vision he explained in his theory of ruin value. He wanted to create modern cities where buildings were built according to certain laws of physics with special materials, intended to last. The result being that when these structures were to collapse after hundreds or thousands of years, they would look like ancient roman ruins.

But this fascination for a post apocalyptic world can also be witnessed if you look at famous successes in the modern era: movies, books, artists or video games.

For example, we could talk about the "Walking Dead" and the huge success of either the comics or the series. Or even the famous Chanel fashion show of Karl Lagerfeld taking place in the Grand Palais with a catwalk disguised as an abandoned city.

The American folk proverb "If you want to destroy a barn, just cut a 45 centimetre hole in the roof and then do nothing", is a good illustration of the inevitable and incredible strength of nature. And this question should be considered when we ask if Mother Nature could completely wipe out any evidence of mankind. How long it would take to recover lost ground and restore the earth?

And finally, as we are supposed to be the most advanced of all species, shouldn't it be possible for us to dream of a way for nature to prosper that doesn't depend on our demise?

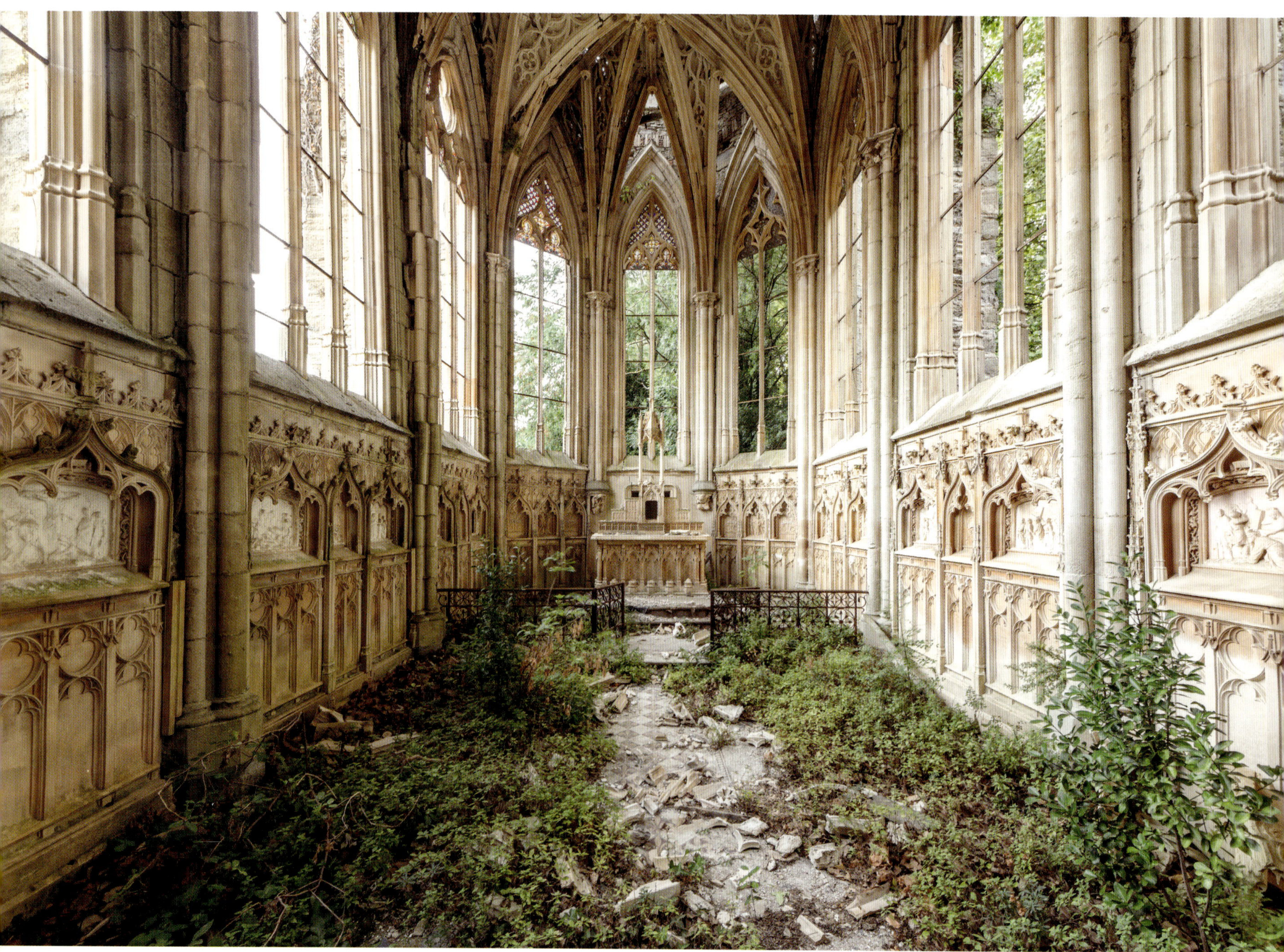

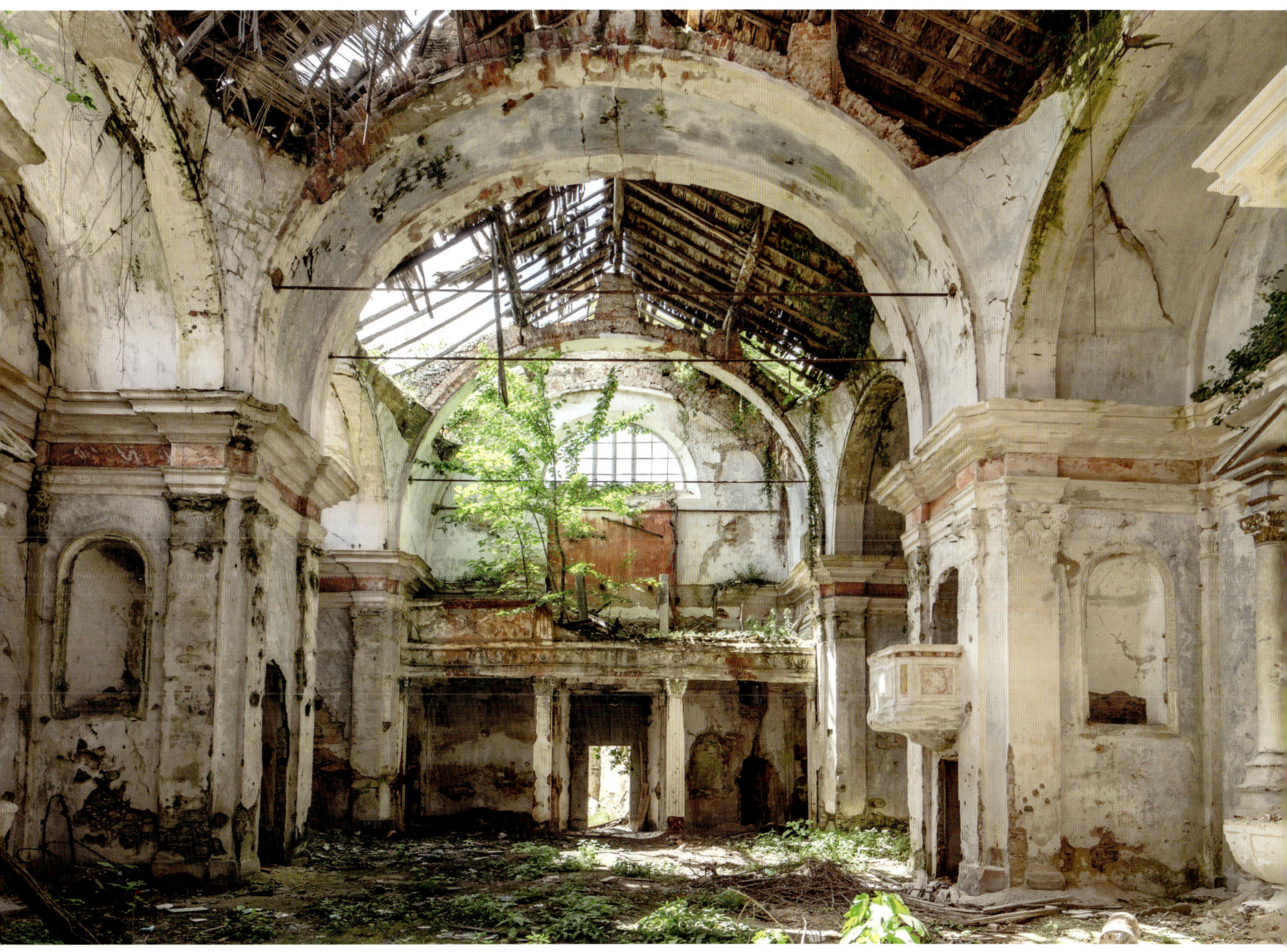

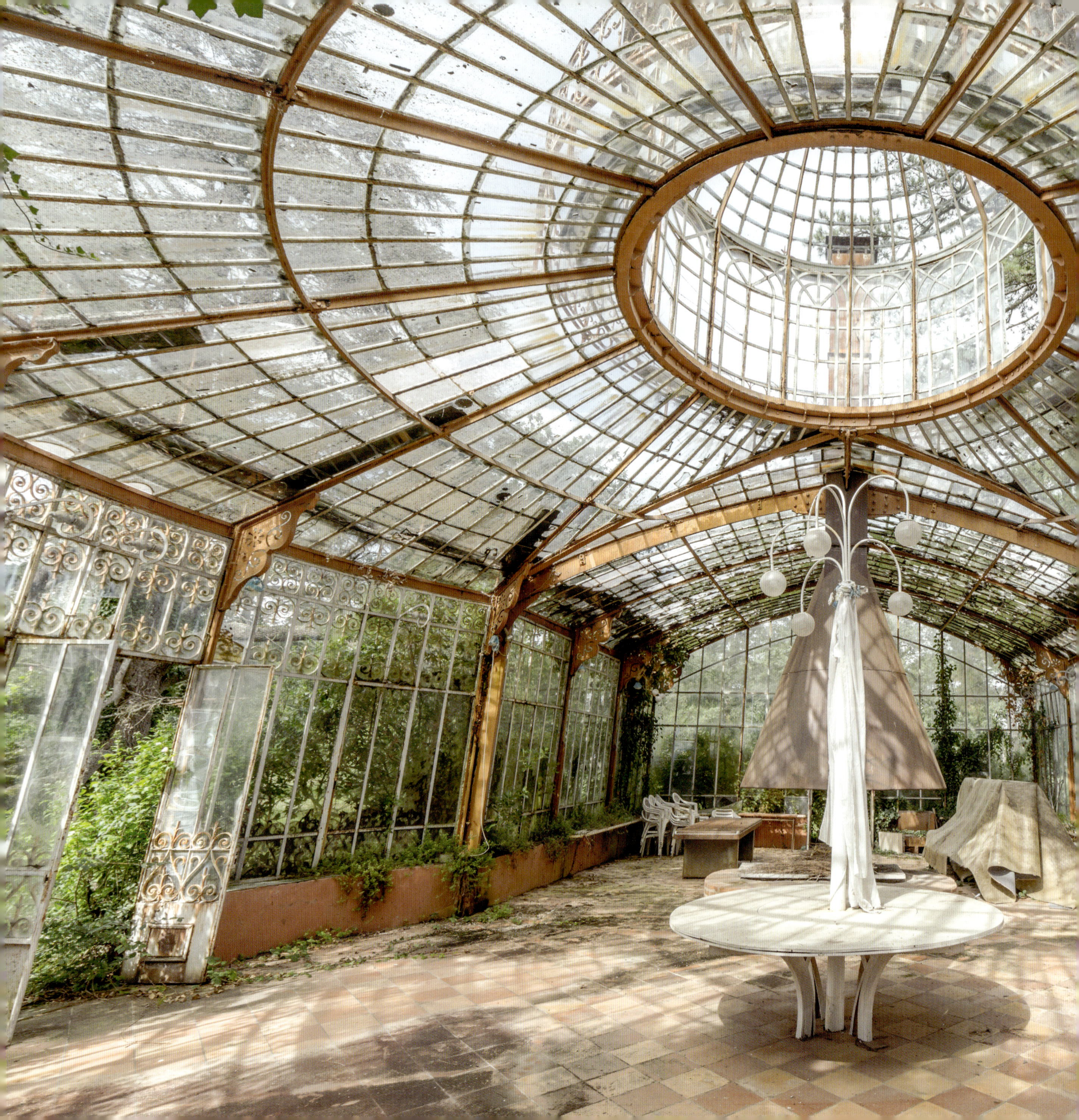

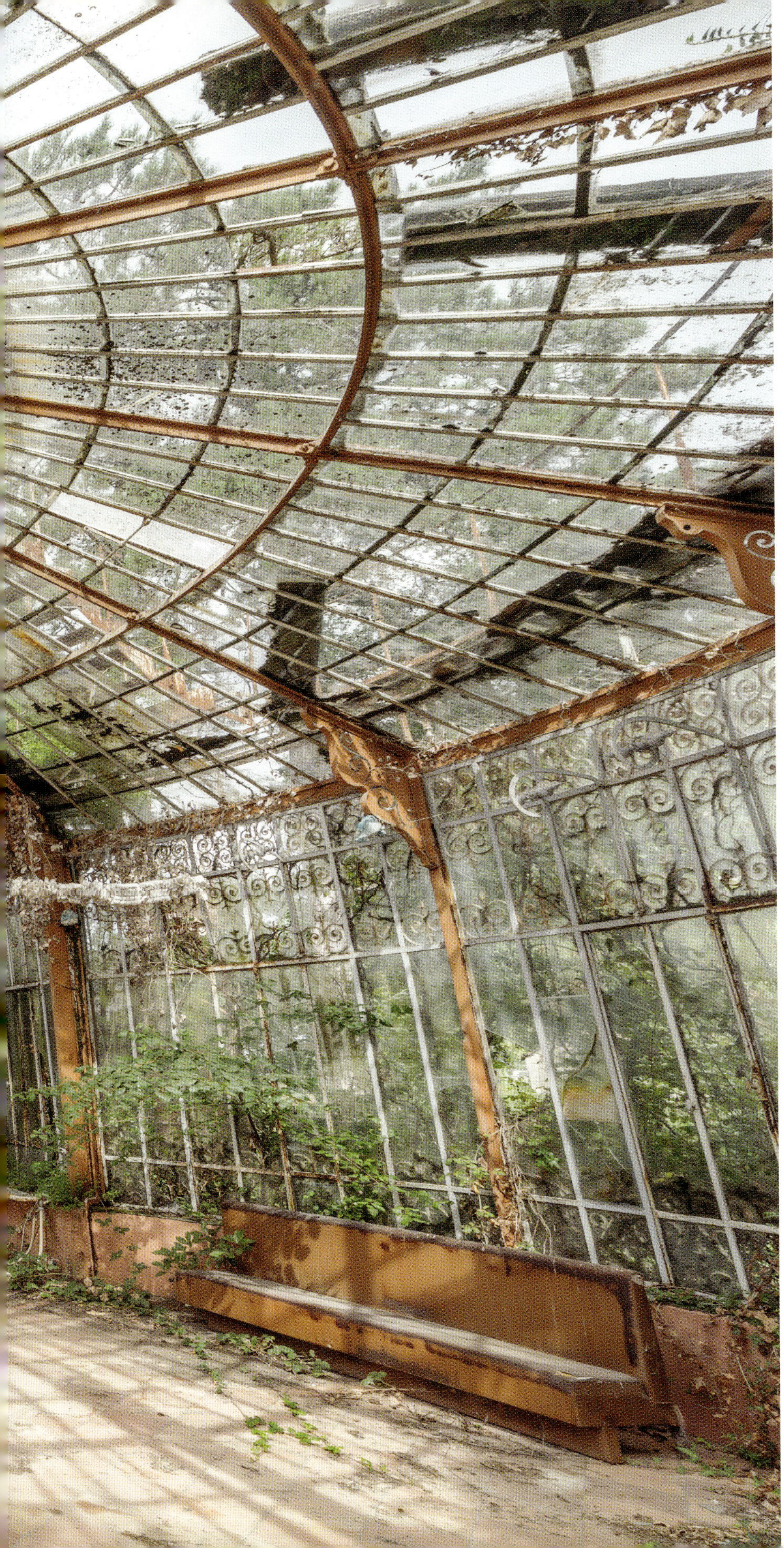

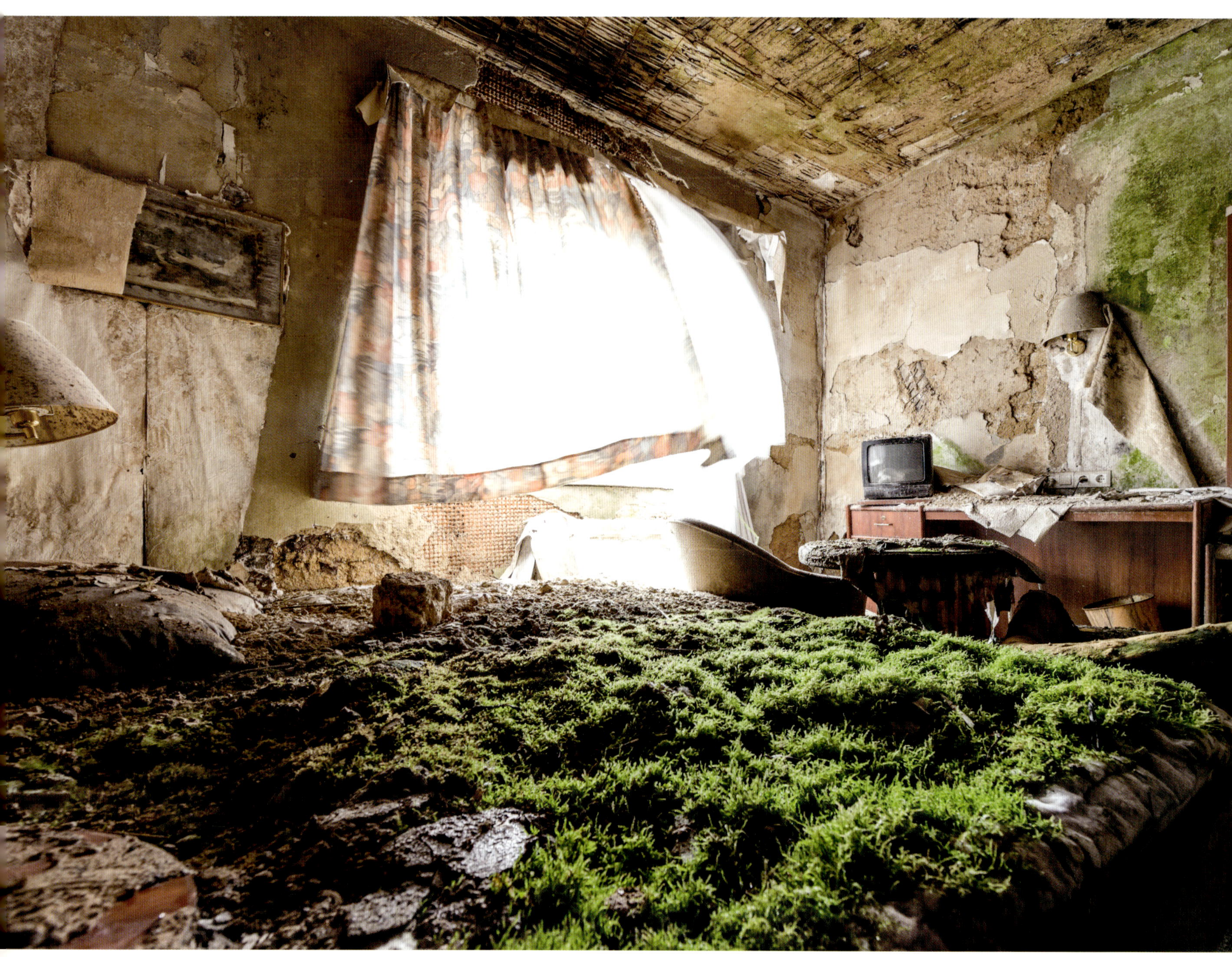

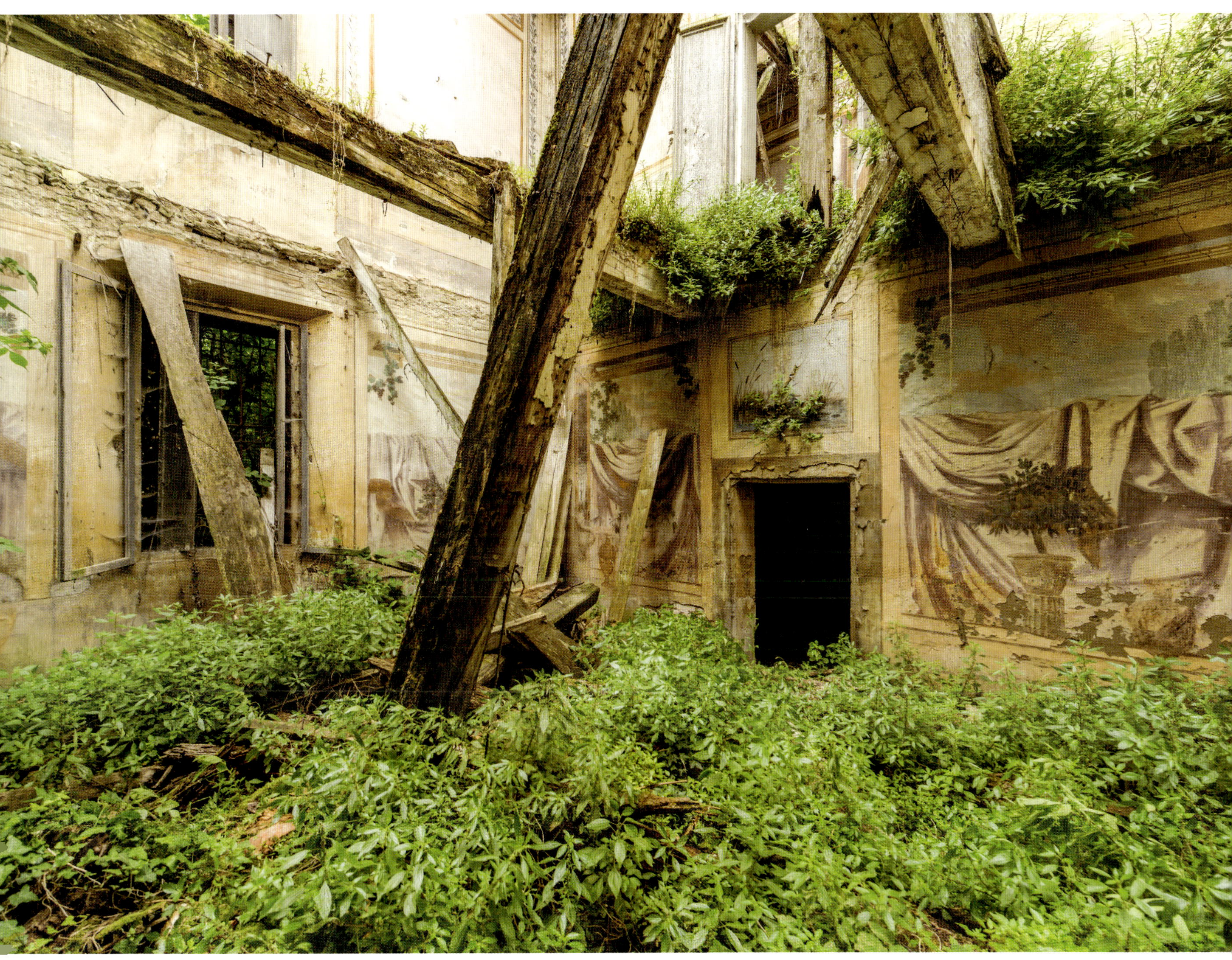

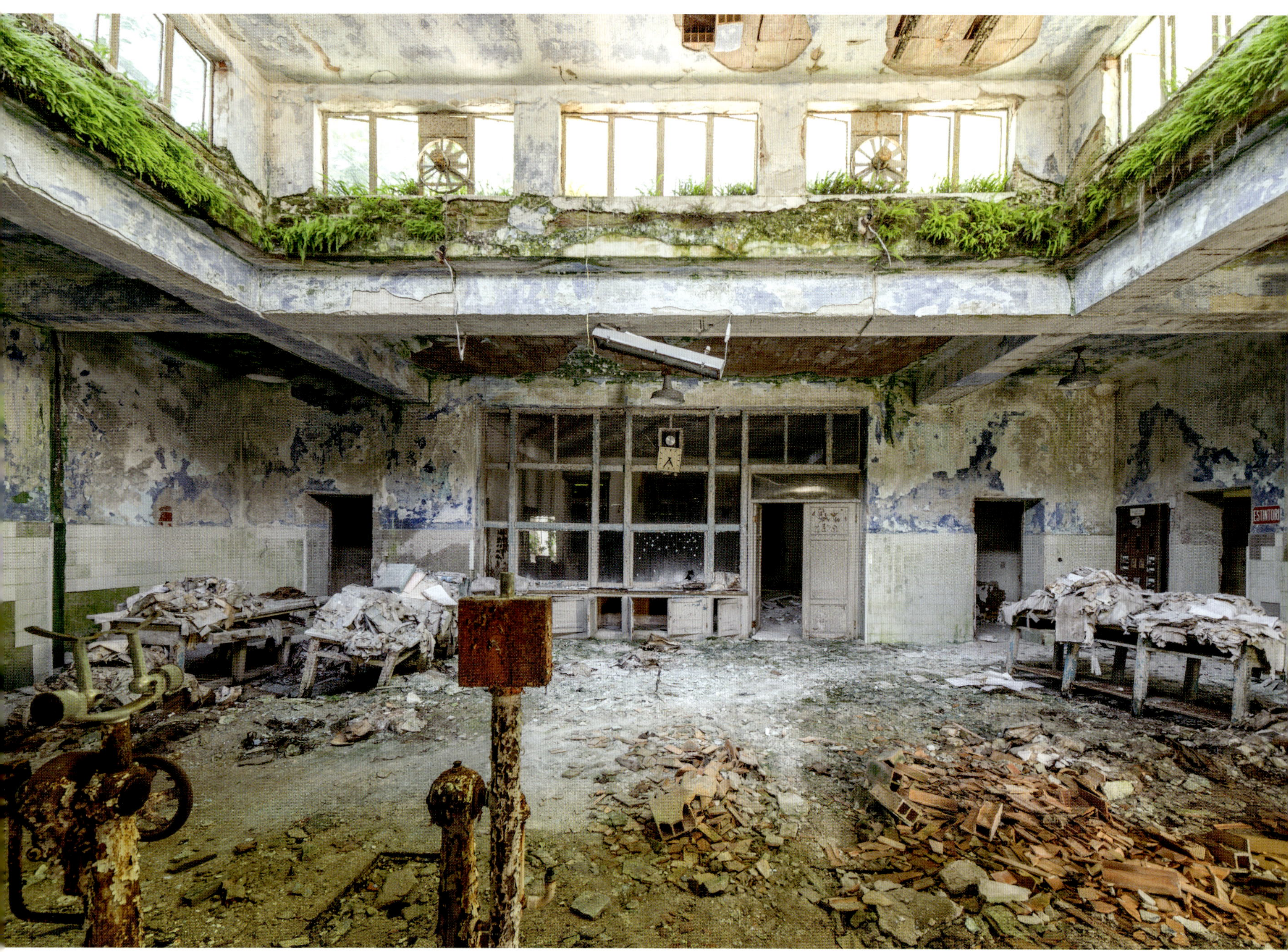

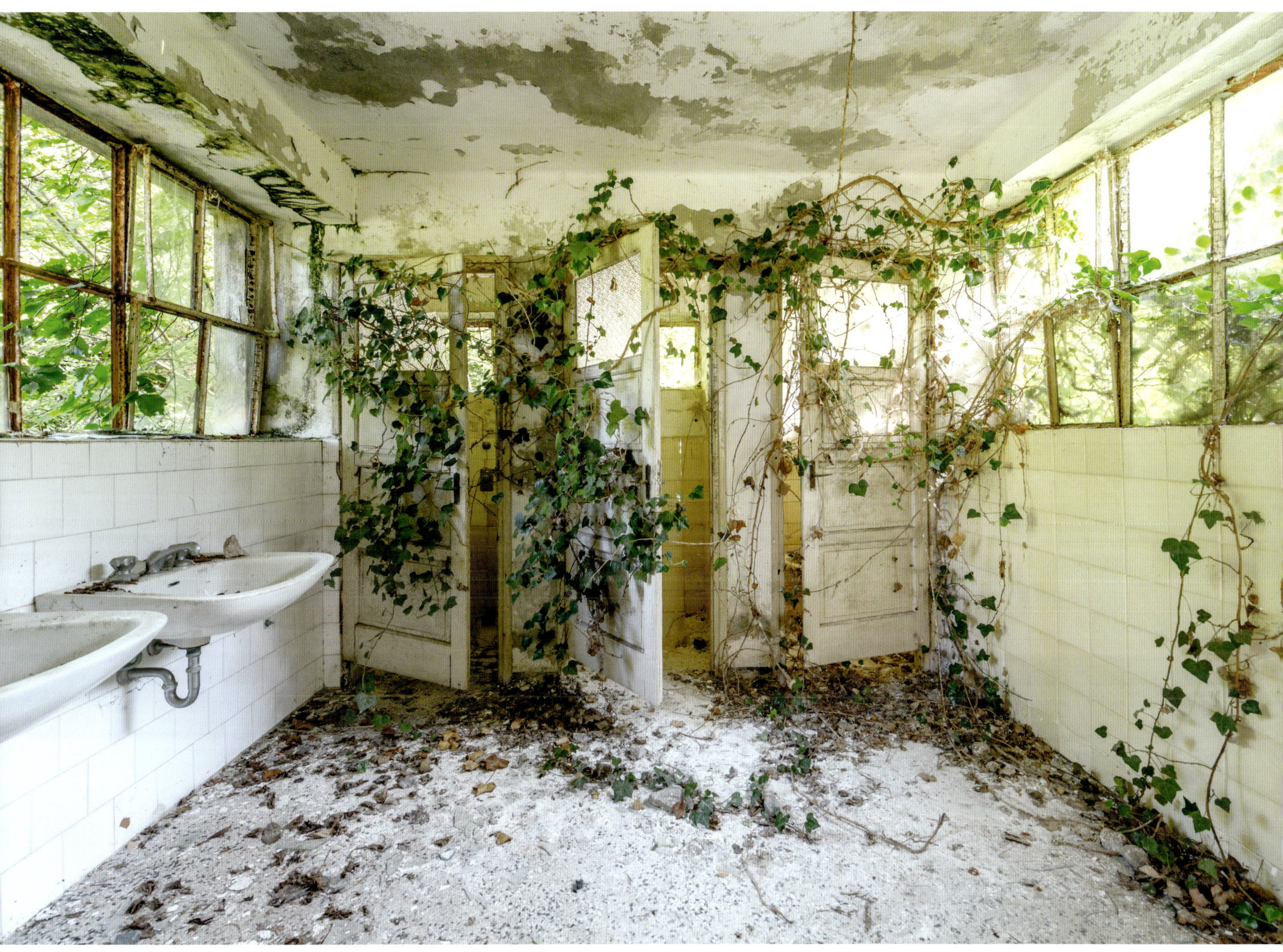

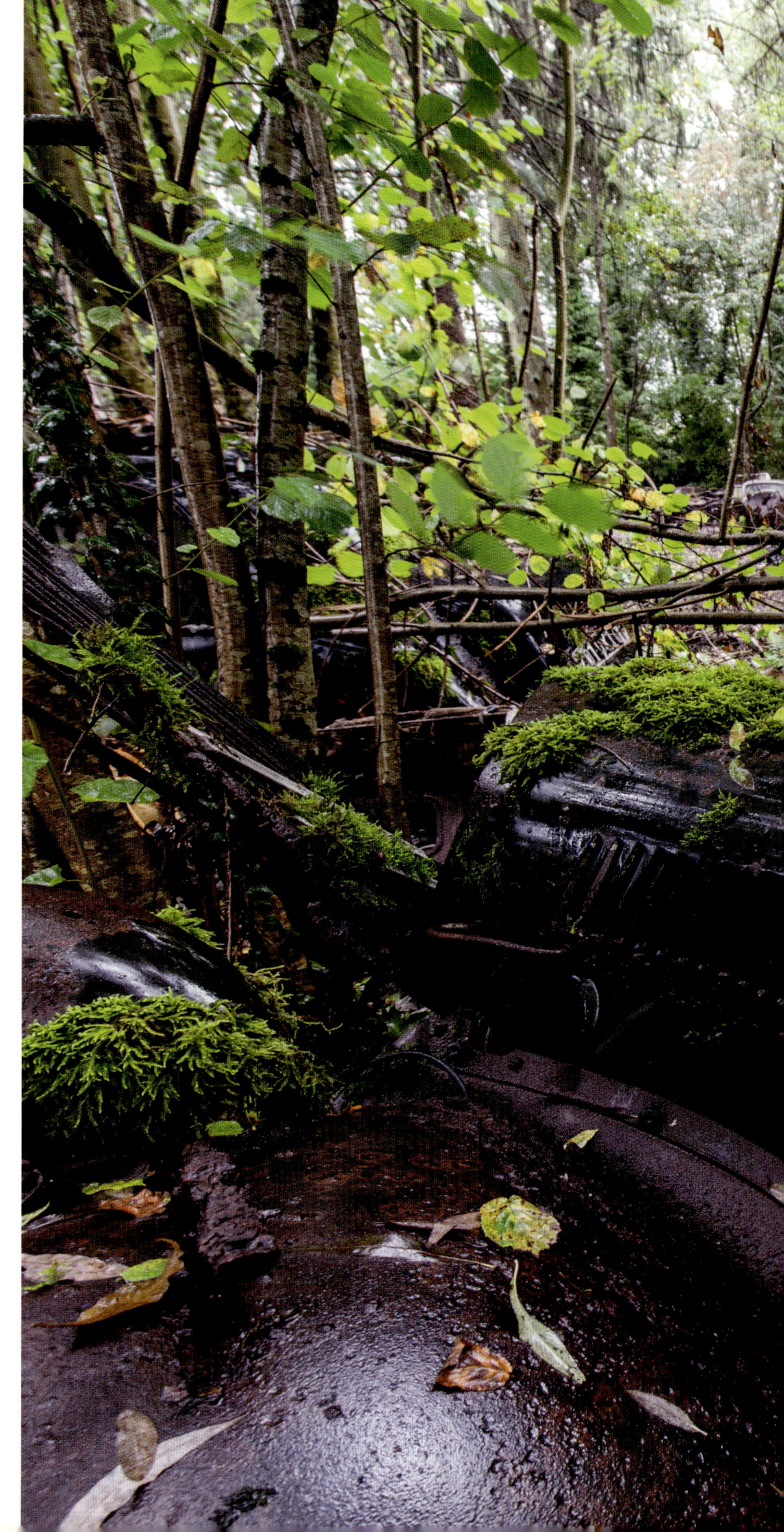

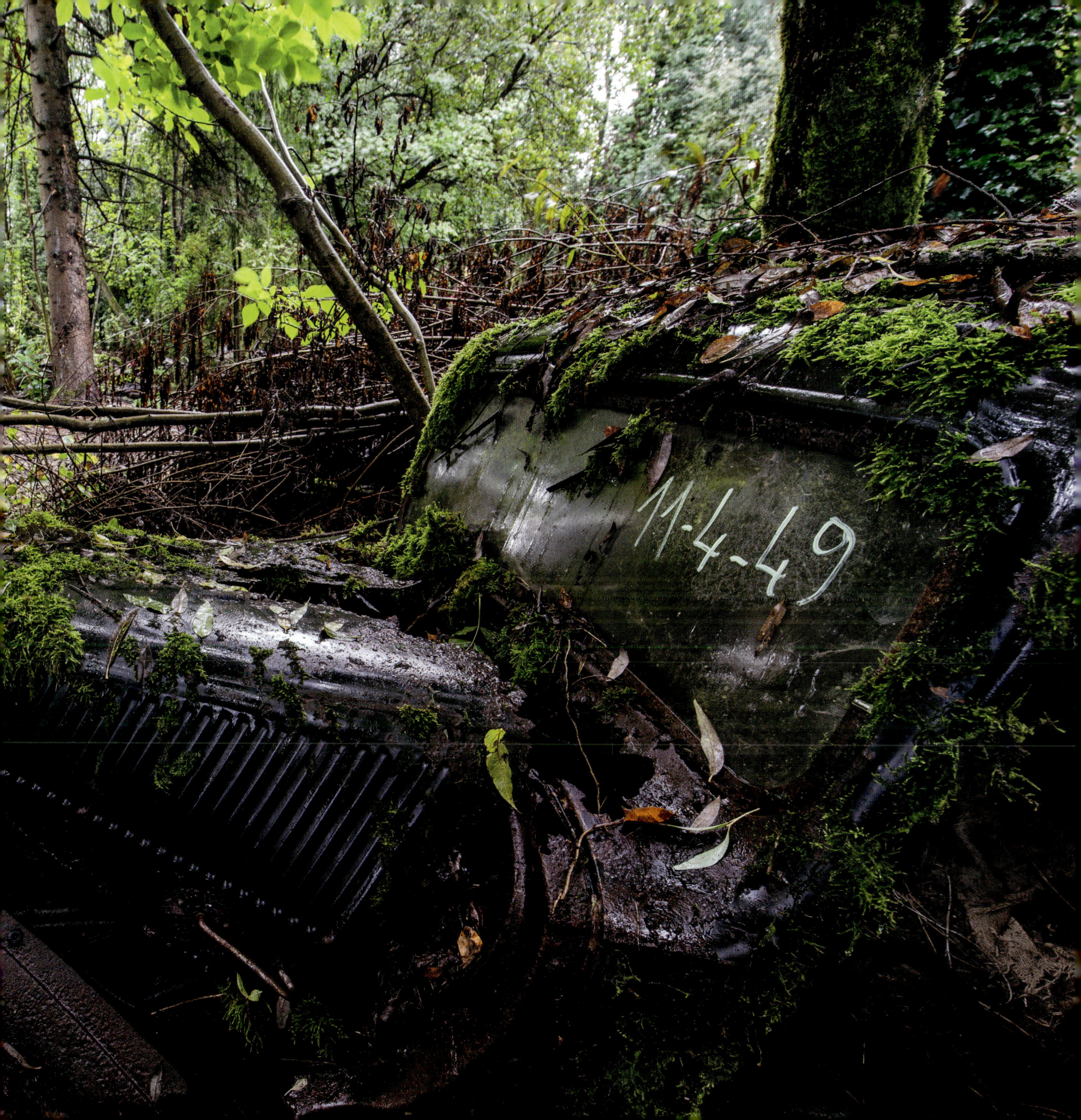

11-4-49

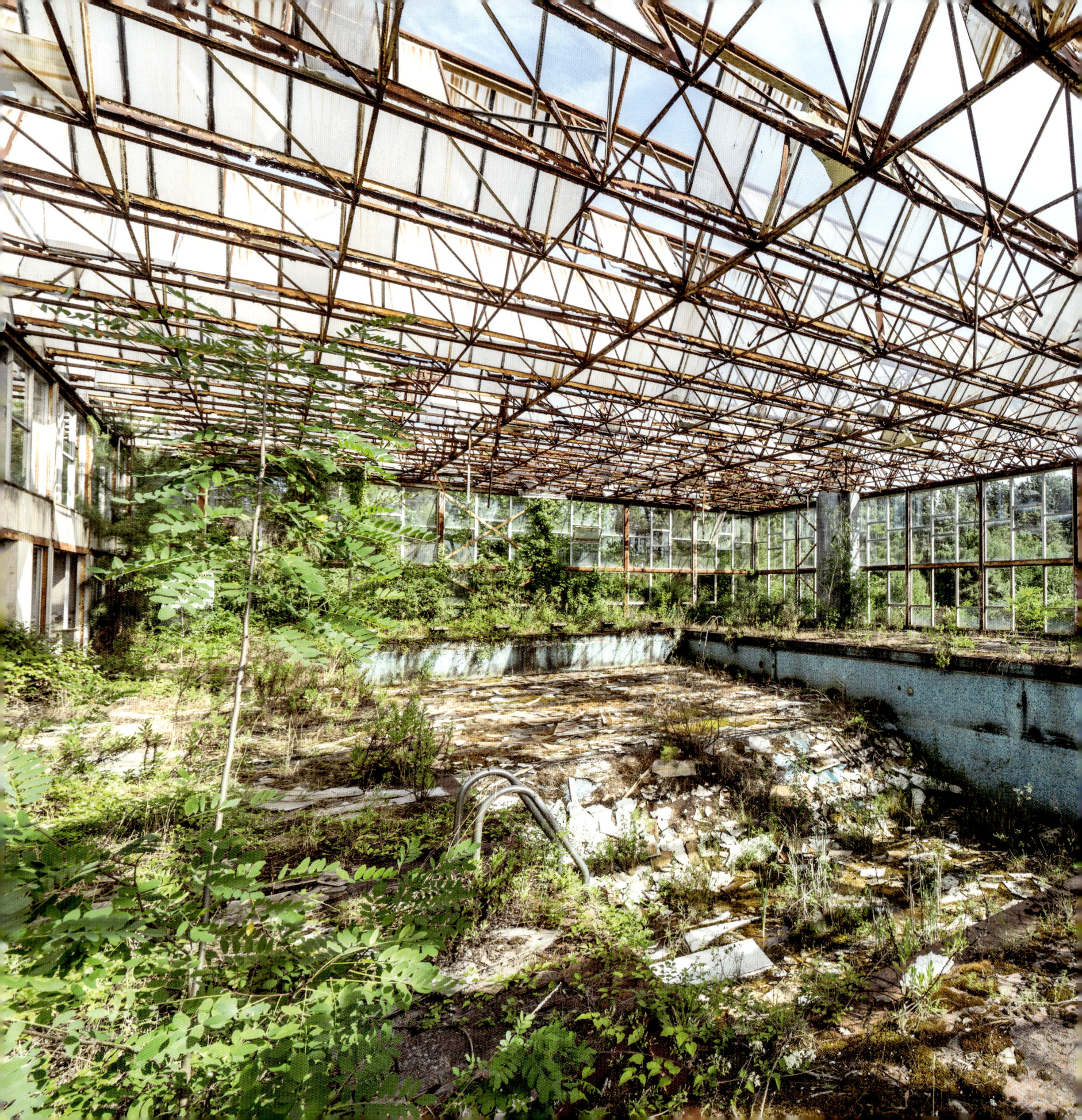

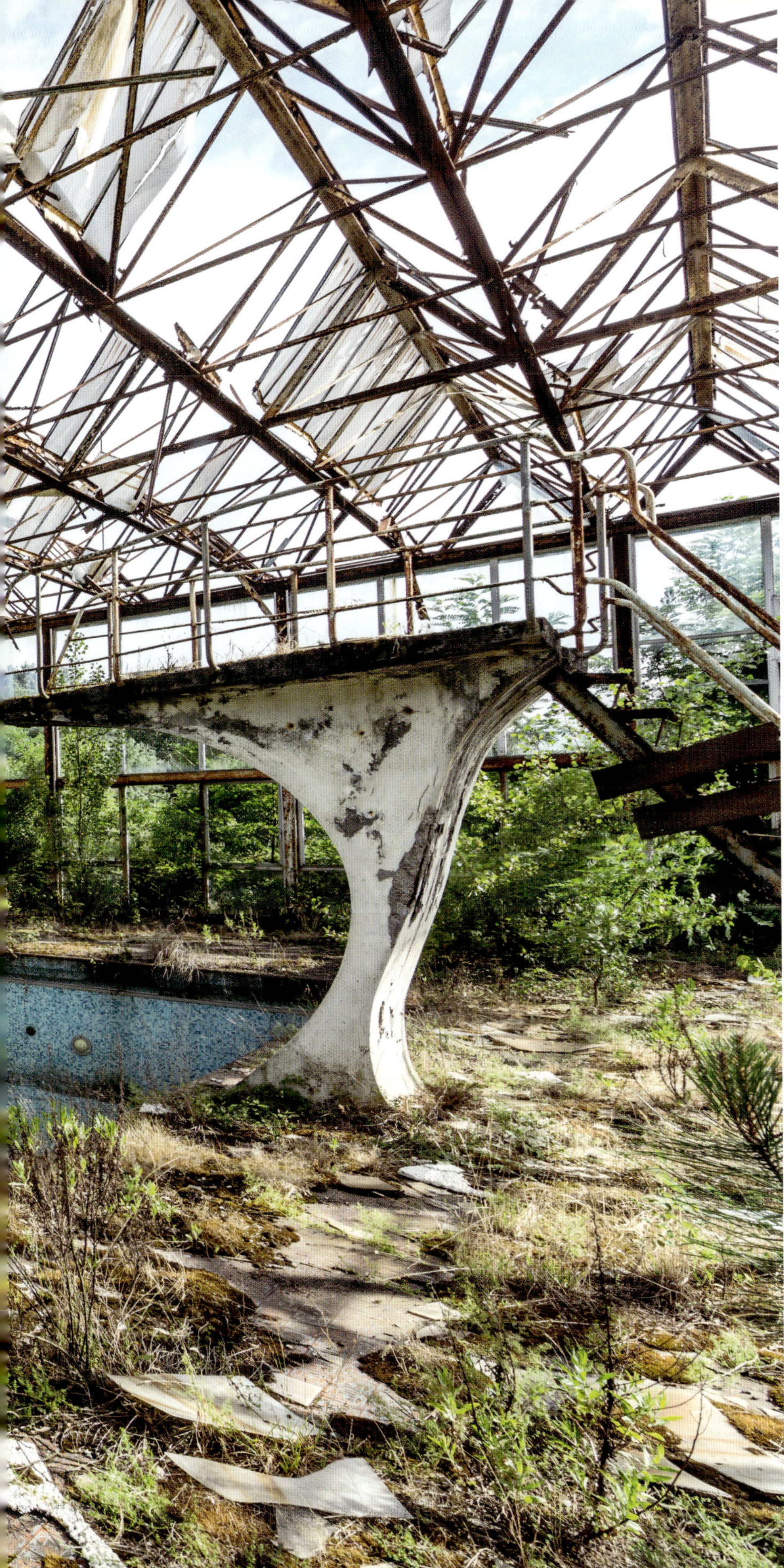

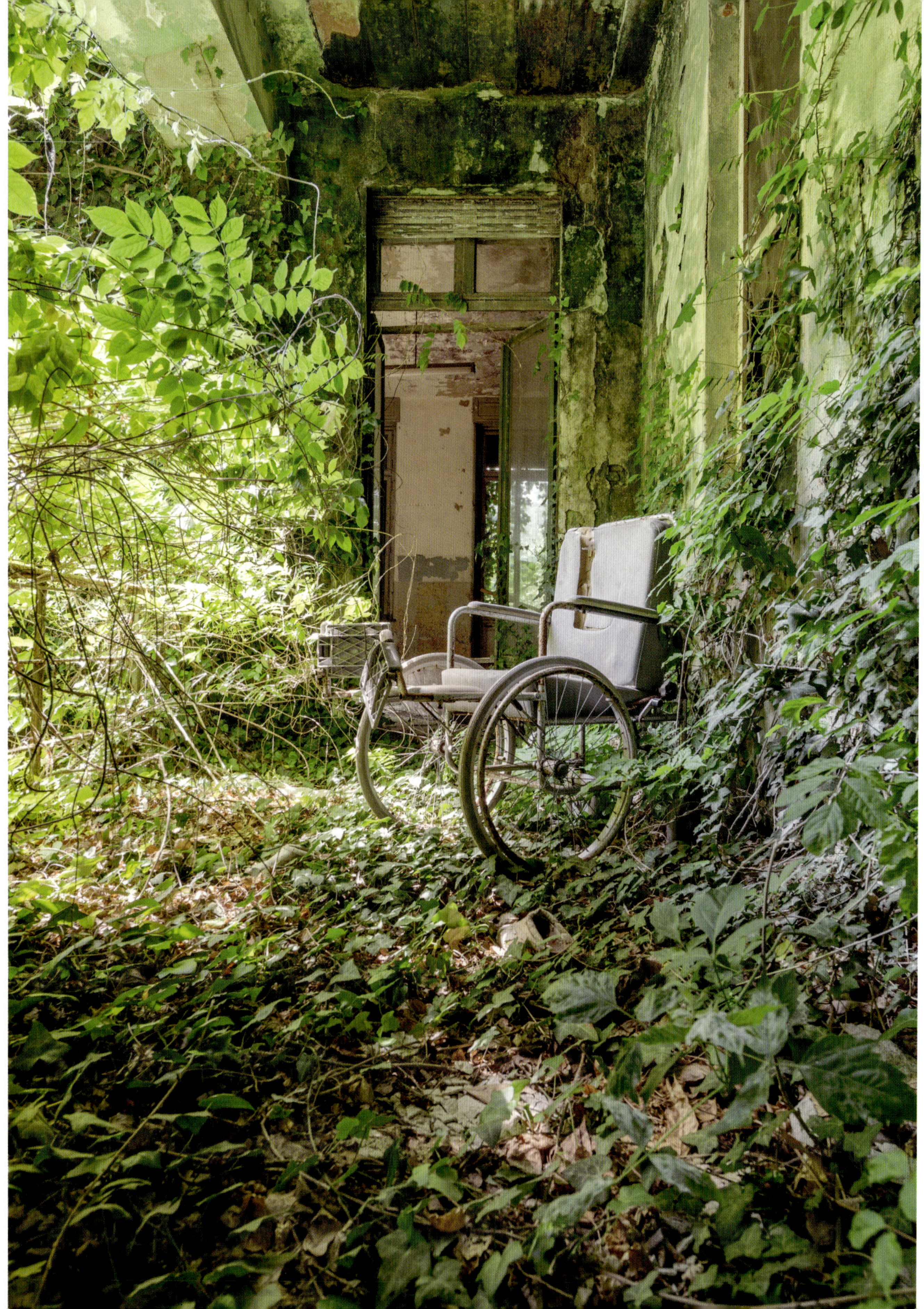

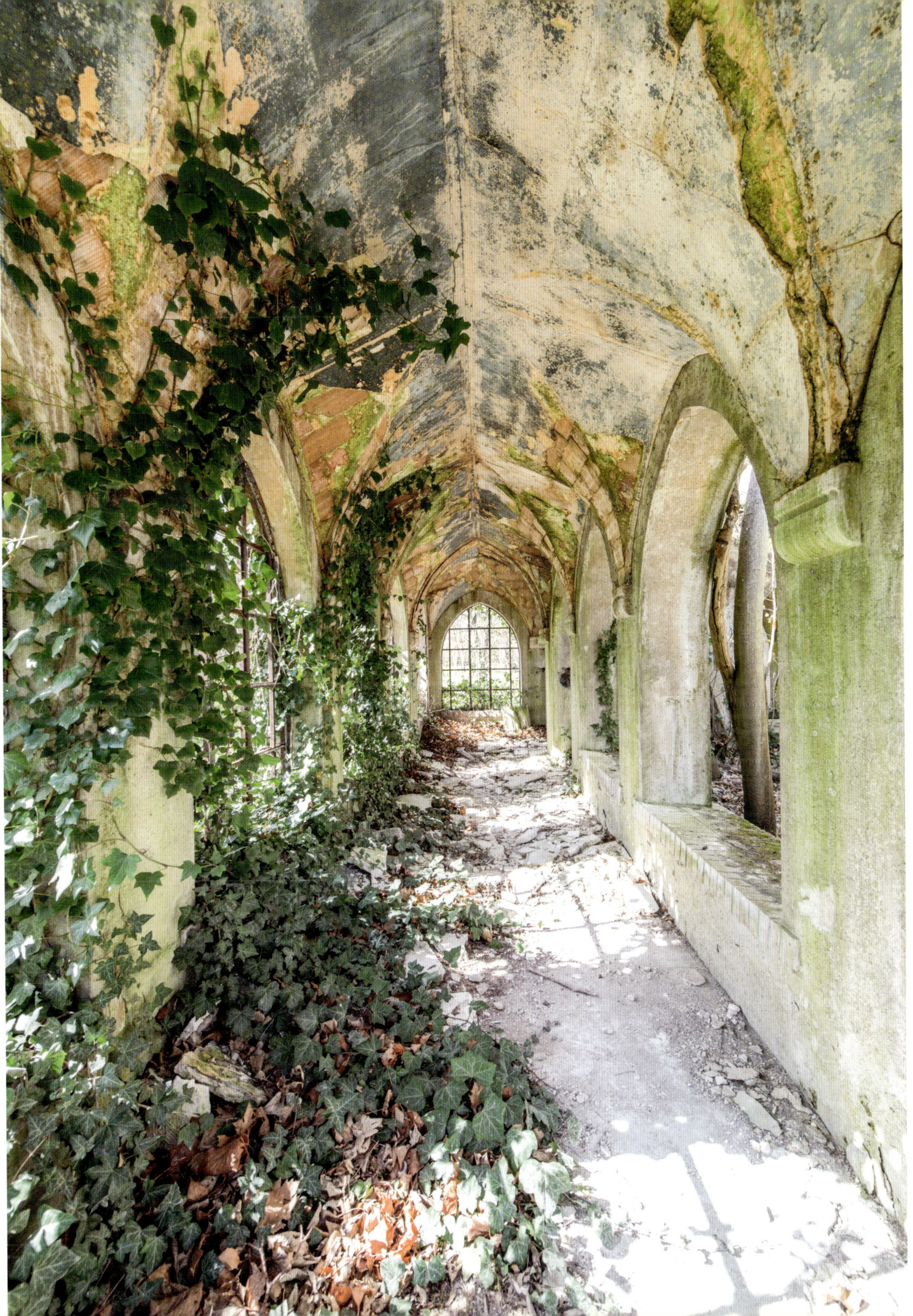

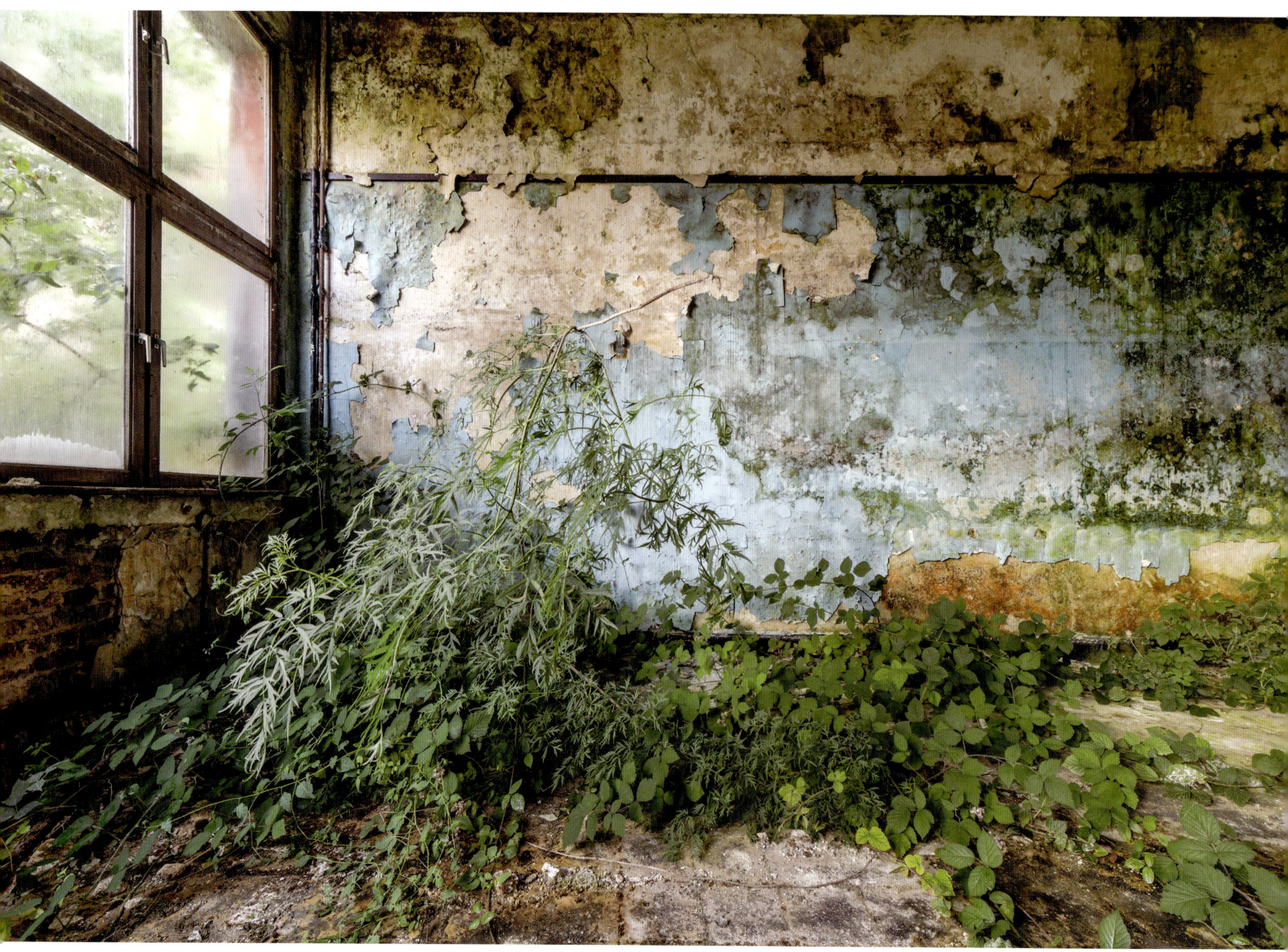

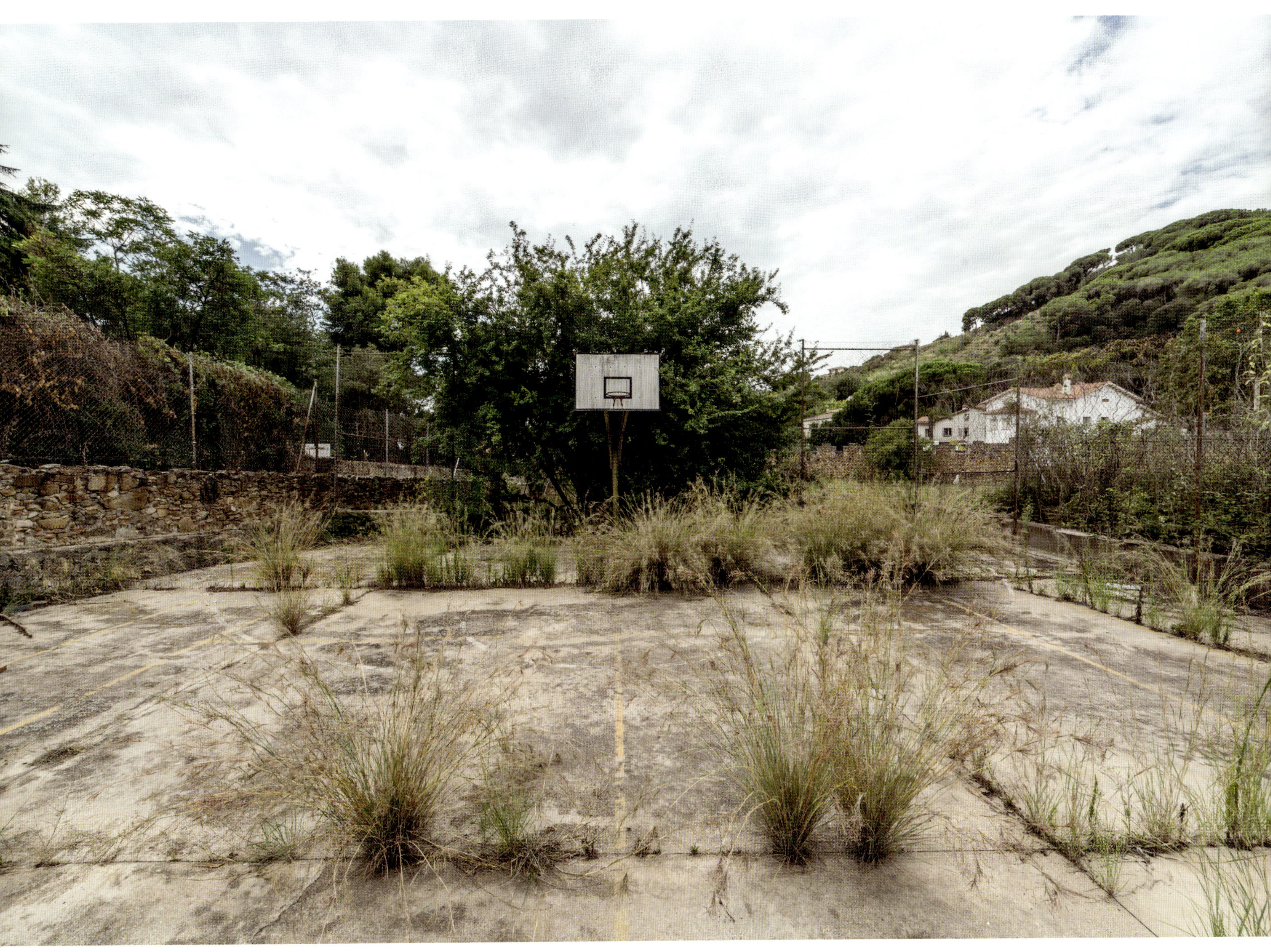

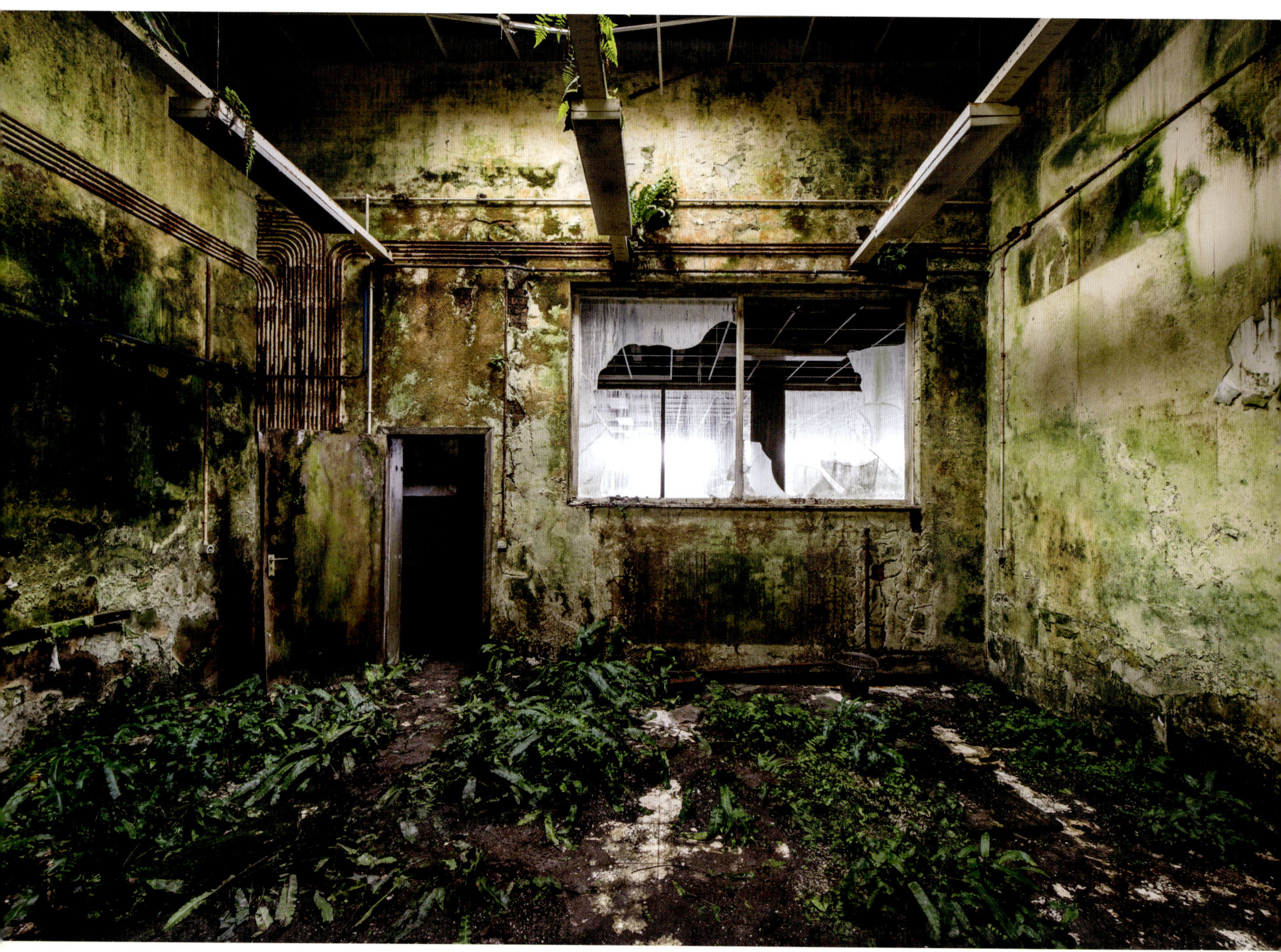

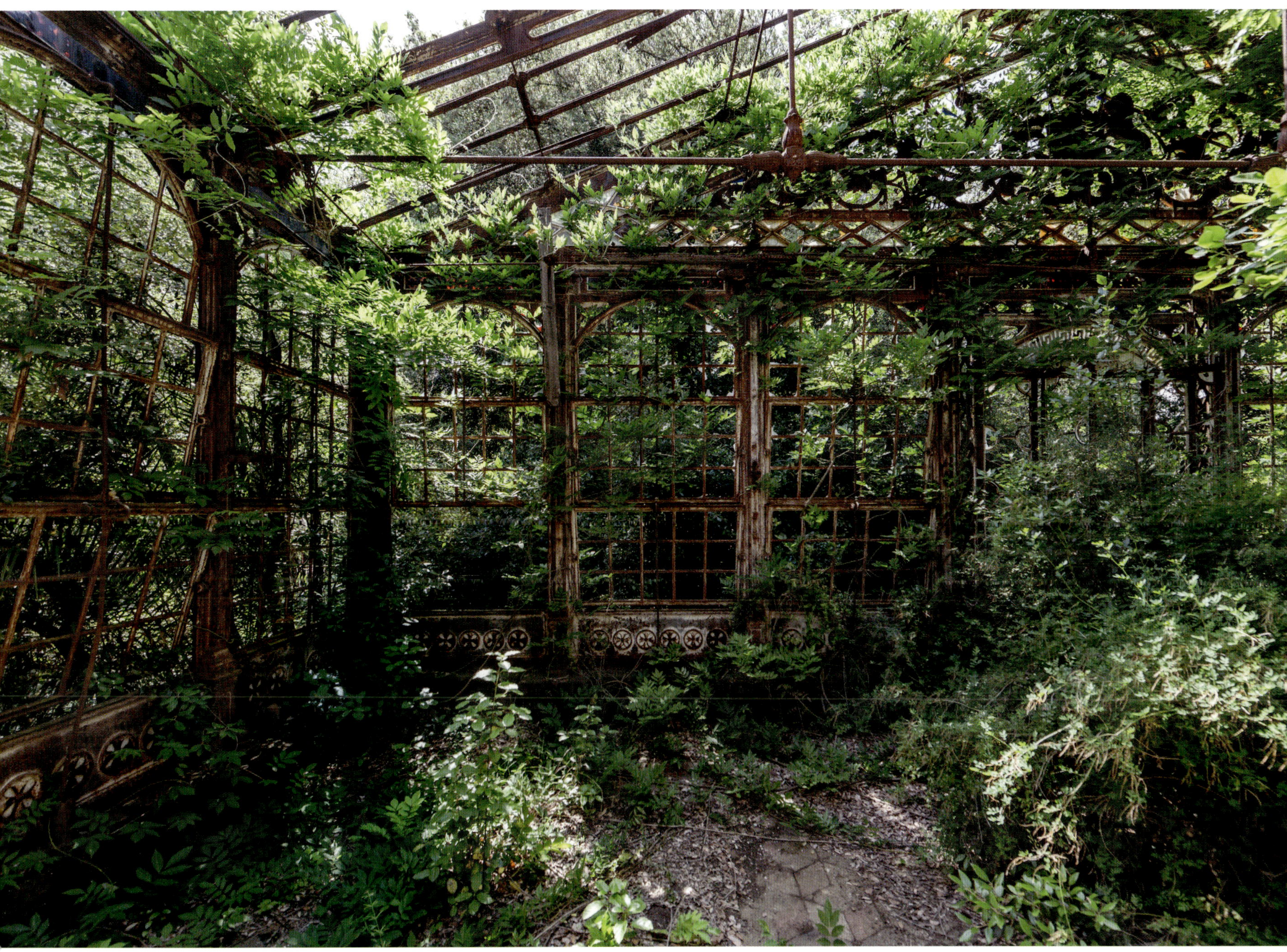

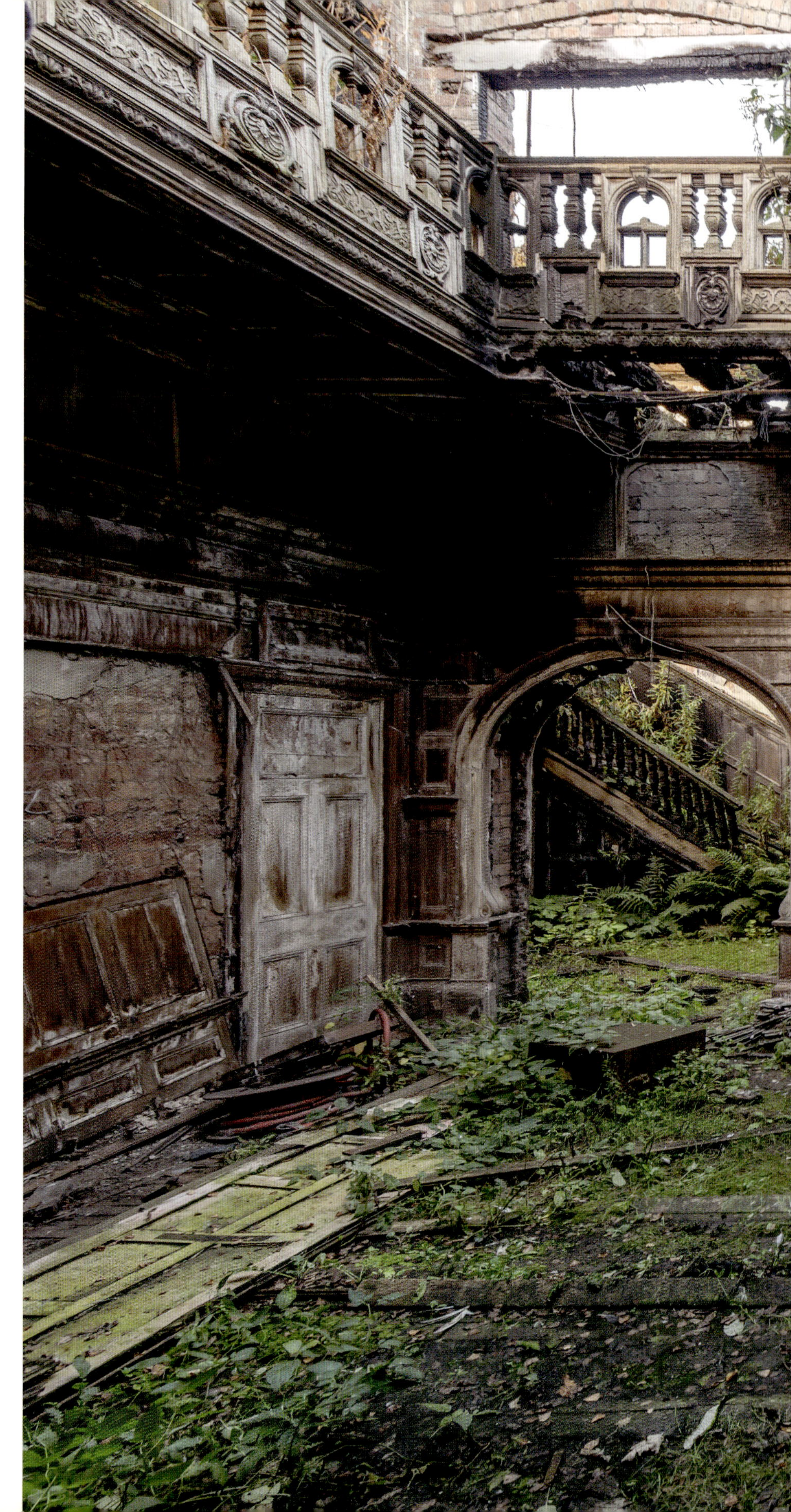

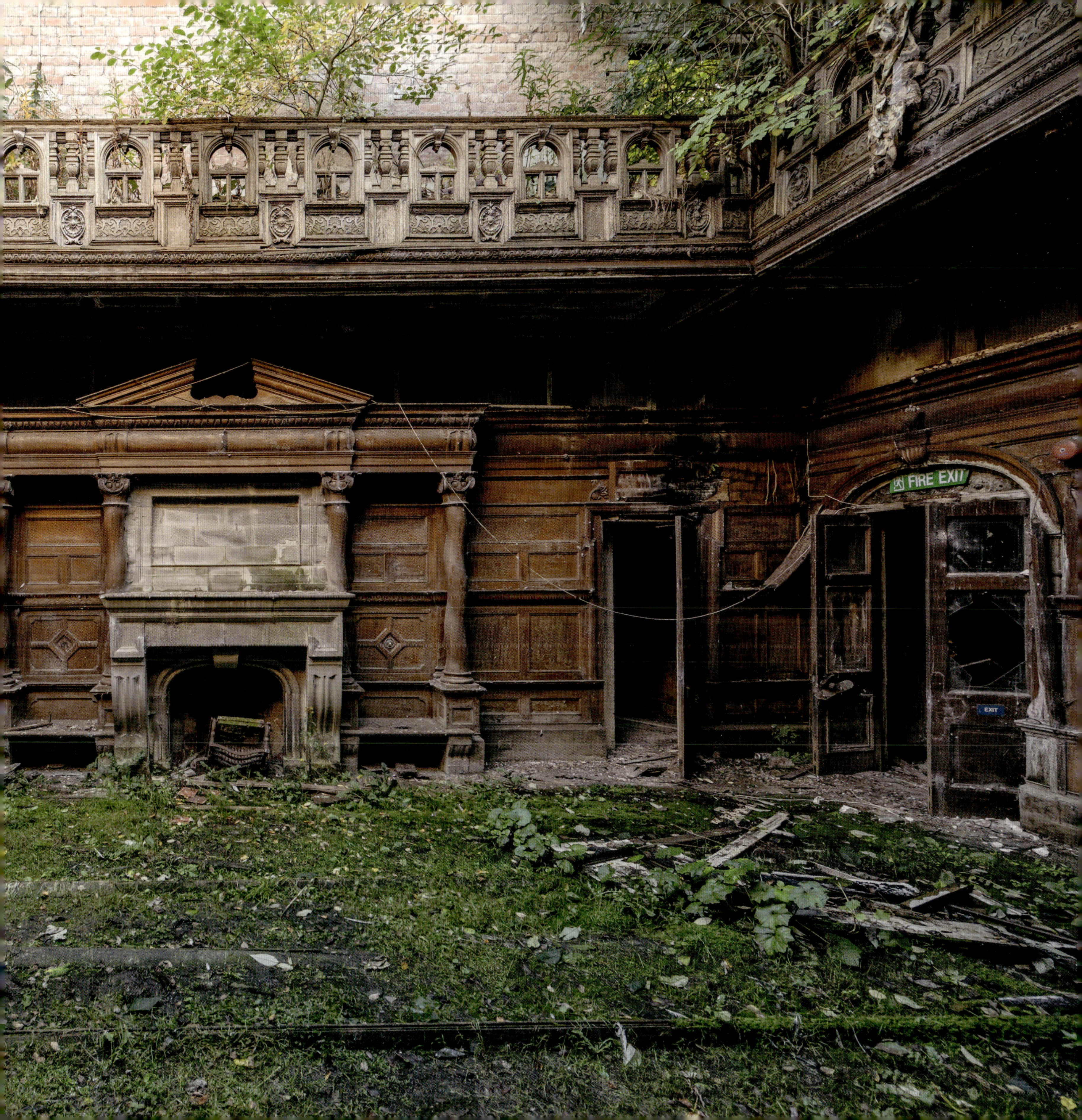
FIRE EXIT
EXIT

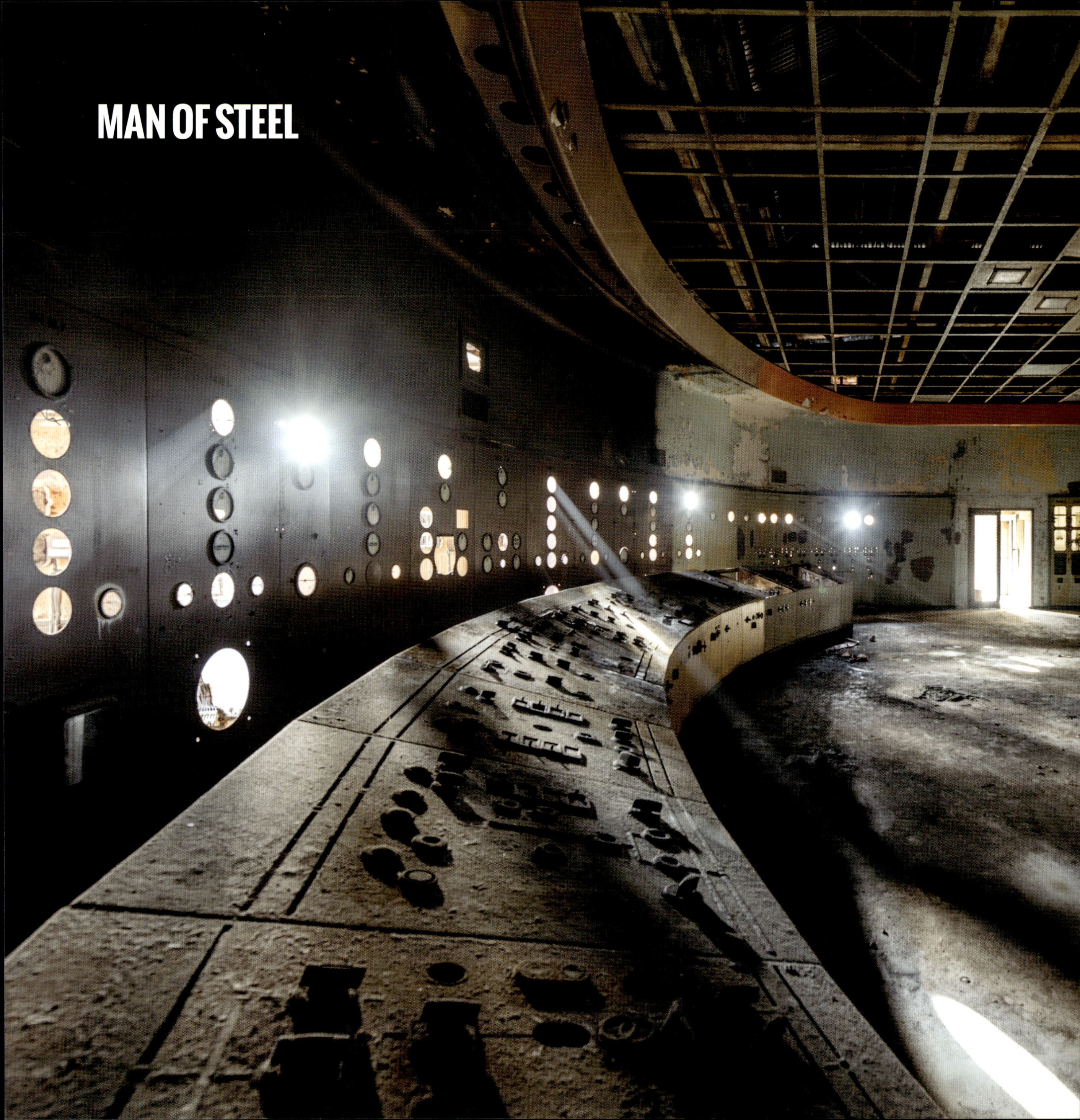
MAN OF STEEL

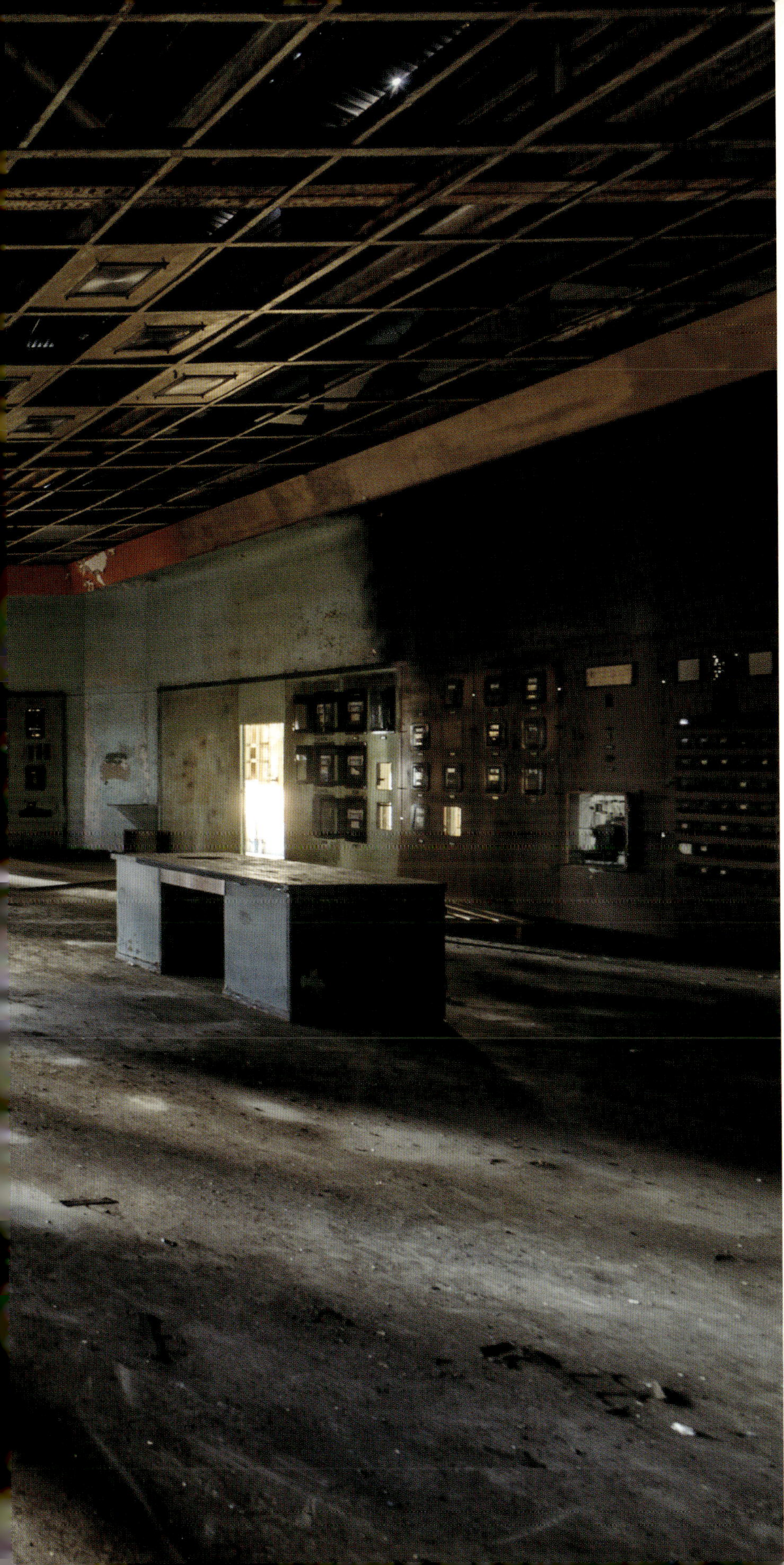

Since the XIXth Century, industrialisation in its first revolution has shaped the landscape of the countries of the northern hemisphere. The transition from hand production methods to new mechanical manufacturing processes marked a major turning point. The working routine was completely changed and with it came a progressive improvement in living conditions.

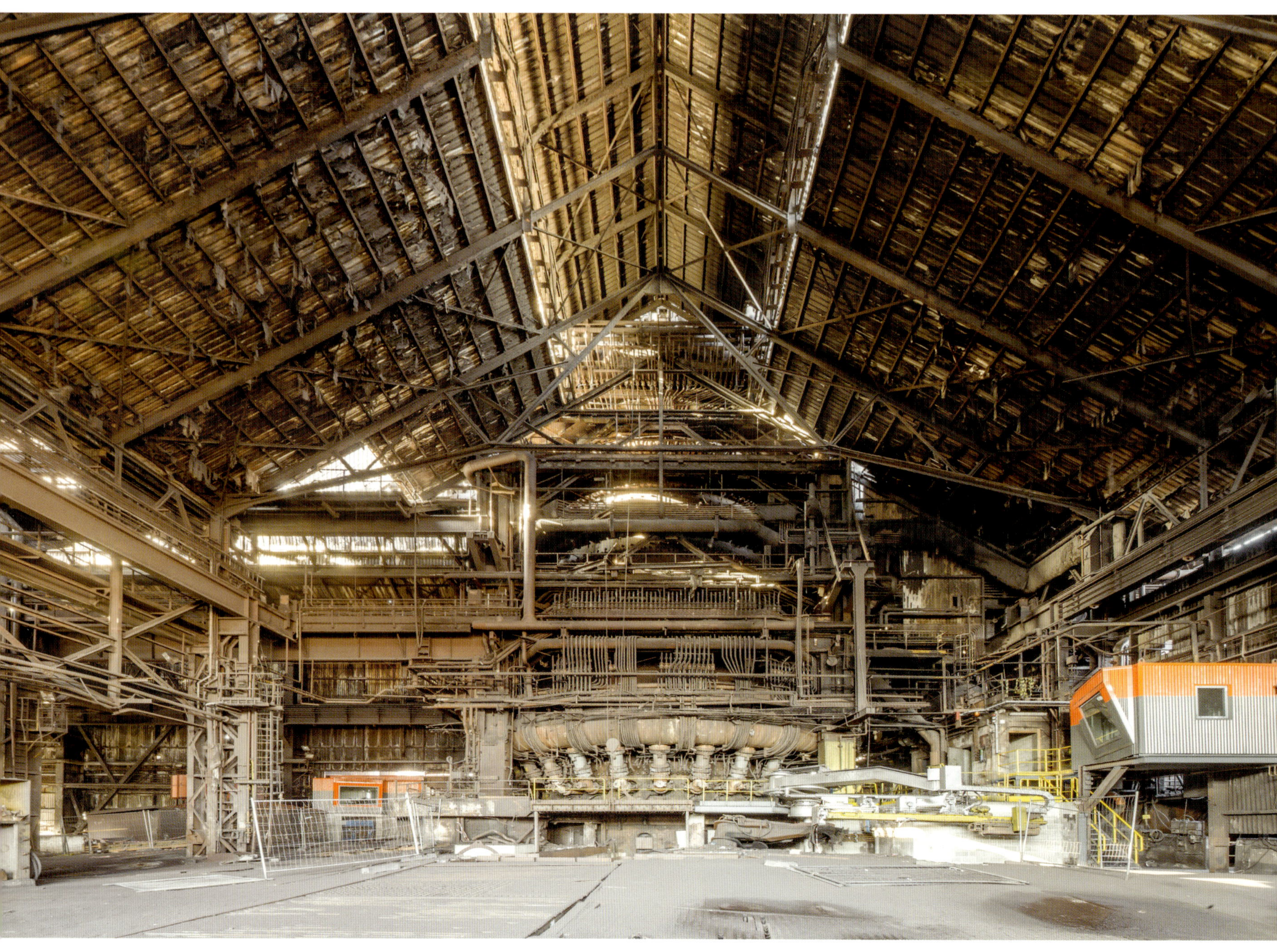

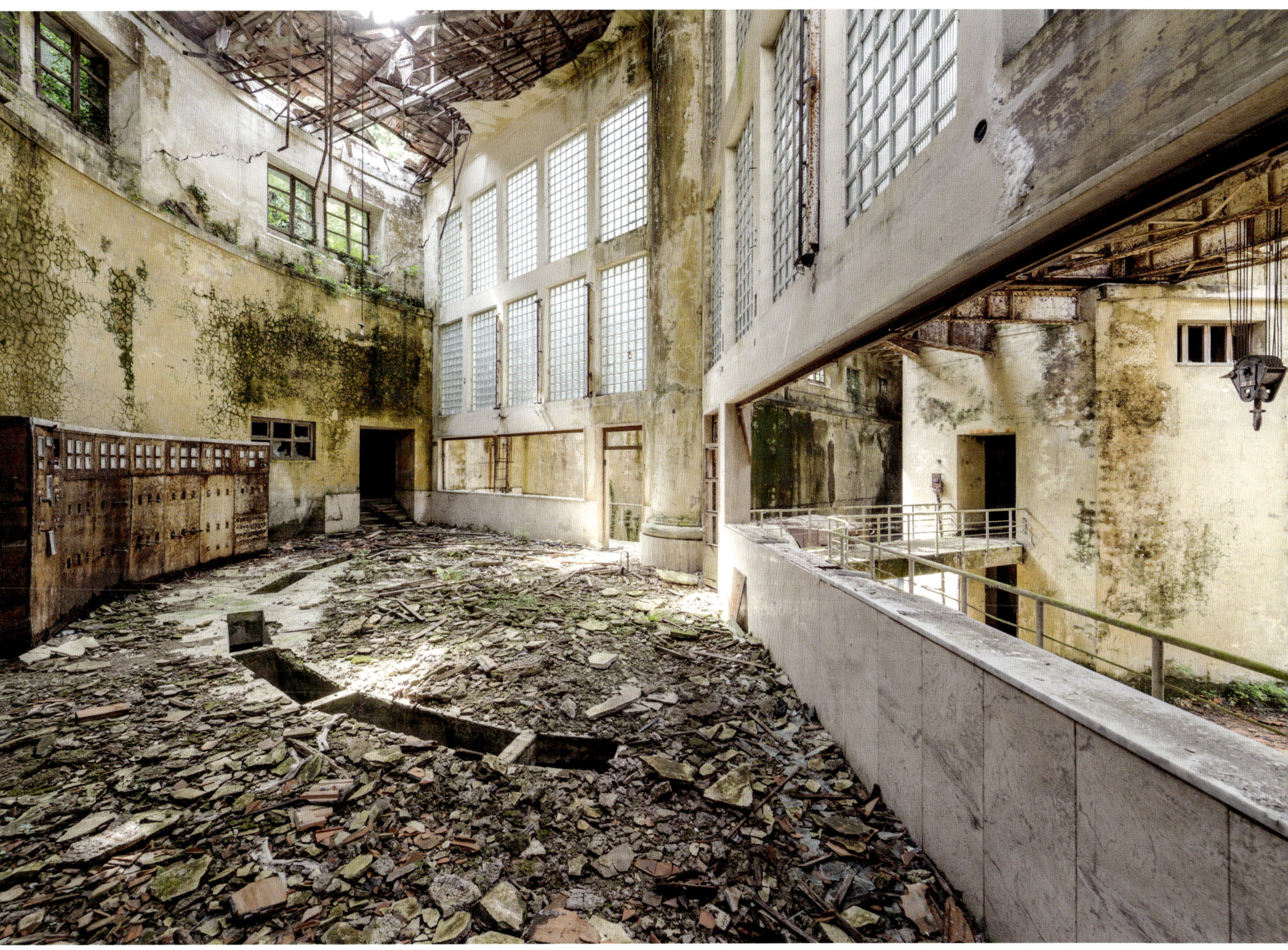

The second wave of the industrial revolution arrived around 1850 with the increase of steel and iron production, the development of the railroads thanks to steam power, the increase in the use of chemicals and petroleum, more widespread use of machinery in manufacturing and of course the introduction of electricity.

But with time, these unique human creations photographed in this chapter, were gradually closed and then abandoned. Causes were multiple but we can talk about three main ones.

Globalization did a lot of damage. Many industries decided to relocate to foreign countries (mainly Asia) where the labour force was much cheaper. The depletion of natural resources, such as coal, is responsible for the disappearance of several sites including mines. The obsolescence of some of the machinery used and the creation of new working techniques put an end to some of the finest locations of our industrial heritage.

For a long time, industrial landmarks and remains weren't really considered as an actual heritage we should protect and were ignored. Mainly, the economic and social traumatism that followed the closures, the pollution issues that appeared and the relative youth of the abandonment. We need to think about the hope that former workers had in their factories re-opening one day.

Recently, attitudes have changed toward our industrial past and many sites have been protected, or even promoted (some of them can be visited like the steel factory of Volklingen in Germany or the Wendel mine in France). Some criteria is necessary to get these sites protected: The age of service of the building and its history, the visibility and size of the site, the originality and the rarity of its architecture, and the accessibility for the public to come and be able to visit without

danger. But a lot of them are still abandoned and fall into further decay a little more every day.

Charles Cooley affirmed in one of his theories: *"To get away from one's working environment is, in a sense, to get away from one's self; and this is often the chief advantage of travel and change"* when he was explaining how men were always interacting with other people and how it had a major impact on how we saw ourselves.

I think it is the perfect way to describe our relation with our work environment and the colleagues we work with. When we are working, we create a different persona, in order to respond to, and fit in with, the expectations of others. The stranger we become will partly identify with its workplace and reflect a part of its spirit.

Of course, jobs are all different from each other, so it is hard to generalise. For example, offices are the most common workplace we share around the world. But I feel it is pretty hard to find some relics of what used to be the working routine of someone in an abandoned office.

I believe it is in our industrial heritage that symbolises this Century and fits perfectly with this definition. These giant cathedrals of steel that are no longer built are left to rust and bear witness to the industrial revolution.

Power plants, cooling towers, mines, paper mills or factories (going from textile to wood, crystal, steel, coal or even sugar fabrication) symbolise the era that you will find in this chapter: their incredible size and architecture. I also want to show another side of manufacturing (for example, cars, fire engines, trains or airplanes) where iron and steel compose these metal monsters, representing their jobs perfectly.

Even though I haven't had the opportunity to go yet, Detroit or "Motor city" would be the best example and symbol of what was one of the most impressive industrial automobile empires, a lynchpin of the American economy. In Europe, northern areas of France, the industrial basin of Charleroi and some German central regions, share the same history and are now full of abandoned factories that were at one time the jewels in their industry.

A lot of the people living in these areas have relatives who worked in these factories, and the factory represents many memories for them. It was the link in a region for everyone to connect to, employing the majority of their population and often the historic symbol of the city.

When the factories close, there is a loss for the entire community, bringing the region down, economically speaking. When you have generations of a family working in the same place, the loss is even more deeply felt. My grandmother used to run a transport company in France and when she sold it, people in the village said a part of the spirit of the village disappeared.

Impressive is the word that is spoken every time I have a discussion about the photographs I have taken in these incredible places. It may be true, that they look other-worldly, despite originating from our past. It is unlikely that we will build structures like that again. It will be too expensive.

Modernisation and technological progress have come a long way. But to my mind, this is why it is so essential that we protect and showcase these locations in the future. Not only because it can be an economic opportunity for these areas to attract tourism, but also because it's an integral part of the culture of a region.

This whole system includes a site; a style of architecture, a machinery and a way of manufacturing things that make it unique. Only money and the will to work durably on these projects can prevail, but we are now little by little treating our industrial heritage like we treat our monuments, and I hope we can save what is left of these "steel giants" before it is too late.

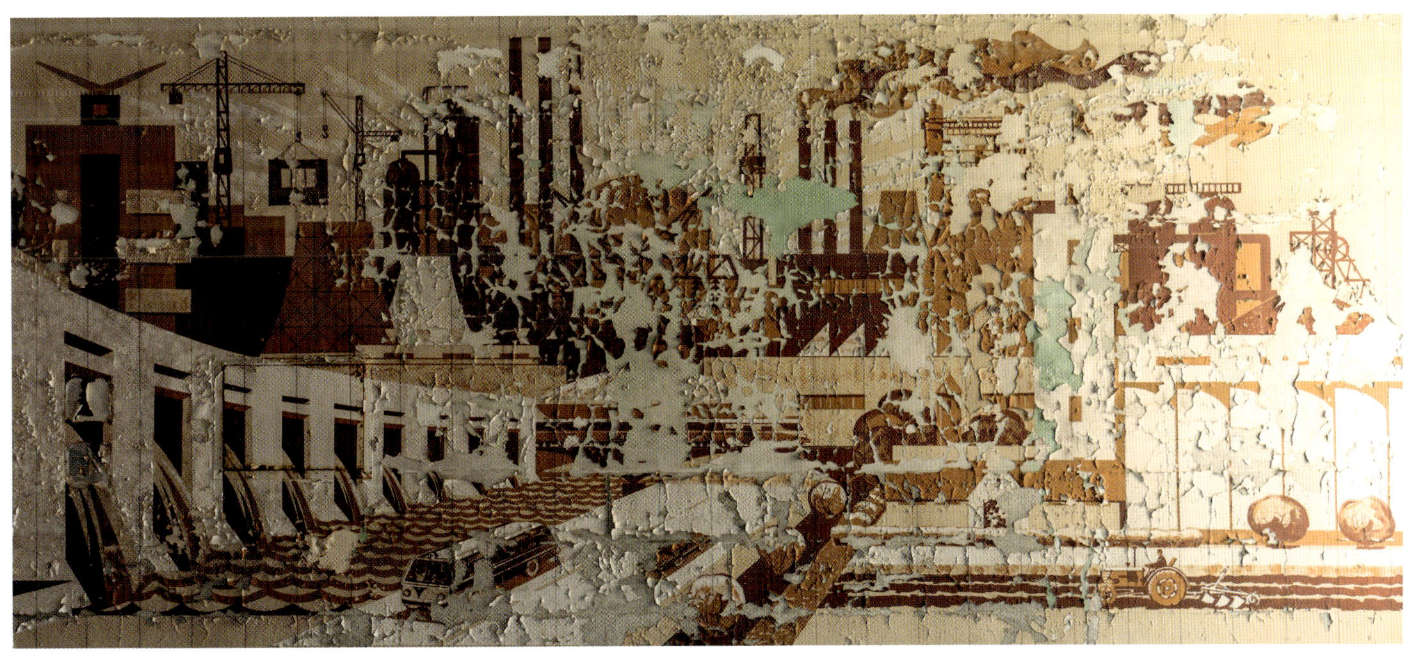

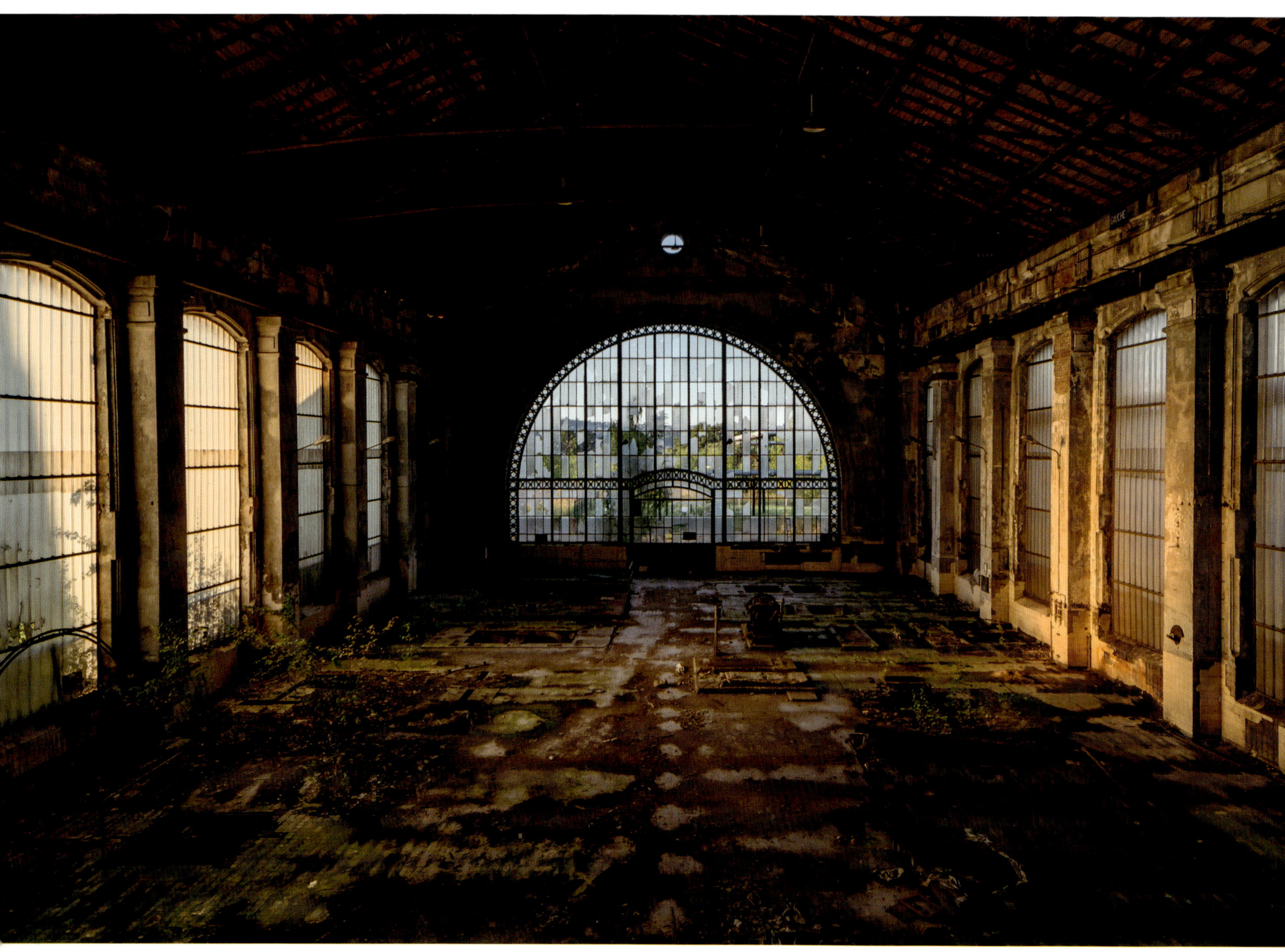

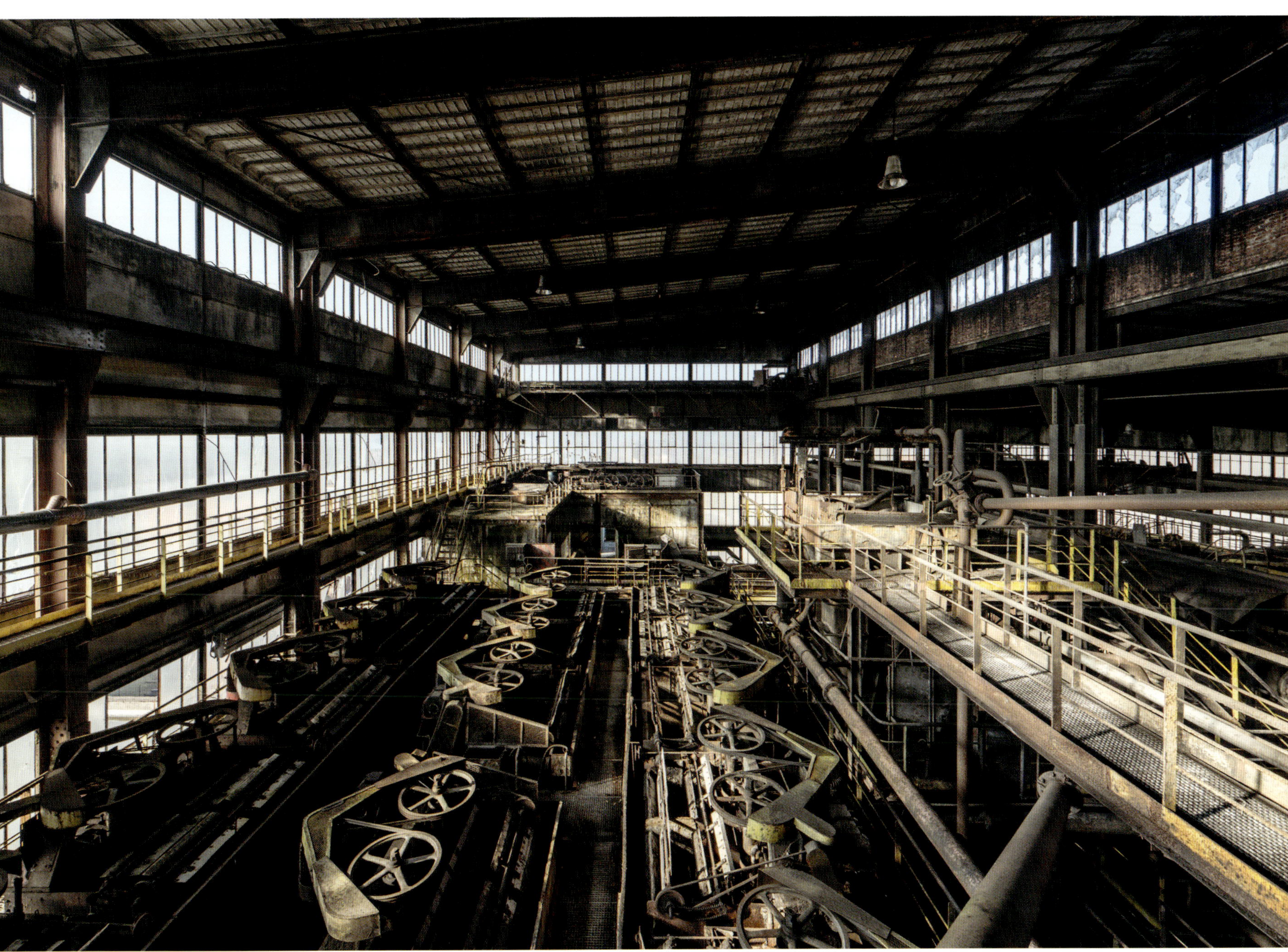

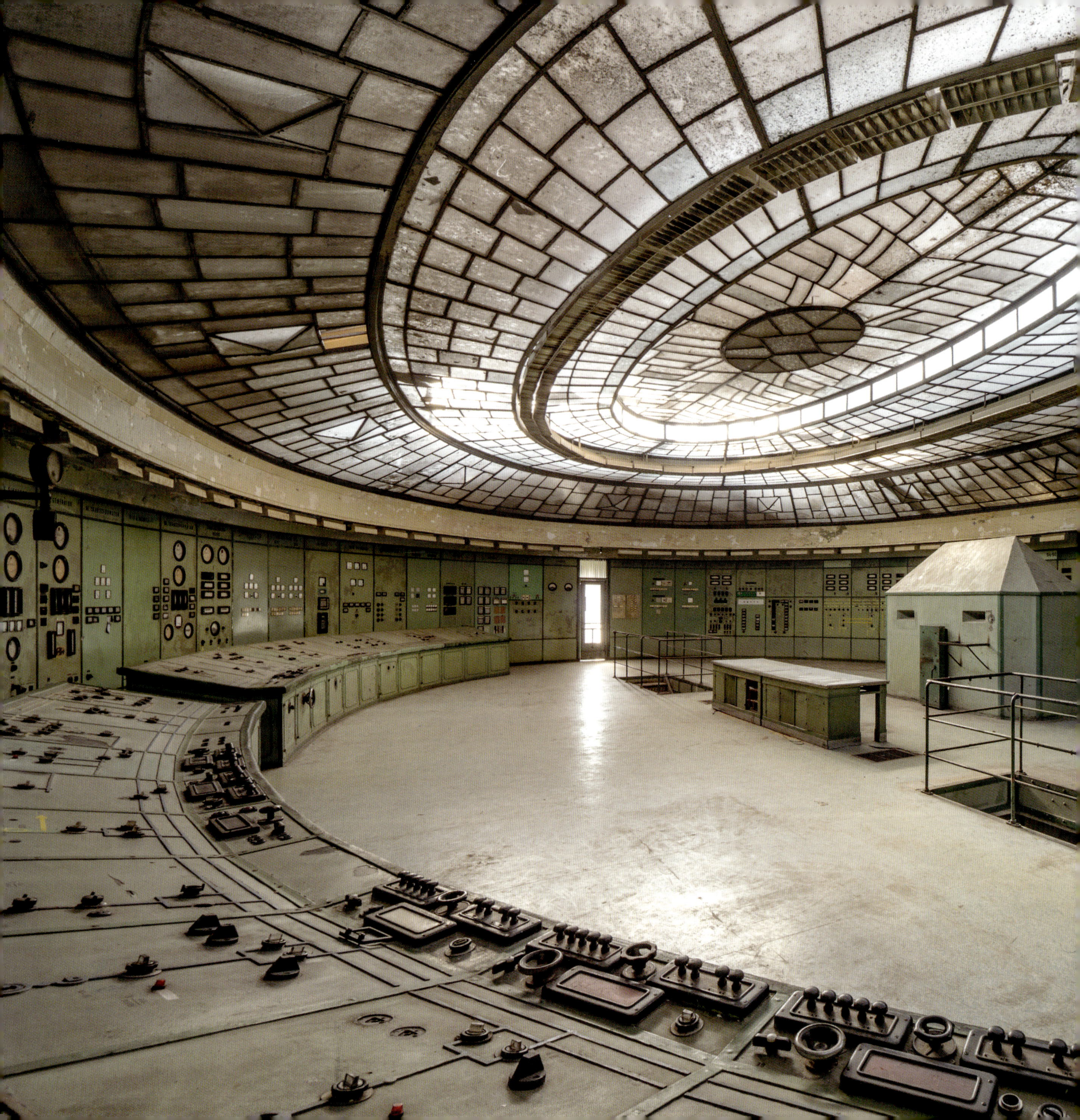

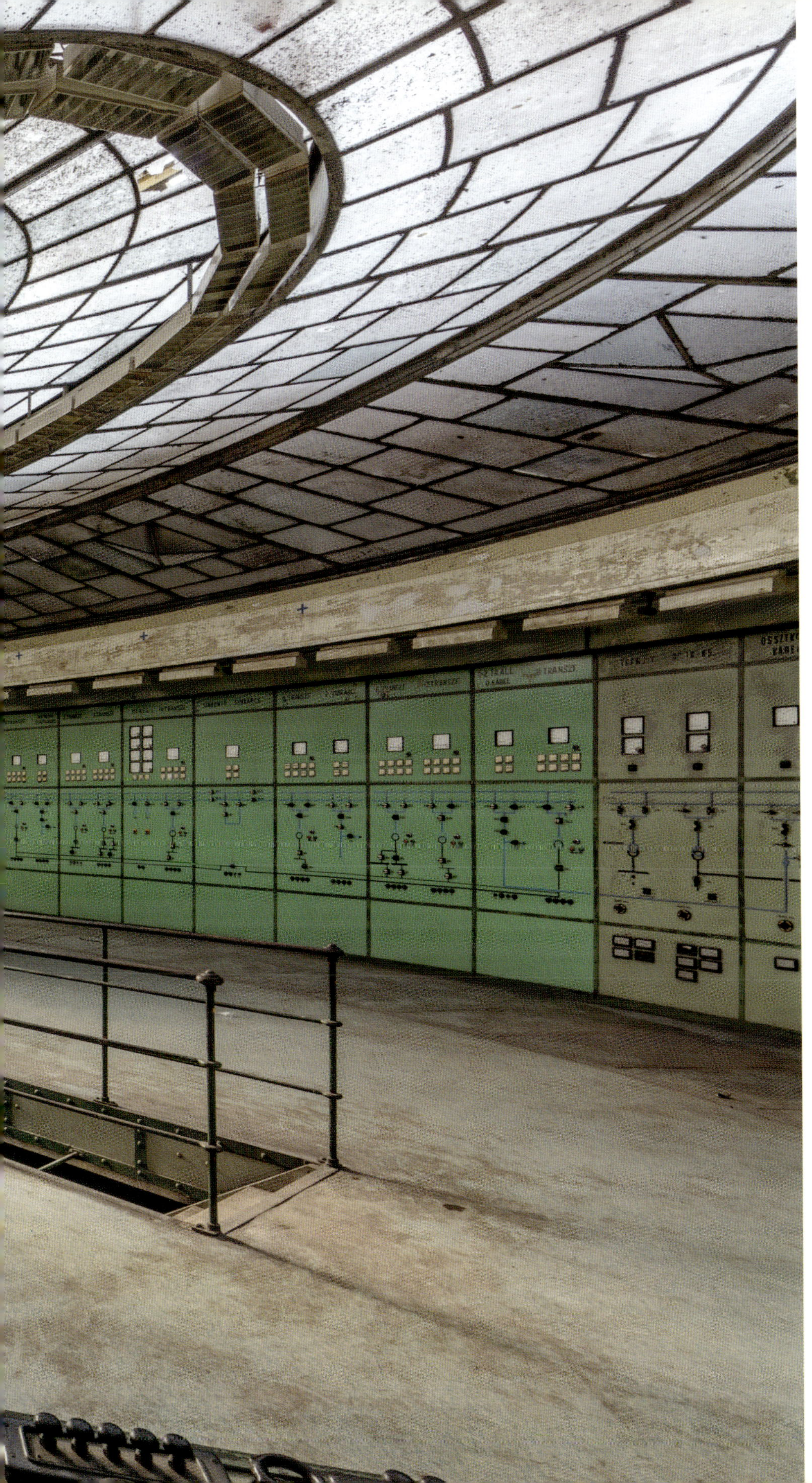

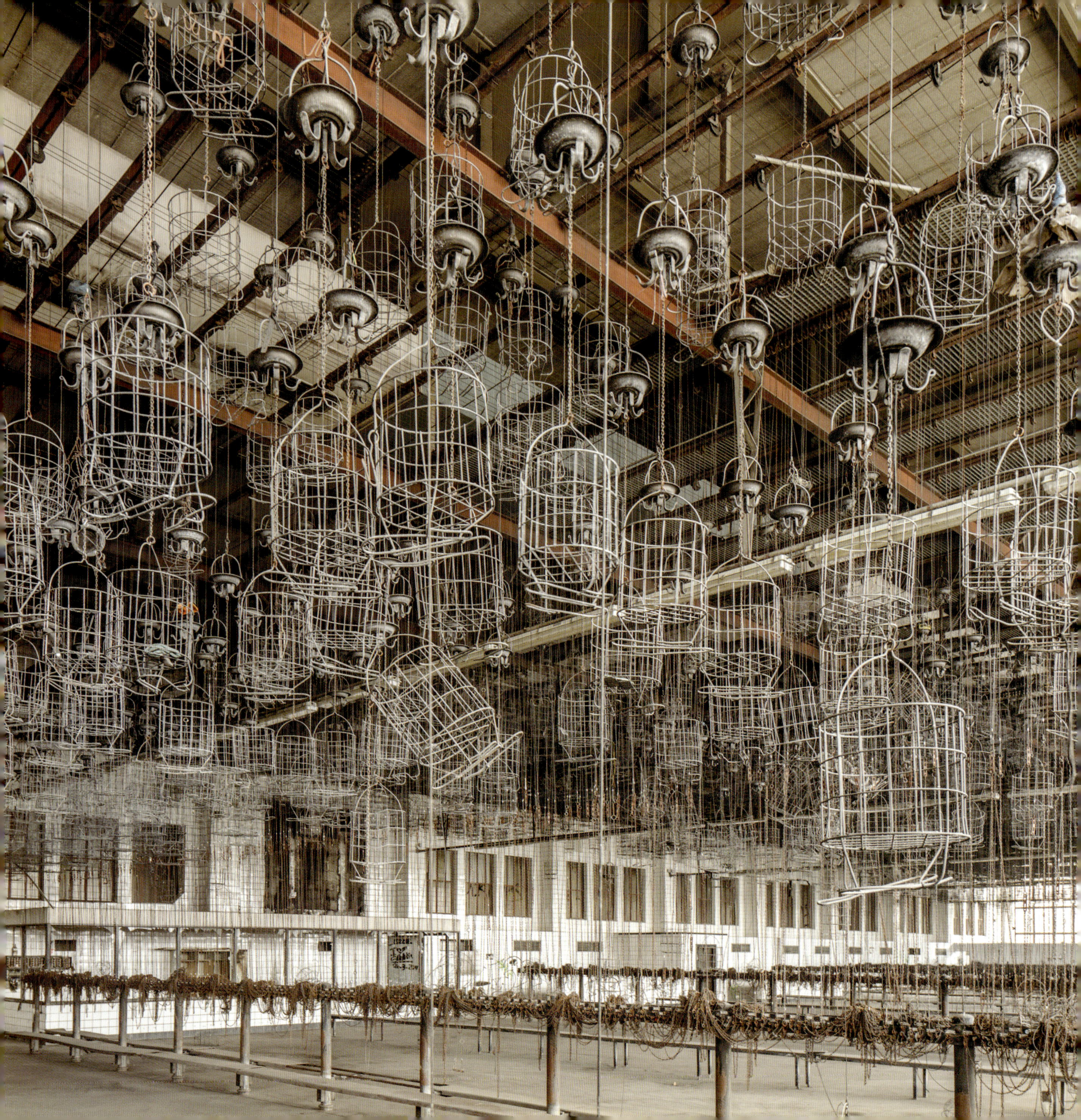

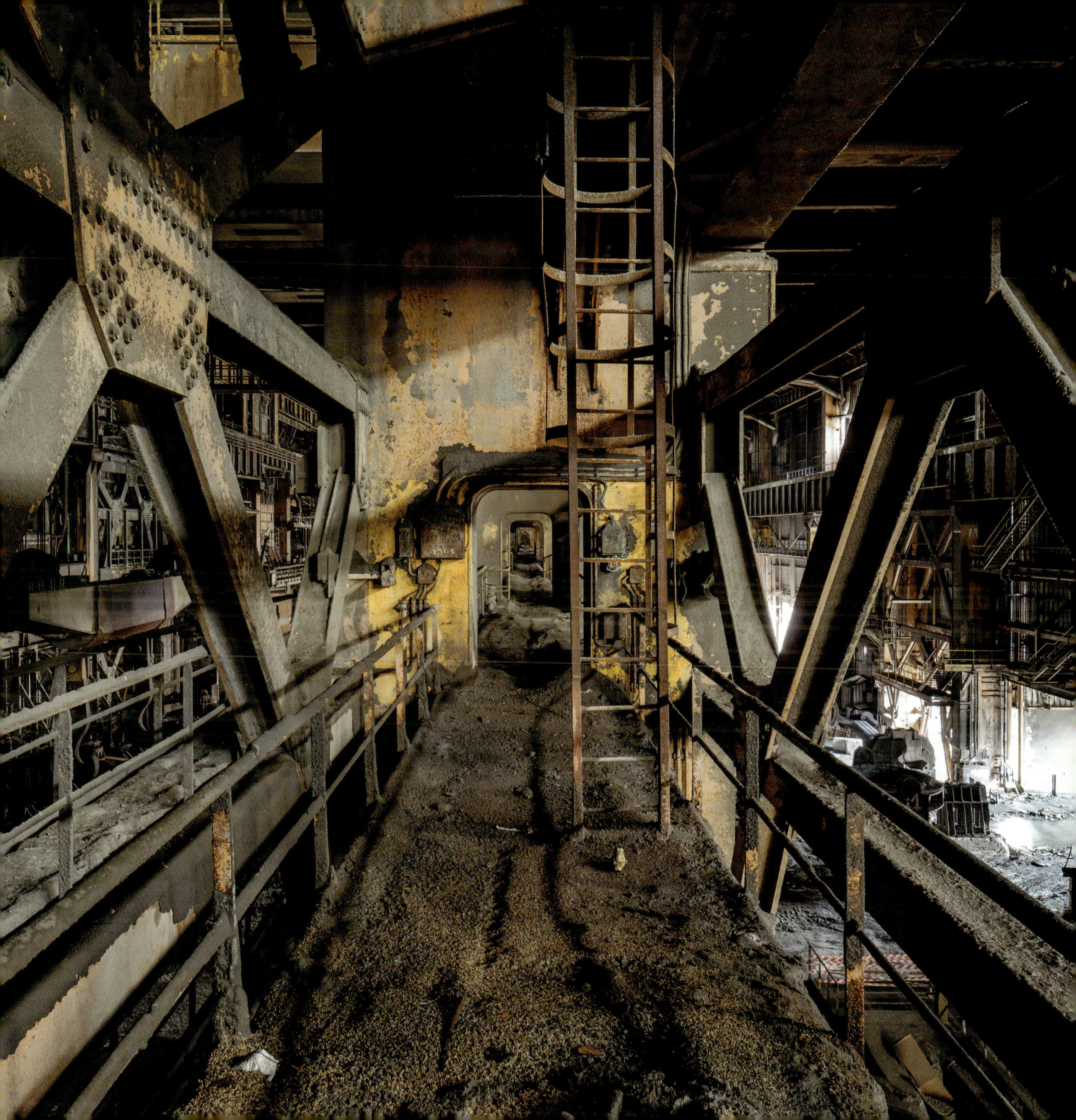

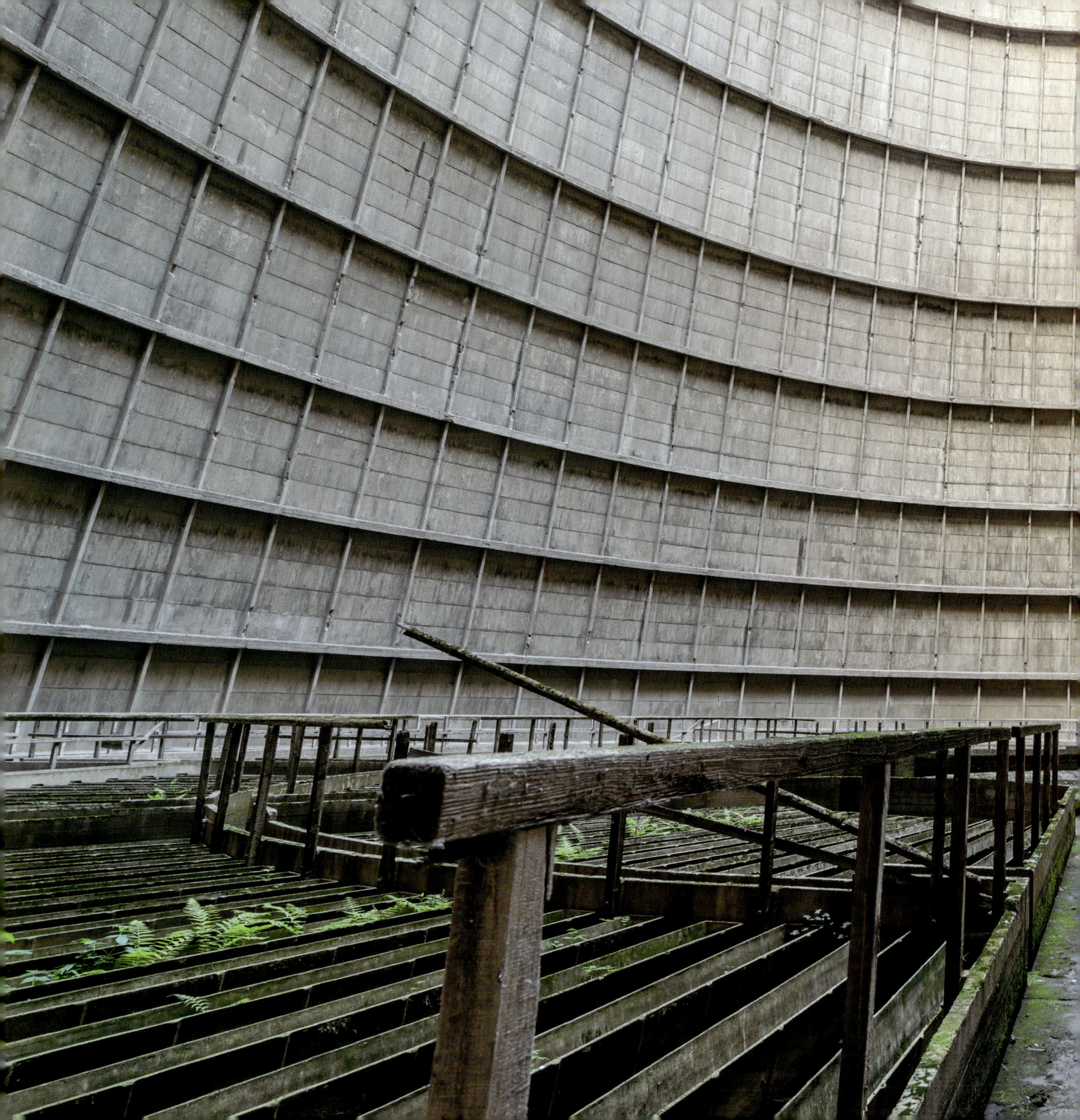

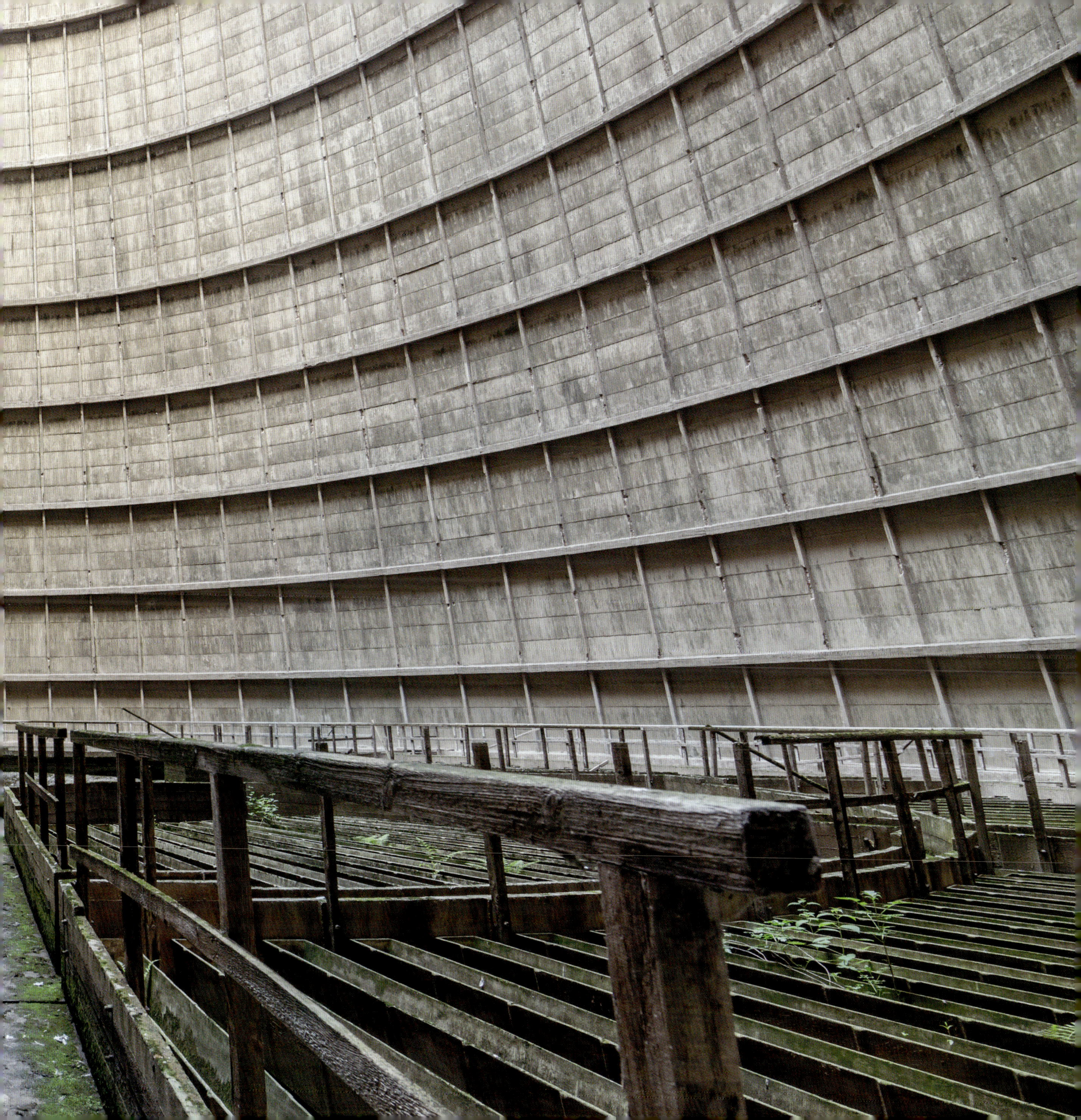

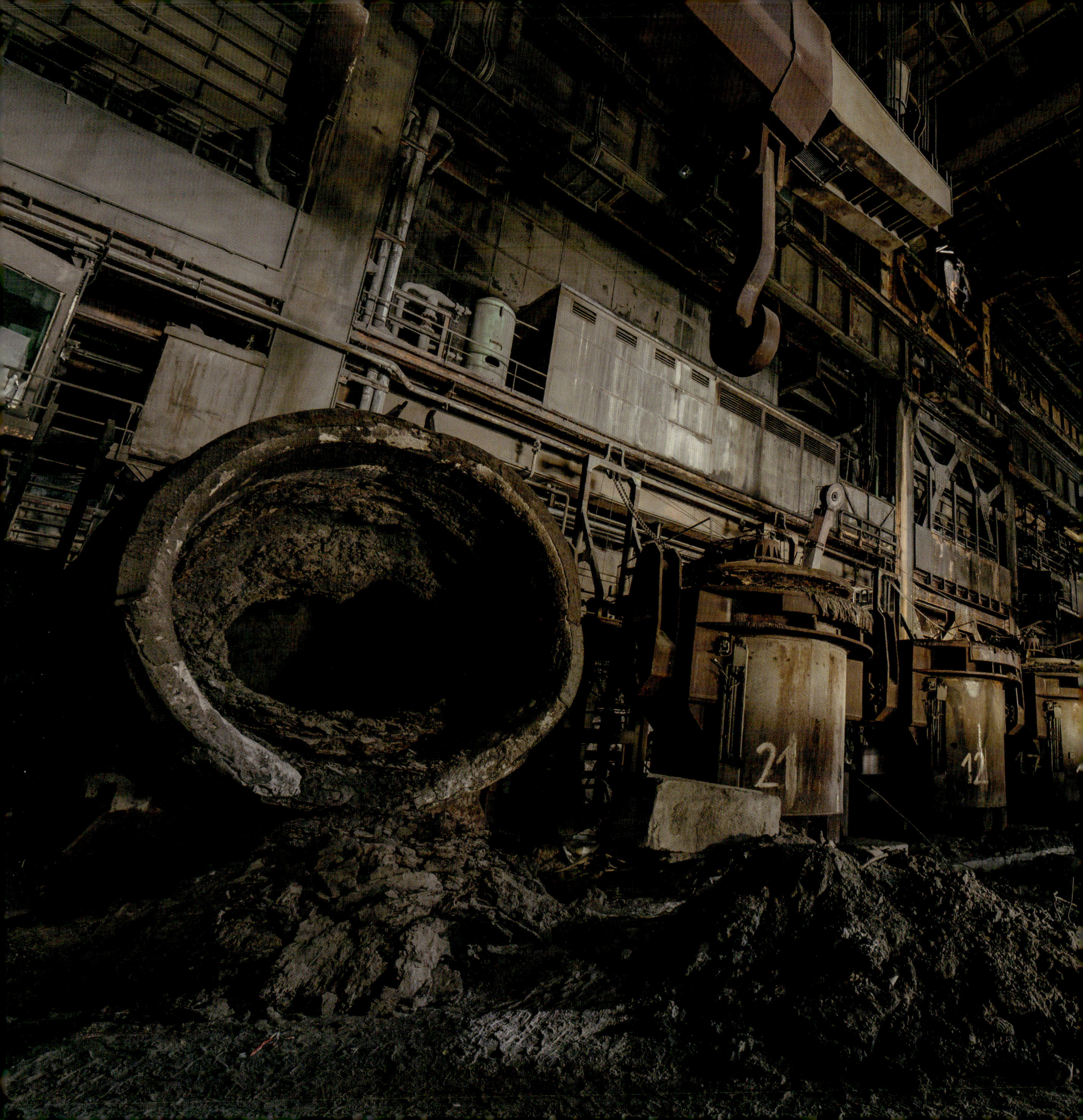

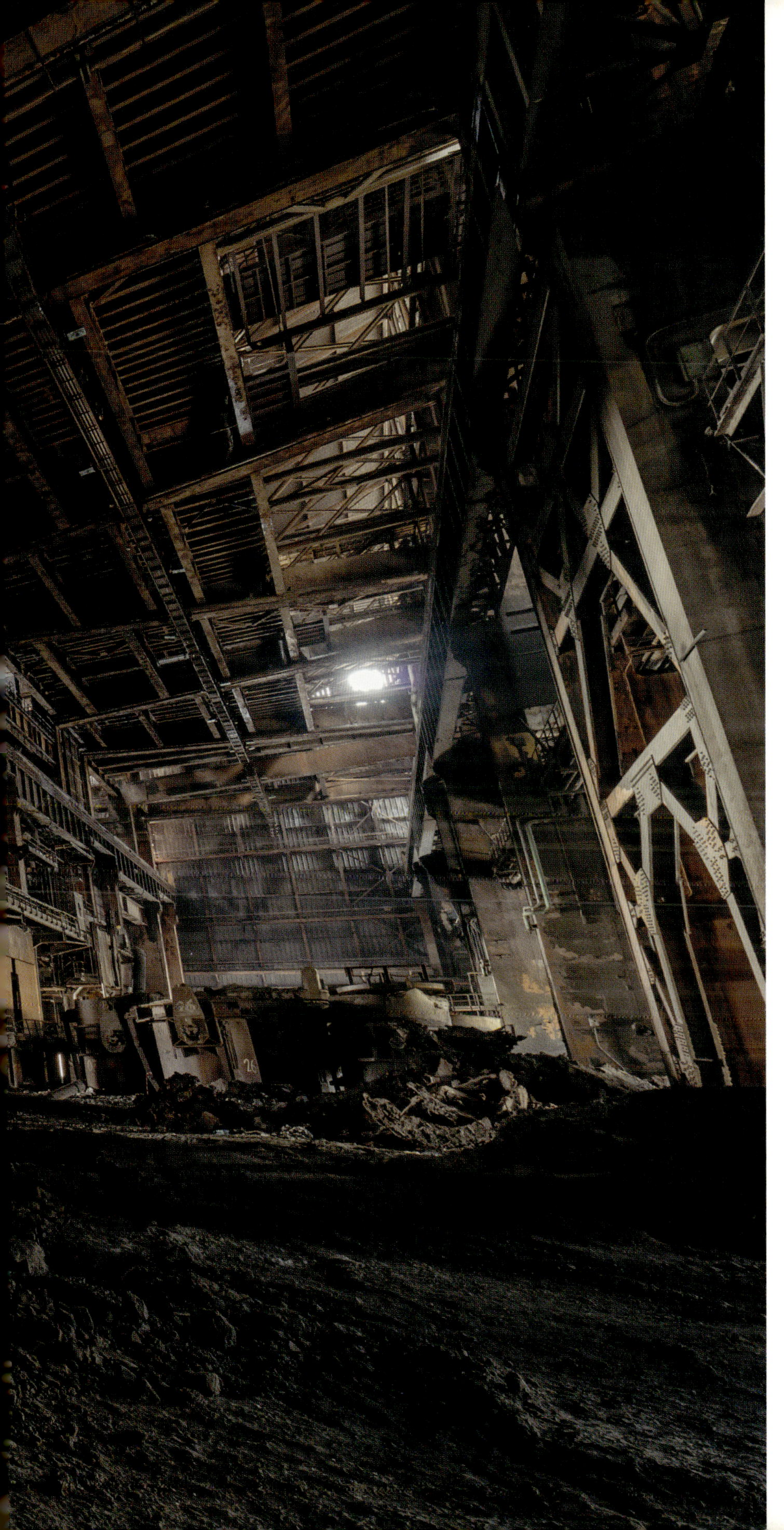

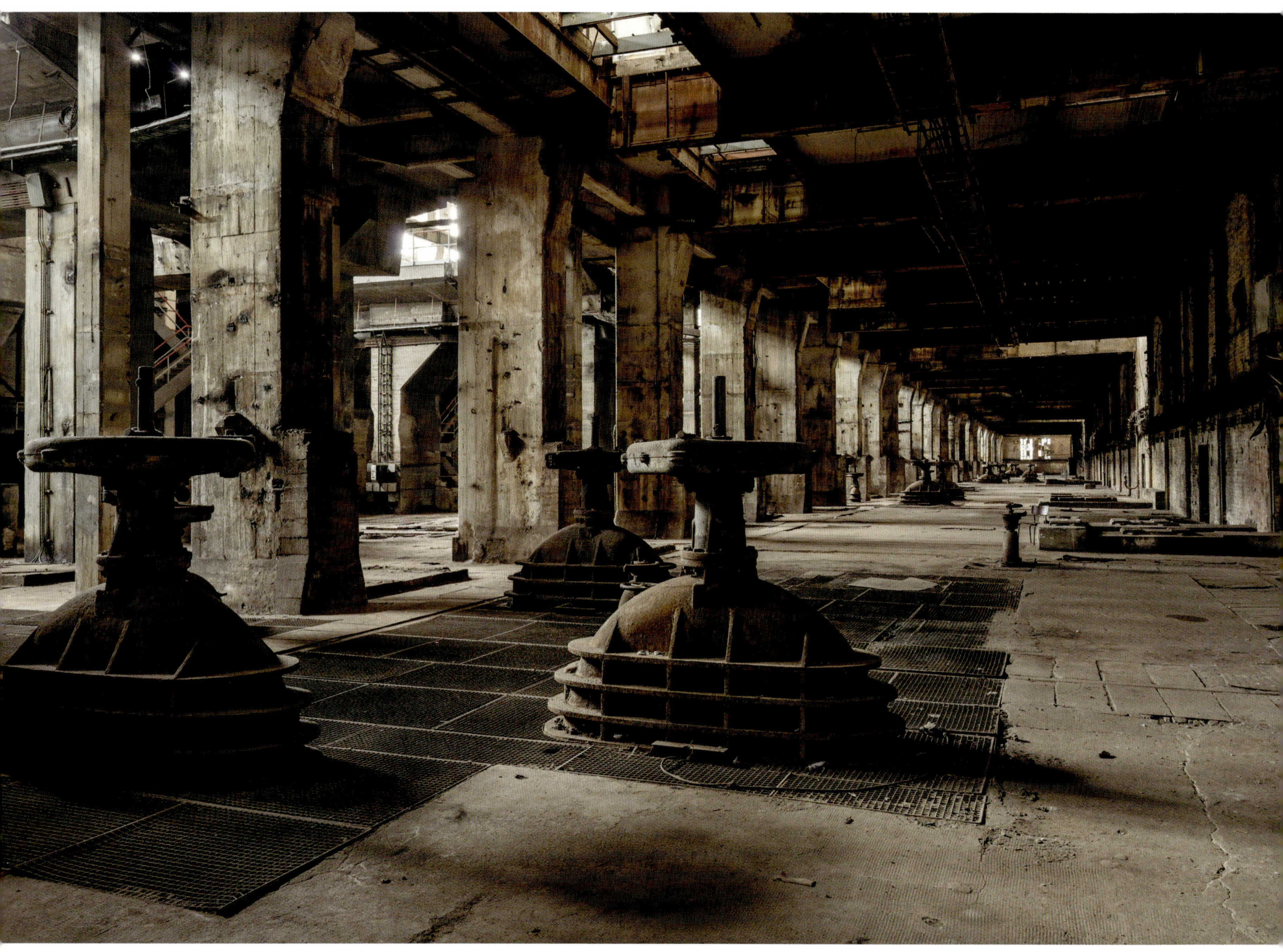

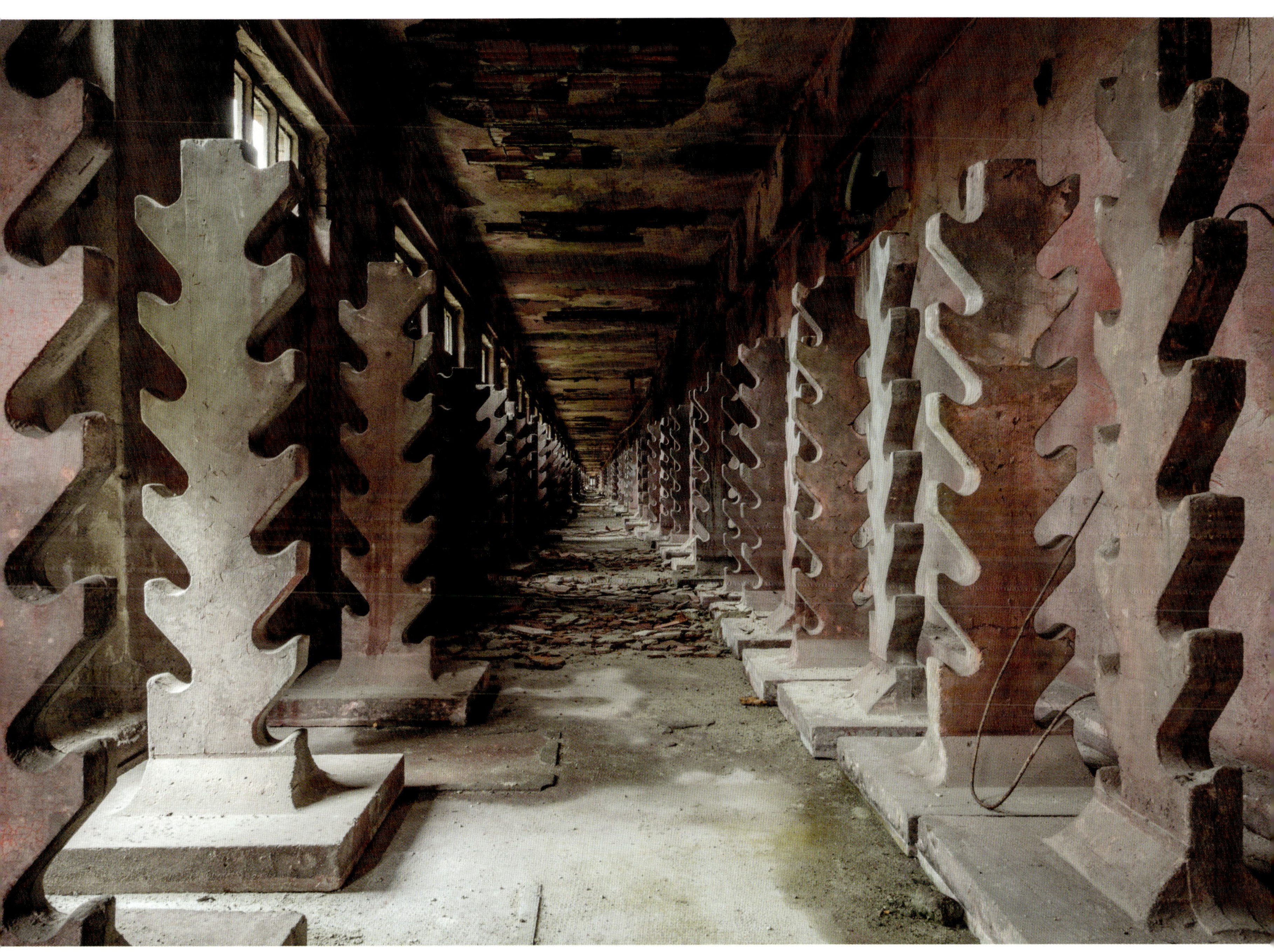

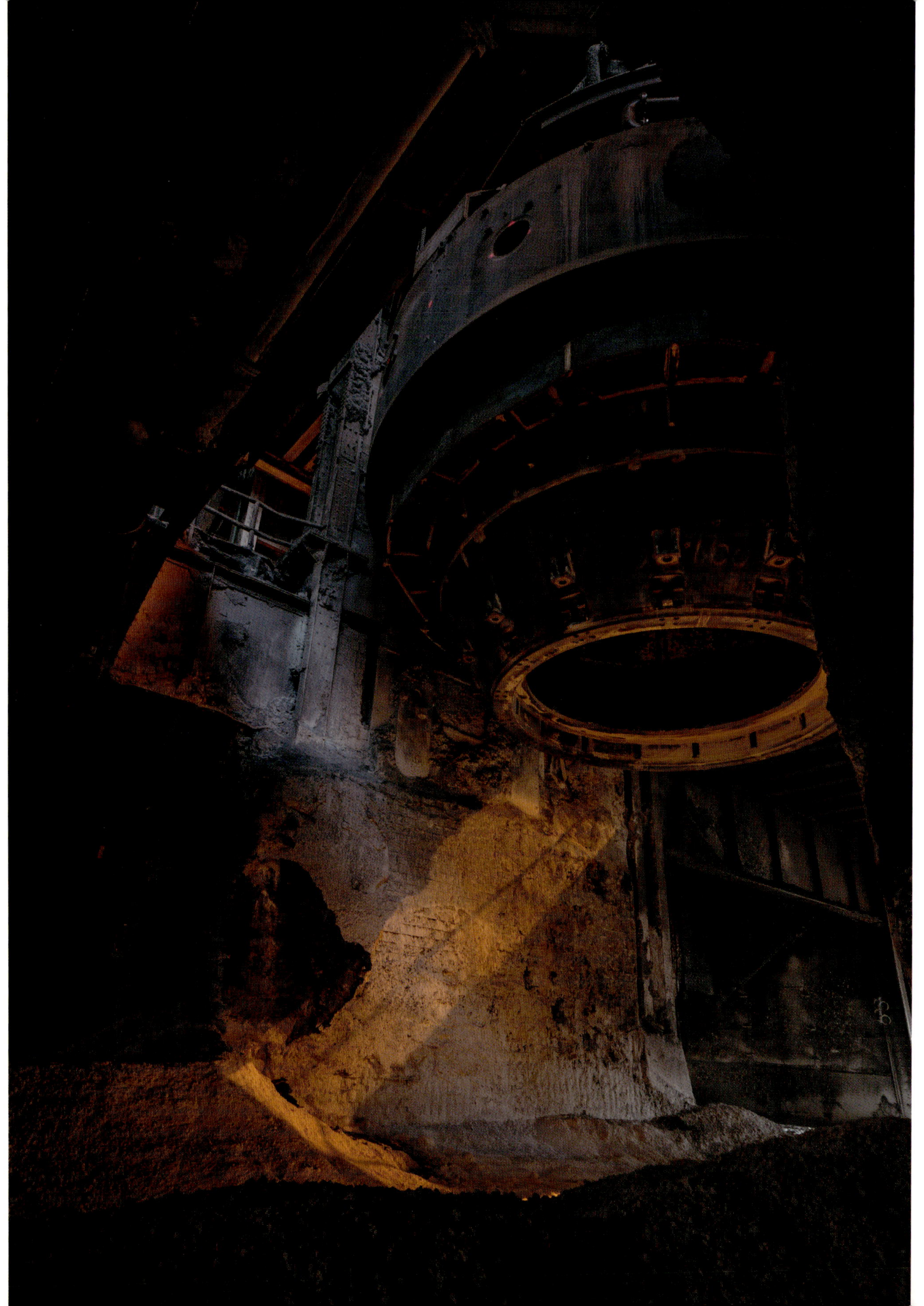

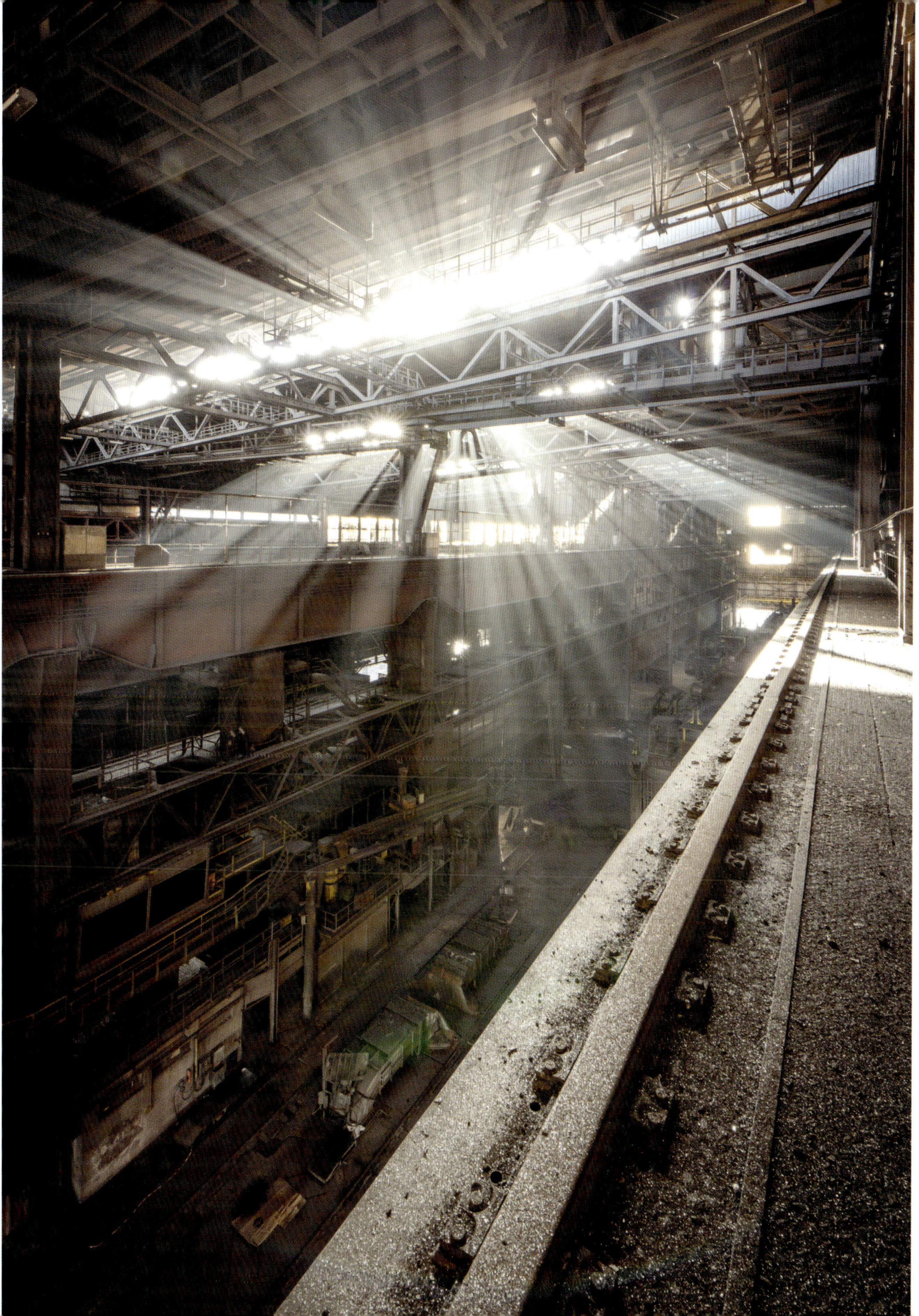

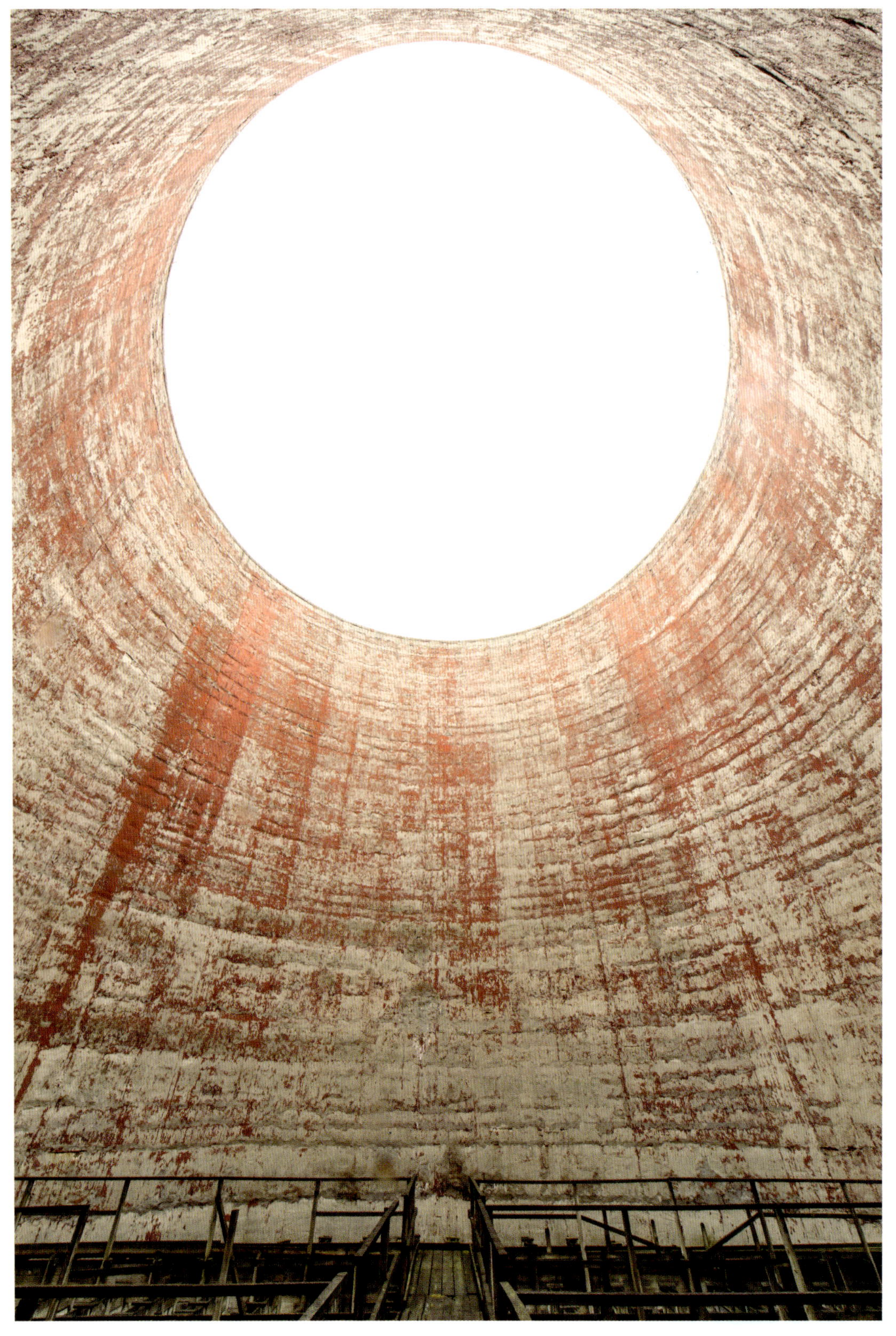

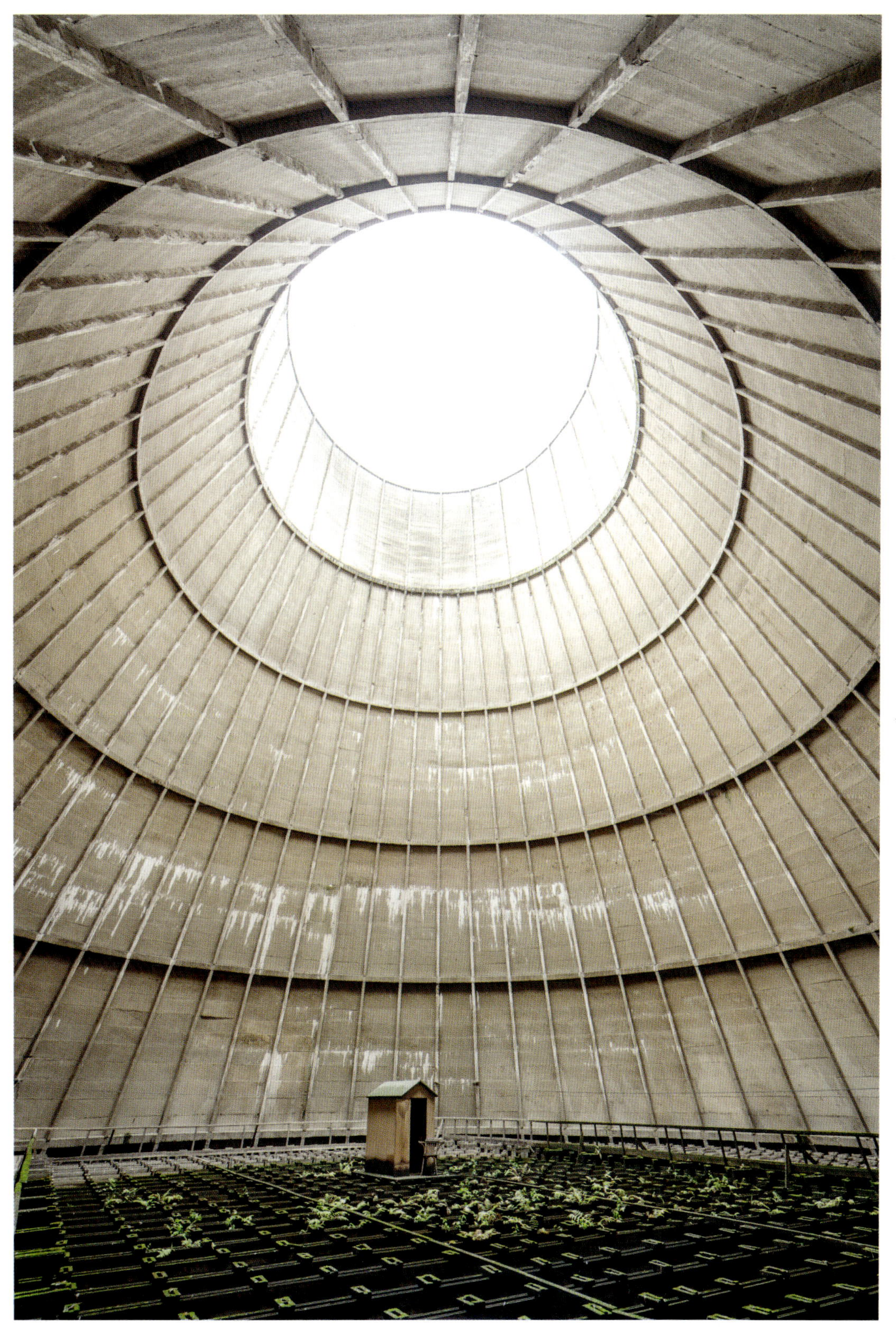

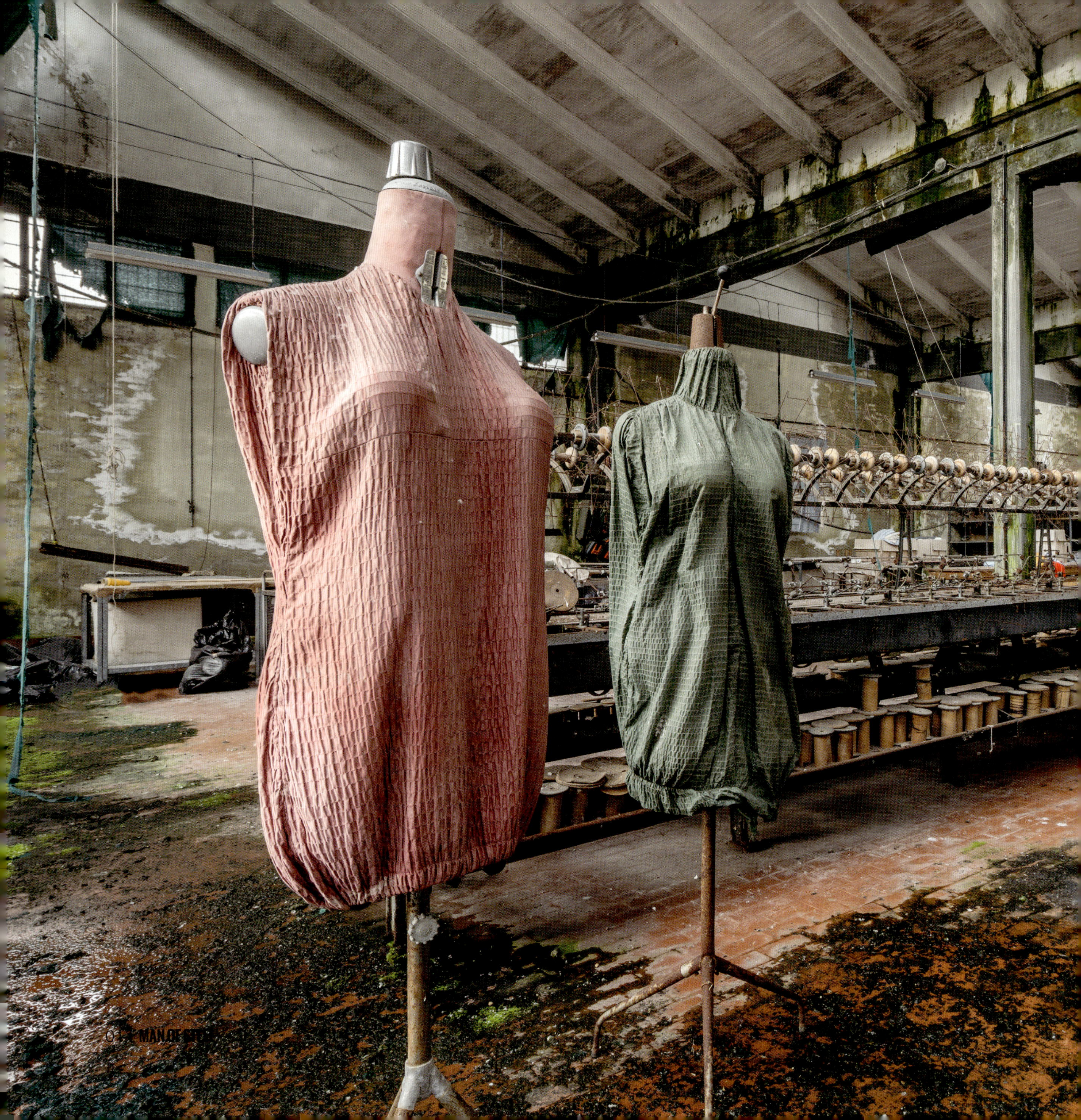
MAN OF STEEL

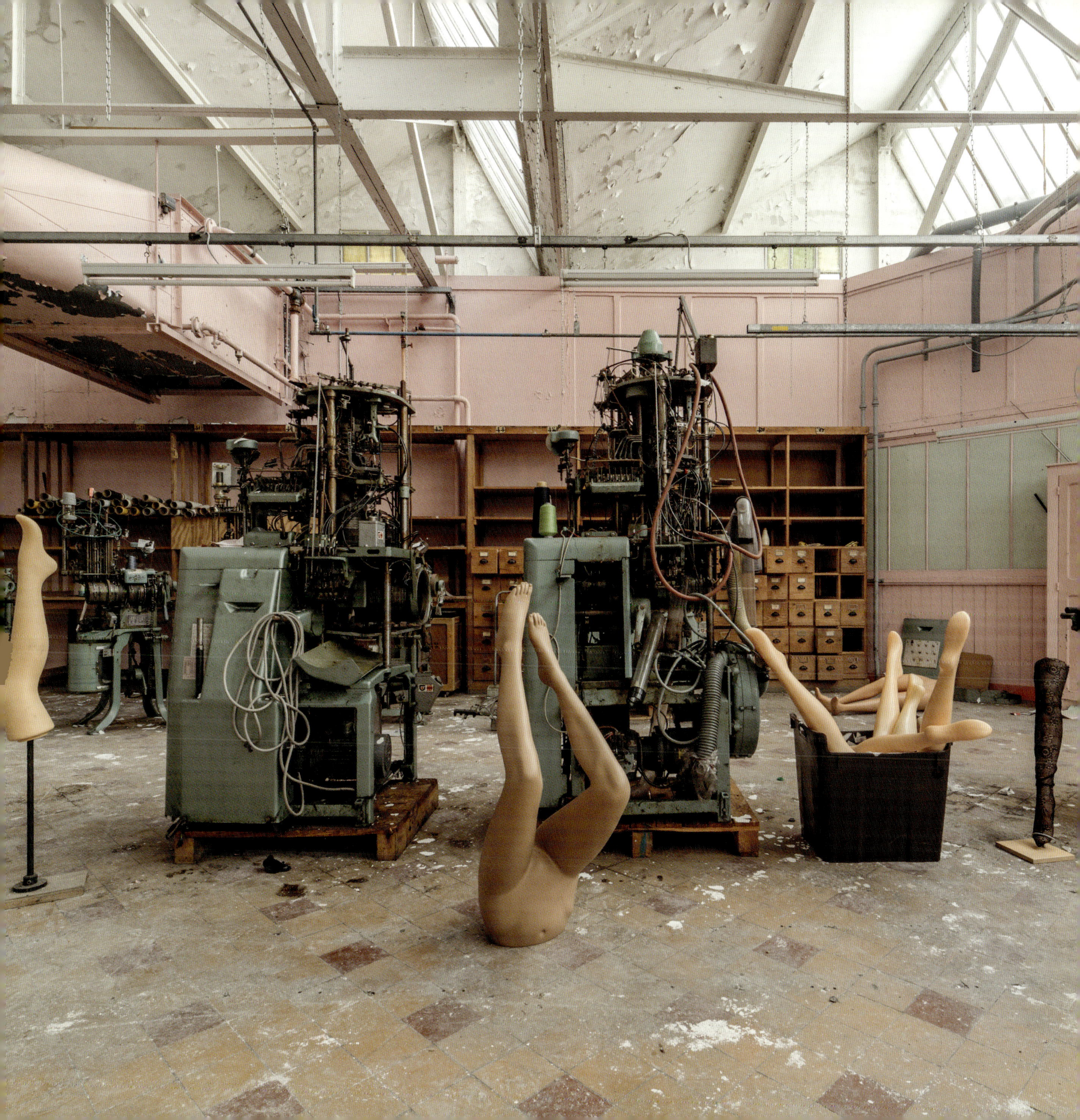

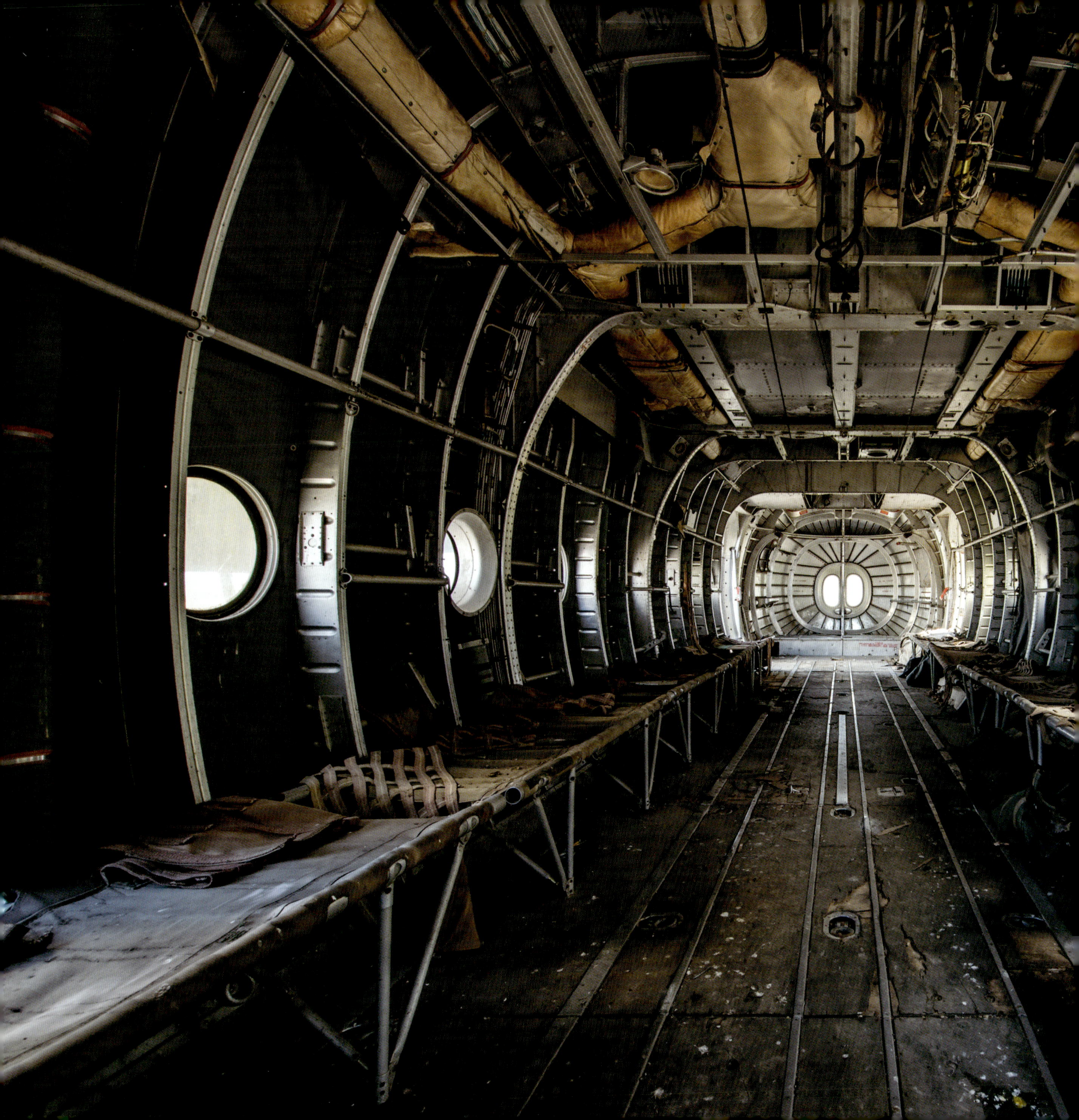

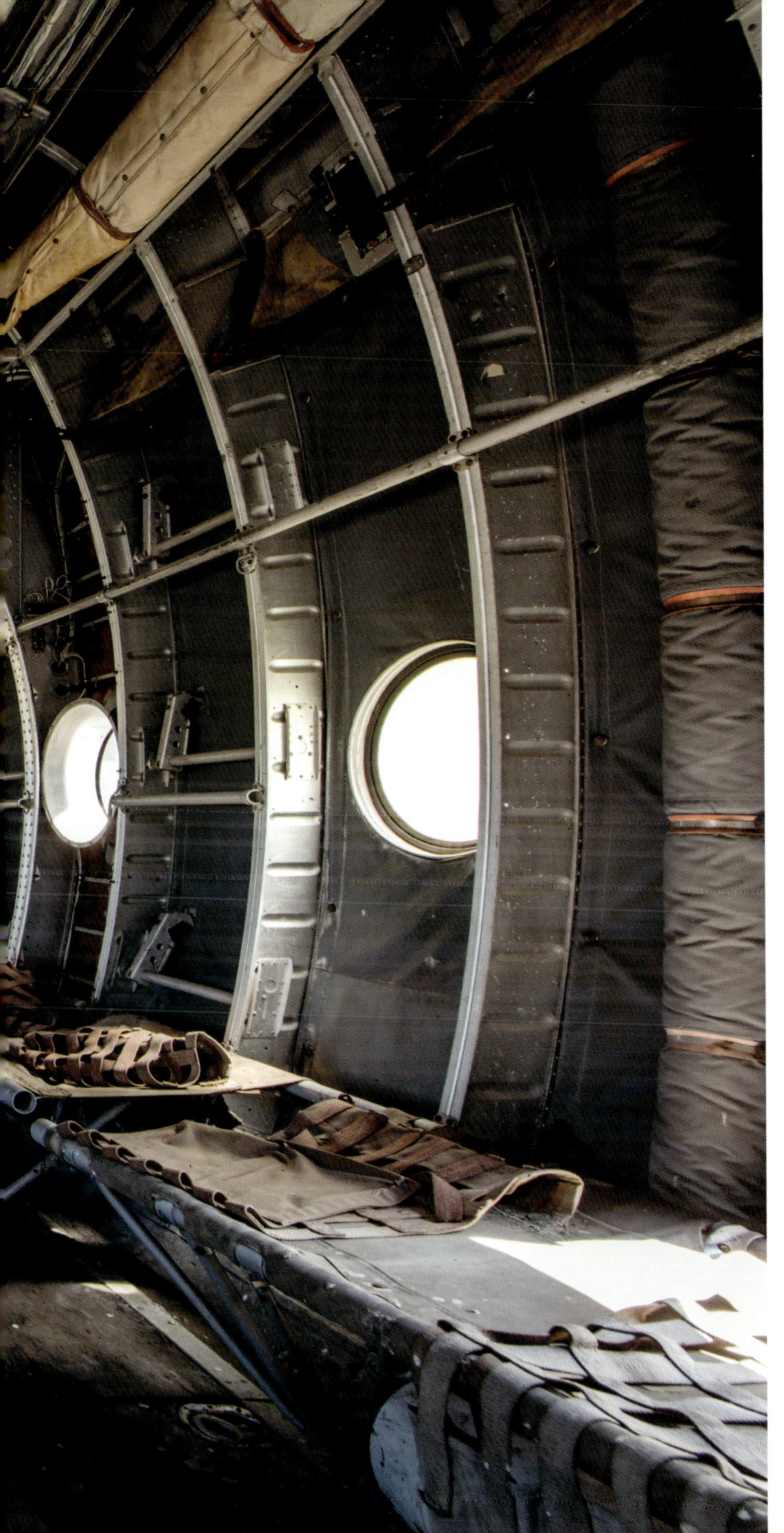

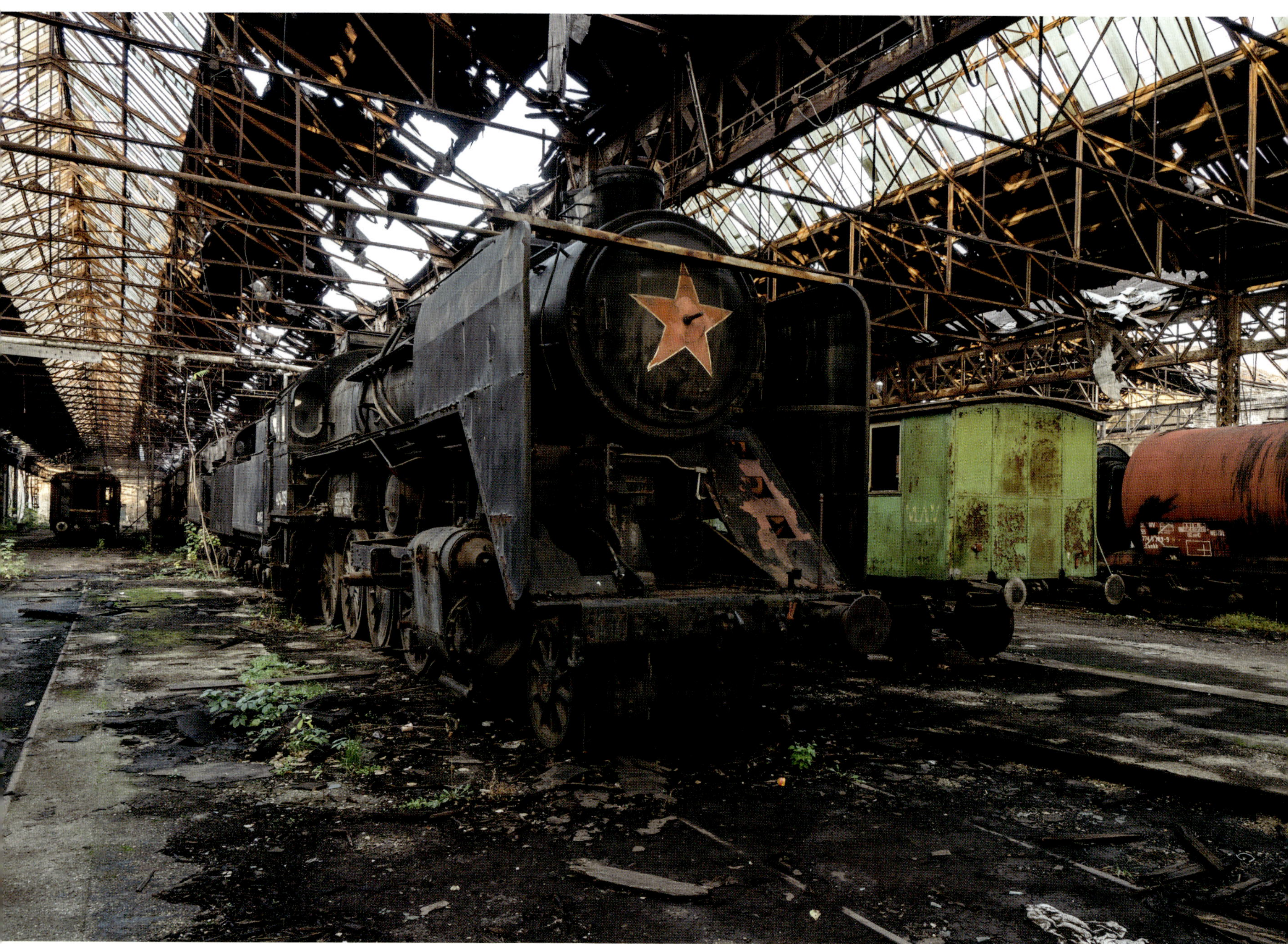

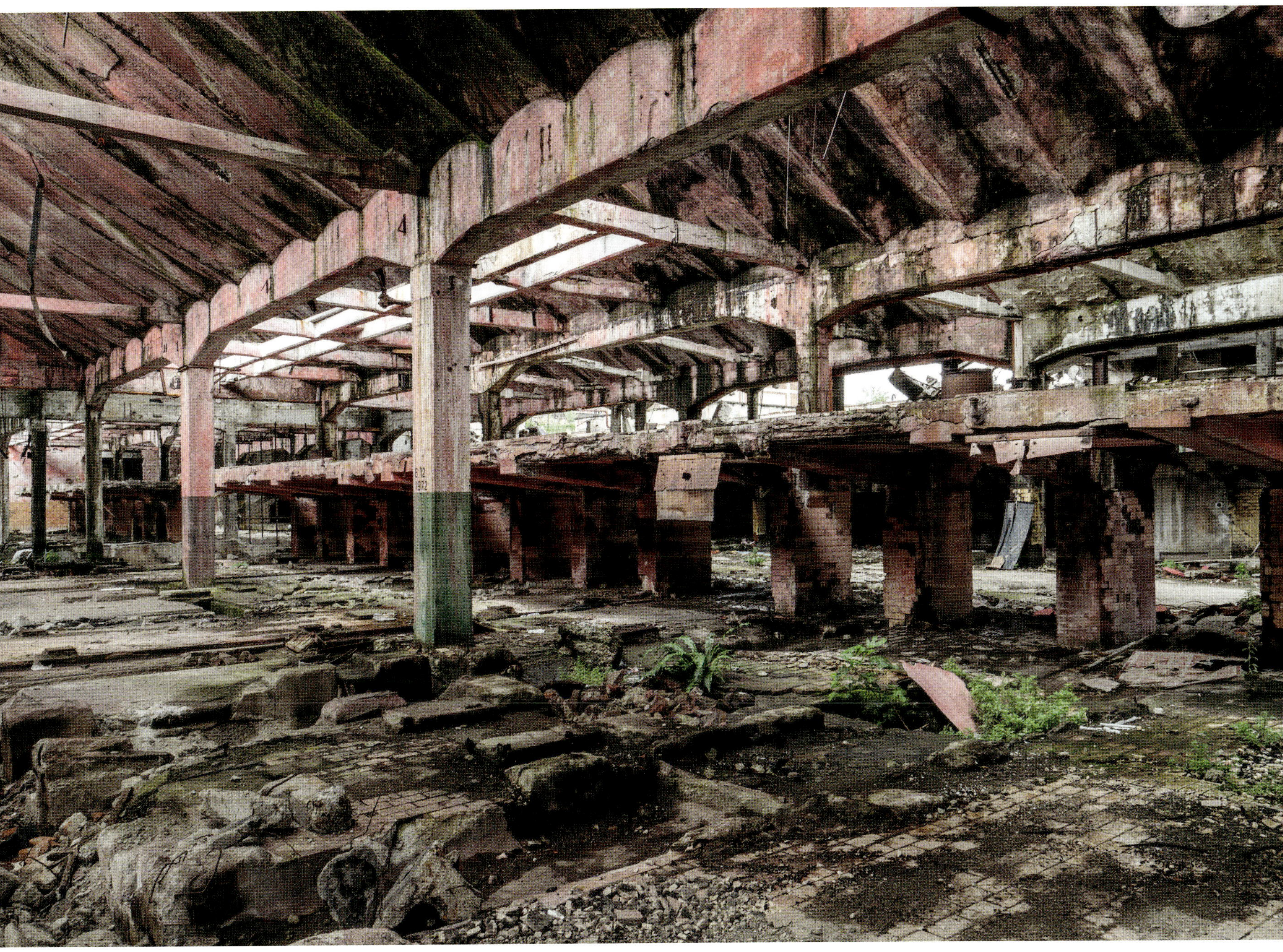

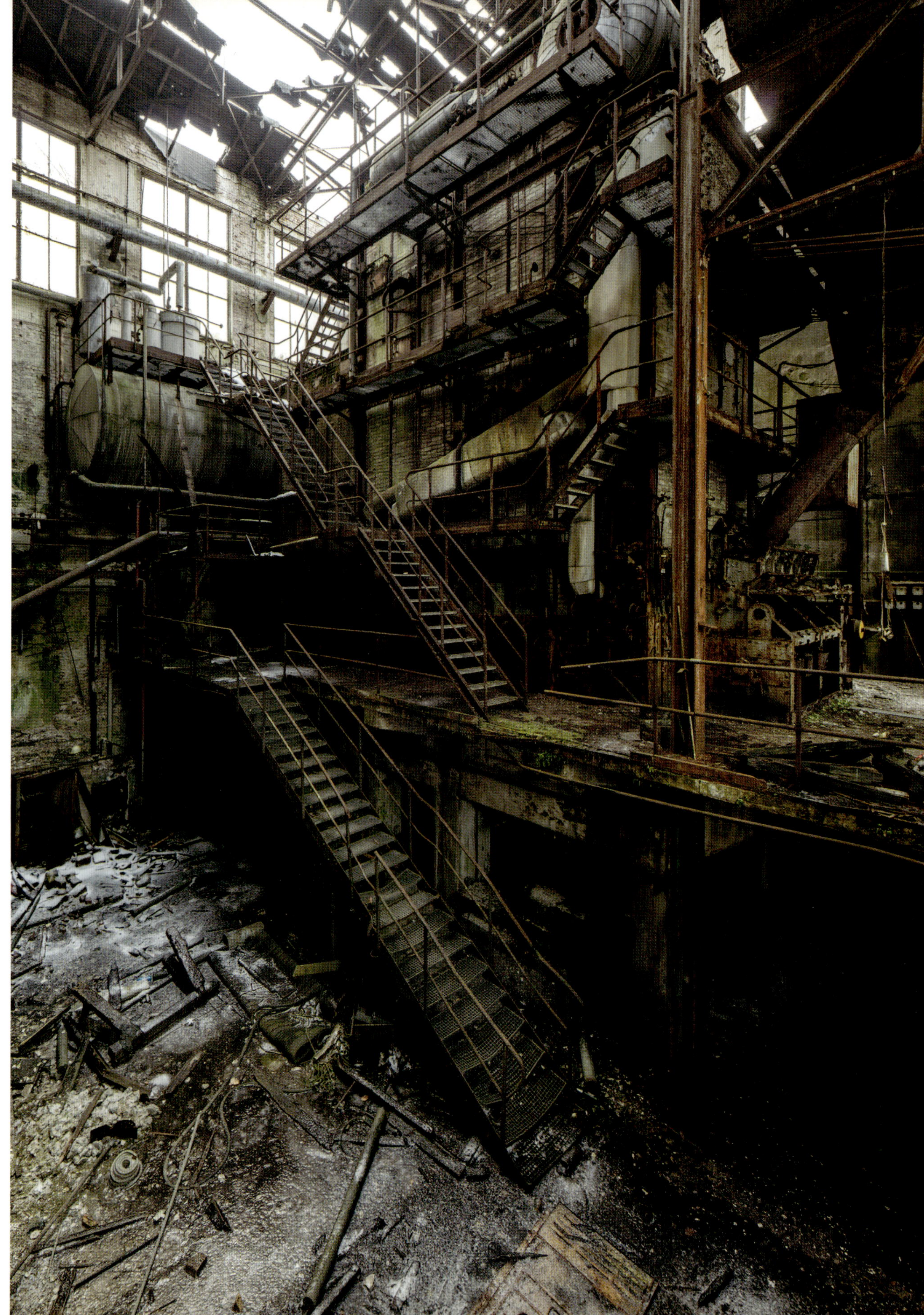

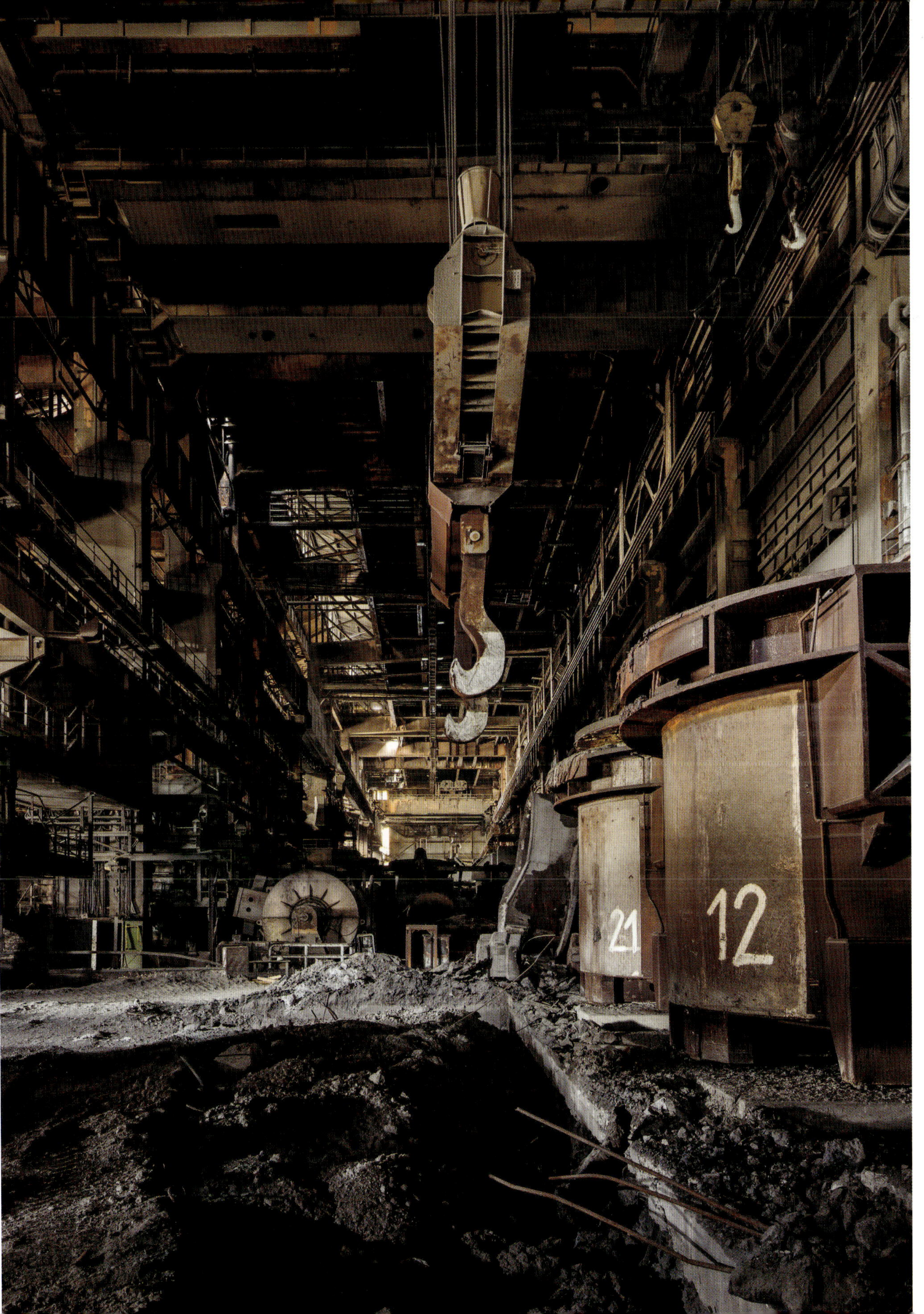

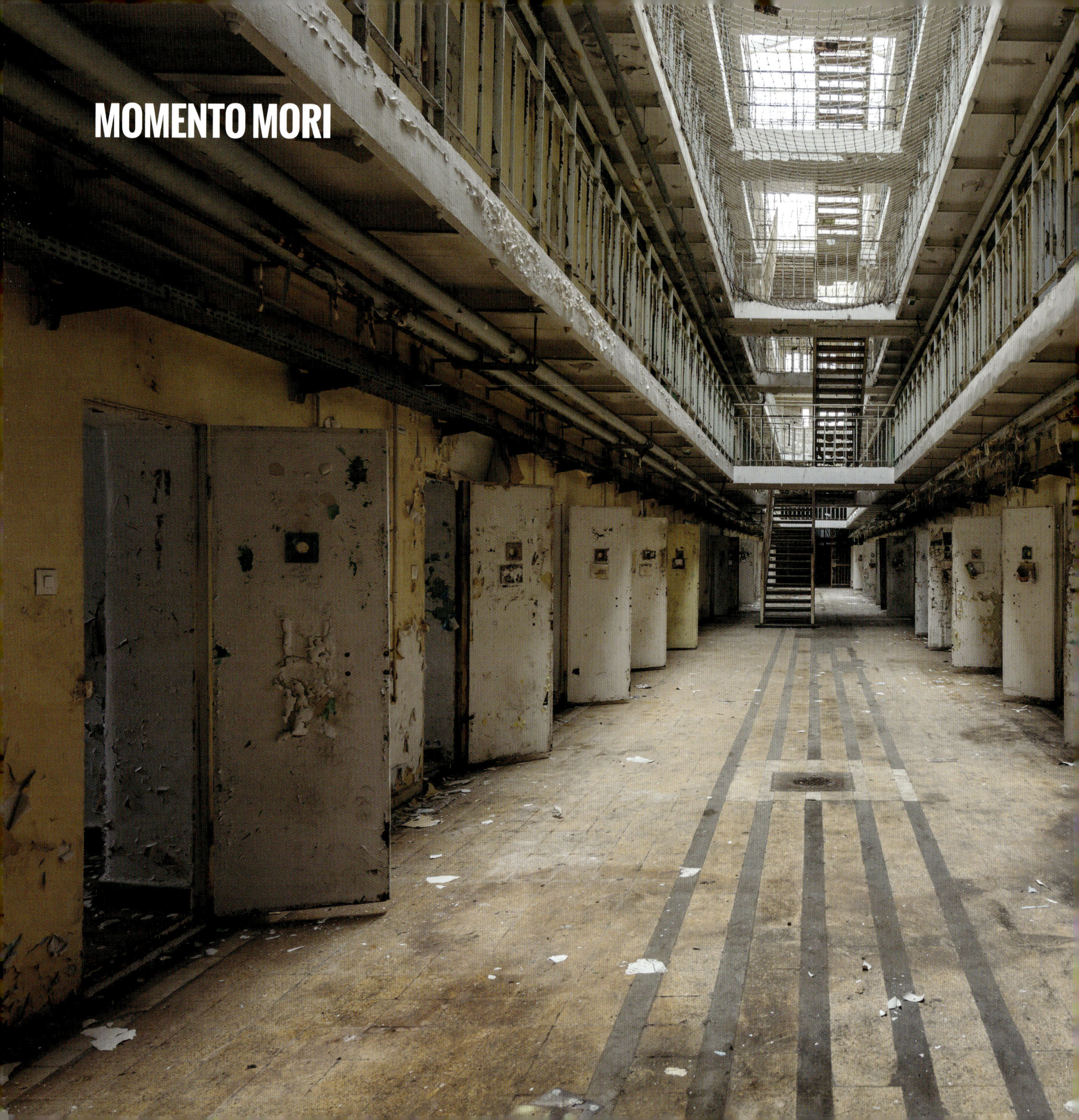
MOMENTO MORI

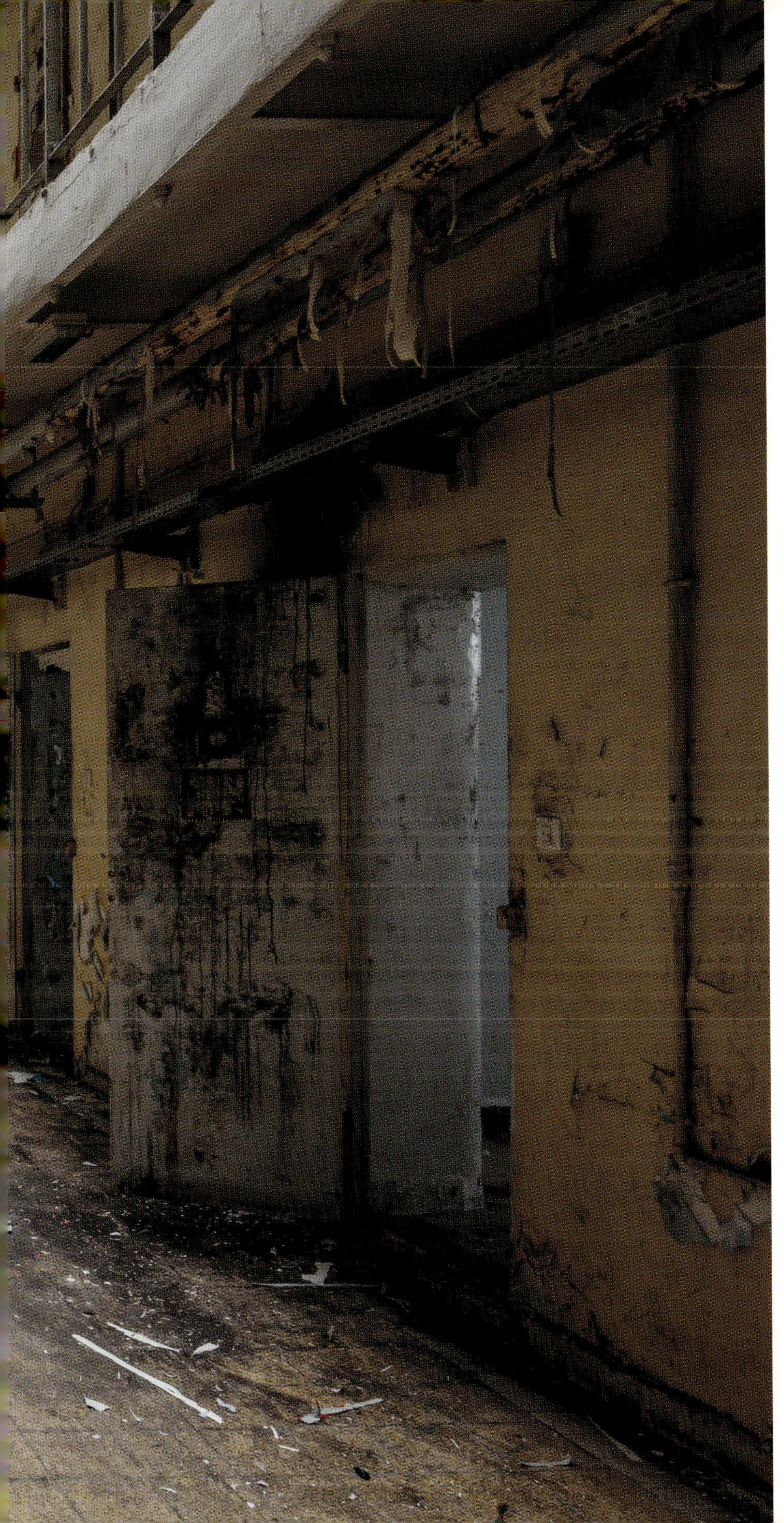

The famous "Memento Mori" in Latin or "Don't forget that you have to die" in English is the religious concept that wants to remind us that we are all mortal and that in the end, we are all going to die.

This spiritual theory has been very popular through time, especially during the middle ages, but it was the Greeks who first introduced this theme. They thought, humans should make the most of each day because tomorrow we might die. Then, during the middle ages, Christians reclaimed and developed this concept in a completely different way. They gave it a moralistic meaning where luxury and pleasures are considered ephemeral compared to the eternity of death and that people should focus on the importance of God and the afterlife in their everyday life so they are not tempted to sin.

Symbolized by the skull, and occasionally by a faded flower, the Memento Mori paintings were depicted as still life in the vanity movement and were pretty popular for artists. All of them wanted to capture death and time in their work. You can often find examples of Memento Mori symbolism in crypt architecture. The Memento Mori was also an important theme in English and French literature during the 17th Century.

Of course, today, the "Memento Mori" perception has completely changed and is defined by a new definition closer to the original Greek thinking. If it was a sign of faith before, it is more now linked to the hedonist point of view. Remember that you have to die one day so enjoy each day like it's the last. This is perhaps how we see the "Carpe Diem" Memento Mori these days. Skulls are now used more as cool art or marketing symbols rather than religious ones.

The fascination for abandoned buildings can be related to the "Memento Mori" concept in the sense that I believe these places today are our own Memento Mori. If before, culture was spread by art and literature, it is now different, we had to create our own Memento Mori adapted to our society. If people need to see how things will look after their death, it means that they are aware of their mortality. They are reminded by looking at my photographs to see what will happen, and therefore are able to feel how to enjoy the time they have left.

At the same time, we are witnessing a similar current in modern culture. Whether it's in movies; video games or books, a lot of art forms are concerned with the future of mankind. For example, the English series "Utopia", the movies "Batman Begins", "Kingsman" or "Twelve Monkeys", the book "The Road" by Cormac McCarthy (among many others) have the main themes of decadence, corruption and the end of humanity. Mankind had a chance but now they have ruined the planet. The villain's role is to create a genocide killing most of the people on earth, to create a new world and a new order where he would be capable of building a new way of living. These too are the new Memento Mori of our society.

That's why the connection between death and humanity interests me so much and why this part of the book is focused on it. Churches, morgues, crematorium, hospitals, prisons… All these locations have a special link with death. The place we die for sure, but also the place where we are sick and hope to get better, where we pray for a better life, for guidance or where we bury our loved ones. Where people are locked up for years and imagine what could have been their life outside the walls, or the place where soldiers trained and lived not knowing if they were going to see their family again. So when you observe them in a state of dereliction, it reinforces the sensation of death and its imminent arrival.

HAUNTING

I believe it is important at this point to touch on the matter of ghosts or spirits that are often related to these places we love to imagine haunted. Some will believe in ghosts, many won't, and more will believe in something in-between depending on a specific location, history or rumour.

We don't all have the same image of what a ghost is. It might be for some the spirit of the person who lived there or it could also be a presence that is felt around you. Many religions or cultures have their own definition for that. But we can all agree on one thing: We have all felt this kind of presence in these abandon places.

The fact that these sites are connected to death more directly than the others can easily heighten our emotions and make us more predisposed to our own imagination. But I don't think knowing if ghosts are real or not is the essential point here. The point is we can imagine what these lost souls must have endured between these walls. Whether it's a prison, a hospital or church, our imagination is enough to perceive the emotions carried by it. Just spend five minutes alone in a prison cell and you will feel it immediately.

Above all, photographing these particular derelict locations is a challenge to eternity and to Mother Nature. Each of these photographs is a desperate attempt to put death on hold by finding some traces of humanity in the remains we left behind. It is as if we had created an opposite form of "Memento Mori" to reverse its meaning to suit us. But while they remind us of the vanity of believing that everything will last forever, that it is still standing after all this time; that we can still leave something for the next generations to see.

"There is but one truly serious philosophical problem and that is suicide" said Albert Camus to start his "Myth of Sisyphus" which focuses on the absurd condition of man's life. Does the eternal quest of Man for a meaningful life and truth in a world devoted to God require suicide? No. He thinks the struggle itself can fulfil anybody's life. "One must imagine Sisyphus happy". And that applies for humanity too I guess. Even if we desperately try to believe that mankind will always leave a trace behind, those traces won't last forever, but the act itself of trying is enough to make us feel invincible.

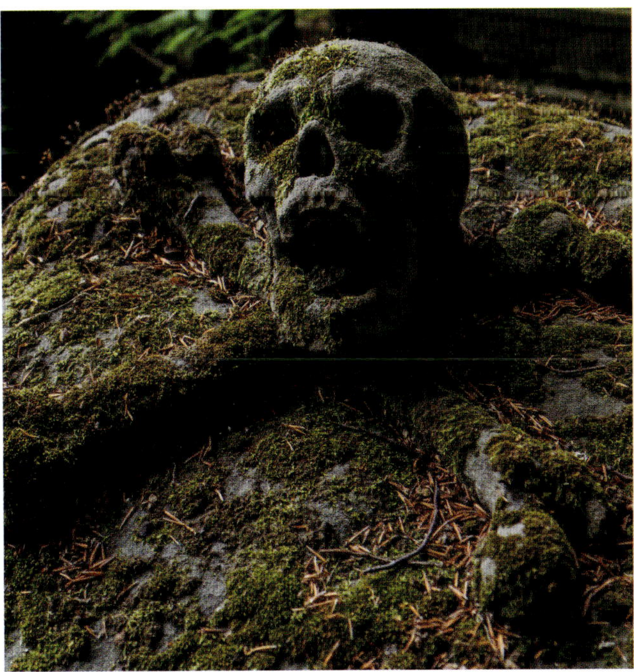

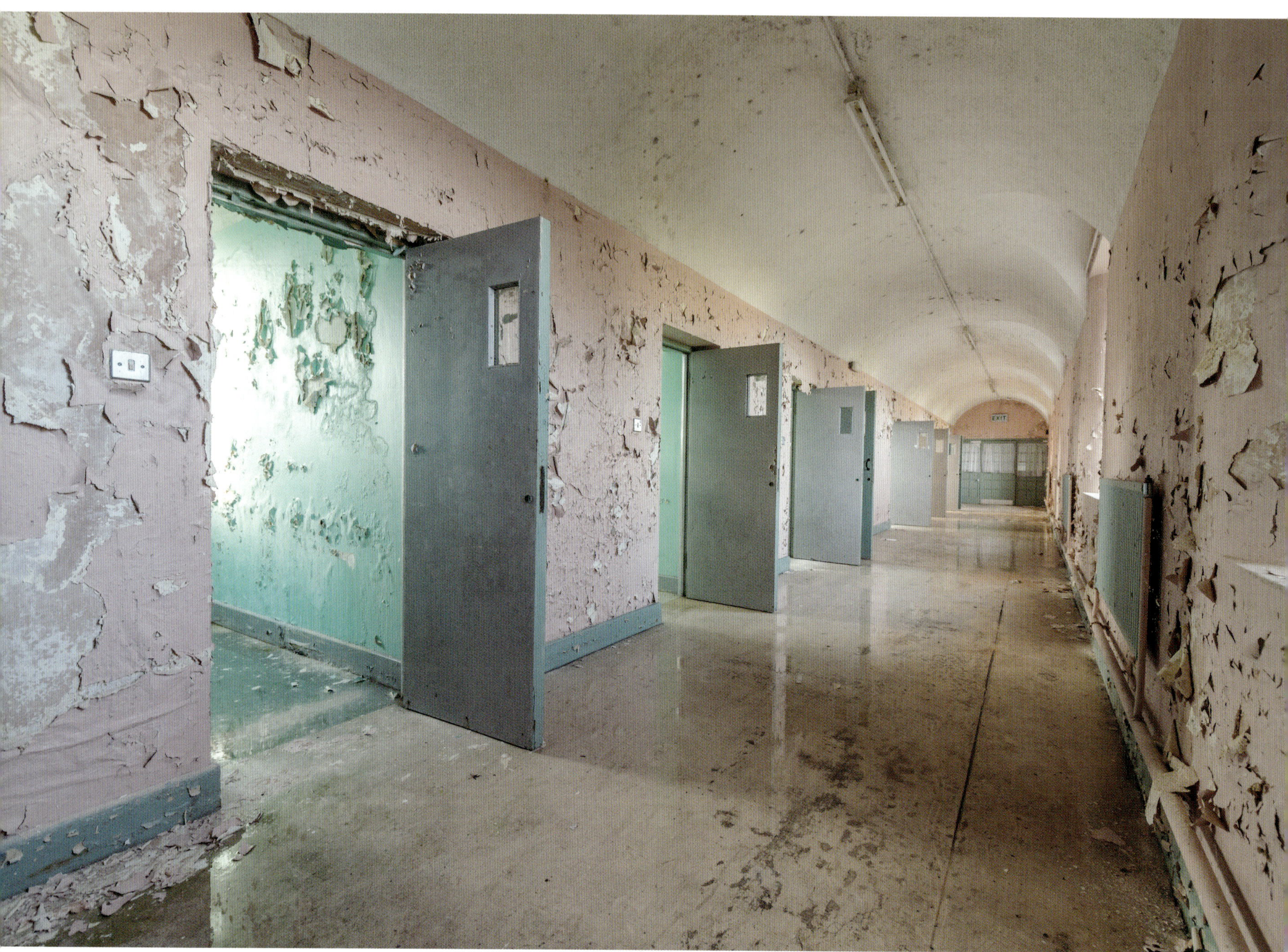

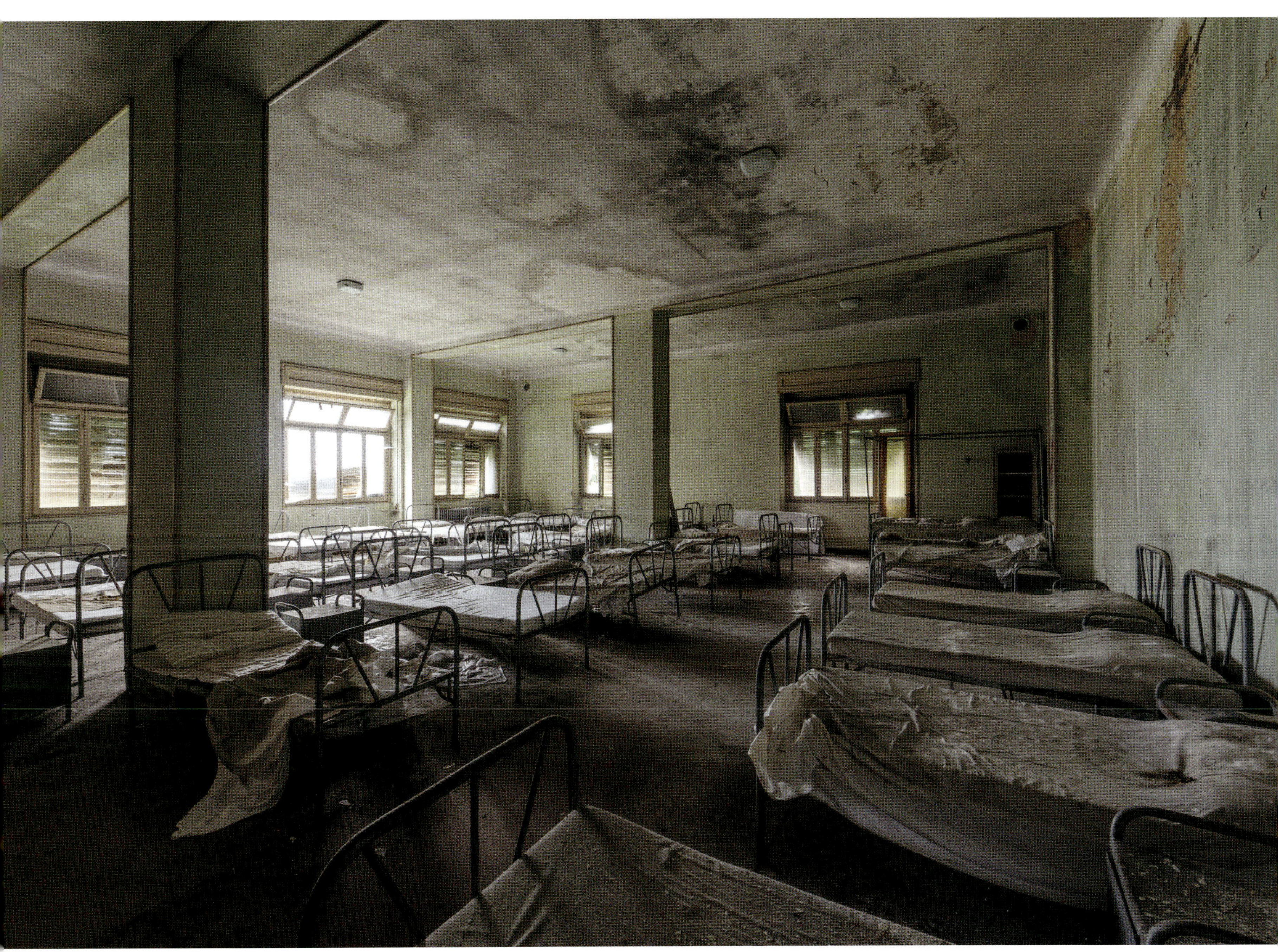

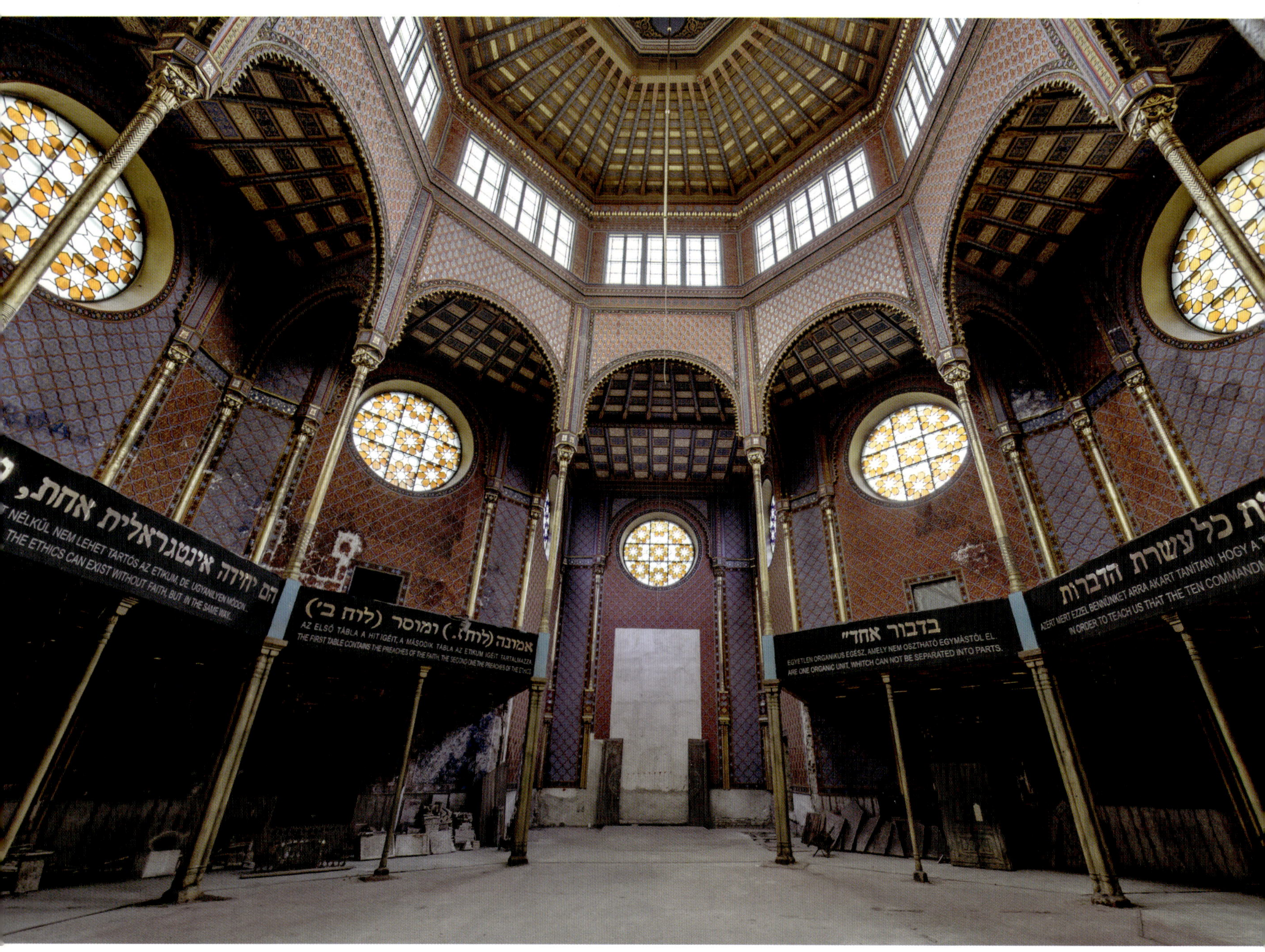
NÉLKÜL NEM LEHET TARTÓS AZ ETIKUM, DE UGYANILYEN MÓDON
THE ETHICS CAN EXIST WITHOUT FAITH, BUT IN THE SAME WAY.
AZ ELSŐ TÁBLA A HIT IGÉIT, A MÁSODIK TÁBLA AZ ETIKUM IGÉIT TARTALMAZZA
THE FIRST TABLE CONTAINS THE PREACHES OF THE FAITH, THE SECOND ONE THE PREACHES OF THE ETHICS
EGYETLEN ORGANIKUS EGÉSZ, AMELY NEM OSZTHATÓ EGYMÁSTÓL EL.
ARE ONE ORGANIC UNIT, WHITCH CAN NOT BE SEPARATED INTO PARTS.
AZÉRT MERT EZZEL BENNÜNKET ARRA AKART TANÍTANI, HOGY A
IN ORDER TO TEACH US THAT THE TEN COMMANDM

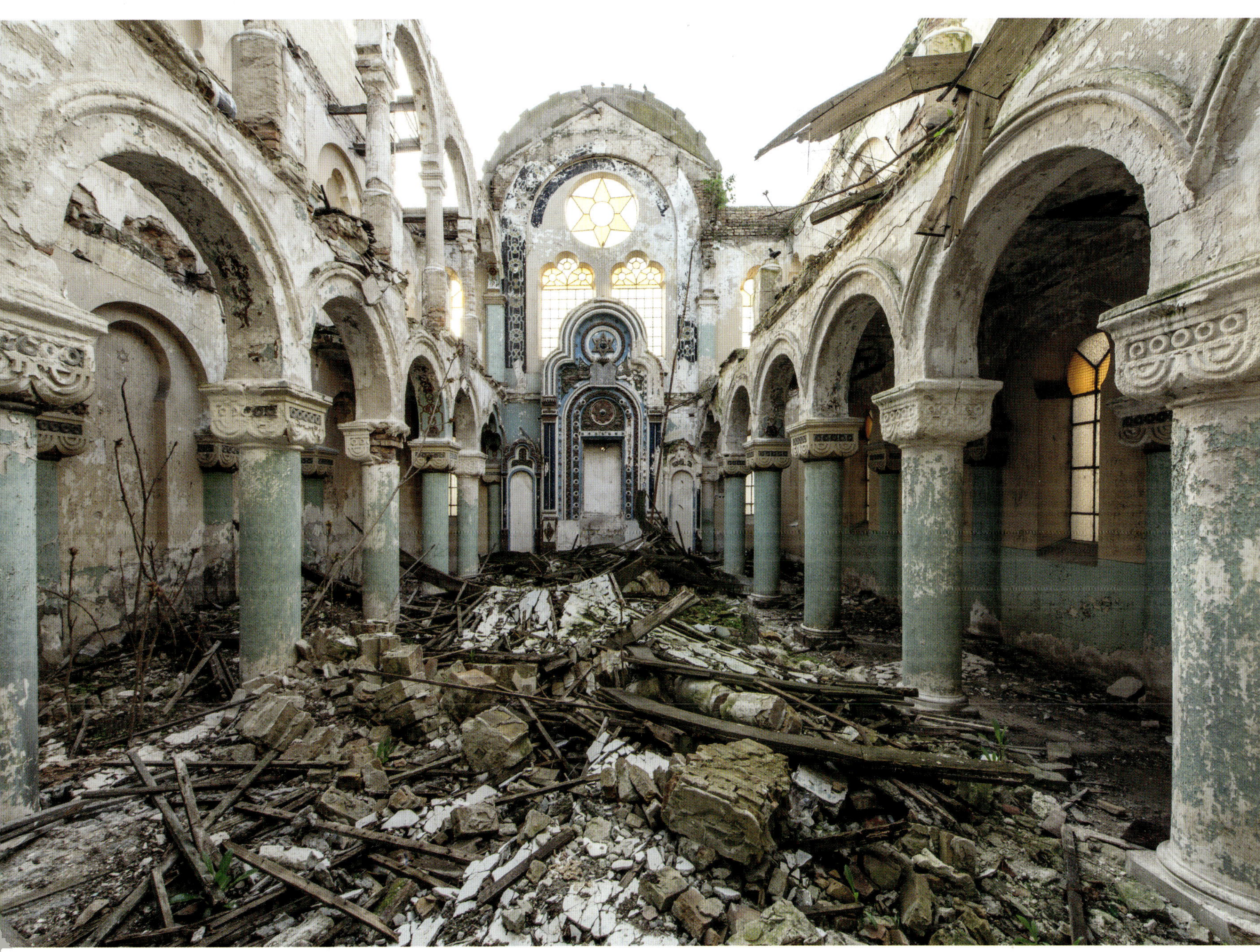

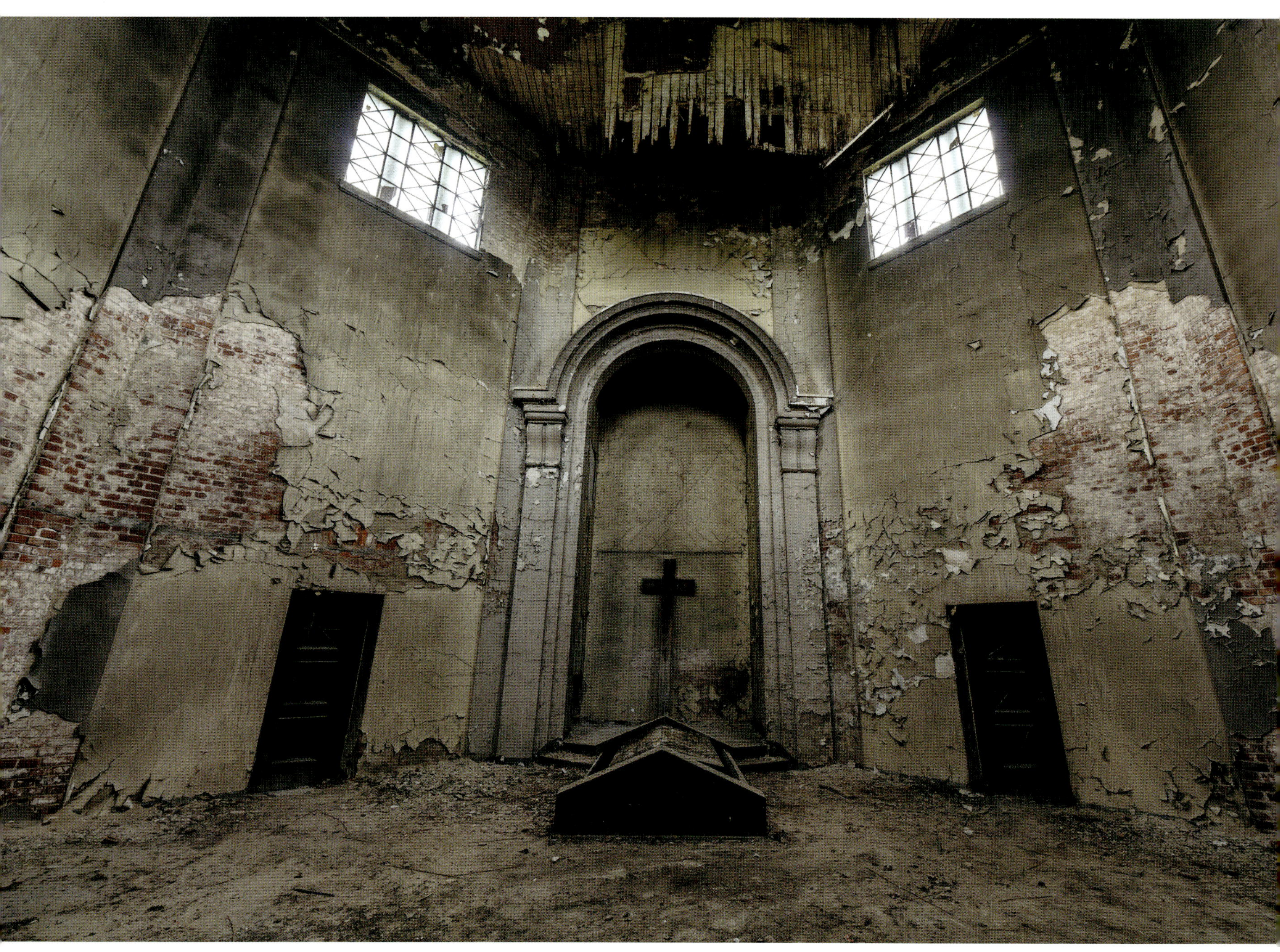

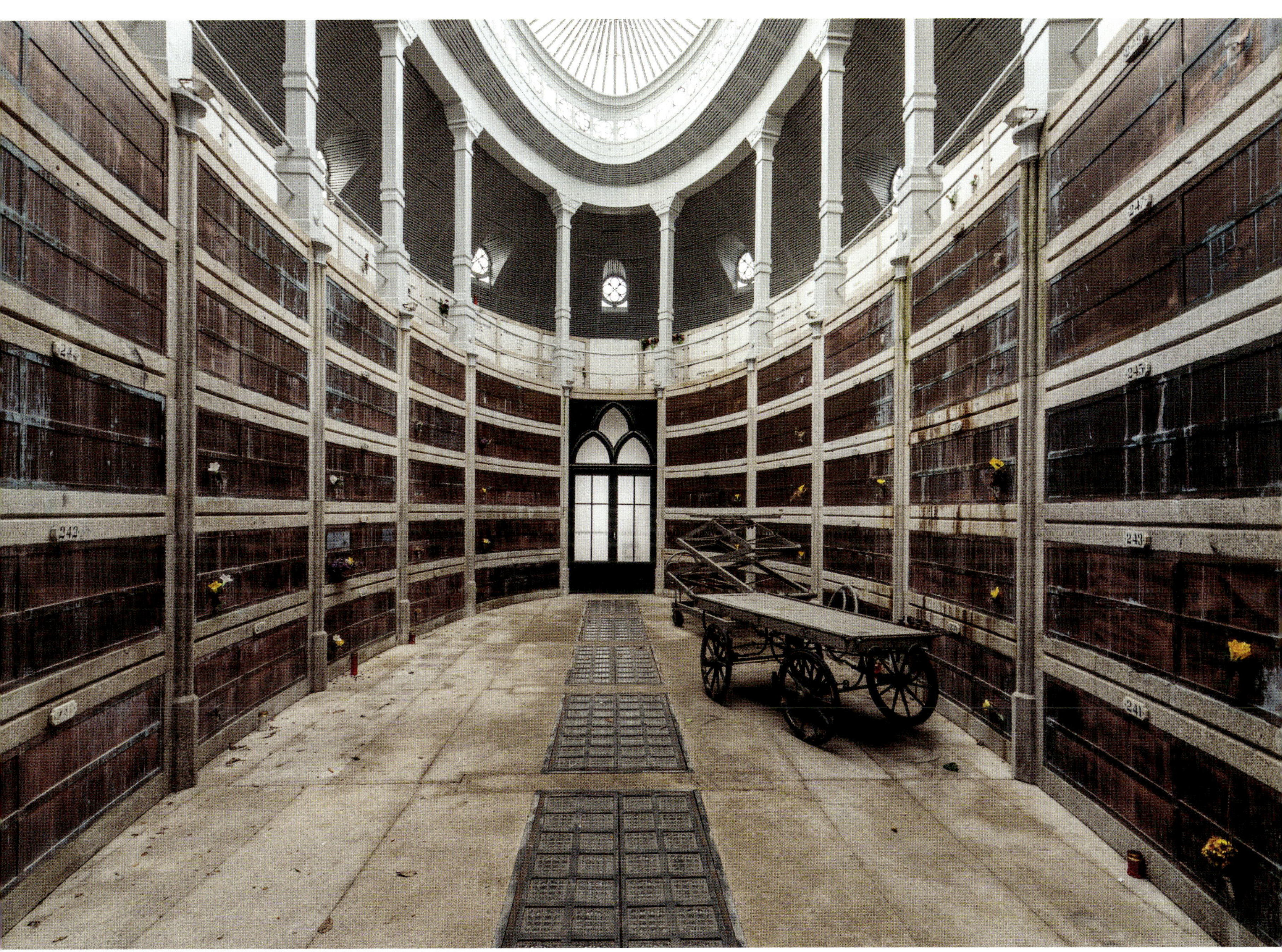

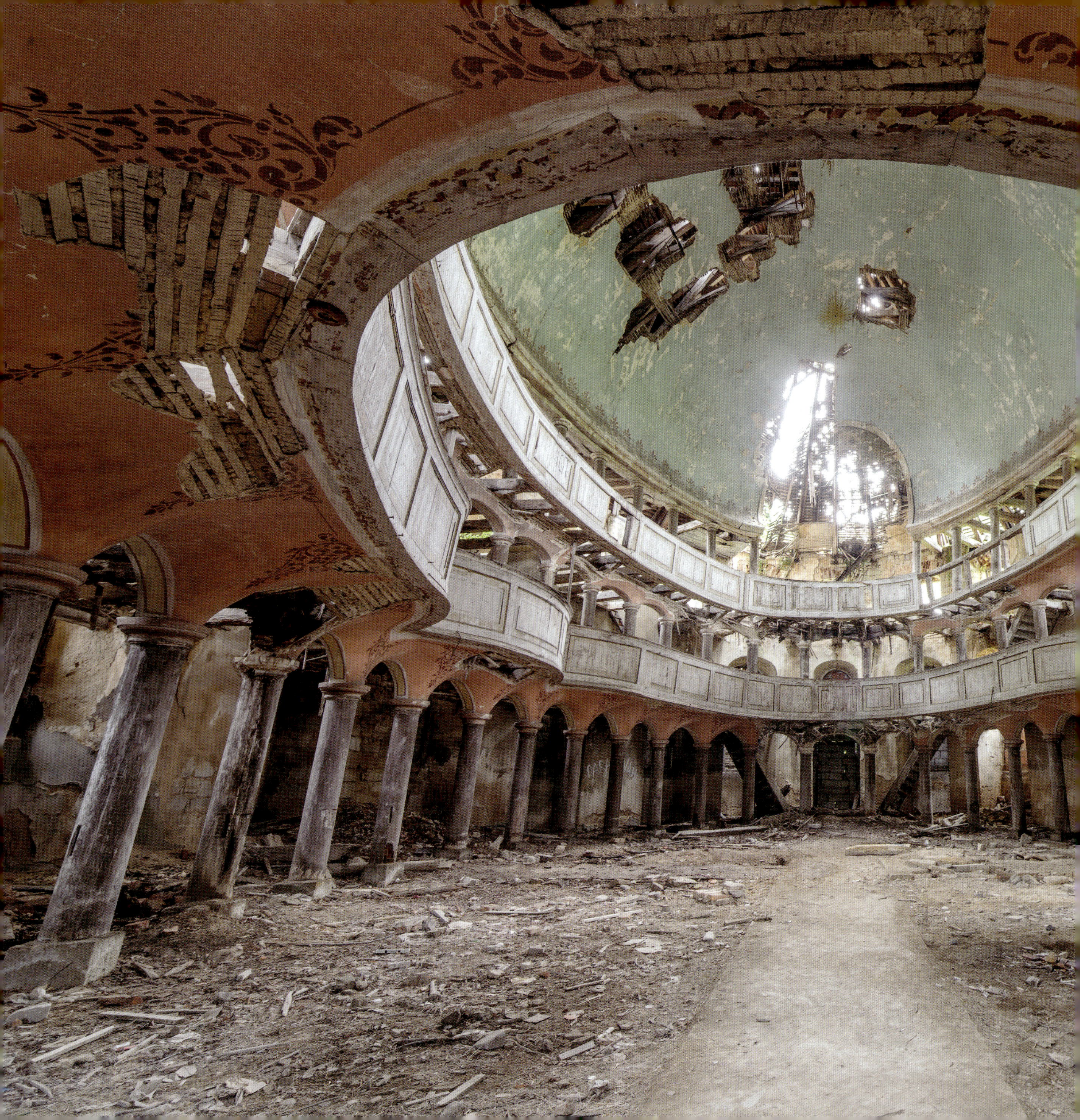

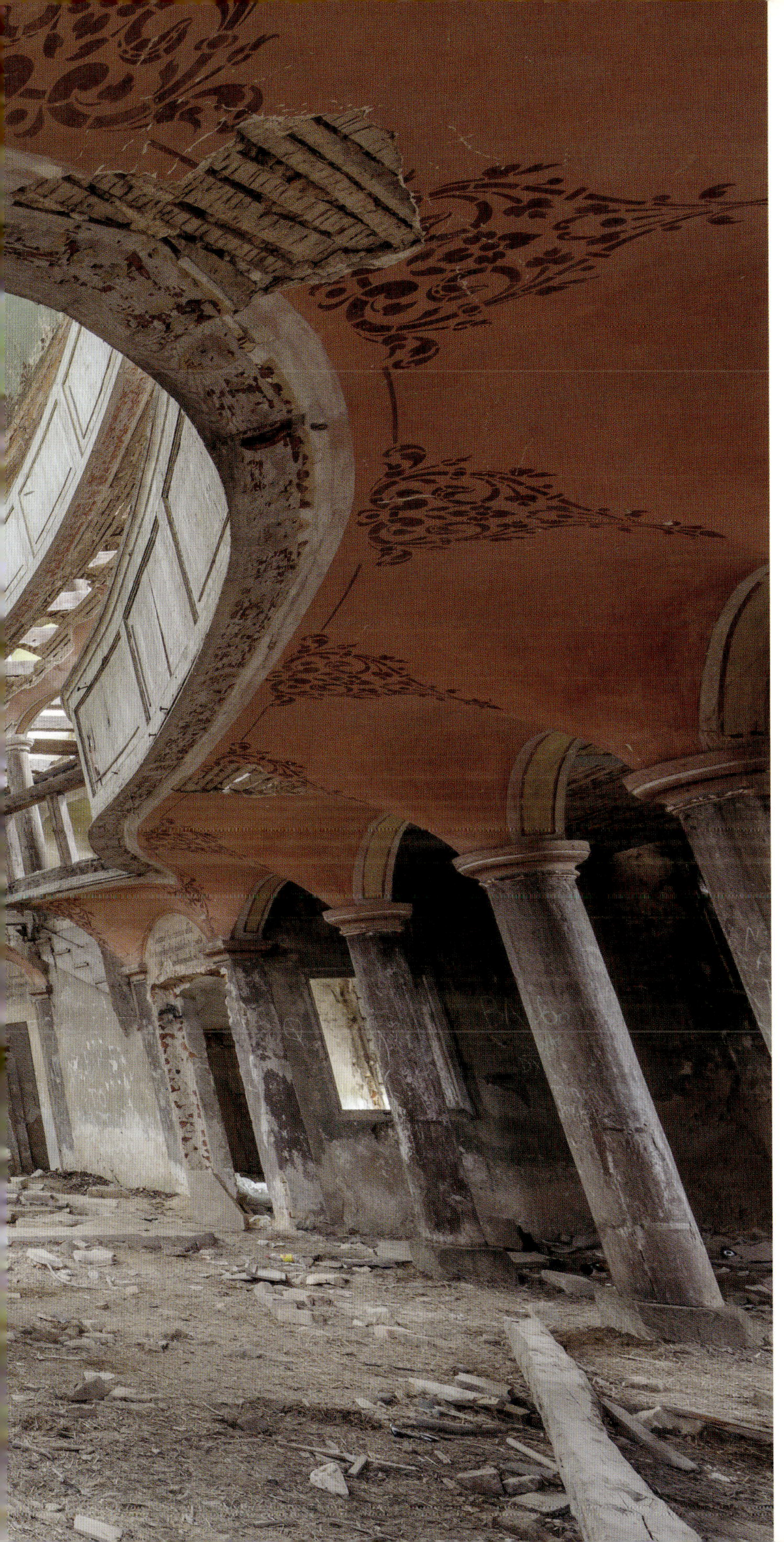

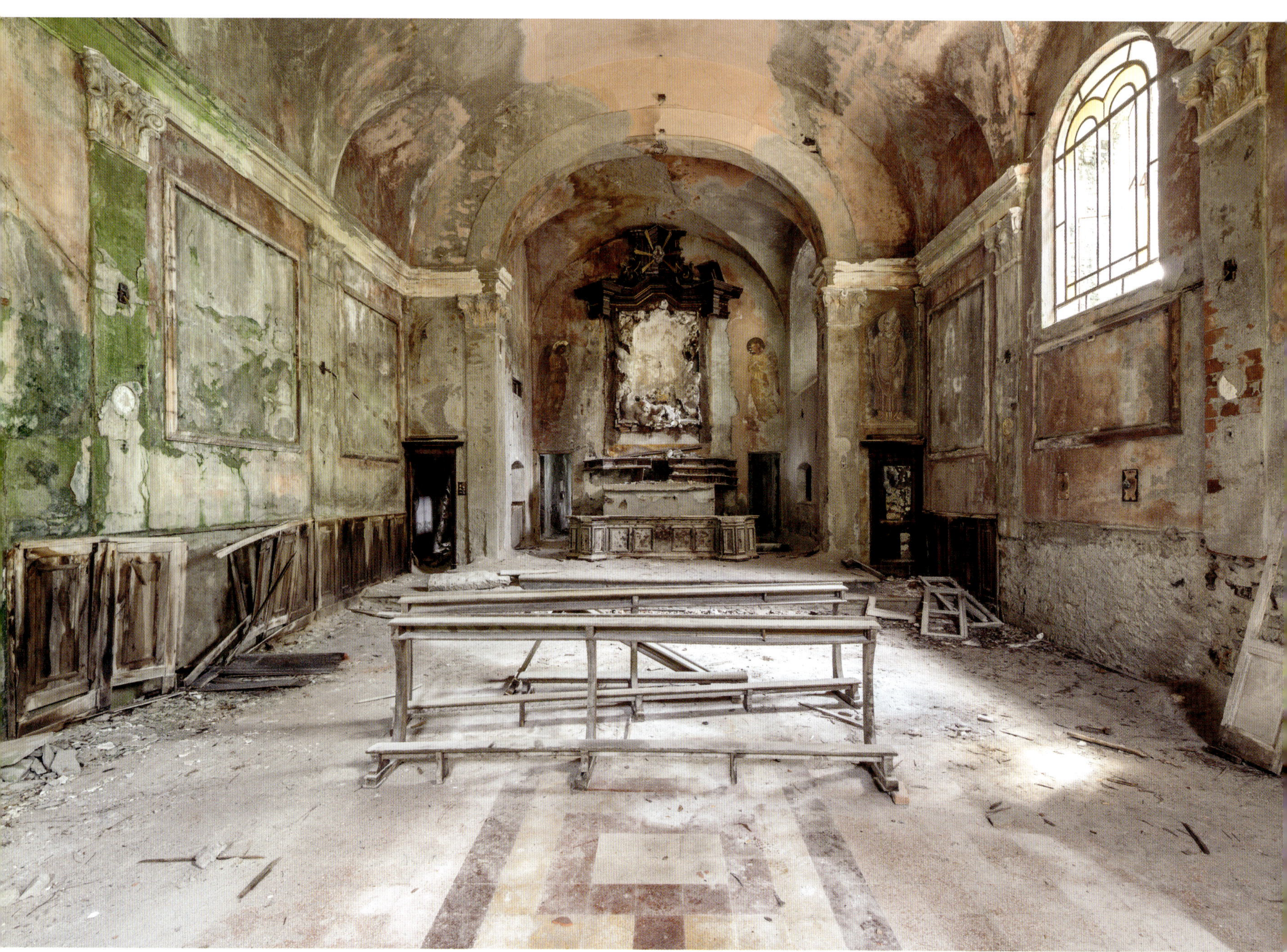

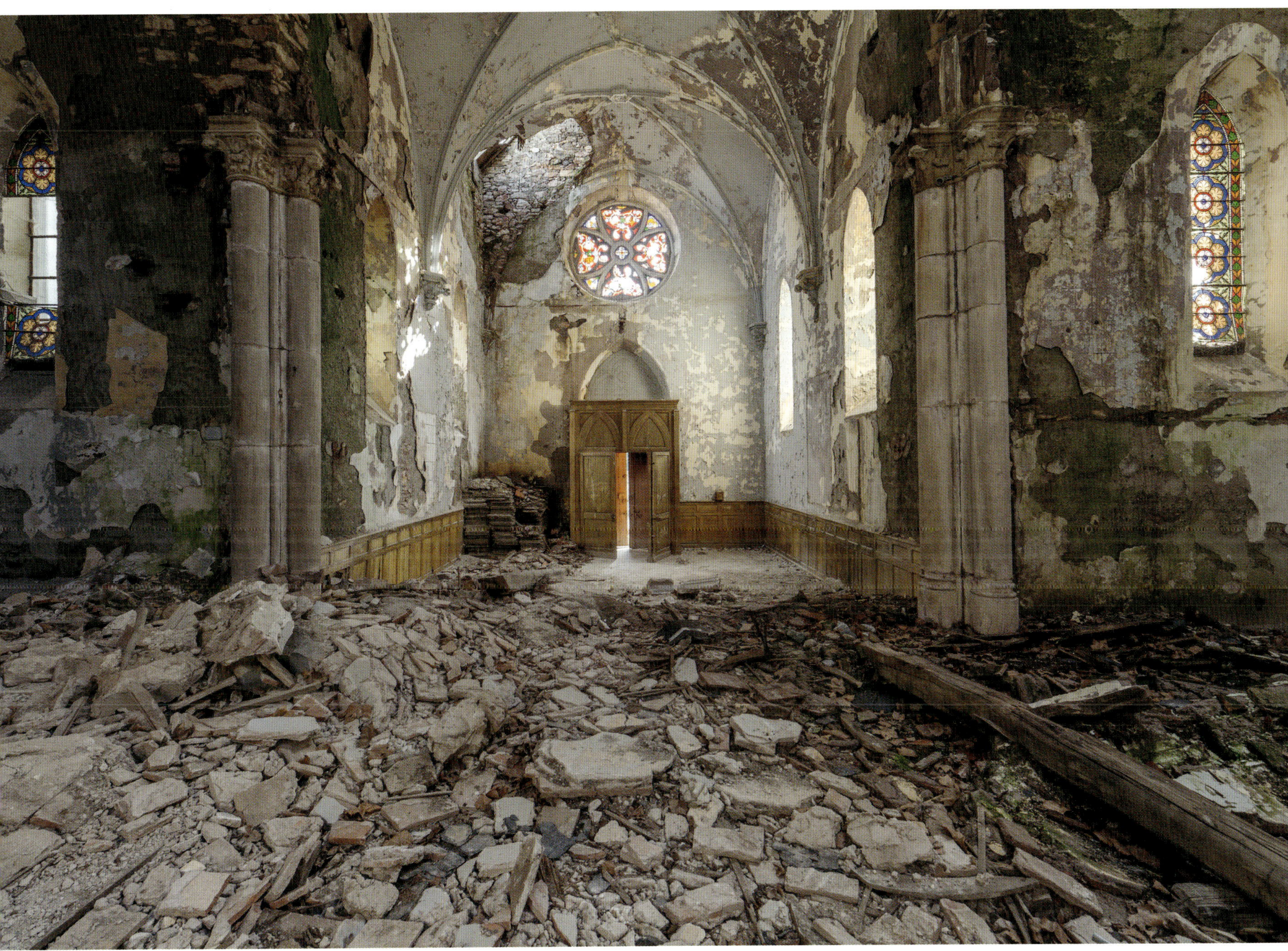

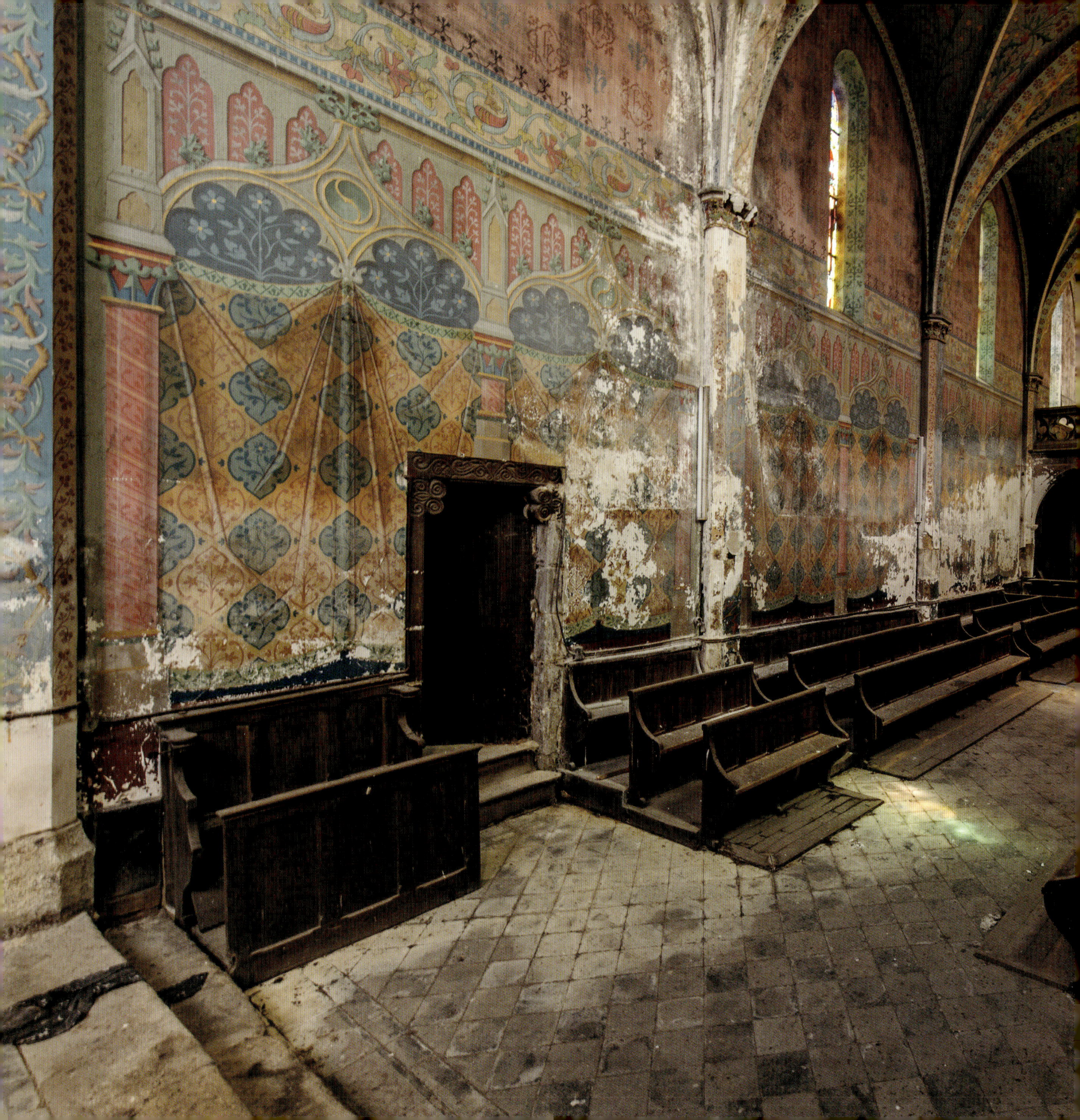

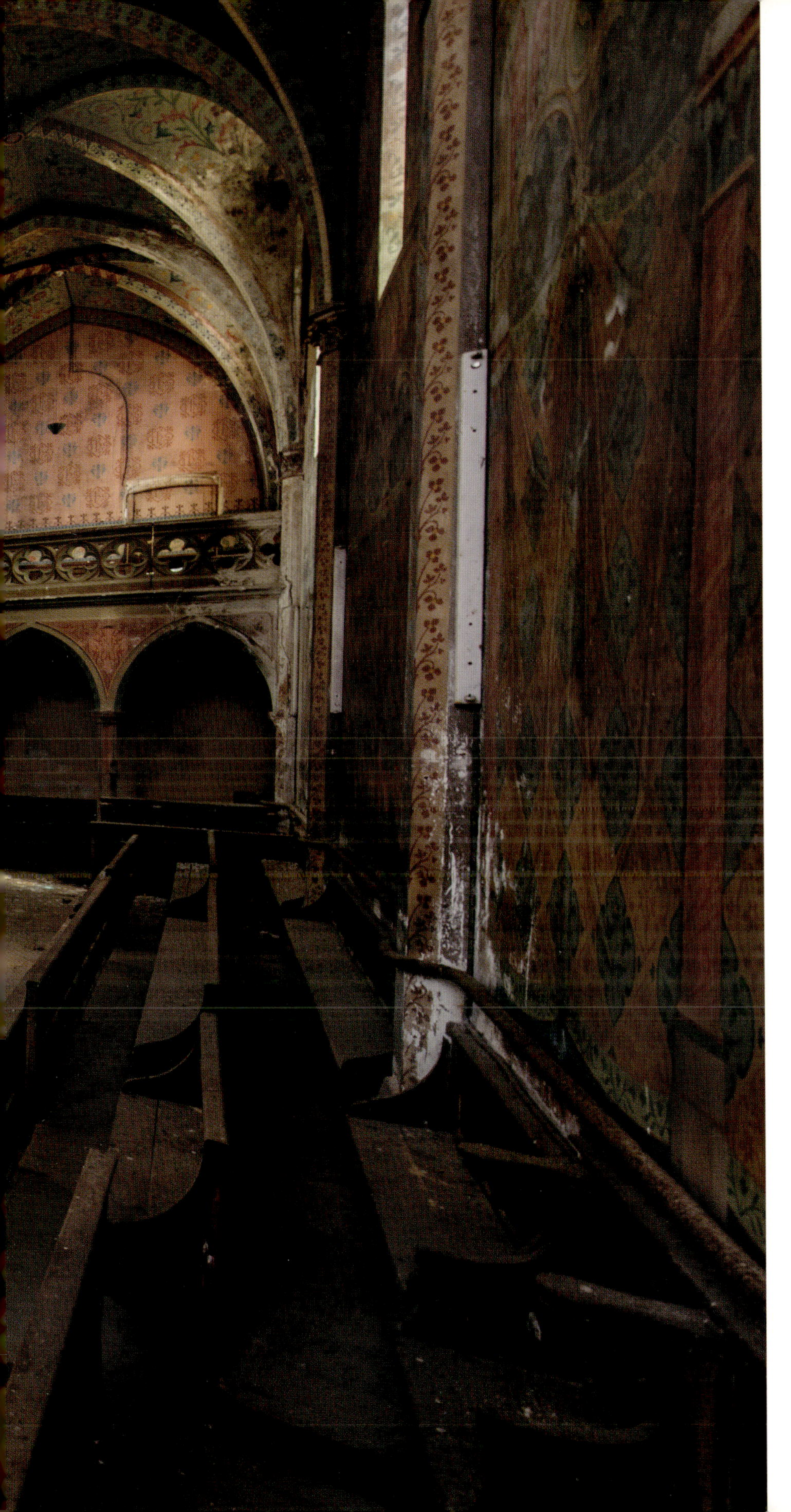

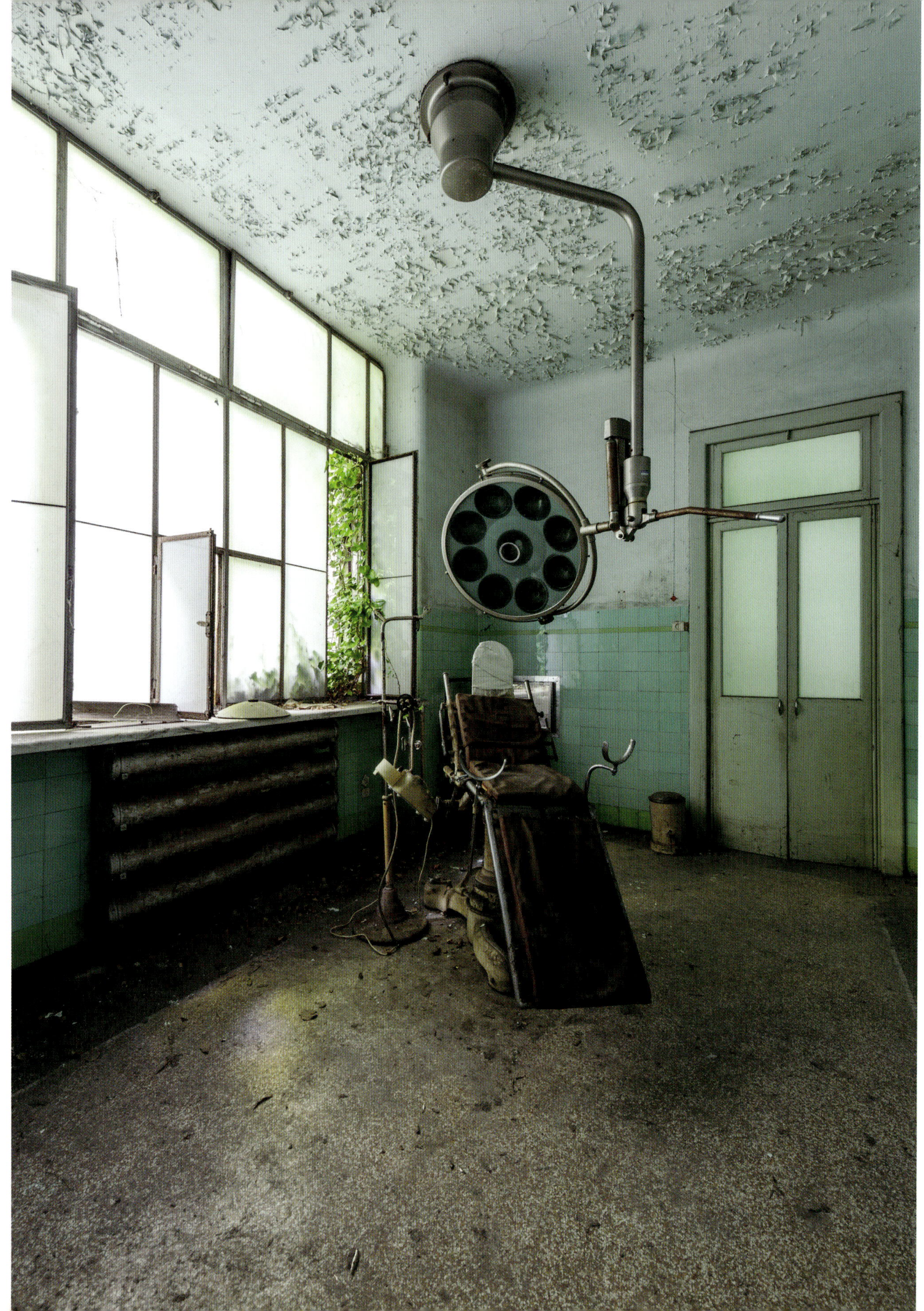

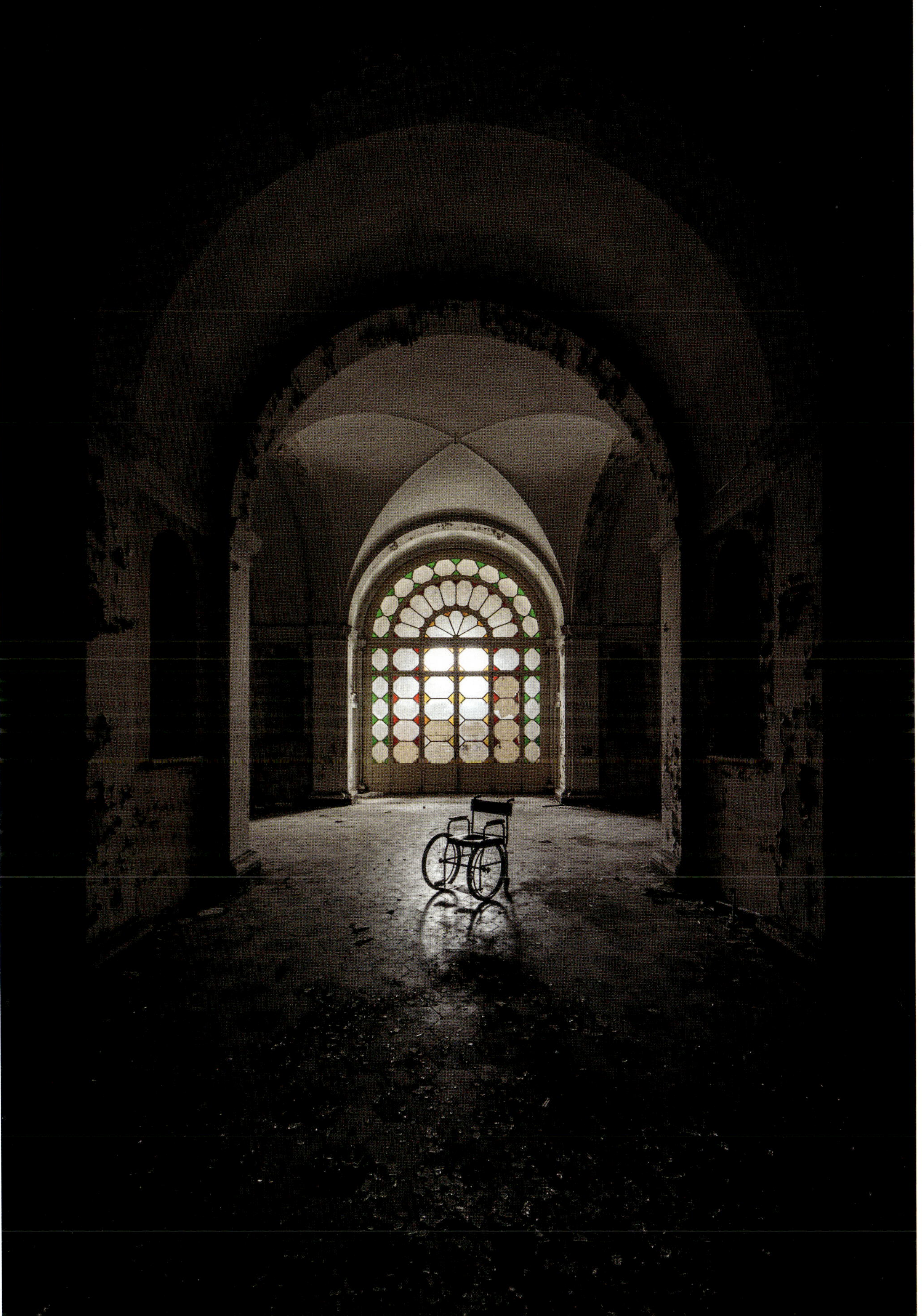

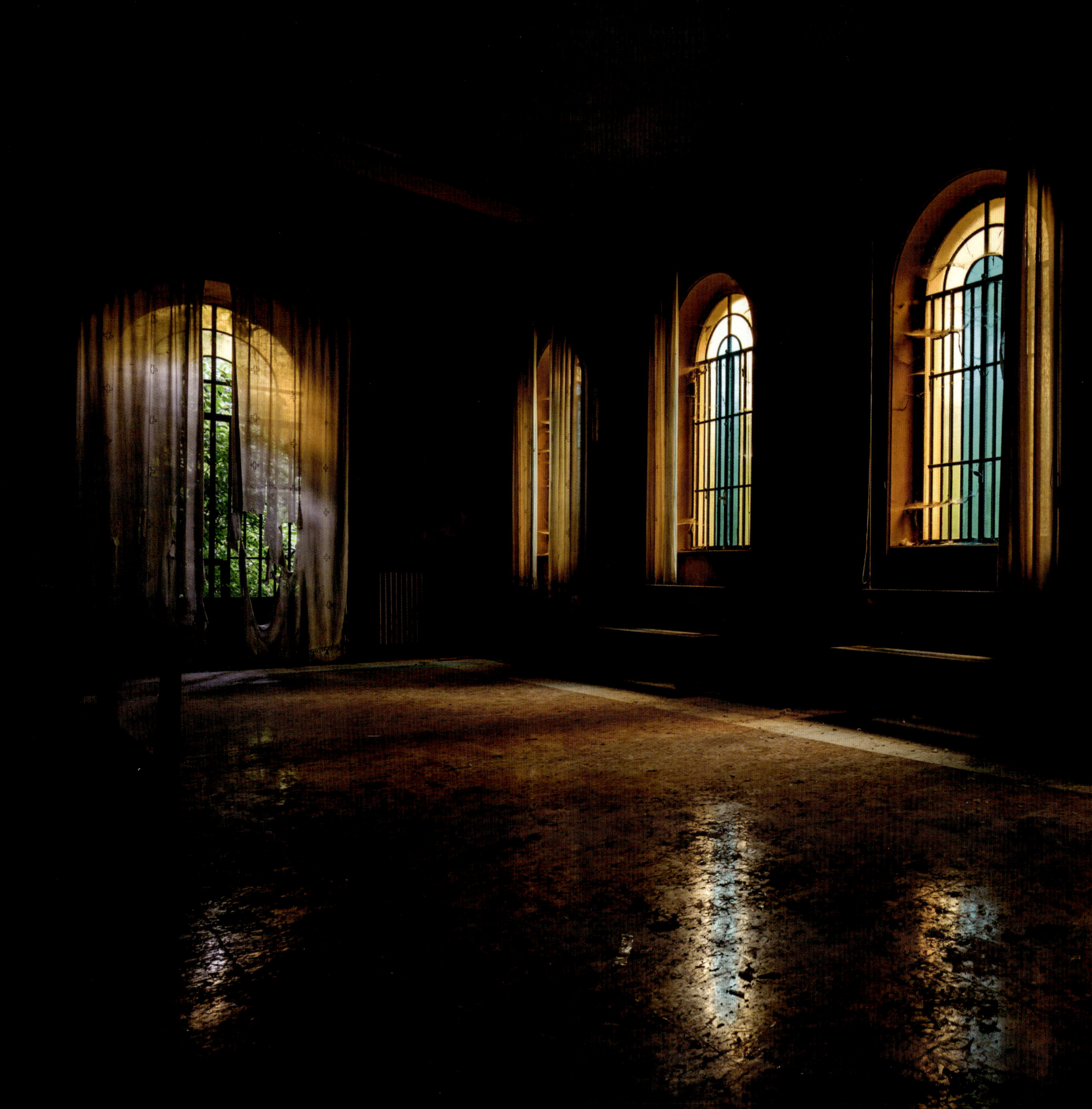

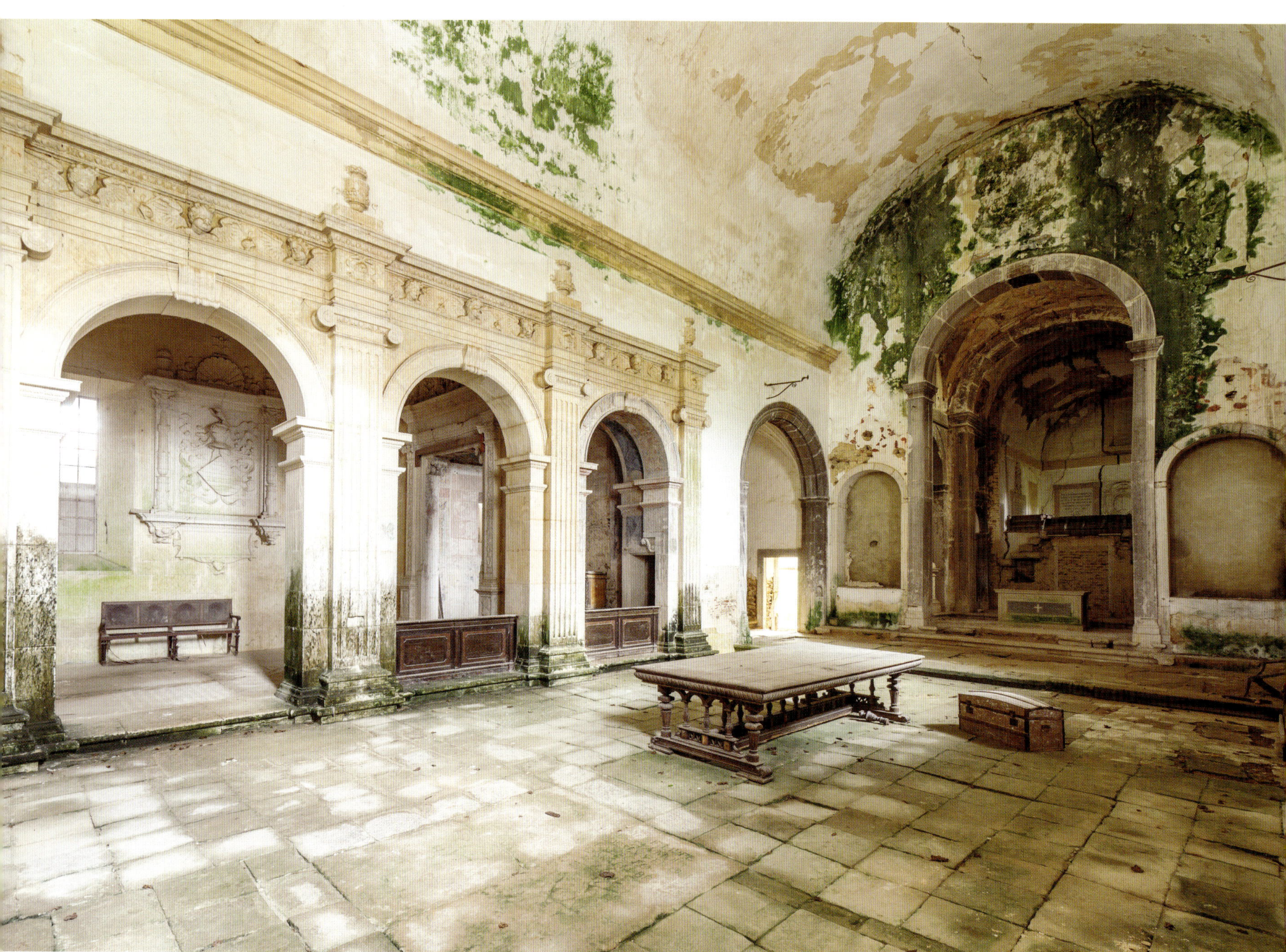

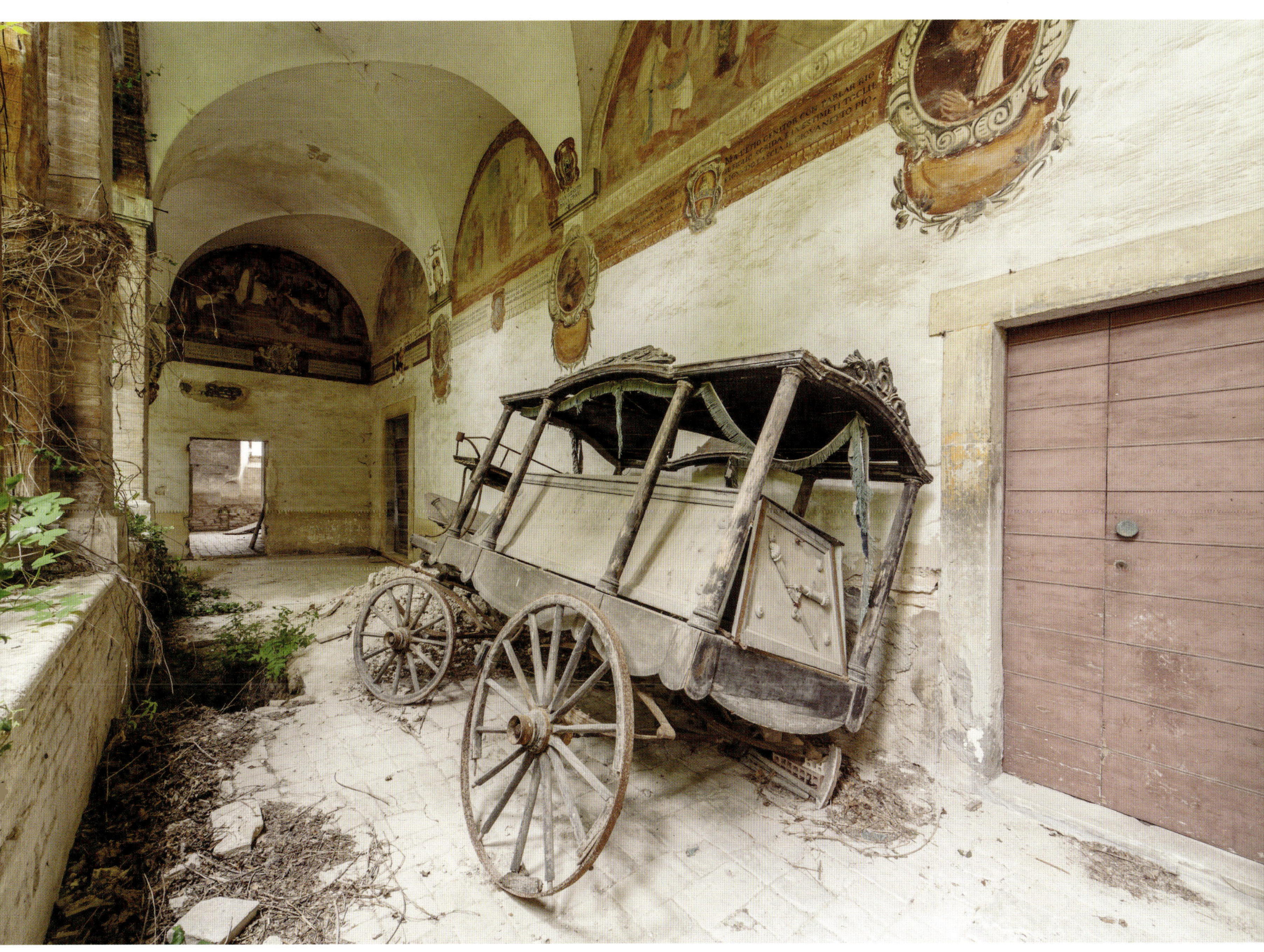

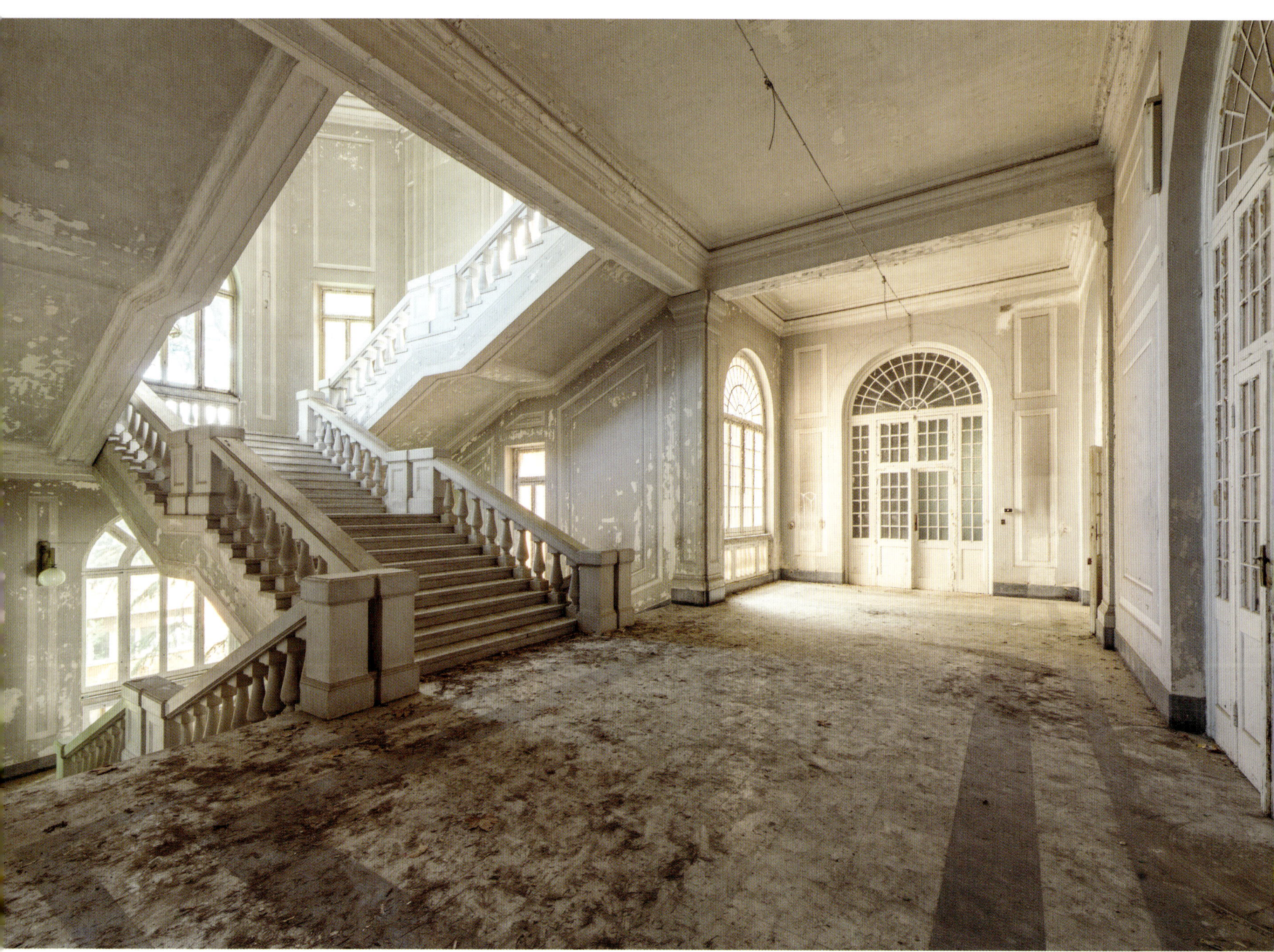

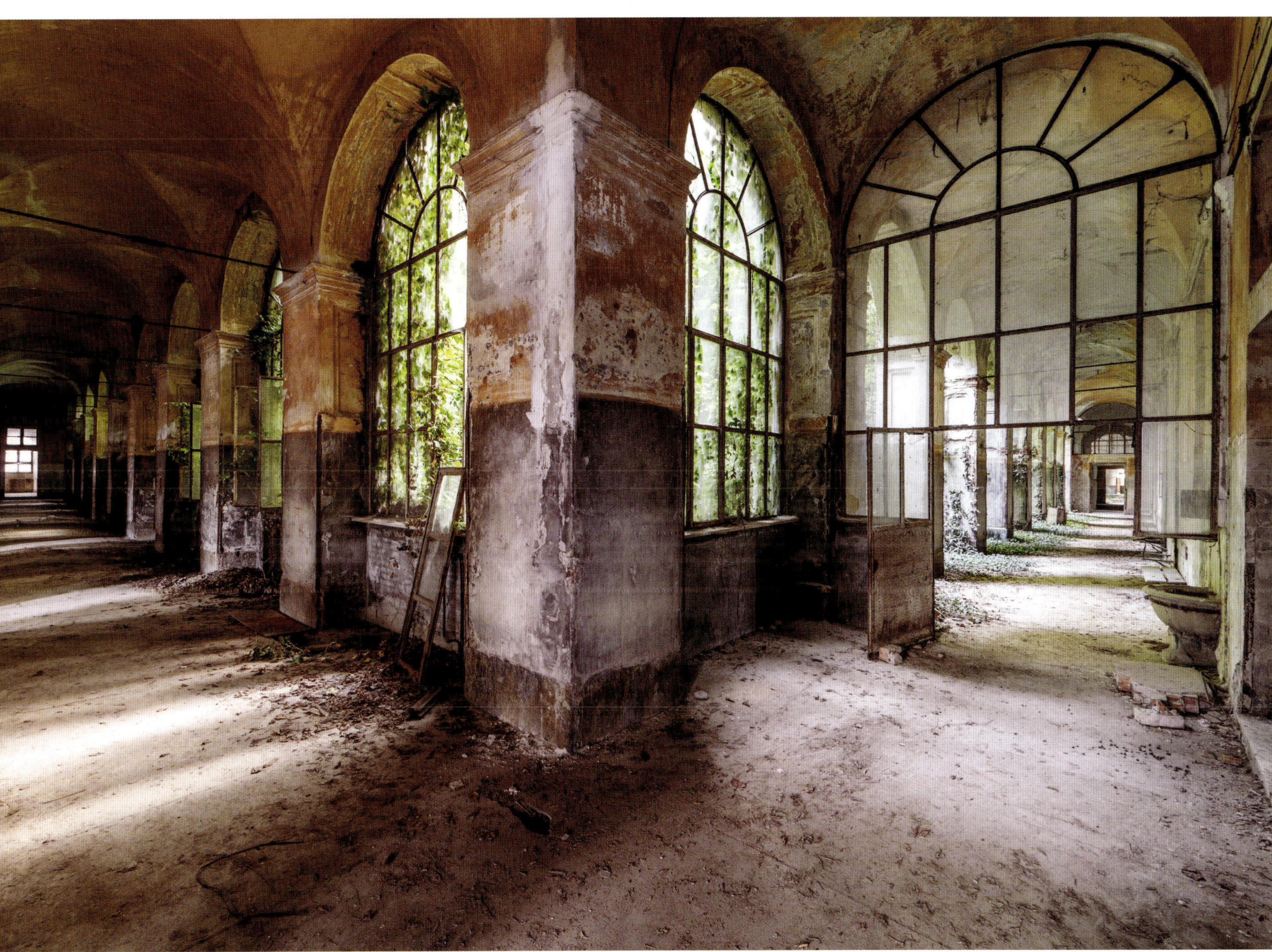

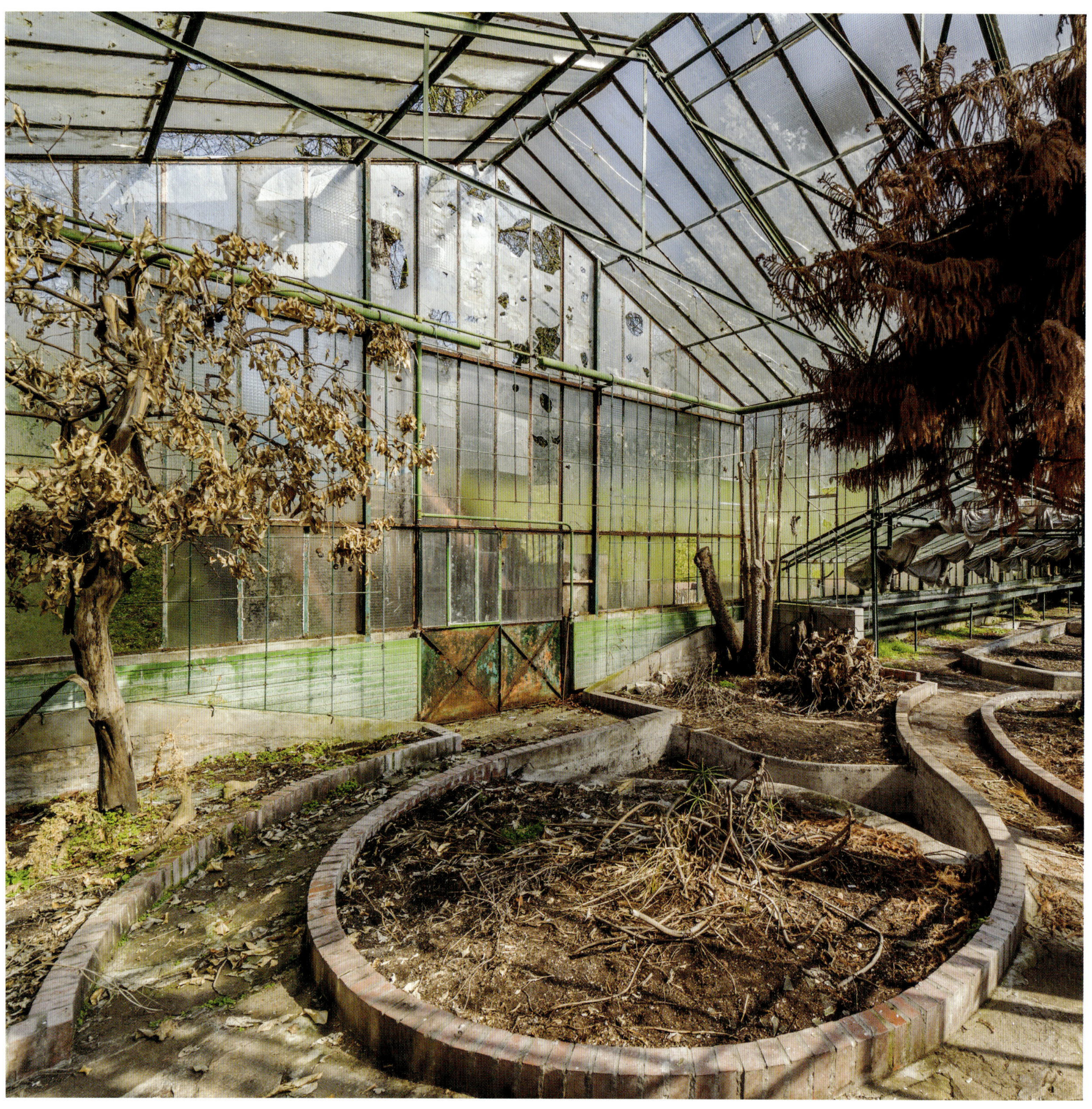

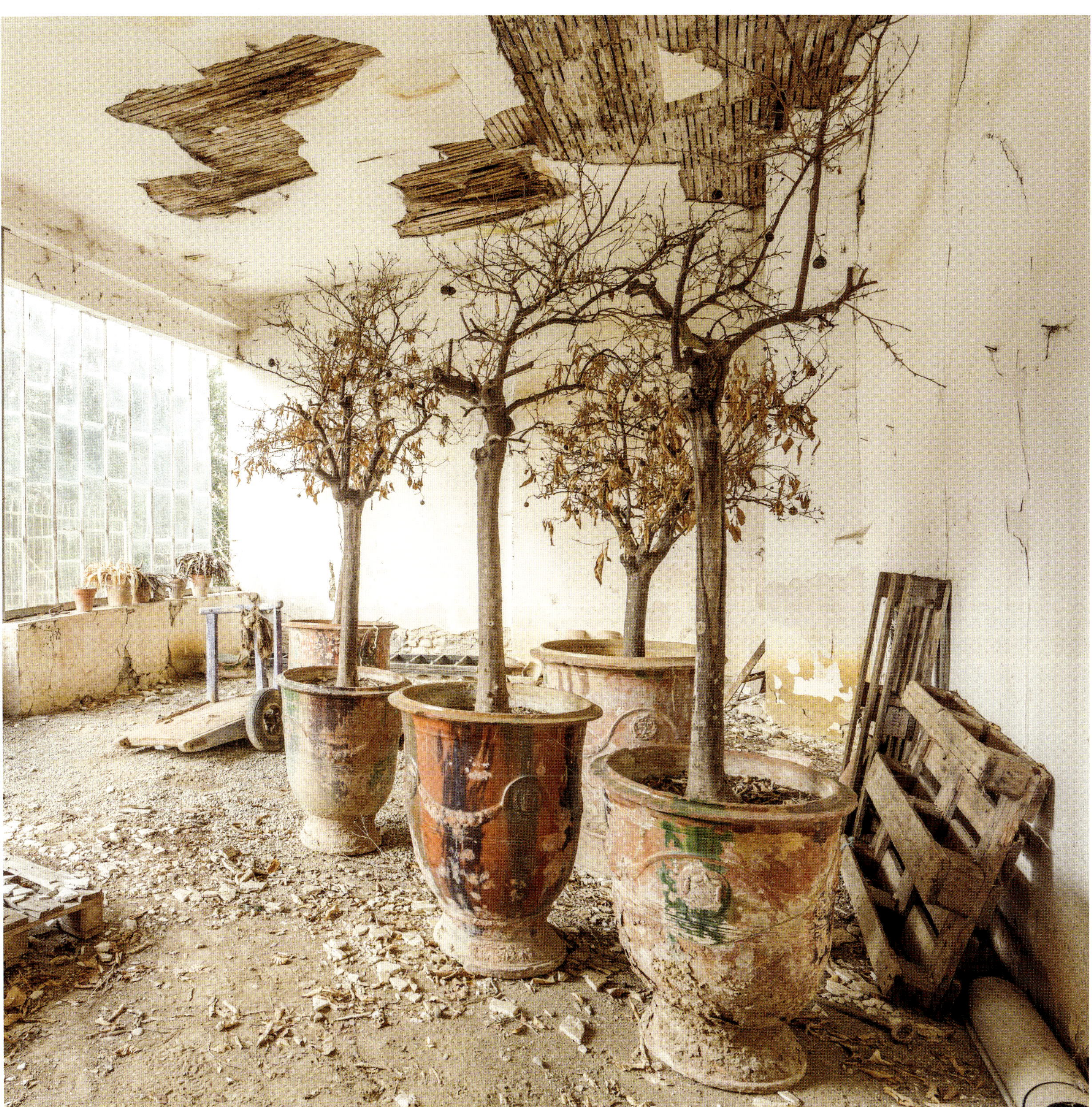

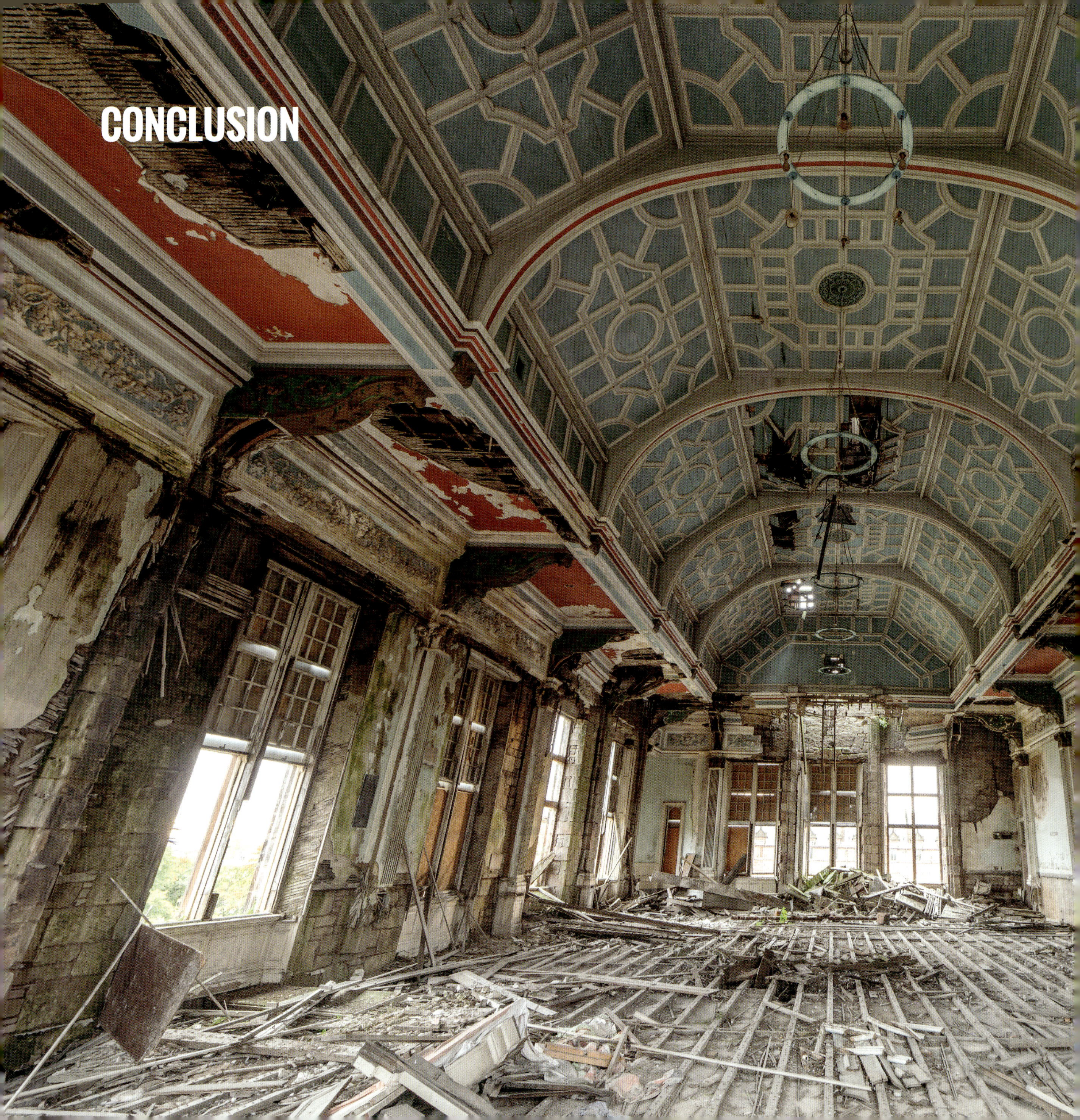
CONCLUSION

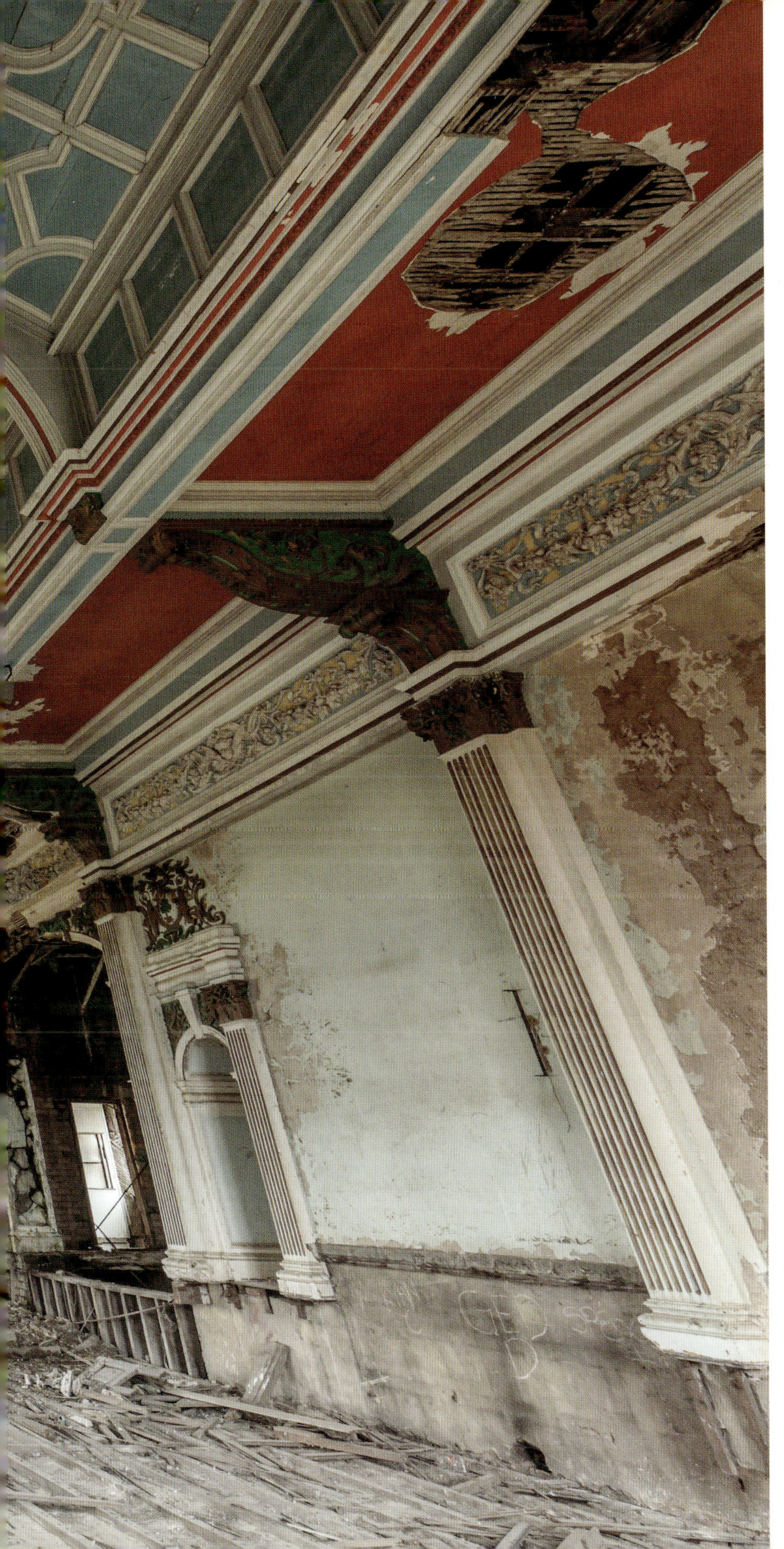

After having wandered in my company through these incredible places and started imagining yourself searching for the ghosts of the past, you might face mixed feelings about these photographs. Firstly, you may feel sad to see the state of decay of these incredible places that used to be full of life, but at the same time, you might feel happy to still be able to witness and explore what remains there for now. For me it is quite easy to understand that the first thing that strikes us about our abandoned heritage is this ambivalence about it, because you are both happy and sad at the same time you discover them.

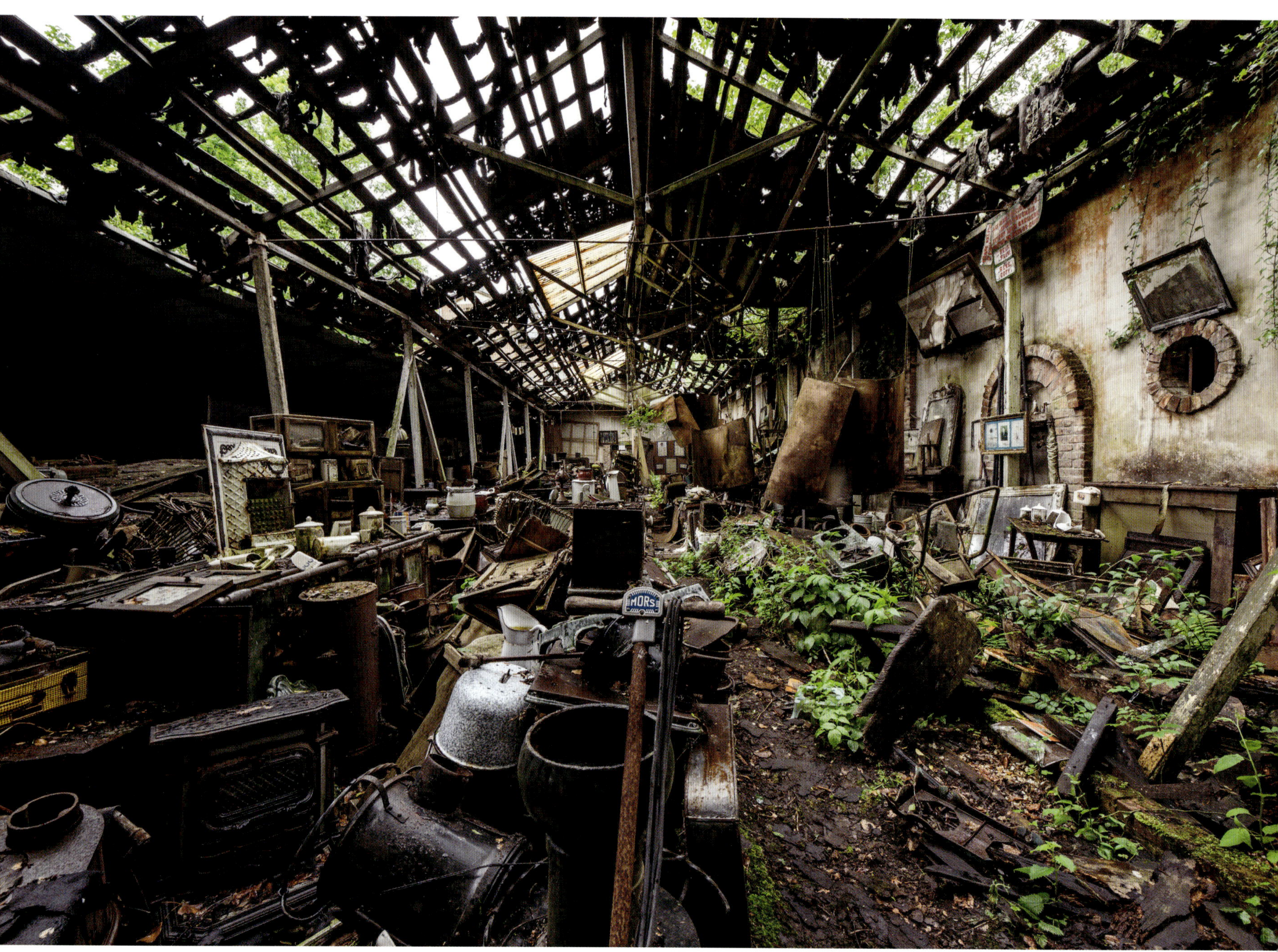

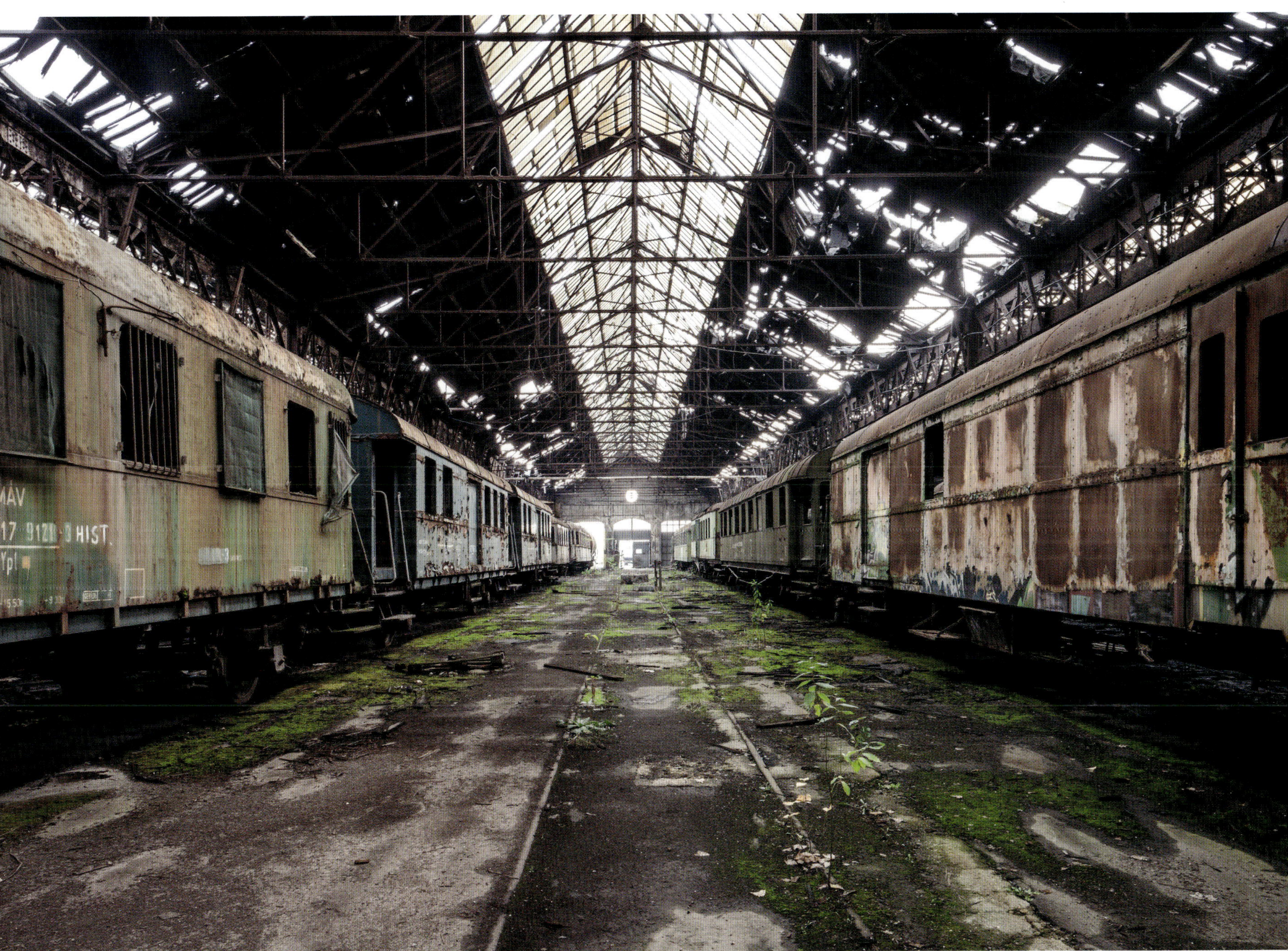

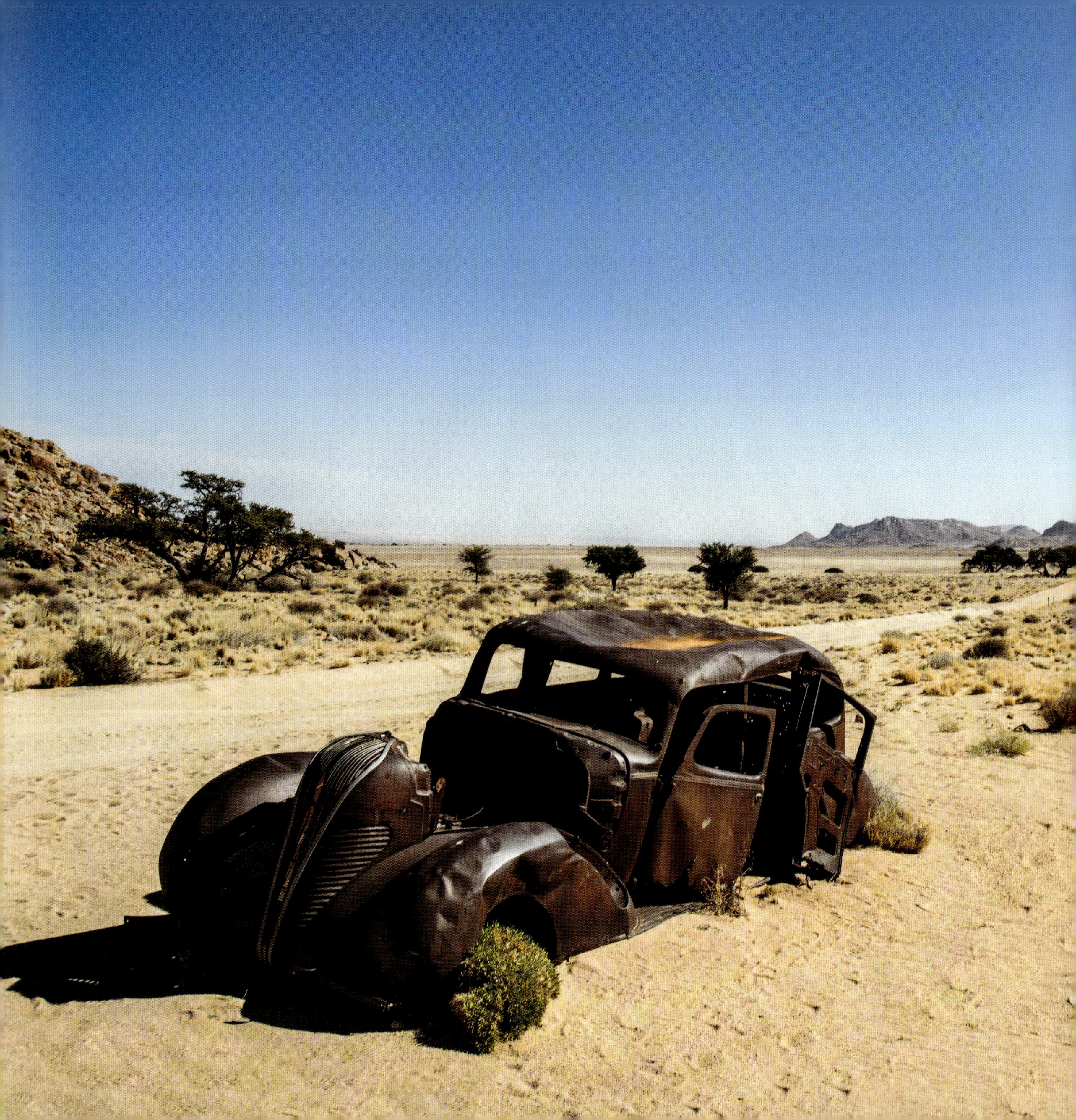

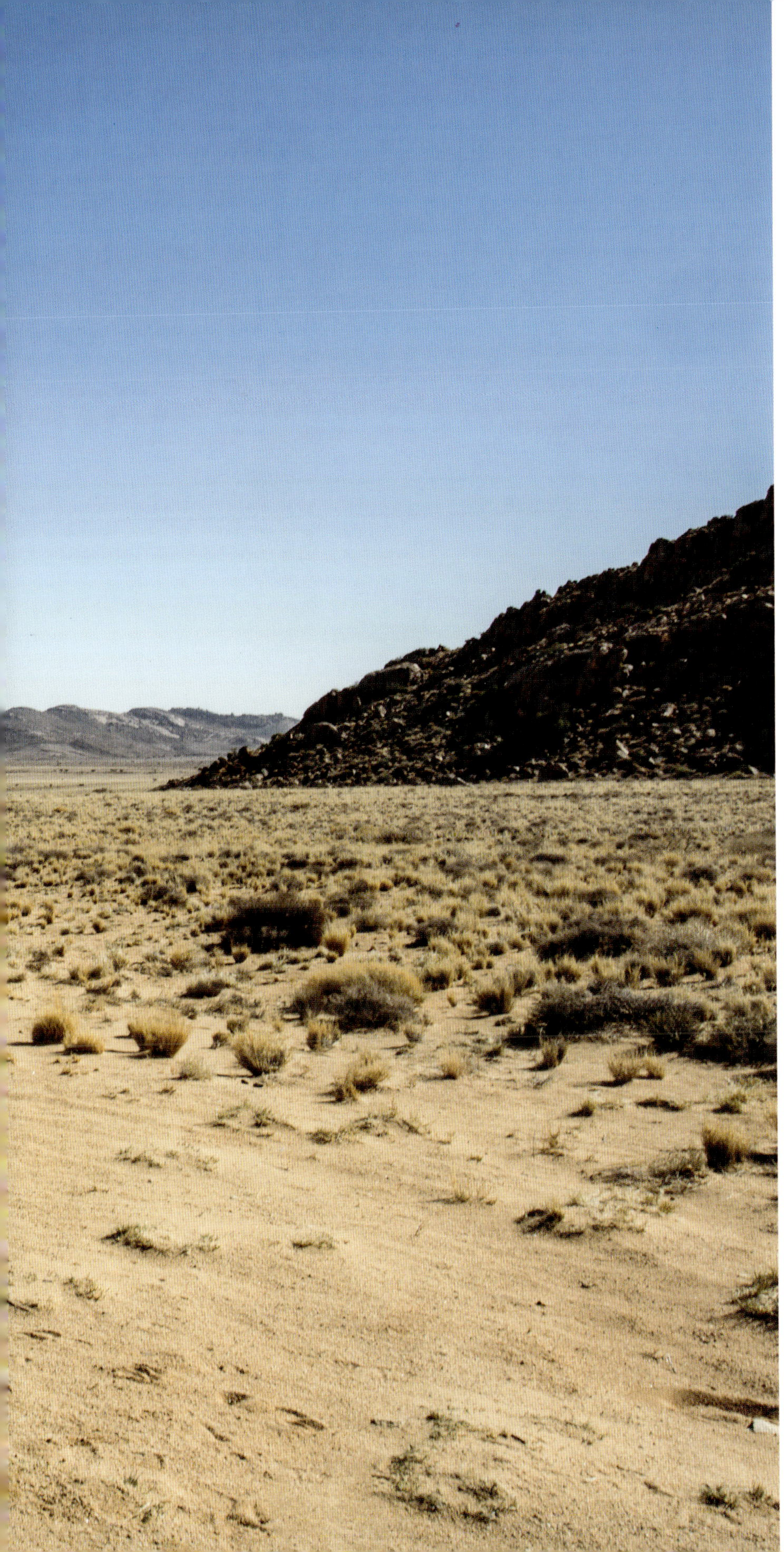

If our constructions are victims of natural disaster and destruction where death is always around; they are also places where life has succeeded and proof that it is still standing there in spite of time. The issue being here that you invariably need to consider the matter as a whole to understand both points of view. There is always a duality in the contemporary obsession for the relics of the past: our desire to admire beauty emerging from chaos is fighting the sadness of witnessing these places falling apart and disappearing little by little.

If the interest in ruins used to be for monuments and the impressive remains of ancient history, new generations are slowly evolving an interest for the more commonplace and unremarkable sites of our ordinary life. We want to see what could happen to our belongings in the future. Our ancestors enjoyed anticipating what their homes or churches could look like in the future because they wouldn't be able to witness it themselves. Now the decline is upon us and we need to see what our reality could become if we were to disappear. That's why we need to find beauty in decay, and why the aesthetic of urban decay has taken on such a huge importance. We need to be reassured, to find something beautiful in the fact that they are abandoned, because we know it could happen to our world very fast.

We need to imagine the world without us, in order to vanquish and exalt our fear and put death and loneliness on hold for a few moments. By contemplating these reverse memento mori I discussed earlier, we make our dreams immortal.

This book is focused on yesterday, but what about tomorrow? What can we do for our cultural and industrial abandoned heritage in the future? Or what can we hope for them? If some buildings can be viewed as masterpieces and have an architectural, historical or scientific interest, some others don't have the same chance because they are not original or interesting enough to be preserved. If time doesn't destroy them, vandals or real estate developers eventually will.

Here lies in the heart of the problem: We can't save them all if we want to be honest with ourselves; we have to choose in accordance with their characteristics. But there are still a great number of buildings that could and should be protected and restored. So, there should be an in-depth thought process from each country's cultural minister and the local population to decide which buildings are the most deserving to benefit from protection in respect of their history, power to attract tourists and their places in the heart of the population.

These which can still be saved, (examples of locations that we can visit officially, like Kolmanskop and Epecuén), show us there is a real growing interest from the public to visit and learn about those places. For that matter, it's no accident that the Coliseum in Rome, Angkor in Cambodia or Petra in Jordan (not to mention many others) are some of the most visited and known places in the world.

Now that we have discovered that hidden treasures can be found around every corner, this new "ruin porn" phenomenon has emerged into everyday life and put abandonment in the centre of our interests. This collection of images is not the only one; there are other great examples in the cultural world (books, video games, movies, series, fashion…) a ubiquity that proves people show more and more enthusiasm for abandoned places and their history nowadays.

So, what concrete future is there for these places? As we have said, the simplest answer will be to modify them into museums so they can still be saved and attract some tourism during their second life. People would be able to visit them in their entirety and learn about the history and how workers used to function there for example. This choice would be more effective for industrial sites or entertainment locations like theatres or swimming pools due to their power of attraction.

It is more complicated with places like castles, houses or offices. Those with a really interesting history or architecture could be turned into museums too, but for those who aren't, there are still solutions. With some renovation coming from the local council or the private sector, they could be transformed into auditoriums, art galleries, schools or even restaurants and hotels. Hospitals and sanatoriums are also being abandoned more frequently. Thanks to their huge size, most of them could be easily converted into social apartments or artistic workshops.

We have also witnessed a specific problem with the growing number of abandoned churches these days. When there isn't enough money to renovate them, to preserve their incredible architecture, they could be sold to other communities or organizations so they don't have to be destroyed (they are even changed into parking lots or shops in the United States). The most important thing is to not let them reach the point where we can't even save their walls anymore.

Of course, some of those abandoned factories, theatres or castles were unique and will never be rebuilt. They were testimonies of an era and are lost forever; but there is a perpetual mechanism to create ruins: Every time that a place is destroyed, another one is abandoned elsewhere. There will always be ruins, as it is in the nature of man.

Every culture is changing and evolving, leaving behind a part of itself. Especially now; we are facing dangerous threats (environmental, geopolitical, social or economic) which have changed our mentality and our way of seeing our future. Modern civilisation has brought more uncertainty that has made us feel the need to see what could become of the world if we continue in this direction without changing how our society works. Let's hope this awareness will come before it's too late.

The future will tell us, it won't be a surprise to see the concept of "ruin porn" getting more and more popular. But while we wait, the most important thing will be to retain the capacity to dream and imagine all sorts of stories while getting lost in these pictures. And I hope that's what you did when you went through these pages with me in my imaginary museum. Each of these photographs represent for me a special memory, a special journey and a special adventure. Behind them, so many different tales could be told that would contain all the passion I feel for these incredible places and their universe.

Every time I enter into an abandoned site, I feel again like a little child and I am grateful for the chance I have to be able to shoot and get lost in them. My personal "Memento Mori" as I like to call them are also here to remind me than nothing can ever be taken for granted. Every cycle has an end, and we always need to be ready to start a new one. I hope each of you will also garner some food for thought from these images. Above all, I hope that the sand timer stopped during the lecture, and that you will take the time to turn it over.

"They reminded me that it was my fate to pursue only phantoms, creatures whose reality existed to a great extent in my imagination; for there are people - and this had been my case since youth - for whom all the things that have a fixed value, assessable by others, fortune, success, high positions, do not count; what they must have is phantoms. They sacrifice all the rest, devote all their efforts, make everything else subservient to the pursuit of some phantom. But this soon fades away; then they run after another only to return later on to the first."

Marcel Proust, "Search of Lost Time"

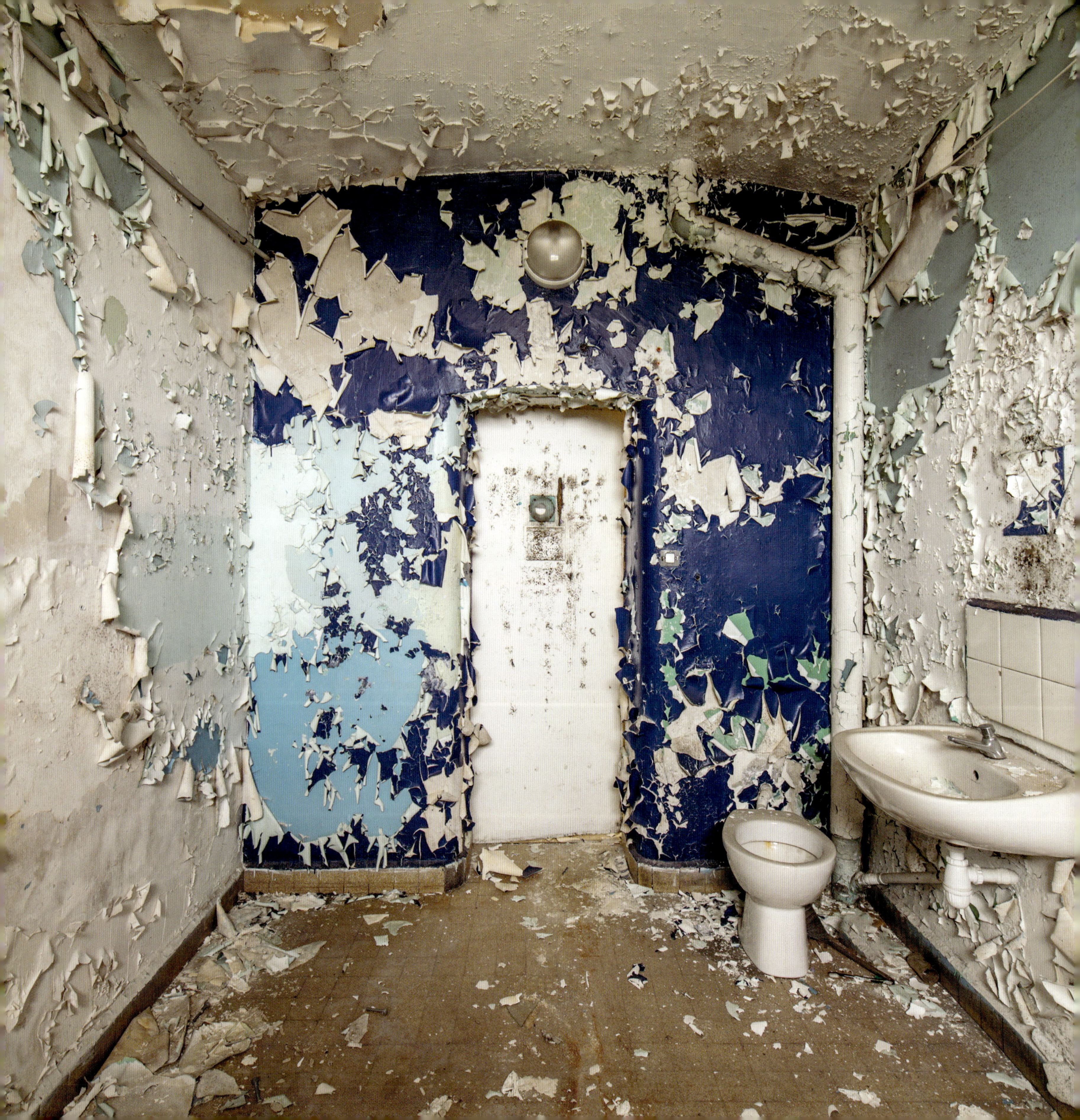

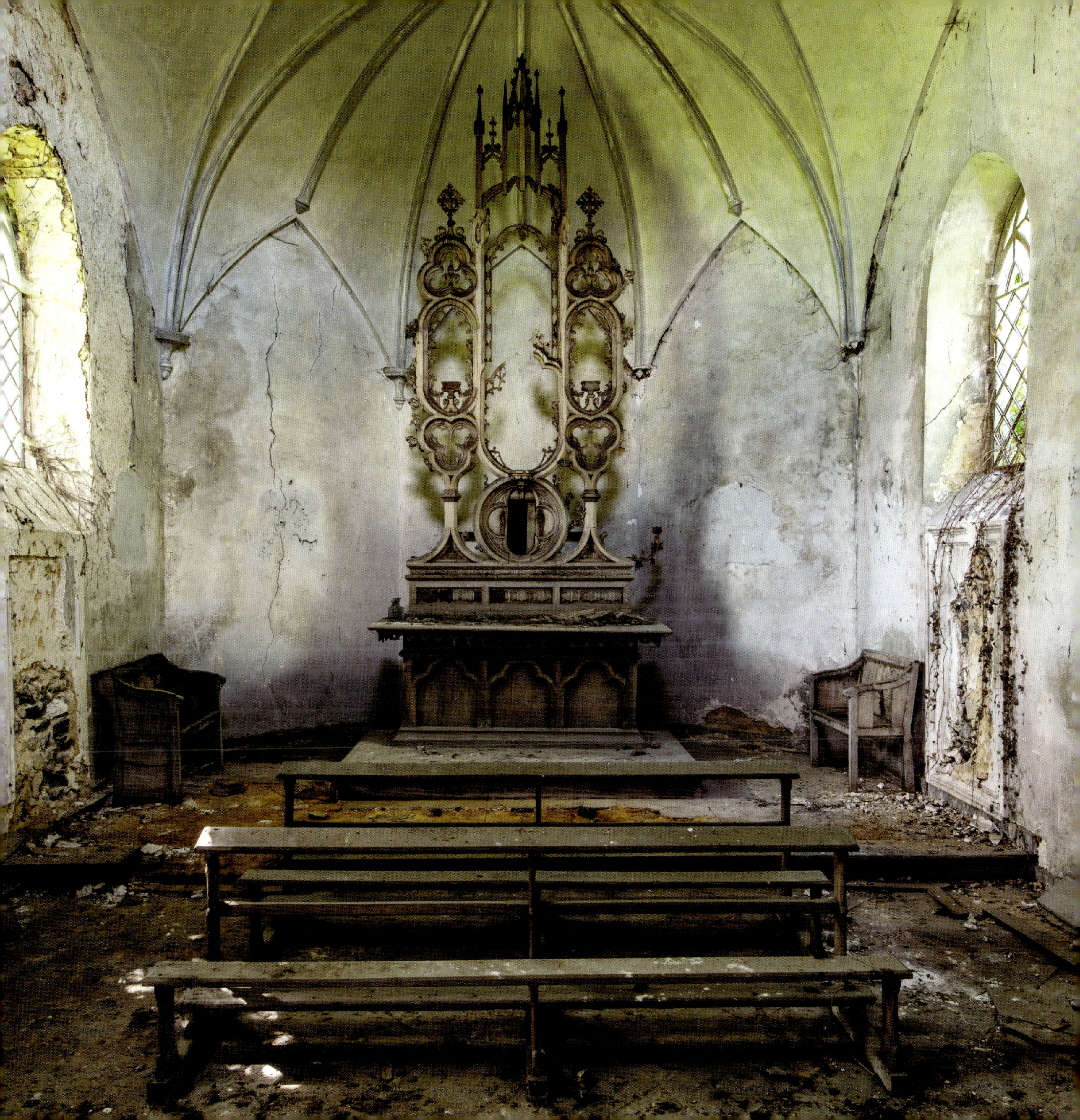

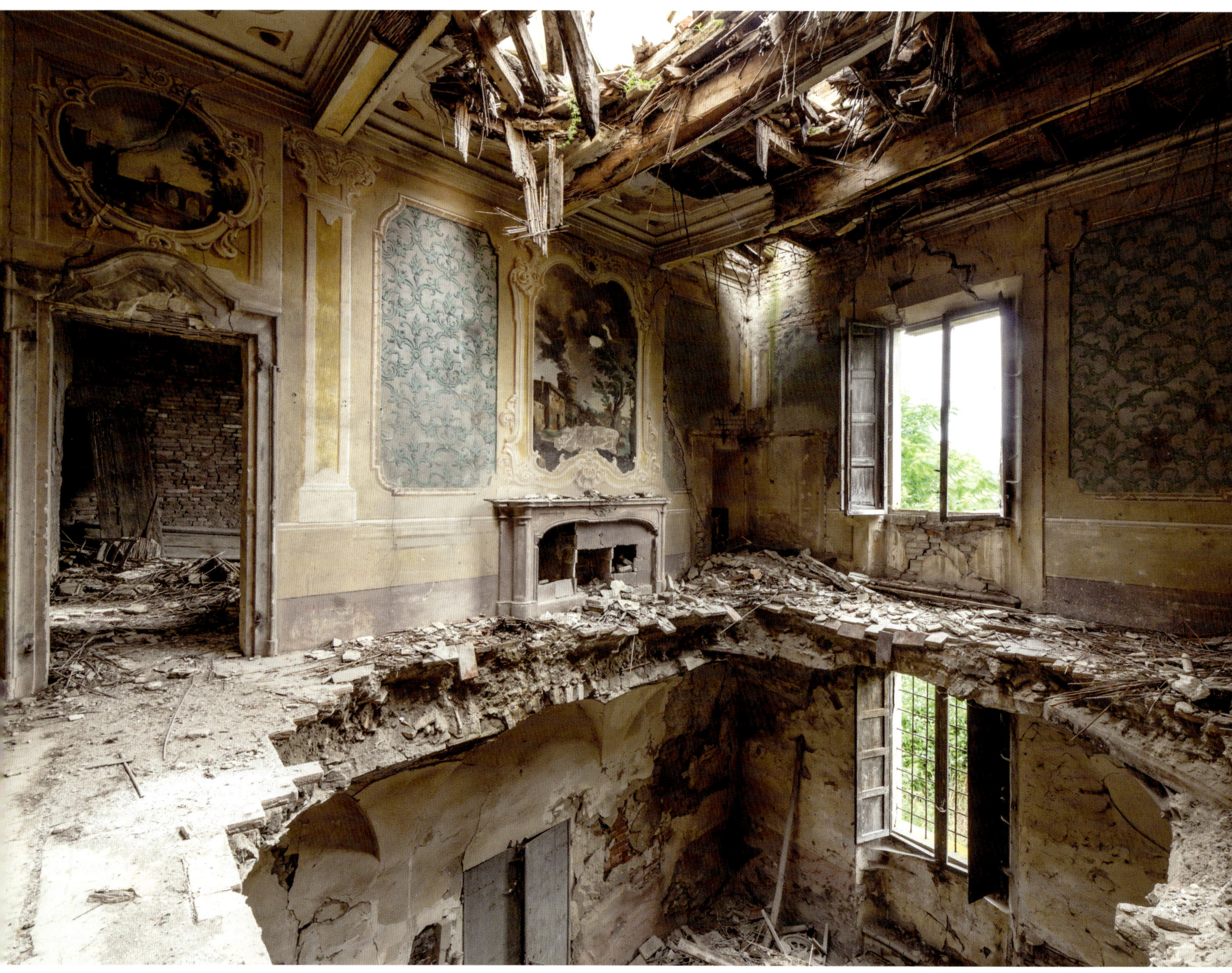

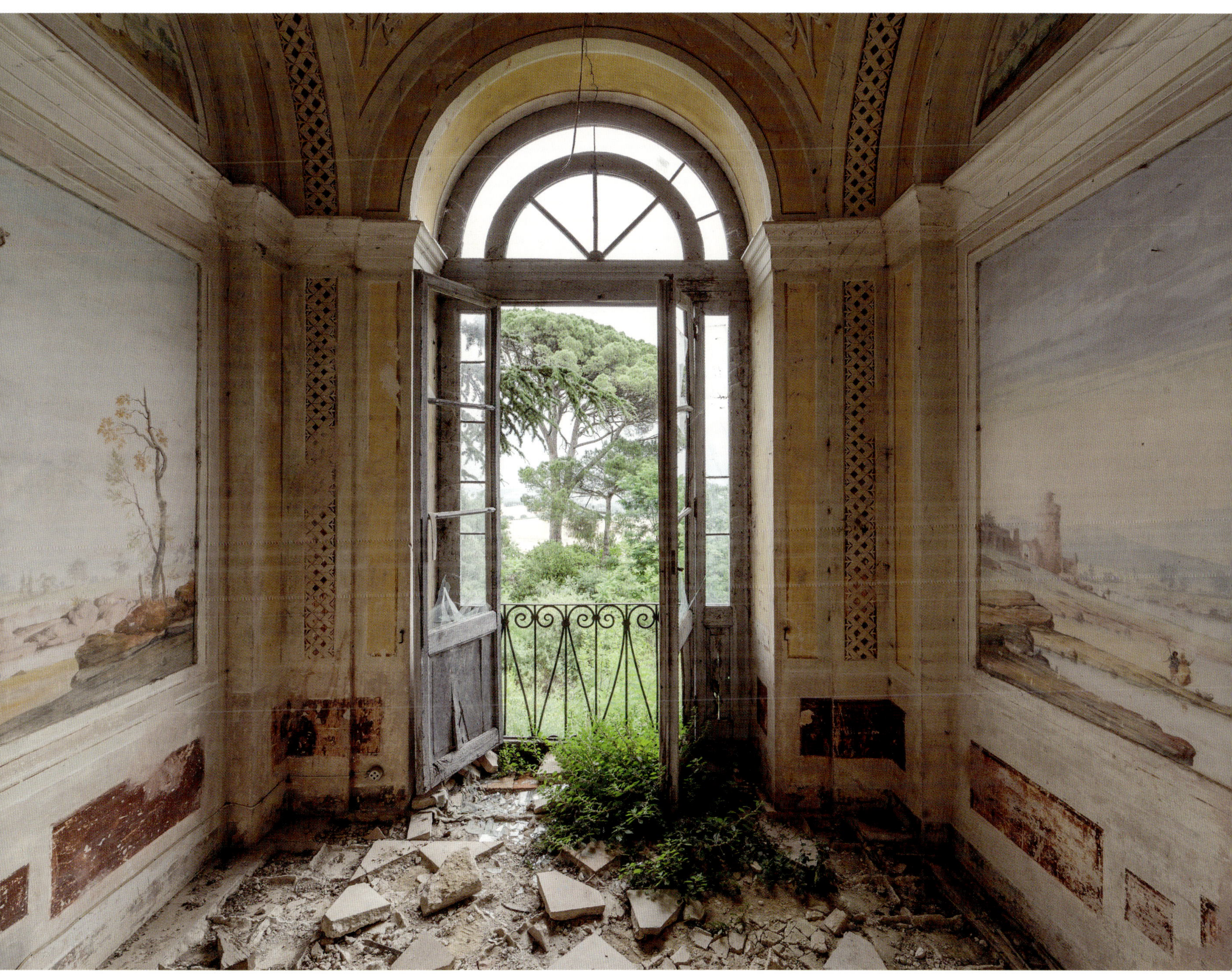

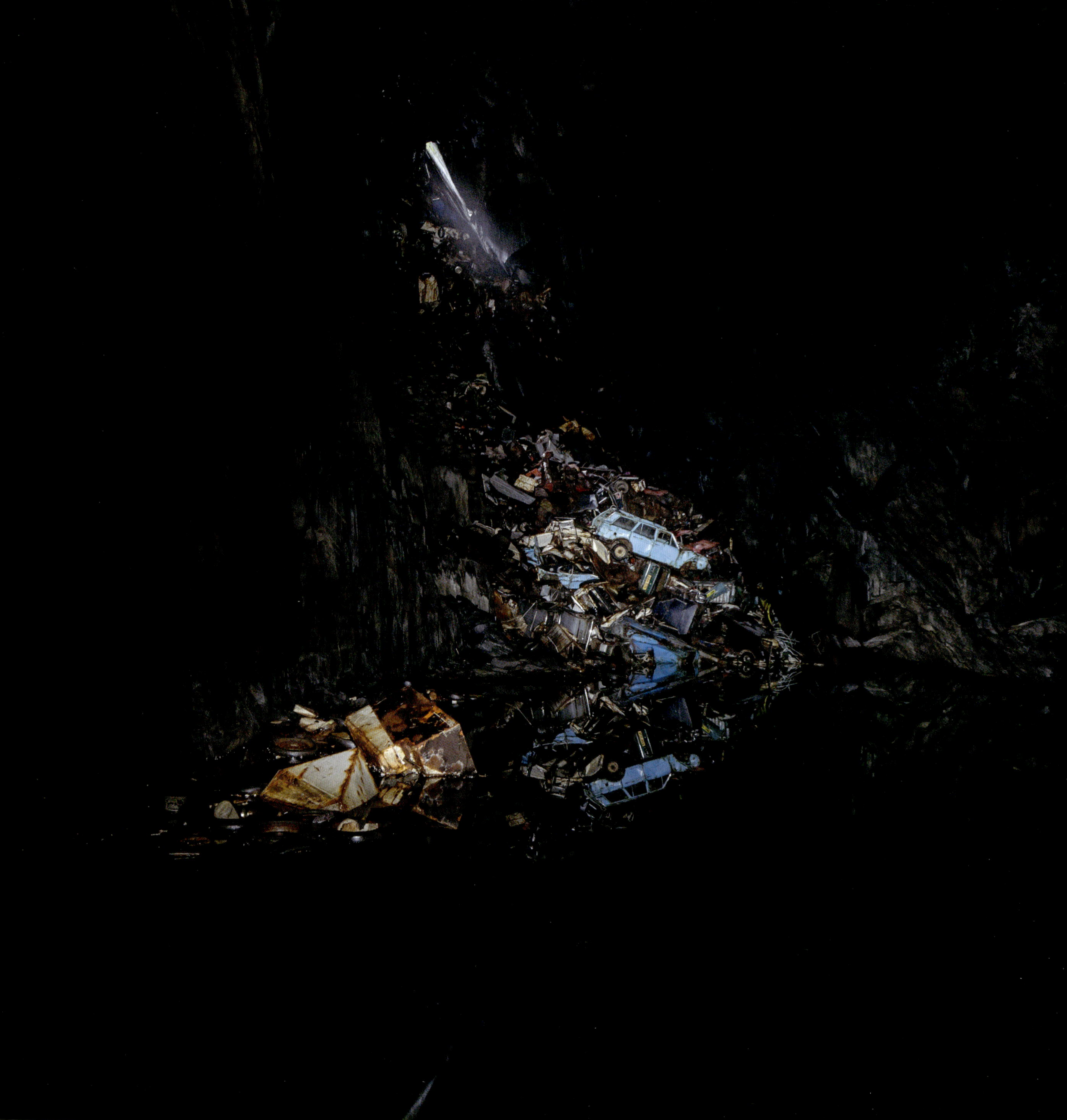